Ralph Weldon

Chronological notes, containing the rise, growth and present state of the English congregation of the Order of St. Benedict

Ralph Weldon

Chronological notes, containing the rise, growth and present state of the English congregation of the Order of St. Benedict

ISBN/EAN: 9783337152550

Printed in Europe, USA, Canada, Australia, Japan

Cover: Foto ©Andreas Hilbeck / pixelio.de

More available books at **www.hansebooks.com**

Pax

Chronological Notes

CONTAINING THE

Rise, Growth, and Present State of the

ENGLISH CONGREGATION

OF THE

Order of St. Benedict,

DRAWN FROM THE ARCHIVES OF THE HOUSES OF THE SAID CONGREGATION AT DOUAY IN FLANDERS, DIEULWART IN LORRAINE, PARIS IN FRANCE, AND LAMBSPRING IN GERMANY, WHERE ARE PRESERVED THE AUTHENTIC ACTS AND ORIGINAL DEEDS, ETC. AN: 1709.

BY

Dom Bennet Weldon, O.S.B. a monk of St. Edmund's, Paris.

LONDON:
JOHN HODGES, 24 KING WILLIAM STREET, CHARING CROSS.
1881.

PRINTED AT THE ABBEY OF OUR LADY OF CONSOLATION,
STANBROOK, WORCESTER.

A CHRONICLE OF THE

English Benedictine Monks

FROM THE RENEWING OF THEIR CONGREGATION

IN THE DAYS OF QUEEN MARY, TO THE

DEATH OF KING JAMES II BEING THE

CHRONOLOGICAL NOTES OF

DOM BENNET WELDON,

O. S. B.

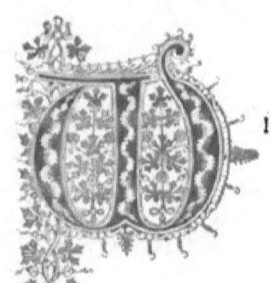

To

The Right Reverend

William Bernard Ullathorne, D.D, O.S.B.

Bishop of Birmingham,

This work,

drawn from the Archives of his Monastic home,

and now first published at his request,

is,

with every feeling of esteem and reverence,

Dedicated by his Lordship's humble servant

The Editor.

St. Gregory's Priory, Downside, Bath.

Feast of St. Benedict, mdccclxxxi.

PREFACE.

The following work is offered to the public as a contribution to the history of the Catholic Church in England during the seventeenth century. There is, indeed, a good deal told us in it concerning the history of the Benedictines in England before that period, but the chief value of these *Chronological Notes* consists in the information which they contain on the reëstablishment of the English Benedictines under the first of the Stuarts, and the chief events in connection with their body down to the death of James II.

Till very recently the supply of works illustrative of the condition of the Catholic Church in this country subsequent to the Reformation has been extremely scanty. The *Collections* of Dodd, the *Memoirs of Missionary Priests* by Bishop Challoner, Mr. C. Butler's *Historical Memoirs of English Catholics*, the antidotal and *Supplementary Memoirs* which Dr. Milner published on the same subject, and the various writings of the late Dr. Oliver, were the best known, and indeed, almost the only works on our history accessible to the Catholic Student. But with the publication of the late Canon Tierney's edition of Dodd's Church history, a new era may be said to have commenced, and the interest excited by his most valuable notes, consisting as they so often did of extracts from the almost forgotten manuscript treasures still in the possession of Catholics, has never since died out. To the influence of this newly-awakened spirit of enquiry and research we probably owe the publication of many able and interesting articles in the *Rambler* and other Catholic serial publications, of the *Records of the English Province of the Society of Jesus*, edited by the Rev. H. Foley, S. J., of Mrs. Hope's *Franciscan Martyrs*, and of several other works of the same kind. Simultaneously with this desire to promote a more general interest in the history of our catholic forefathers, there has arisen a wish for the reproduction and publication of the original records from which the works above enumerated drew their information. What the *Calendar of State Papers* and the numerous historical publications issued under the direction of the Master of the Rolls, have done for the general history of our country, has been done in some measure for Catholic history, by Mr. Lewis' translation of Sanders' *History of the Schism* and by the First and Second *Douay Diaries* edited by the Fathers of the London Oratory. These works, we cannot doubt, are an evidence of, as they are an answer to, the wish so often expressed, that we should have the opportunity of forming our own opinions on the thoughts and actions of our Catholic ancestors, and be enabled to enter more surely into their feelings and opinions on those internal disagreements and troubles which, even more than the open persecution of which they were so often the valiant victims, bore them down, and, to a great extent, neutralised their noblest efforts. This wish is admirably summed up in a letter of the Very Rev. Father Knox, of the Oratory, which I may be pardoned for quoting here :

"What is wanted just now, it seems to me, is original documents, printed just as they were written. They will form the material for future histories. But unless the documents are given themselves in their integrity, readers have no means of testing the views of historical writers ; and there are so many disputed and debatable questions in our Catholic history of the Post-reformation period that we need a full publication of the sources to be able to form correct judgments on these points."

It is hoped that these *Chronological Notes* will, in some measure, help to supply this want, as they contain the only full and consecutive account that has yet been published of the restoration and remodelling of the English Benedictine Congregation, a not unimportant element in the English Catholic world of the seventeenth century. Of the history of that body in pre-reformation times much has been written. Its connexion with the conversion of our forefathers and the spread and development of the Anglo Saxon Church, necessarily attracts the attention of all students of the history of our country ; and when we consider that the labours and holiness of St. Augustine and his companions were perpetuated or renewed in an Aldhelm and a Boniface, a Bede and an Alcuin, a Dunstan and an Anselm and many another saintly teacher and zealous pastor, we can understand the claim that the monastic order had on the reverence and love of Catholic England and the large part that the monks of old played in the civil and religious history of our country. Their widespread monasteries, their broad acres, their stately churches, bore witness to the piety of the faithful towards the benefactors of their race ; and the spell which in the Middle ages had such influence over men, was not unfelt in later days by many, who, though aliens from the Faith of their fathers, could not view unmoved the noble ruins of what that Faith had built up. And thus it is that we see in the works of Dugdale and Stevens, of Spelman and Willis in former times, and in our own days of many well known writers, (of one of whom, the Rev Mackenzie Walcot we have lately had to deplore the loss), an evidence of the lasting interest which the history of English Monasticism has for the student, the architect, and the antiquary. And it is matter for congratulation that the works of recent writers have almost without exception evidenced a thorough appreciation of the monastic ideal and its beneficial influence upon society, notwithstanding that it had been customary for writers of a previous generation to bestow upon the Religious Orders a more than ordinary share of that rancour and bigotry with which everything Catholic was assailed.

Of course it would be unreasonable to assert that the high standard which marked the most flourishing period of Benedictine history was uniformly maintained. The changing phases of society, the long continued civil wars, the ravages of those frightful pestilences which were the scourge of mediæval Europe, all combinded to interfere with the perpetuity of those sage reforms which the fourth Lateran Council (1215) had promulgated. Hence we are not surprised at finding that two hundred years after that date some further efforts were needed to restore the Order to its pristine vigour. In England the first step towards a reform was taken by King Henry Vth, who as we are told by Thomas

Walsingham (himself a monk of St. Alban's), summoned the Abbots and Prelates of the Order of Black monks to meet him in the Abbey of Westminster. There accordingly, in 1421, sixty Abbots and Conventual Priors, and more than three hundred monks, learned men, and procurators of those Abbots who were unable to attend in person, assembled to meet the King, "whom certain false brethren had prejudiced against their Order by asserting that many both Abbots and monks, had fallen away from the primitive institution and observance of the Monastic State" and that a reform was urgently needed. The historian explains the disorders which had arisen by stating that the death of the greater number of the Abbots and senior monks in the great pestilences of 1407 and 1413 had exposed the monasteries to the dangers which naturally followed from the accession to posts of office and dignity of those who were young and inexperienced. The King, then, accompanied by only four persons, one of whom was Edmund Lacy, Bishop of Exeter, went to the Chapter House of Westminster Abbey where the representatives of the Benedictine body had assembled to meet him. After a discourse by the Bishop, the monarch earnestly addressed the monks reminding them of the piety of his ancestors and others in the foundation and support of so many religious houses; he exhorted them to rectify whatever abuses had of late crept in and to return to the former strictness which had of old made the Order so renowned, and repeatedly begged of all to pray unceasingly for himself, his kingdom, and the Church.* Under the direction of the Abbot of St. Alban's, William Heyworth, a man "much admired for his great holiness and piety, beloved both of God and men for the strictness of his life and the excellency of his government,"† several articles of reform were drawn up which it was agreed should be submitted to the ensuing Provincial Chapter of the Congregation for approval and to the Apostolic See for final confirmation.

In the meantime a movement had commenced among the Benedictines of Germany and Italy which was destined in after years to make its influence felt in England. The Decrees of the council of Lateran (1215) ordering the holding of triennial chapters had long been neglected in Germany, with results which proved only too clearly the wisdom of the Pope who had in the first instance promulgated that salutary ordinance. The Fathers of the Council of Constance therefore, insisted on the practice being revived (1414), and among the twenty five chapters which they devoted to the reformation of the Monastic Orders they specially insisted on the Abbots of the Province of Mayence assembling every three years in General Chapter as had been decreed two centuries previously. Accordingly a Chapter was held at Peterhausen near Constance in 1417, where of the hundred and thirty-one monasteries comprised in the Province, only three were unrepresented. The regulations drawn up at this assembly were afterwards approved by the Emperor Sigismund, (Jan. 17, 1418), and put in force throughout the Province.

The soul of the movement was John Dederoth, Abbot of Rheinhausen; to him was owing the reformation of the Abbey of Clus near Gandersheim, which had hitherto resisted the reforms of the Peterhausen Chapter, and after accomplishing that difficult task, he betook himself to the half ruined Abbey of Bursfeld

---

* Thomas Walsingham, Historia Anglicana. Vol. II. p. 337, Ed. 1864.
† Stevens' addition to Dugdale. Vol. I. p. 262, Ed. 1722.

which was destined to become the centre of the Benedictine revival in German

Another name which is inseparably connected with his is that of John Rhode, who, at the solicitation of Archbishop Otho, had left his Carthusian solitude to take upon himself the government of the great Abbey of St. Matthias at Treves. He assiduously seconded all the labours of the holy Abbot of Bursfeld, and through their united efforts the reform was extensively propagated. On the death of Abbot Dederoth in 1439, his successor John de Hagen took up his unfinished task, and the Council of Bâle, appreciating the importance of the work which was being accomplished by these "Reformers before the Reformation" deputed twelve Abbots, John Rhode being of the number, to visit and reform all the houses of both monks and nuns throughout the German Church. The Statutes of Bursfeld were gradually introduced into other monasteries, and from the community of Bursfeld were selected those monks who were required for the infusion of new life and regular observance into the other houses of the Order. Thus, little by little the influence of the Abbey of Bursfeld grew, till in time it came to be regarded as the head of the reformed monasteries of Germany. Its first General Chapter was held in 1446 ; the Apostolic See approved of the new congregation in 1458 and 1461, and extended to it the privileges recently conceded to the congregation of St. Justina of Padua which was doing a similar work in Italy. From that date the great German Monasteries, one by one adopted the reforms and were aggregated to the Bursfeld Congregation, which by the year 1502, reckoned on its roll ninety of the chief Abbeys of the Empire.

Nor must we omit to mention the part taken by Cardinal Nicholas of Cusa, Papal Legate in Germany (1451—1453,) in this great work of the renovation of the Order of St. Benedict. His zeal seconded by his immense popularity brought about the reform of nearly every monastery of the order in Austria, Styria, Carinthia, Salzburg and Bavaria ; while under his personal influence the communities of several important Abbeys* in the North of Germany were incorporated into the Bursfeld Union.

The history of the foundation of the Congregation of St. Justina in Italy is even more remarkable.† There was in the suburbs of Padua an ancient Abbey of Benedictines formerly in great repute but at the commencement of the 15th century reduced to a state of great penury both spiritual and temporal. Its revenues had been almost entirely lost, and the regular places were in such a state of ruin, that there was hardly sufficient accomodation for the Abbot and three surviving monks who formed the community. But within the church lay the bodies of St. Prosdocimus, the first Bishop of Padua, and of St. Justina, his convert, the Patroness of the Monastery. There came daily to visit the sepulchres of these Saints a holy old Priest of Padua, Mark by name, parish Priest of St. Mark's Church in the same town. To this simple and saintly man God made known that the Abbey of St. Justina was about to be restored, and that by the merits and prayers of the Saints and Martyrs who therein reposed it would become once more a veritable house of God and the home of his faithful servants. The author, under God, of this reform was indicated to the priest Mark, as Louis Barbo, at

---

* Among others those of Treves, St. Michael's at Hildesheim, St. Martin's and St. Pantaleon's at Cologne.

† An interesting account of this movement is given by Moehler, Histoire de l'Eglise. IIme Period, Chapter IV. § V.

that time Prior of the Canons Regular of St. George in Alga at Venice, who on visiting Padua was told by Mark, of the position and work prepared for him by God, but who laughed at predictions which he considered to be the result rather of his old friend's affection than of the inspirations of the Giver of Lights. The transfer of St. Justina's to the Olivetan monks, and Barbo's own promotion to the Abbey of St. Cyprian di Mariano seemed to show that Mark was no true prophet. But ere long all was changed: Barbo resigned his claim to St. Cyprian's; the Republic of Venice at the request of the old monks of St. Justina's annulled the transfer of their house to the sons of Blessed Bernard Ptolomeo, and to crown all, Pope Gregory XII by the unanimous advice of his Cardinals and at the suggestion of his nephew the Cardinal Gabriel, (himself to be one day Pope under the name of Eugene IV) gave the Abbey of St. Justina to the young Prior of St. George in Alga; and to the great joy of all, and of none more than of the old priest Mark. Louis Barbo was installed in his new dignity. With the ready help of the few monks whom he found there and with one or two others (including some of the Clerks of his old monastery of St. George), the new Abbot set about the restoration of St. Justina's; but the difficulties which he met with, and the desertion of his first disciples, almost discouraged him from persevering in his holy work. At length after many months of uncertainty and darkness, when every attempt which he made to withdraw from his post had failed, Abbot Barbo was cheered by the arrival of a postulant from Pavia, Paul de Strata, to whom he gave the habit of St. Benedict on Easter-day, 1410. A young friend of Paul's, of the family of the Salimbeni, coming to the monastery to endeavour to entice his comrade away, was himself overcome, and in his turn became a fervent novice. The constancy of this young man in resisting the solicitations and even violence of his friends and kindred to alter his determination and to make him give up the idea of becoming a monk, caused such a stir in the town that the work upon which Abbot Barbo was engaged became known and many hastened to enrol themselves among his followers. Sixteen students of the University were among his first novices; each year saw an addition of about twenty monks to his community, till at last it became necessary to establish new foundations to accommodate the numerous religious family of S. Justina. In this way the Abbey of St. Fortunatus at Bassano, another at Verona, of St. Nicholas at Genoa, of the Holy Spirit at Pavia were founded the monks of St. Denis at Milan, St. Mary's of Florence, and St. George's at Venice embraced the reform, and in a few years the regular observance of St. Justina's had been introduced into the greater number of the Italian monasteries. The Cardinal Gabriel of Sienna above mentioned introduced sixteen monks from the Venetian Abbey of St. George into the ancient Patriarchal monastery of St. Paul at Rome; and when later the Arch-Abbey of Monte Cassino adopted the reforms of St. Justina's, the reigning Pope Julius II gave the name of the *Cassinese Congregation* to the whole body of the reformed Benedictines of Italy.

The good effected by Abbot Barbo and his monks was not confined to Italy and the Benedictines. The Portuguese Gomes who had made his profession at St. Justina's was chosen to reform the Cistercians, Sylvestrines, Minorites and other religious orders in the neighbourhood of Florence, and afterwards passed to his native country to extend there also the spirit of zeal and regularity which had marked his career in Italy. To Placid Pavanello, Abbot of St. Paul's at

Rome was entrusted the renovation of the Vallombrosians; Archangelo Rossi and others of the Cassinese Congregation were commissioned by St Pius V to reform the Cistercians of Tuscany. In 1547 the Benedictines of Dalmatia were formed into a Congregation on the model of that of Italy and a century later distant Poland received a colony of Monks from the Arch-Abbey of Monte-Cassino, whose new home, the Abbey of Castro Cassino in Lithuania became the centre of Benedictine influence, as it was the model of monastic observance in that country (1693).*

How far these widespread efforts at a better order of things among the monks of Germany and Italy were known to and appreciated by their brethren in England it is impossible to say. We know so little of the internal life of the English monasteries in the fifteenth and sixteenth centuries that it is useless to conjecture what were their views on the monastic revival on the Continent; but there is one incidental piece of evidence that shows that the influence of that movement was not entirely unfelt in this country. Richard Kiddermynster, Abbot of Winchcombe, was called on some affairs of his Order to Rome in the year 1500; and we read that during his stay of more than a twelvemonth in the centre of Christendom, he improved himself much in learning and particularly that "he informed himself of "several useful regulations belonging to a monastick life." On his return to England he taught the lessons which he had learned and practised abroad, so that in his Abbey of Winchcombe monastic discipline was observed to the greatest nicety, while the diligent pursuit of learning and the numbers who attended the cloister schools made the monastery seem like a little University.†

The state of the Religious Orders naturally attracted the attention and claimed a share in the zeal of those noble-minded Bishops whose names lent lustre to the reign of Henry VIIth. Amongst others Fox, Bishop of Winchester, had some thoughts of founding a College at Oxford for the benefit of the monks of his Cathedral, but he was dissuaded from the project by Hugh Oldham, Bishop of Exeter, who prophetically told his friend there were more monasteries in England already than could stand long.‡ Another prelate whose early endeavours for the reformation of abuses seem to have been dictated by an enlightened zeal was Cardinal Wolsey; and to him Fox wrote that for three years he had been giving all his study, labour, and attention towards that object, and especially towards a revival of the primitive intention of the Monastic Life.§

Such facts are indications of the importance which was attached to the condition of the religious houses, and doubtless the still unpublished documents relating to the last years of the old Hierarchy will throw much light on this section of Ecclesiastical History. If there is little evidence that Winchcombe Abbey was but one of many houses wherein the regularity and fervour of the

---

* See Rohrbacher, Histoire de l'Eglise, Vol. XXI. p. 235, and Mœhler's Histoire; Hme Period: Chap. IV. § V.

† Dodd's Church History, I, 229; Wood's Hist. et antiq. Univ. Oxon: I 1. p. 247. In a dispute concerning ecclesiastical exemptions in 1515, Abbot Kiddermynster vigourously opposed Dr. Standish, Provincial of the Franciscans, who in this question sided with the court. Dr. Standish was condemned by the ensuing convocation of the Clergy, but was promoted by the King to the See of St. Asaph in 1579. A full account of the dispute is given by the Rev. H. Blunt in his *Reformation of the Church of England*, p. 395

‡ Dodd's Church History, I, 183.

§ Blount's, Reformation of Church of England, p. 363.

new foreign congregations were known and emulated, there is certainly as little to show that the better part of the English monasteries had fallen to so low a state as was the case, for instance, with St. Justina's or Bursfeld before the grace of renovation was given to them. There is nothing to make us suppose that the monks of Croyland had so soon degenerated from the regularity and piety which had moved the Saint-like monarch, Henry VI, to desire admission into their fraternity,* nor that the community of Westminster had done anything to forfeit the high esteem which had raised their Abbot, Thomas Milling, to the Bishopric of Hereford under Edward IV, and which, under Abbot Islip, had procured them such favour in the sight of the seventh Henry: Glastonbury, St. Edmund's, Whitby and others of the "divers great and solemn monasteries" seem to have fully merited the praises for "Religion right well kept and observed" for which an extremely zealous Parliament, in proceeding to the dissolution of the smaller houses, returned thanks to God. The many honourable names of men distinguished in ecclesiastical and literary affairs that were found among the monks up to the very end prove that their condition was not so black as their enemies gave out. Christ Church Monastery at Canterbury under Priors Sellying and Goldstone would have reflected credit on any age. The good repute of the English Benedictine body is likewise evidenced by the considerable list of its members who were judged worthy of the Episcopal office.†

The services which the monks rendered to learning by their patronage of the newly discovered art of printing constitute a lasting claim to the gratitude of

---

* "In the year 1460, King Henry VI coming to *Croyland* and being delighted with the Religious Life of the Monks, stay'd three days, desiring to be admitted into their Brotherhood, that is to partake of their Prayers and other Acts of Piety; which being granted him, he in return gave them his Charter whereby he confirmed their Liberties." &c. Stevens' Addition to Dugdale, I, 374.

† The following is a list of those monks who were promoted to the Episcopate in the forty years which preceded the dissolution of Abbeys:

1495, September 4th, D. William Senhouse or Sever, Abbot of St. Mary's, York, made Bishop of Carlisle; translated to Durham, January 27th, 1502.

1500, January 8th, D. Miles Salley or Sawley, Abbot of Eynsham, appointed Bishop of Llandaff.

1505, April 4th, D. John Thornden or Thornton, S. T. D. Prior of Wallingford, appointed Bishop of Syrin, i. p. i. as Auxiliary to Archbishop Warham.

c 1512, D. Thomas Chard, appointed to the See of Salubria, *in partibus*, as Coadjutor to Hugh Oldham, Bishop of Exeter.

1515, D. Robert Wilson, Prior of Drax, appointed Bishop of Negropont, i. p. i. as Auxiliary to the Archbishop of York. He was translated to Meath, Feb. 27, 1523.

1520, April 16th, Robert Blyth, Abbot of Thorney, nominated to the See of Down and Connor in Ireland.

1521, August 9th, D. William Sutton, Prior of Avecotte, appointed Bishop of *Paraden*: i. p. i., as Auxiliary to the Bishop of Coventry and Lichfield.

1524, April 28th, D. John, Prior of Tynemouth, appointed Bishop of *Polotcy*: i. p. i. as Suffragan or Auxiliary to the Archbishop of York. The same title seems to have been borne by another Benedictine, John Stanywell, Abbot of Pershore, who died in 1553.

1532, May 15th, D. William Fawell, Prior of St. Nicholas' Exeter, nominated Bishop of Hippo, i. p. i. He died Archdeacon of Totness, July 4th, 1557.

In the same year the Cathedral Prior of Winchester also received Episcopal consecration.

1539, August 27th, D. Gabriel de S. Sevo, nominated to the See of Elphin; he was translated to Ferns, June 3rd, 1541.

See Dodd's Church History, **Maziere Brady's Episcopal Succession, Gam's** Series Episcoporum, &c.

posterity. As the Benedictines of St. Alban's in Mentz were among the earliest to encourage printing in Germany, as the monks of Subiaco were the first to welcome the new art into Italy, so in England the same merit may be claimed for the monks of Westminster in whose Almonry the first English press was set up in the days of Abbot Milling. The Abbeys of St. Alban's and Tavistock, and apparently those of Abingdon and St. Augustine's at Canterbury also, were not long in procuring presses for their own use. *

It is not intended to give in this place a detailed account of the visitation, and suppression of the religious houses. So much has been said on the subject by well informed writers † that till it receives fuller illustration from the further research of able and conscientious students it will be impossible to say what has not been well said already. On one point, the serious charges which their enemies made against the monks, we will quote the words of a well known journal which, in a few sentences, gives a common sense view of the whole question : ‡

"The historiettes concerning the depravity of monks and nuns at the Reformation were mostly invented to give a colour to the wholesale rapacity of the Court, and no doubt the sanguinary reign of Mary was the revanche. The Roman clergy had been not only injured but insulted ; not only robbed but lied against; and in their blind fury at deeds which would not admit of palliation, they cauterised their detractors with excesses which nobody will care to justify. At the same time as a mere matter of common sense, it is simply beyond the range of imagination to conceive, either in the Middle Ages or our own day, men and women devoting their lives and their substance to religion, whether in its contemplative or in its active aspect, and yet being so amazingly inconsistent as to convert their cloth into a cloak for secret sin.

The folly of one who invests all his spare savings in a huge insurance policy, keeps the premium going for twenty years, and with the money in his hand deliberately allows his policy to lapse in the 21st. year, is as nothing to this. Indeed, we fail to see the point of people who expect, in return for vows of celibacy and holy poverty, of obedience and devotion, to earn a glorious hereafter—unless they have arrived at the conclusion that their belief is illusory—deliberately descending to a lower moral standard than that adopted by the world. It is not business. It is buying shoddy in the dearest market."

It is not pretended that every single community of the very numerous houses in England and Wales wherein the Rule of St. Benedict was followed, was at the time of its dispersion in the highest state of Regular discipline. The genuine records of the time show that there were occasional shortcomings among the monks, as there were, are, and must be to the end of days in all human societies. The letters relating to the affairs of Christ Church Monastery at Canterbury, for instance, give us an insight into the troubles which beset the Prior or Warden of a monastic College in one of our Universities. Dom John Langdon, Warden of Canterbury College, Oxford, thus writes to the Prior of Christ Church :

"Another cause of my writing at this time is this; I have had trouble late with some of the brethren that be sojourners with us, especially with them of Peterborough, which, as you remember, by their ungodly demeaning in D. William Chicheley's days went from us to

---

* See Dibdin's Typographical Antiquities of Great Britain, Vol. I, Life of Caxton, p. ci.
† See The English Monastic Houses ; their accusers and defenders. Dixon's History of the Church of England ; and Blunt's Reformation of the Church of England, &c.
‡ From an Article entitled "Veil and Cowl," in the "Whitehall Review," of March 2nd, 1878.

Gloucester College, and since they were taken again to us in D. Humfrey's days. And now they be as frowardly disposed or worse than ever they were. It were too long to write to you the process of their guiding, therefore what they have done and propose to do I have committed unto my fellowship to inform you especially to D. Thomas Eastry. The said brethren of Peterborough be now at home in their monastery, and shall be till Michaelmas, wherefore I pray your fatherhood to write on to their Abbot, desiring him to give them charge, if they shall come again to us, that they be guided as scholars should be, for they be no students. And also, that worse is, they begin to set all men at debate, and especially (the) other sojourners amongst us."*

This letter was written about the year 1493: There is another letter in the same collection written by the Cathedral Prior of Coventry to the Prior of Christ Church, explaining the circumstances which obliged him to dismiss a certain monk from the monastery of Coventry : † and at a slightly later period certain charges were made against the monks of Hyde Abbey, by Winchester, which even if true, hardly justify all the severe things that have been said against the monks ‡ Well would it have been if they had in every case been as careful as the sainted founder of their Order to avoid whatever might be made use of by their adversaries to the vilification of their state and the undermining of the Church of God. §

In estimating the ease with which so many venerable monasteries were overthrown it must be borne in mind that for some years previous to their final suppression many steps had been taken by those in power to render that suppression more easy. One of these and perhaps the chief, was the appointment by the court of compliant and suborned men, already apostates at heart, to highest positions in the religious houses. No one was more prominent in this disgraceful intrigue than the highest ecclesiastical authority in the kingdom, the Primate Cranmer. We find him writing as follows to the King's Vicar General, Lord Cromwell (August 15th, 1535) :

---

* Christ Church Letters, Camden Society, pp. 59-60.
† "Moreover Father, the said Sir William Catesby informed me that you marvelled greatly of dismissing of a brother of mine. The truth is thus: D. Richard Blake, for some time being in Oxford, which you knew as I supposed, being at home in our monastery, unknown to me sued for a capacity, his conversation being not virtuous nor good, exciting others to the same. And when I had very certainty of it, I moved him to the contrary, and he would have made conditions with me, which I would not be agreeable to. I knew his conditions such, my conscience to be saved, rather to part with him than to keep him still, in so much as he had obtained a capacity; and by council, saying that he was sure of an annual service, dismissed him from my congregation. If he have given you any other sinister information, I pray you heartily let me have knowledge in writing, that I may answer thereto." Letter XXIV. p. 29.
‡ See *Liber Monasterii de Hyde*, edited by Edward Edwards, Esq. Preface, p. lxiii.
"The complaints relate for the most part to certain anticipations, by some of the more youthful monks, of the teachings of what has lately been called muscular Christianity, as shown in their addiction to the practice of long-bow archery in the Hyde meadows, and to that of keeping late hours, sitting for long discussions sometimes to the hour of eight in the evening, and even beyond it (and, it is much to be feared, occasionally over a potation to freshen their talk), instead of betaking themselves to bed immediately after supper, according to the good wont of their predecessors. It was also alleged that their train of servants was now so numerous as to diminish the old almsgiving, long honourably characteristic of Hyde Abbey."
§ See S. Bedæ opera, Ed. Colon. T. VII, p. 344 ; "Forsitan (S. P. Benedictus) secularium latratus vitabat qui bonos monachorum mores, canino more devastant : et hoc credunt in illis quod suis malis actibus agere non recusant."

"Moreover I understand the Priory of Worcester shall be shortly void, which if it be so, I pray you be good master unto Mr. Holbeck, doctor of divinity, of the house of Crowland, or else to Dane Richard Gorton, batchelor of divinity, of the house of Burton-upon-Trent. And if the priorship of Worcester shall not be vacant, yet I pray you be good master unto these two, when you shall find places meet for them: for I know no religious men in England of that habit, that be of better learning, judgment, conversation, and all qualities meet for an head and master of an house."*

Three years afterwards the Archbishop was similarly employed; and this time to the undoing of his own Cathedral monastery:

"My very singular good lord, in my most hearty manner I commend me unto your lordship; and whereas I am informed that one Sandwich a monk of Christ's Church in Canterbury, and Warden of Canterbury College in Oxford doth sue for the preferment of the prior's office in the said house of Canterbury, these my letters are most effectuously to desire your lordship, if any such alteration be,† to bear your favour and aid to the Warden of the manors of the said house, a man of right honest behaviour, clean living, good learning, good judgment, without superstition, *very tractable, and as ready to set forward his prince's causes* as no man more of his coat; and in that house in mine opinion there is no better man. I am moved to write to your lordship in this behalf, in as much as I consider what a great commodity I shall have if such one be promoted to the said office, that is a right honest man, and of his qualities: and I insure your Lordship the said room requireth such one; as knoweth God.‡

In the same year, the Primate again endeavoured to promote his and the King's ends by procuring a prelacy for a certain Mr. Hutton. He writes to Cromwell, (August 15th, 1538):

"In my last letter I prayed your lordship to remember Mr. Hutton that he might be made an Abbot or a Prior, which I doubt not that your lordship will effectuously attempt with the King's majesty."§

That such attempts upon the liberty of their elections were not readily acquiesced in by the monks, is manifest from the letter of Robert Silvester, Prior of the Canons Regular of Gisborn and his fellow Visitor, Tristram Teshe, who were obliged to write to their master Cromwell of the defeat which they had sustained at the Abbey of Whitby through the manly resistance of "Sir Robert Woodhouse, Prior claustral of the said monastery" and his adherents, "which perversely resisted and withstood your lordship's pleasure and commandment." ‖

The almost unanimous fidelity which the religious orders, and especially the Benedictines, showed to the cause of the Catholic Church against the vigourous heresies which were then springing up in Germany and England; their opposition to the divorce of King Henry VIII from Katharine of Arragon, and their opposition to the novel claims of their temporal monarch for ecclesiastical Supremacy in his own dominions, have been spoken of by many writers both Catholic and Protestant.¶ Thus at Westminster on April 27th, 1533, "the preachers have

---

* See Remains and Letters of Cranmer, Parker Society, 1846.
† Alluding, apparently, to the contemplated removal or retirement of the then Prior Goldwell, "a man of unstained reputation, the last survivor of the circle of Warham, More, and Colet" (Dixon, History of the Church of England, II, 226). Prior Goldwell had long proved a thorn in Cranmer's side, opposing the Archbishop for abusing the Pope (Dixon's History, I. 330).   ‡ Cranmer's Letters and remains.   To Crumwell, Letter 220, March 17, 1538.
§ Cranmer's Letters &c.—Letter 235; p, 376.
‖ Letters relating to the Suppression of monasteries Camden Society. cxxiii, p. 249.
¶ See an article on "English Martyrs" in the Dublin Review. April, 1877.

ing been desired to admonish the people to pray to God for the King and Queen Anne, one who preached at Westminster not only spoke against the marriage but told the people publicly to pray for the King and Queen Katharine, and for the Princess."* In 1534 when Latimer had been broaching novelties in Bristol, D. Robert Cirecster, Master Prior of St. James' Benedictine House in that city, was one of those who were most zealous in opposing him, "approving purgatory, pilgrimages, the worshipping of Saints and images, also approving that faith without good works is but dead, and that our Lady being full of grace is and was without spot of sin."† To Catholic readers the following words of the same heretic Latimer to Lord Cromwell will read as the highest praises of the monks of the noble Abbey of Evesham:

(Christmas Day, 1537). "My Doctor Barnes hath preached here.... I would wish that the King's Grace might see and hear him: but I pray you let him tell you how two monks hath preached a late in Evesham, and I wist you will hearken to them and look upon them; for though they be exempt from me, yet they be not exempt from your Lordship. I pray God amend them, or else I fear they be exempt from the flock of Christ, very true monks, that is to say, pseudo prophets and false christian men, perverters of Scripture; sly, wily, disobedientiaries to all good orders; ever starting up, as they dare to do hurt."

These are but a few of the many instances that might be quoted to show that in general, the monks were on the side of the Church in its struggle with the powers of the world. That this was felt by the court party is manifest from the unscrupulous efforts of every kind which were made to shake their constancy. By the promotion of unworthy men to the greater Abbeys, by the great bribes of all kinds which were offered to those who would resign, by the terrors inspired in the beginning of their troubles by the cruelties exercised on the Holy Maid of Kent and her supporters,‡ and afterwards on so many Abbots and Priors of various Orders, and Priests, secular and regular, the submission, ruin and dispersion of the religious was brought about.

It little availed the monks of Tewkesbury that they forcibly resisted the King's Visitors at their first coming: their Chapter House, Cloisters and other offices were burned to the ground to avenge the insult.§ It little availed the premier Abbey of St. Alban that its Abbot, Robert Catton, some time Prior of Norwich, waxed hourly "more obstinate and less conformable" when the Grand Inquisitors made their "communications or motions" concerning a surrender; telling them "that he would rather choose to beg his bread all the days of his life than consent to any surrender"; for he was deprived of his office and a more pliant Superior appointed in his stead to give up the Abbey into the King's hands. ‖ Evesham was resigned by a young monk Philip Hawford or Ballard who feared to have it said of him, as he told the commissioners "that he was compelled to resign for fear of deprivation; but this was only when the lawful Abbot, Clement Wych of Litchfield, "not choosing to surrender, was persuaded by Cromwell to resign his pastoral staff."¶

---

* Calender of State Papers. Henry VIII. 1533, April 27.
† Letters relating to the suppression of monasteries. Letter **V.** p. 12.
‡ For an able defence of the Holy Maid, a Benedictine nun of St. Sepulchre's, Canterbury and her companions, including two Benedictines, two Franciscans and two secular priests, see the Article, "English Martyrs" in the Dublin Review, April, 1877.
§ See Steven's addition to Dugdale, I, 513. ‖ Suppression of monasteries. p. 249.
¶ Monasticon. II. p. 9.

Hyde was given up by a courtly Prelate, Salcot, **Bishop** of Bangor, who held the Abbey *in commendam*. The Abbot of Gloucester would not sign the deed of surrender, so the Prior did it for him. The Cathedral Priors of Canterbury and Bath as though to hide themselves after their forced surrenders, refused preferment in the new establishments, which arose in place of their late monasteries, and spent the remainder of their lives in retirement.

John Reeves of **Melford, the last Abbot of St.** Alban's "intrepid, prudent, learned, affable, upright, and a lover of his vow and his religion" died of grief a few months after the destruction of his house which he had been powerless to avert. * The fate of the Abbots of Colchester, Reading, and Glastonbury was even more tragic. Of the first named of these three houses Colchester fared the worst, or the best, according to the manner in which its history is viewed. Its Abbot, Thomas Marshall, who had formerly been Abbot of St. Wereburg's at Chester was imprisoned in the Tower of London for refusing to consent to the King's wishes, and appears to have been executed in January, 1539. In the same year his successor John Beche, the last of the Abbots, was hung before his monastery gates in December, † and the monks sent adrift, even though Sir Thomas Audley ‡ the Chancellor wrote to the King's Vicar General for the preservation of that house, where the many poor people who dwelt in the King's own town of Colchester had daily relief from the charitable fraternity.

The noble end of the Abbots of Reading and Glastonbury was the last scene in the history of the destruction of monasteries. The satisfaction which these executions, or rather martyrdoms, gave to the protestant party ought to be made better known than it seems to be. Some extracts from the *Zurich Letters* will indicate the jubilant tone in which the revilers of the monks alluded to their downfall, Bartholomew Traherou, a favourer of the reformation writes from London (February 20, 1540) to the exiled Bullinger.

"I have nothing to relate at present except that all the monks in this country have lost the appellation, that some of the principal monasteries are turned into schools of studious men, and that three of the most wealthy Abbots *(Glastonbury, Reading and Colchester)* were led to execution a little before Christmas, for having joined in a conspiracy to restore the Pope."

Four days later another protestant, John Butler, thus wrote to Bullinger.

"More than all this, wonderful to relate, the monasteries are every one of them destroyed or else will be before Shrovetide; of the most opulent of which, namely Glastonbury and Reading the two Abbots have been condemned for treason and quartered, and each of them is now rotting on a gibbet near the gates of the Abbeys over which they respectively presided. A worthy recompense for **their imposture**."

---

* Monasticon III, 116. See also a little work "Scraps from my scrap book," p. **118.** Concerning St. Edmundsbury Abbey, John Aprice thus wrote to Cromwell: "The Abbot.... seemeth to be addicted to the maintaining of such superstitious ceremonies as hath been used heretofore, as touching the convent we could get little or no comforts among them, although we did use much diligence in our examination, and thereby with some other arguments gathered of their examinations, I firmly believe and suppose that they had conferred and compacted before our coming that they should disclose nothing.... There depart of them that be under age about eight, and of them that be above age upon a five.... The whole number of the convent before we came was sixty, saving one, besides three that were at Oxford." Monasticon III, **170.** † See Blunt's Reformation of the Church of England, p, 345.
‡ Suppression of monasteries, **pp. 245, 246.**

In the same strain wrote Nicholas Partridge from Dover (Feb. 26, 1540) to the same Bullinger:

"But since you have sent me such excellent tidings respecting your church, I will also relate some circumstances not perhaps to be despised. There does not, exist here a single monk at least in name.* Punishment has lately been inflicted on three principal Abbots, who had secreted property to a great extent, and had conspired in different ways for the restoration of popery."

Turned out of their homes, the monks **and nuns** were in most cases put to great **suffering and endured many** privations from the difficulty of obtaining a **livelihood. Some** no doubt were provided with livings :† others, as the historian of Oxford tells us in his *Fasti* (Vol I, p. 61), retired to Canterbury College, Gloucester **College, Durham,** St. Bernard's, St. Mary's, and other halls which were full **of them. Many** went abroad, others wandered about their native land in the greatest penury.

The sufferings of the Benedictine Nuns, as of those **of the other Orders, were in many cases** extremely severe. The high reputation **which so many of their Communities bore** for regularity and benevolence, the **fact that they were the only schools for the** young, and that they were the **centres of charity for the country around** them, induced the King in many cases **to refound them** for a few brief months ;‡ but the evident utility of their mission, **and the holiness** of their inmates could not save such houses as Shaftesbury, Holywell, Polesworth, or **Godstow from the** hand of the destroyer.

The popular sympathy for their sufferings and hard lot was shown **by the** demand of the Devonshire insurgents a few years later, for the restoration of at least two Abbeys in every county ; § a demand which at the same time **indicates** the loving, trusting regard which the poor of England still entertained **for their** tender hearted guardians.

With the reign of **Mary began a happier time, and those who under the** tyranny of the past reigns had **been in hiding for conscience** sake **or had** wavered in their faith, **now** that there was **freedom once again,** declared themselves **true** Catholics. The Archbishop, Cranmer, was **reported** to have said Mass in

---

* The last person to wear the religious habit in England during the persecution was Thomas Empson, a monk of Westminster, who for his constancy in refusing to adopt a secular dress, was imprisoned and probably executed. See Dodd's History, I, 535.

† A few of the compliant abbots were provided with bishoprics during the Schism, as Salcot of Hyde to the See of Bangor and subsequently of Salisbury ; Thomas Spark, a monk of Durham, to the Suffragan See of Berwick ; Wharton, Abbot of Bermondsey, to the See of St. Asaph's ; Rugg, Abbot of Hulme, to Norwich ; Holbeach, Prior of Worcester, to the new See of Bristol ; Abbot Chambers to the new See of Peterborough ; Abbot Kitchen to Llandaff ; Wakeman, Abbot of Tewkesbury, to the new See of Gloucester ; and John Salisbury, Prior of St. Faith's, to the new Suffragan See of Thetford.

‡ The pious monarch having deprived the Austin Canons of their Priory of Bisham in Buckinghamshire, refounded the same for an Abbot and twelve Benedictine monks, towards whose support some of the lands of Chertsey Abbey were assigned. Bisham Abbey soon met the fate of similar institutions of an older and more honourable foundation.

§ The 14th article of their demands was as follows : "We will that the half part of the Abbeylands and chantry lands in every man's possession, however he came by them, be given again to two places, where two of the chief Abbeys were within every county ; where such half part shall be taken out, and there to be established a place for devout persons, who shall pray for the king and the commonwealth, and to the same we will have all the alms of the Church boxes given for these seven years."

Canterbury Cathedral for King Edward's soul, but he denied the charge to the Privy council saying: "It was not I that did set up the Mass in Canterbury, but it was a false, flattering and lying monk (—whom the Archbishop afterwards named to be the Benedictine suffragan Bishop, Thornton—) with a dozen of his adherents which caused the Mass to be set up there, and that without mine advice or counsel."[*]

Another monk of Canterbury was among the earliest to preach openly the Catholic doctrine on the Holy Eucharist in London.[†] A monk of Westminster almost lost his life in defence of the same mystery, on Easter-Day, 1555.[‡]

In the general revival of Catholicity under Queen Mary several Bishops of the Order took a prominent part. Wharton of Hereford, formerly Abbot of Bermondsey was one; he received his appointment on the 17th of March, 1554, and on July 6th of the same year the Papal Legate confirmed the choice, after the Bishop-elect had been absolved from the schism into which he had fallen "rather by some fear than by any other cause."[§] On the 18th of November, (1554) John Holyman, a monk of Reading who had all along remained true to the Church was consecrated the first Catholic Bishop of Bristol in place of the intruded Holbeach; Bishops Salcot of Salisbury, Chambers of Peterborough, Kitchen of Llandaff, and Thornton, Suffragan Bishop of Dover, were also among those whom Cardinal Pole absolved and reinstated in their Sees.[‖] Unfortunately they were not granted many years wherein to labour and thus repair in some degree the havoc which heresy and irreligion had caused in the Church, in England. Bishop Chambers died in 1556; Bishops Thornton and Salcot in 1557; the Bishops of Hereford and Bristol in 1558. Their survivor, Bishop Kitchen, who managed to retain his see till his death (October 31st, 1563), is entitled to an honourable mention solely by his obstinate refusal to consecrate Parker to the Archbishopric of Canterbury; the momentous results of that refusal need not be dwelt upon in this place.

The years of Mary's reign were too few to allow of the religious houses being reestablished in all places where they had formerly existed. The Bridgettine nuns of Sion, the Dominicans in Smithfield, the Observants, and lastly the Benedictines of Westminster Abbey, were among the few who who were refounded.

A brief account of the restoration of the monastery of Westminster (November 21st, 1556) is given in the *Chronological Notes*; of its history during the short period of its renewed existence some few details have been preserved in the diaries and other records of the time. Dr. Feckenham, a monk of Evesham, who had been appointed Abbot, seems to have contemplated the possibility of restoring the venerable Abbey of Glastonbury: the following petition of four of the monks of that house who had joined the new Community at Westminster may well be reprinted here. Their address to the Lord Chamberlain and the Queen was, (with a few variations in the spelling), as follows

---

[*] Cranmer's Works. Parker Society, I, 429.
[†] See a Confutation of unwritten verities, p. 65, Parker Society. "I will rehearse one sermon, made in Queen Mary's beginning by a monish monk, and so leave off their vain and wicked lies. A new upstart preacher, being some time a monk of Christ's Church in Canterbury stept into the pulpit in St. Paul's Church, saying that the very body of Christ is really and naturally in the Sacrament of the Altar. &c."
[‡] See Wood's Ecclesiastical Antiquities of London, p. 265.
[§] See on these appointments *Brady's Episcopal succession*.
[‖] Salcot, Kitchen and Chambers were absolved from the Schism on January 26th, 1555.

To the Rt. Honble. Lord Chamberlain.

To the Queen's Majesty.

Right Honourable in our most humble wise, your lordship's daily beadsmen, some time of the house of Glastonbury, now here monks in Westminster, with all due submission we desire your honour to extend your accustomed virtue as it hath been always heretofore propense to the honour of Almighty God, to the honourable service of the King and Queen's Majesties, so it may please your good Lordship again, for the honour of them, both of God and their Majesties, to put the Queen's highness in remembrance of her gracious promise concerning the erection of the late monastery of Glastonbury, which promise of her Grace hath been so by her Majesty declared that upon the same, we, your lordship's daily beadsmen, understanding my Lord Cardinal's Grace's pleasure to the same, by the procurement here of our reverend Father Abbot, have gotten out the particulars; and through a warrant from my Lord Treasurer our friends there have builded and bestowed much upon reparation: notwithstanding all now stands at a stay. We think the case to be want of remembrance, which cannot so well be brought unto her Majesty's understanding as by your honourable lordship's favour and help. And considering your lordship's most godly disposition, we have a confidence thereof to solicit the same, assuring your lordship of our daily prayer while we live, and of our successors during the world if it may so please your good lordship to take it in hand.

We ask nothing in gift to the foundation, but only the house and site, the residue for the accustomed rent, so that with our labour and husbandry we may live there a few of us in our religious habits, till the charity of good people may suffice a greater number; and the country there being so affected to our Religion, we believe we should find much help amongst them toward the reparations and furniture of the same, whereby we would haply prevent the ruin of much and repair no little part of the whole to God's honour and for the better prosperity of the King and Queen's Majesties, with the whole realm. For doubtless, if it shall please your good Lordship, if there hath ever been any flagitious deed since the creation of the world punished with the plague of God, in our opinion the overthrow of Glastonbury may be compared to the same; not surrendered, as other (Abbeys), but extorted; the Abbot preposterously put to death with two innocent virtuous monks with him; that if the thing were to be scanned by any University or some learned Counsel in Divinity, they would find it more dangerous than is commonly taken; which might move the Queen's Majesty to the more speedy erection; namely it being a house of such antiquity and fame through all Christendom, first begun by St. Joseph of Arimathea who took down the dead body of **our** Saviour Christ from the cross, and lieth buried in Glastonbury. And him most heartily **we** beseech to pray unto Christ for good success unto your honourable lordship in all your lordship's affairs, and now specially in this our most humble request that we may shortly do the same in Glaston for the King and the Queen's Majesties as our Founders and for your lordship as a singular benefactor

Your Lordshiy's daily beadsmen of Westminster,
John Phagan
John Neott
William Adelwold
William Kentwyn.*

Though the restoration of Glastonbury was not effected before Queen Mary's death, the hope of one day seeing its glories revived was not quickly extinguished. A holy old monk of Glastonbury, Austin Ringwode by name, who died in the **winter** of 1587, is said to have predicted that "the Abbey would be one day **repaired** and rebuilt for **the** like worship which had ceased." †

---

* Monasticon Anglicanum. I. 9.
† See Dr. Lee's Church under Queen Elizabeth, Vol II, p. 101. "A prophecy, long ago fulfilled, is one of the points of the following notice. The restoration of Glastonbury Abbey is by no means so improbable as our forefathers may have supposed. An old monk of Glastonbury, Austin Ringwode, who, having the fear of God before his eyes, though turned out from his sacred home, dwelt in a cottage **no** great distance from it, and through many long

But the brief reign of Mary was not long enough for **the fulfilment of** all these pious hopes. The funeral discourses which Abbot Feckenham preached at the obsequies of **the** Queen, though it touches but lightly on the prospects of Elizabeth's reign, sufficiently indicates the gloomy forebodings with which men awaited the coming troubles. Choosing for his text those words of Ecclesiastes (IV, 2, 3,) "Laudavi mortuos magis quam **viventes** sed feliciorem utroque indicavi qui necdum **natus** est," he proceeded in **the course** of his address to speak as follows :—" Let **us comfort ourselves in the** other sister whom God hath left, wishing **to** her **a prosperous reign in peace** and tranquillity with the blessings that the prophet **speaketh of (if it be God's** will) *ut rideat filios filiorum et pacem super Israel* ; ever **confessing that although** God **hath** mercifully provided for them both, yet *Maria optimam partem elegit*, **because it is still a** conclusion, *Laudavi mortuos magis quam viventes*. And **now it only remaineth**, that we leaving to speak of **these two noble ladies, look and provide for ourselves, and** seeing these daily casualties **of death gather our faculties and put ourselves in a** readiness **to die."***

Having **made** up **her mind to** separate herself **from Catholic** Christendom, Elizabeth proceeded to undo **all** that her sister had done on behalf of the Church. The religious houses and among others, the Abbey of Westminster, were again suppressed, and on July 12th, 1552, (the day after the summer festival of St. Benedict) the monks were forced to quit their venerable cloisters. What **became** of them all we are not told, particulars of only three of the Westminster **community** having been preserved. One of these, D. William Copinger, an intimate friend of Bishop Gardiner, on refusing to conform to the newly established order of things in the first year of Elizabeth's reign, was committed prisoner to the Tower where he died soon afterwards. † Abbot Feckenham, who had already endured four years imprisonment during the reign of Edward VI, **was, after** Elizabeth had in vain endeavoured to shake his constancy, committed a second time to the Tower. Thence he was taken and removed to the custody of Horn, the pseudo-bishop of Winchester, who to rid himself of so unwelcome a guest, procured his removal for the third time to the Tower, whence he was afterwards taken **to** the Marshalsea **prison, and then for** a time allowed to remove to lodg**ings in** Holborn though **he still continued a** prisoner at large. During this **period of comparative** freedom, Dr. **Feckenham employed** himself in **various**

---

years, observing without relaxation **his old rule, constantly interceded with God for his miserable and afflicted countrymen. He lived** under **the spiritual direction of** Father Bridgewater, in the greatest retirement and on **the** sparest **diet** ; gave himself up constantly **to** prayer, self denial and fasting ; and in his later years, was favoured with celestial visions **of** a most consoling nature. To some friends who went to tender him assistance when he **was** smitten down with a sore plague, he predicted that "many weeful troubles" would "fall upon the people because of their sins : that "the lands would be untilled for divers years, and that a bloody war" would overtake the country as a punishment. He furthermore averred that **some** of those living would not die until they had beheld these portents. He said moreover, **that** "the Abbey would be one day repaired and rebuilt for the like **worship** which had ceased and that then peace and plenty would for long time abound."

Dr. Lee refers to a tract "A true relation of Master Austin Ringwode" &c. published in London in 1652, wherein the first part of the prophecy is assumed to have been fulfilled by the Civil War.

* A sermon on the death of Queen Mary. British Museum, MSS Cotton. **Vesp. D.** xviii, fol. 94.

† See Dodd's Church History, I. 524, with the authorities there quoted

good works; the building of a hospice for the poor who frequented the mineral waters of Bath being one of the last efforts of his beneficence.* In 1580 the Abbot was again confined in prison, this time with many other noble confessors in the unhealthy Castle of Wisbeach, and there, five years later, he died the **death of** the just. Dom Sigebert Buckley, who had received the Benedictine **habit at** Westminster during Mary's reign, lived on for many years, and **was the means,** under God, **of** perpetuating the old English Congregation **of the Black Monks,** of which he was probably the last professed member.

Scattered notices are found of others who survived long into Elizabeth's reign and even later. Thus in May, 1579, a blind old man who had formerly been a monk of Westminster visited the new Seminary at Douay in the Company of Dr. Allen, its president and founder.† Probably many **of** the English monks had betaken themselves to the Continent.‡ Others we know found a welcome in Catholic Ireland. "In the course of fourteen years about twelve hundred monks escaped to Ireland, where they repaid the hospitality with which they were received by preaching, and strengthening the faith of their hosts. In Elizabeth's reign they were hunted like wolves and shot like carrion crows, till the few survivors from bullet, steel, nakedness and hunger, died out in the most inaccessible places. F. Latchett, a monk of Glastonbury, was imprisoned for twelve years, **and tortured** twenty **times;** but he at last escaped, and died in the wilds of the Galtee mountains at the age of 101."§ The history of the Nuns of the Order, who **were** turned adrift by Henry and who were true to their holy calling affords us many edifying incidents. Thus Dame Isabelle Sackville, the last Prioress **of** Clerkenwell was, through the kindness of her friends, enabled **to** support three of the religious of her convent till her death in her ninety-first year in the **twelfth year of the** reign of Elizabeth. Sybilla Newdigate, last Prioress of Holywell **in London is** supposed to have **perished** of want. Towards **the very end of** Elizabeth's reign two of the nuns of Godstow died of want, one, **Dame Rose Herbert,** at **Hackney,** another near **St. Alban's;** Dame **Isabel Whitehead,** formerly a

---

* See the *Bath Herald*, November 29th, 1879. In 1576, during the **mayoralty of** Thomas Turner, **the** Chamberlain of the city: "Delivered to Mr. Feckenand, **late Abbot of** Westminster, three tonnes of Tymber and 10 fote to build the House for the poor, **by the** White Bath, 33s., 4d. To him more 400 Lathes at 10d. the 100, 3s, 4d."

In the British Museum (Sloane MSS. A. 3919) is a manuscript of **about 400 folio pages** the work of Abbot Feckenham which bears the following heading:

"This booke of sovereigne medicines against the most common **and knowne diseases both** of **men and** women was by good proofe and longe experience collected **of Mr. Dr. Ficknam** late Abbot of Westminster **and** that chieflie for the poor which hath **not att all tymes the** Learned phisitions att hande.

† Records of the English Catholics. Douay Diaries, page **153.**

‡ Thus Father Stratford, the author of a small black letter **book on "the Irish Abbeys** and **Monks,"** who had been a monk of Reading Abbey, died at Tours **iu** 1549, at the age of eighty seven years. See Burke's Historical Portraits of the Tudor Dynasty, II, 217.

§ See the Dublin Review (art: *English Martyrs*) for April, 1877, quoting from the "Accompte of the noble English Fryers" by Paul O'Dempsy, O. S. F. apud Burke "Men and Women of the Reformation." Vol. II, p. 64. In Dr. Burgo's *Hibernia Dominicana*, (at page 559), an account is given of the treachery which Elizabeth exercised in 1602 towards a shipful of Benedictines, Cistercians and Dominicans, forty-two in all, who had been induced to accept a safe conduct out of Ireland, but were, by the Queen's orders drowned off Scattery Island near the mouth of the Shannon.

nun of the monastery of Arthington in Yorkshire, died a prisoner in York Castle. (March 18th, 1587.)

Thus the ancient English family of St. Benedict's Order was gradually becoming extinct when that wonderful revival of Catholicity began which had its origin in the zeal and energy of Dr. Allen. It was not long before the hearts of many of those who were being trained in the Seminaries which he had been mainly instrumental in establishing were turned to the Order of St. Benedict: and the internal differences which disturbed the peace and unity of the new Colleges caused several both priests and clerics, to seek admission into the Benedictine Order in Italy and Spain. To this twofold movement, of those, namely, who were attracted by the edifying lives of the monks to seek to enter among them and of those who, while they sought to avoid the uncongenial surroundings which had made their seminary life distasteful, were yet anxious to devote themselves to the spiritual needs of their countrymen, must be assigned the rapid development of the Benedictine Mission into England which is sketched in the following pages.

Of the author of these *Chronological Notes* it behoves us to say a few words. Ralph, or, as he was afterwards called from his religious name, Bennet Weldon, was the seventeenth and youngest child of Colonel George Weldon of Swanscombe near Gravesend. He was born in London in 1674, and our author thus chronicles the events of his early life in some memoirs which have come down to us.

"At London I first saw light on the 12th of April, S. N. 1674, and was christened at home by Dr. Hornet, or Horneck, minister of the Savoy. My Godfathers were Sir Francis Clarke and Sir John Cotton's eldest son; my godmother the Lady Barkham: the name they gave me was Ralph, which had no other ground than this, that for some generations the family had affected to conserve a succession of two names, viz. Ralph and Anthony; and that my mother being at Swanscombe, the seat of the family, a place very renowned in English history for the Kentish men there conquering the Conqueror, William I, my cousin Elizabeth Weldon, now Mrs. Barrow, as they were viewing the tombs of the name in the Church, takes water from the font and sprinkling my mother tells her she would baptize the child she bore a Ralph. Thus I had my name from my great grandfather's tomb, as noble and stately a monument as one shall see in Westminster Abbey, as I have been credibly assured, for I have not seen the place myself, though I was very near it once but had not time to go.* The inscription on the tomb is this:

To
The Grateful memory of Sir Ralph Weldon, Knt. whose body lies here entombed. His

---

* In Murrays *Hand-book for travellers in Kent and Sussex*, 2nd. occurs the following passage referring to Swanscombe Church. (p. 33.) "In the chancel is the monument of Sir Anthony Weldon, Clerk of the Kitchen to Queen Elizabeth and James I., who in his piteful reminiscences has supplied us with one of the best pictures of the British Solomon, and who sat himself to Sir Walter for some part of the character of Sir Mungo Malagrowther. The monument of Lady Weldon is opposite and in the S. Chancel are other Weldon Memorials, including a stately altar tomb with recumbent figures for Sir Ralph and Lady Weldon: d. 1609.

The Church here was attached to the manor, which soon after the Conquest was granted to the family of Montchesni, who long held it. In it was one of the many shrines which lying on or not far from their road, pilgrims to Canterbury were accustomed to visit. The Shrine here was that of S. Hildefertho whose aid was invaluable in all cases of insanity or "melancholia."

wife, the Lady Elizabeth Weldon, out of her dear affection and respect, erects this monument.

He was chief Clerk of the kitchen to Queen Elizabeth ; afterwards Clerk Comptroller to King James, and died Clerk of the Green Cloth on the 12th November, in the year 1609, and of his age 64, having by the said Elizabeth, daughter to Leven Buffkin, Esq. four sons, Anthony, Clerk of the Kitchen to King James, Henry, Leven, and Ralph, and six daughters, Catharine and Elizabeth, Anne, Mary, Judith, and Barbara.

His grandfather served King Henry VII, and was master of the Household to King Henry VIII, whom likewise Thomas Weldon his uncle served and was cofferer to King Edward VI., and Queen Elizabeth, and died Clerk of the Green Cloth.

> Let this suffice for those who hereby pass,
> To signify How, when and what he was :
> And for his life, his charge, and honest Fame
> He hath Wel-don, and so made good his name."

Our author then gives an elaborate account of his reasons for thinking that the family name was the same with the famous one of Guelpho or Welpho in Germany, "from whence, by what I have seen, I am persuaded it came with the Saxons into England."—Regarding the diversity of spelling, he says, a little further on," Those that are strangers to us, because it sounds sweeter pronounce and write our name *Welden*, but we of Swanscombe hold stiffly to the *o*."

Sir Anthony Weldon, the grand-father of Ralph held the offices of Clerk of the Green Cloth, Clerk of the Kitchen, and Clerk of the Woodyard under King James I. By his wife Eleanor, daughter of George Wilmer, Esq, he had twelve children, eight sons and four daughters. The eldest son, Ralph, "became a Colonel, and Governor of Plymouth and enjoyed the estate, which is at least even now, as I was assured in 1700, without exaggeration, seven or eight hundred pound sterling a year ; adorned with great honours, as particularly a famous piece of homage every year on St. Andrew's day on Rochester Bridge, as the tide goes under, and the Royalty, as I think they term it, of Rochester Castle." The second son, Edward, "was shot through the head as he entered triumphantly a place he had taken for the Great Duke of Muscovy." Then came Anthony, "who became very famous in the Wars in the Low Countries, and after he had spent three fair estates, perished at sea in a great expedition he had undertaken for the Great Duke of Tuscany." The fourth brother, Henry, after the death of Edward, returned from Muscovy and lies interred at Swanscombe. Thomas, the fifth son, married a considerable fortune, and passed his time quietly at Goudhurst in Kent. George, the father of our author, became a Colonel, and "had a great hand in the King's restoration." Of the daughters, Elizabeth "married Mr. Hart, a family of great account ;" Eleanor "unhappily married Mr. Say, one of the Judges of King Charles I, and, by a just Judgment of God, that man's posterity is now come to nothing ;" Susanna became the wife of Mr. Charnock, and her sister Mary appears to have remained unmarried.

Colonel George Weldon was bred up for some time under Sir John Pennington, Vice Admiral under the Earl of Northumberland. On the breaking out of the Civil Wars in the reign of Charles I, Sir Anthony took up the Roundhead cause and induced his eldest son to throw in his lot with him. But George remained true to his King, and was accordingly banished for seven years by his own father, and "what was yet harder, for his father's sake was never looked on notwithstanding all his loyal services acted on behalf of the Stuarts, as ensue hereafter."

These loyal services were of a very varied nature, In 1647 he was engaged against Lord Fairfax and Cromwell in their march upon London. "Afterwards he was privy to all the actings of Colchester, being several times in action with Col. Will. Mayr and Lieut. Genl. Mayr and by reason he repulsed his father's orders to take a command of horse under Harrison against his Majesty at Worcester in that rebellious **service,** Sir Anthony his father utterly deprived him **of** his affection, **and at** his **death** refused to see him, neither did he leave him **so** much as £5; and **all this was upon** no other account than that of his being **loyal to his sovereign."** Besides " he ventured all that he had and his very **life in destroying the Committee of** safety; he received a commission for raising four **thousand horse against Lambert,** when he was in the North; and materially aided the **Duke of Albemarle** (then General Monk) in securing Coventry and **Northampton.** For these services he was three times **earnestly** recommended by the Duke to the King's notice, but was not so fortunate as to meet with any reward." How this came about is thus narrated:

"**One** thing that contributed to his remaining thus unrecompensed, was that **as** the King **(Charles II)** returned triumphantly home, and he, among other his faithful servants, attended him on horseback as his Majesty was passing from Dover, the horse my father rid grew **all on a** sudden into freaks; and, as he was not far from the King, it gave the King's horse **a kick,** and leapt with its rider into an arm of the sea and broke his leg. The tide was out and **so he** escaped drowning. The Right Hon. Earl of Bridgwater sent his coach and took him up; and while he was curing, which lasted some time, all was distributed at Court; so that when he was able to appear he experienced the truth of the English proverb *Out of sight out of mind*—The King excused what had passed, promising fair for the future, as soon as possibly he could, which proved never, as we have seen.

Besides all this, he was entrusted with many concernments for King Charles I. for which he suffered very much and as he attended on his Majesty for **a** time after the English had got him from the Scotch, wherever he waited on the King, as he could not imagine the wicked drifts and fetches of those perverse men who at last took the King's life away, as he was astonished at the rudeness and brutality of the people to their Sovereign, with his own hands he would so cane their sides to their duties that they dared as well be hanged as forgot themselves while he waited; which the suffering King took so kindly with his other loyal services, that he declared that, if ever it pleased God to settle him on his throne quietly again, he would highly advance him.

In one word, this most loyal and worthy gentleman who had never really acted against the King by thought, word or deed, but had ever made it his whole care and study, to serve their Majesties, and had been the refuge and azyle of their friends, as I said in 1700, authentic testimonies thereof, under their hands **and seals of many persons** when they were so straightly pursued, that they expected nothing **but death—yet all this** did not hinder Mr. Weldon's dying unrewarded, and neglected **and brought to hard shifts,** Anno Domini 1679, at 12 o'clock, at noon on the 30th of March, **interred on the 2nd of April** following.

He married twice, first to a cousin german **of the** Countess **of** Anglesey and the **old** Countess of Buckingham. This gentlewoman was a widow. He never had child by her, but right and title to £3300 sterling a year. She dying, he made her a noble funeral, and sometime after married my mother. It was in the time of the detestable regicide Oliver; for they were not only married by a parson, but by a Justice of Peace. Her name was Lucy Necton, of a family of much ancienter date than the Conquest, seated in Norfolkshire. Her grandfather possessed £3000 sterling a year in old rents, which they say would now make £6000 sterling a year. This Gentleman marrying a Stuart, nothing less than a first Cousin to King James I, when he came to the crown of England, she lived so highly puffed up with the thoughts of her royal blood, that she brought this estate to only £100 sterling a year, bringing her son up at the Inns of Court, that by the dint of his wit, he might help himself to another estate as he could. But King James I who had been his Godfather and given him his name, pitying his circumstances, gave him also offices at Court, so that at his death, he left betwixt his three daughters £1500 sterling a year. The eldest married Sir John Gaddesden, in Hertfordshire; the youngest was my mother; the middlemost dying, her portion was divided betwixt the other two. By this means my mother brought £800 sterling a year to my father, land of inheritance. This presently was made use of to make good my father's right and title by his former wife, of which he recovered £1500 sterling a year, King James II, then Duke of York, rising up in the house of Lords and speaking in the behalf of my father's cause, whom he honoured with his royal favour and esteem, and was sorry to see in such turmoil of law, while his cause was just. This was the final trial of all the bustles about that estate. Ten thousand pounds sterling cash was flung away in these affairs, to my certain knowledge, and my father was so disgusted, that he lost all appetite of pursuing the rest. Several families concerned in restoring the usurped estate, were impoverished sadly by these lawsuits, and a Lord undone, and the said £1500 a year tricked away from him. By my mother he had many children, of which I am the seventeenth and last. Few lived; only my sister and three males; but so that, betwixt each of our births there was seven years space. Of my oldest brother I say nothing now, reserving his memory to the year in which I was sent to England upon his account. My brother Charles came over in '88, in order to be a monk here, but, went first to Tyrone to the Mauritian Benedictine Seminary, to review his humanities; but here he, in a short time, ended his days like a Saint. How and when he became a Catholic, I know not. I suppose he saw me so young and green, that therefore he would never speak to me of such a thing, but he never ceased with my mother till he saw her reconciled to the Church in the time of King James II. But then, under the usurper William III, teased to death by her protestant relations, in whose hands she chanced to be then alone, she became so indifferent to outward communion in religion, that she would neither hear Priest nor parson—declaring that she put all her confidence and trust in the merits of her Redeemer and Saviour, Jesus Christ. She died about her great climacterical year, April 26, S. M, 1702, and was nobly interred, according to her birth, in Aldgate Church, at London, in the vault her grandfather and the Lord Darcy built there for them and theirs, where lies her father Mr. James Necton, and her Mother Madam Theodosia, daughter to one of the Kings at arms in England, and who, in marrying a second time had taken to husband Major General Gibson.

I see no ground for any reproaches to be made to me upon **this mishap I did all that was possible for me to do, in 1700, when I saw her last, but was always repaid with the above-** said Declaration. Yet seeing that she ended with all the piety **that was possible for a person** in those circumstances, heartily sorry for all offences, entirely resigned, composed **and easy**, possessing her senses entire to the last moment, **I have reason to** hope well for **her possessing** the infinite mercy of God, and with so much the more **reason by** how much I am **thereto in-** duced by what Monsr. Habert tells us in the life of the great **Cardinal Berulle**; **that a nun**, having apostatized from her profession, and tottering after that **in her** faith, was recommended to the said Cardinal's piety. He to the utmost that could be expected from his great sense of God and religion, acquitted himself of his commission, offering himself in a manner, a living sacrifice for the said soul, by much prayer, and severe corporal affliction, to obtain her grace. Some hopes he had, but they lasted not long: for "inimicus homo" undoing in the night what he did in the day, as she had abandoned her nunnery, so she abandoned the faith she had been brought up in, and for the over measure of her wickedness, became a minister's wife, and away with him ran to Geneva, and there died so. After many years of Monseigneur Berulle's being continually afflicted in mind for her, as a lost soul, an extraordinary holy pious creature, whose true worth and virtue he very thoroughly knew, declared to him the lost soul was to **be** found in heaven; **for that**, through an extraordinary and singular **grace** of God, expiring she had made **such an act of** contrition for all her miscarriages, **that God** had received **her into** his Mercies—A **most prodigious and** singular example.

After a sickly childhood[*] he was by his father's last earnest desires on his deathbed, " continually kept at some public school or other " till, on his recovery from a great sickness in 1684, he was taken by his mother to Westminster, that he might enjoy the air of St. James' Park. There "an honest Catholic" made him acquainted with Father Joseph Johnston,[†] who, after sufficiently instructing

---

[*] He says of himself, "I was nursed up with strong Spanish wines **as Sack, and** such like, with Naples biscuits, and nothing else but such things."

[†] On the foundation of the Royal Benedictine Monastery at St. James' **Palace of which** Fr. Johnston was a member, Weldon elsewhere writes "James II. rightly **surnamed the**

him in the Catholic faith, received him into the Church. **He thus recounts his conversion.**

"**For** as near as I can remember, my dipping into the clear **fountain of the Church was on the 12th of October S. N. on a Saturday, 1687,** when I made **my abjuration at the Royal convent of St. James'** in the hands of R. F. Joseph Johnston; **and was admitted to the most holy Sacrament of the Altar, on** the Monday following, October **14, in the said chapel, which I have therefore ever since** particularly loved, and much **grieve to see it in the power of** erroneous darkness.

My Mother **was very** vigilant to cultivate **my tender** greenness with the best and noblest principles of morality and honour and **conscience, and** took care that I prayed morning and evening &c, but as she **was not** learned, **as few are in** the affairs of religion, so she **could not** teach me much thereof; **but I** hearing **my brothers** arguing with her about the schism. God enlightened with his grace my tender **reason, I** argued with myself, without telling them my thoughts,—that those whom God **made use of,** to plant the Church, were **men of** most extraordinary holy lives; while it was evident **that King** Henry VIII **was a man of most** infamous shameful life; wherefore I concluded it **was never by** such that God ever makes any alterations in Church affairs, and by consequence, **that his** pretended *Reformation* **was** but an execrable *deformation,* and that therefore **I would** never remain any longer in it, come what would of my change. And so, without asking any leave, I became a Roman Catholic, resolved to die in the truth thereof. The day I abjured, I was sent to visit a young gentleman lately come from Constantinople, in order to my undertaking as much ; but I went, and first made my peace with God at St. James' ; and then I went about the human amusements ; but after that I had sealed up my holy deed by the most holy Sacrament of the Altar, my **mother** finding **out** the affair, I knew not how, was in such a toss, that, had I been murdered **she could not** have been **in** more. But God **gave** me **grace** to support the storm : **and crossing the Park of St. James' I fetched Revd. Fr. Johnston, who** calmed it. I cannot

---

Just, **of** most holy memory, **no** sooner had the English **imperial diadem on his** professed Catholic hands (*sic*), but he thought himself of its old props the Benedictine Crozier. (Reader consult the histories of England, you will find this no piece of arrogant pride **but a** great truth humbly hushed up in a word): and therefore resolved his royal Consort's Chapel should be attended by a Convent of Benedictine Monks. Thus **the** Royal Chapel of St. James', (the Franciscans being placed with the Queen Dowager at Somerset House), came into the Benedictines **to whom** his **Majesty** had shown much affection before, having two of them attending his **Duchess when** he was **Duke of** York, to wit, the RR. FF. **Lionel Sheldon and Nicholas or Poss, as we have** seen before, besides those King Charles **II,** his royal brother, maintained, **under pretence of** their being **part of the** clergy composing **the** Chapel of his Queen. **The monks** thus **placed at St.** James' were as follows : 1. **V. R. F. Augustine** Howard. **2. V. R. F.** Francis Lawson, **3.** F. Maurus Nicholls, **alias Poss, 4. F. Joseph Aprice. 5. R. F. Philip Ellis, of Weddesdon** in Buckinghamshire, **professed at** Douay **the 30th. of** Nov. 1670, **whom** the King **before** the Revolution, honoured with **a mitre** in this **Chapel of** St. James', **6.** R. F. Thomas Aprice, 7. R. F. Bennet Gibbons, **8.** R. F. **Maurus** Knightley, 9. V. R. F. Bernard Gregson. **10.** F. **Cuthbert** Parker, whom the King ordering to be otherwise disposed of, the V. R. F. Augustine *alias* Thomas Constable, of the Castle called Eagle in Lincolnshire, professed at Douay the 22nd of August, 1649, came in his place. **11.** F. Bernard Lowick, de Humili Visitatione B. M. V. 12. R. F. Joseph Johnston. 13. F Cuthbert Marsh was added for his preaching so eloquently. 14. F. Gregory Timperley. 15. Br. Thomas Brabant, **a** pious, industrious, laborious Lay-Brother of Douay house deceased **not** long ago at London to the great grief of all that know him 16. Br. Austin Rumley, Lay-Brother of Dieulwart.

And such was the affection of his Majesty to the habit, **that when he** assisted **at his** Royal Chapel at Whitehall, (for he often resorted to that of St James'), **he would have** one of our Fathers by the credence in his habit, that seeing St. Bennet **in his children, he** might be ever mindful of him. I have seen it as I say, and wondered at **it,** till the V. R. F. Francis Fenwick told me this as I have delivered it, and he was the person that used to be there, which seemed to me therefore strange, because the Chapel of Whitehall was served by the ecular Clergy and some Regular Clerks as one may term them."

ut admire that she had so much honour and virtue and dread for the great sacrament of religion, that she never offered, in all her taking on, to call me back from what I had done; but lamented what would become me, for that, by this, I had forfeited all the kindness, favour and assistance, I had to expect from friends, in the desolate circumstances her and my father's misfortunes had cast us into. But she was soon eased of this concern, Fr. Johnston proposing to her a Monachal condition for me, which I was mighty desirous of from the first time I had seen the Chapel, desiring nothing more than to spend my life in the service of God in the habit of St. Bennet. Accordingly, I set out after Easter in 1688, took shipping at Dover the 29 of May, and arrived at our house of Paris the 5th of June N. S., the eve of the great solemnity of Whit-Sunday. But as I was too young for the habit, I was sent to the Mauritian Benedictine Seminary of Pontlevoy, by Blois, from whence I set out hither on the 5th. Dec. 1699, and on the 17th of the same month, by the order of R. F. Prior, Fr. Francis Fenwick, then occupied abroad, Rev. Fr. Maurus Nelson, Sub-Prior, clothed me, as it was a Sunday, a little before Compline, and out of honour to our great Patriarch, I chose his name, anno æt. meæ 25, and on the 13th of January, 1692, also a Sunday, I made my profession.* Rev. Fr. Francis Fenwick did the ceremony, in presence of Rev. Fr. Joseph Sherburne, President: —so that my clothing and profession happened on two days singularly consecrated by the Church to the honour of the Eternal Wisdom of God, without my having sought after [it].— Thus came all about what many had often said of me, when in my tender infancy, they never saw me better pleased than in setting up altars and rearing stately temples pro modulo meo of what I could lay hold of: Though there was no likelihood of my ever becoming a Catholic,

* At the same time as **Bennet** Weldon, Br. Joseph **Kennedy was likewise** professed. Br. Bennet gives the following account of his fellow novice.

"This F. Joseph alias William Kennedy is son to Sir Richard Kennedy, Knight and Baronet, 2nd baron of her Majesty's court of Exchequer in Ireland. He was sent to London in 1682 to the Inns of Court, where his brother, Sir Robert Kennedy, who managed his father's concerns, was to pay him fourscore pounds a year. In this famous town he became a Roman Catholic. Fr. Joseph Johnston was the instrument of his conversion. Rev. Fr. Joseph, President, received his abjuration at our Royal Chapel of St. James', and gave him here at Paris, on the 28th of August 1687, the habit himself very solemnly, with his own religious name of Joseph, before many considerable persons, for whom afterwards there was not only a formal but splendid treat in the convent. But his brother Sir Robert Kennedy dying, **he** was sent by his Superiors into Ireland to look after his affairs. While he was thus busied, King James II, of glorious memory, came into the country, and empowered him to act for him **on** the lands about his brother's estate, to raise soldiers &c, and made him Governor of Wicklow, a castle on the sea shore. But Fr. Kennedy managing with his sister, a notable Dame, his brother's estate, and having the person of his little nephew, Sir Richard Kennedy, in his hands, his most earnest desire was to get away secretly his nephew, without the friends knowing anything thereof and bring him for France, and here bring him up a Roman Catholic, with all education suitable to his quality. The design miscarried, the friends took alarm, and raised the country against him, deferring him to the Viceroy, my Lord Tyrconnel, who to avoid the consequences of shocking and vexing the Protestants, at that time found himself in a necessity of issuing out orders against Mr. Kennedy, as disturbing the king's peace, so that he **ran** risk of his life for his undertaking. In fine, in 1690, reaching Paris again in the begin**ning of** November, **on the** 6th of the said month he put on his habit again and we were pro**fessed 1792** together **as is** said. Afterwards Fr. Johnston being Prior, made him his Procurator. Orders he had **taken** before. at Cambray, having been sent to Douay, for the dislike some had taken to his conduct here, though a man of an honourable and virtuous carriage. But the very Scriptures (The Bible) show how Saints themselves sometimes disagree, while each endeavours for that which seems to him to be best. He had not been 2 months Procurator or Cellerarius, but he was called by the President into the mission, where he is very much esteemed, and has seen his nephew who cannot bear his uncle a grudge for so much good he sought to procure him in his infancy; but like a gentleman incline to satisfy him on his estate: For Fr. Kennedy had a very handsome income, which he gave up very freely with himself before the Altar, and had not the orangian Revolution happened, his debts could have been paid, and the house helped by his fortune: for I do not find his debts **as I have** heard them represented. There are papers in the house where he gives a very clear account of them, as also of his estate, and what was owing to him himself."

yet they said more, that I must become a religious man. Besides that, in that little age, it was a mighty satisfaction to me to be carried in arms to Westminster Abbey, on whose ground even my father was born in a great house standing almost close to the Abbey Church, above the Northern Porch.

The Easter following my profession, R. F. Fenwick, delighting to encourage those whom he saw sensible of their duties, as he told me himself, would needs do me the honour of taking me for his companion to St. Germain's en Laye, where he was most highly obliging and kind, making me to kiss the young prince's hand, etc. ; but when we went to the Rt. Hon. **Alexander** Felton, Baron Gosworth, Lord High Chancellor of Ireland, he presently asked who I was. R. F. Fr. Fenwick had no sooner told him, but he presently again answered with great demonstrations of a high esteem of my father, expressing much civility to me upon it,—a sign my father's integrity and worth was sufficiently known to the better part of the state. And King James himself, in a visit he here honoured us with, upon the account of my father took particular notice of me, in our great room as we call it. Besides that, before he came to the crown, when Jeffreys was very severe to my Brother-in-law, fining him £2000 sterling, after he had committed him to prison for only a few words he had hastily and inconsiderately let fall, tending to the blame of those who had condemned a man, my mother no sooner appeared before his highness, and told whose widow she was, but as soon as over he heard the name, he most graciously assured her, her business was done ; and presently all the pursuit ceased, to the very great astonishment of even Jeffreys himself.

After spending about two years at St. Edmunds', Br. Bennet, thinking himself called to a life of still greater retirement and perfection, besought the Very Rev. F. President General of the English Benedictines for leave to withdraw to the Abbey of La Trappe, where a strict reform of the Cistercian Institute had recently been introduced by the celebrated De Rancé. Failing to obtain the approbation of his superiors for this scheme, Br. Bennet nevertheless persisted in his design, and encouraged by letters of the holy reformer, (who herein seems to have acted with less than his ordinary discretion), left Paris and set out for perfection and La Trappe. De Rancé received his new postulant with all possible kindness but after a sojourn of about eight months among his new brethren (from July 4th, 1694, to March, 1695), he found that he had made a mistake and returned somewhat crest-fallen to St. Edmund's. After a brief stay there he was sent to La Celle en Brie where the English Benedictines of the Paris house had a small dependency or priory. The retirement of La Celle suited the studious tastes of Br. Bennet, and he remained there till the April of 1696 when he was recalled to Paris to his great grief "being sorry to exchange the quiet of that solitary place for the noise of so great a town." The following year, (1697) he was again placed at La Celle for a few months, and in 1698 obtained the permission of his Superiors to reside among the French Benedictines of St. Maur in the Abbey of Jumièges in Normandy. His stay there was cut short by certain family affairs which made his presence necessary in England. He thus accounts for this unexpected change in the quiet tenour of his life.

"Through the Orangian Revolution and the wars ensuing, not having any account of my friends, I acquainted Rev. Fr. Hitchcock, then Prior, that I desired to inform myself how affairs stood with them, but especially my elder brother, whom at my entrance into religion I knew to be in a very flourishing condition in the East Indies. R. F. Hitchcock herein very willingly and very obligingly employed good Br. Thomas Brabant who at London did the business of the Congregation ; upon enquiry he found my brother returning home had been made away, and (he) expressly set down in his letter that my brother's fortune was counted five hundred thousand pounds sterling."

His elder brother, Colonel George **Weldon** had held the post of Deputy Governor of Bombay, and the fortune which he had accumulated and the rumours of foul play which reached Br. Bennet at Paris made him desirous in the interests of his mother and sisters to do what he could to recover some portion of his brother's property which was almost their only support. He set out from Paris in the company of Sir Richard Moore, nephew of Prior Hitchcock, and proceeded to Dunkirk.

"When I came to the sea shore, not finding a conveniency to pass over at Dunkerq, and Sir Richard being in the humor of staying there, I went alone to Calais. The weather being contrary, the packet boat could not stir; but there coming an express from the King of France to his ambassador at London, passage was offered me in a little fisher boat with it, mighty uneasy I was to go over in such a small thing, and when I was in it I was ready to come out of it again; but I knew not what overpowered me and held me there; from midnight we laboured till three o'clock in the afternoon the next day against wind and tide, viewing Dover and not being able to reach it, when all on a sudden it pleased God to send a favorable gale of wind which presently carried us in, the sea being become then almost without motion and the sun shining very pleasantly as the moon had done all night; though then the waters were so rough to the little vessel that I several times expected that what with the waves and what with the wind we should have turned over."

The history of Colonel George Weldon which his brother the monk recounts in great detail is too long to be set down here; but it seems from that account that the Colonel was poisoned on his way home from India. Here is an extract from the narrative:

"While they joyfully repair home the Lady (Mrs. G. Weldon) falls sick and proves poisoned; breathing forth her last gasp 25th. of April S. V. 1697. The corpse, adorned with jewels to the value of £500 sterling, was committed to the sea, the ship being under sail and far from land, and reached not land till two months after, when it touched on an Island called Morusha's, (I know not whether I spell the name right; as it belongs to the Hollanders, possibly it has its name from some Prince of Orange called Maurice) at Carpenter's bay. Here the Captain began to persuade my brother to leave the ship and take his diversion on land to solace his grief and melancholy which he contracted for the loss of his lady: wherefore at night through excercise he had gotten a good stomach insomuch that he eat the best part of two pullets, and never was better in his life as to health; but as he loved salad, he met that supper with a fatal one; for presently he found himself all on a sudden in a moment seized with such violent pains, that if he had been racked he could not have endured more; and so on the 2nd of July. S. V. of the same year he also expired in vast torment. Some have declared that the authors of this barbarity seeing the wind stood fair for them to be gone from that place, they stifled him with pillows that they might not be frustrated of profiting of the wind by expecting till the poison had wrought its full effect..... They buried him in the Island, and over him reared up a monument such as the times of Barbarism in the uncivilized ages used to set up for remarkable persons."

The efforts which the Weldons made to recover the property of the murdered man and bring his murderers to justice proved unavailing, and so Br. Bennet after spending some months in England returned to the continent. "Seeing," he says, "that I could do nothing in England either as to them or the reclaiming of my mother, as I have said, and that I had no character for the mission, my conscience spurred me to my convent again to there live according to what I had vowed before the Altar." Before proceeding to Paris, however, he spent about six weeks with the monks of St. Gregory's in Douay.

What Br. Bennet says about his having no character for the mission is no exaggeration. Though a person of extremely regular life and studious habits,— we are told that he never missed a conventual duty when in health, and spent nearly sixteen hours daily in study and writing,—he was of a very retiring scrupulous nature, so much so that he would never be induced to take Priest's Orders, and remained throughout his life a simple monk.

The remainder of his career presents few incidents. He passed a few weeks among the Maurist monks at Treport in the autumn of 1701; he spent about a twelvemonth at La Celle two years subsequently and returned to Paris in November 1704 and spent there the remainder of his life. His death occurred on the evening of November 23rd, 1713, when he was in his 40th year. His literary labours were undertaken at the suggestion of Father Bernard Gregson, President General of the English Benedictines, who persuaded him to employ his leasure in collecting materials for a history of the Congregation; two folio Volumes of this work, the result of his industry, are still preserved. Another work of Br. Bennet's is now in the Library of the British Museum.* This is entitled "A course and rough first draught of your History of England's late most holy and most glorious Royal Confessor and Defender of your true Faith King James II...... Ut aliqua Serenissimi Regis Jacobi II haberetur notitia in Bibliotheca Domus suæ hæc exscripsit mensibus Maii, Junii, Julii et Augusti 1706 Frater Benedictus Weldon à Sancto Raphaelo Archangelo Monachus Anglo-Benedictinus Monasterii Sancti Edmundi Regis et Martyris suburbiis Lutetiæ Parisiorum Sanjacobæanis.

The Chronological Notes are an abridgment of the two folio volumes of his Historical Memoirs of the English Benedictines and were finished in 1709, though a few additions were subsequently made. Two copies of this work are preserved at St. Gregory's, Downside, and from them the present Edition has been prepared. The spelling throughout has been modernized, though proper names have been given as they stand in the manuscript. The same remark may be made regarding the names of the monks and nuns in the appendix. This will account possibly for such variations as Belasyse and Bellasyse, Kennet, Kennett, Middelton and Middleton, and similar cases.

The editor in conclusion begs to return his best thanks to the many kind friends who have supplied him with the catalogues of the professed religious which appear at the end of this volume.

---

* Additional MSS. 10, 113. The work was purchased for the Museum Library at Heber's Sale in February, 1836.

CORRIGENDA.

Page 51, *for* Berkgate *read* Merkgate.
„ 89, last line, *for* Rayner *read* Reyner.
„ 122, line 11, *for* Cank *read* Cauke.
„ 143, line 8, *for* 1624 *read* 1623.
„ 154, line 8, *for* conseut *read* consent.
„ 168, line 8, *for* Frier *read* Frere.

IN THE APPENDIX.

Page 4, *for* 1122 *read* 1182.
„ 5, *for* D. John Baines *read* Barnes.
„ „ *for* Badd *read* Budd.
„ 8, line 13, *for* R. F. Moundeford, *read* R. F. John of St. Martin, Moundeford.
„ 32, line 17, *for* as *read* are.
„ 35, Anno 1784, *for* Thielmans *read* Thielmans.
„ 36, line 21, *for* Jeromima *read* Jeronima.
„ 40, Anno 1776, *for* Harkham *read* Markham.
„ 42, line 29 *for* Gillibord, *read* Gillibrord.

To

THE VERY REVEREND & VENERABLE FATHER
FATHER BERNARD GREGSON,
PRESIDENT GENERAL OF THE ENGLISH CONGREGATION
OF THE HOLY ORDER OF ST. BENEDICT,
PATRIARCH OF THE WESTERN MONKS,

THE COLLECTOR WISHETH ALL PROSPERITY
& GIVETH ACCOUNT OF HIS STUDIES.

Very Reverend Father.

When I consider all human societies or public weals whether profane or sacred, so much the more careful I find them of maintaining the glory their predecessors or beginners have achieved, by how much the actions of those worthies have been deeply imprinted in their minds. Wherefore Divine Grace having made me a member of one of her sacred societies, I have always delighted to consider her operations in those she hath set me for patterns and examples in this course of life to which she hath called me. This hath been the cause that not content with the lives of the Saints of this great Order, recorded through all ages by so many illustrious pens as are the chiefest storehouse of modern erudition, I have also been glad to behold the latter glories of so sacred a weal. Hence come these Chronological Notes on modern times that fresh examples may inspire new courage to maintain by sanctity and purity of life, the first achieved glories of a society so magnificently holy, as the Church of God hath beheld with joy, the most illustrious Order of Saint Benedict, of which the English Congregation (as all monuments of antiquity over and above attest) hath been a most egregious and singular part and ornament: the glory of whose worthies I have here attempted to echo, but how successfully I abandon to your Very Reverend Paternity's pious judgment and charitable censure.

I have not here recorded all, but have chosen the most remarkable, not questioning but that many of them whom I have not mentioned deserve as honourable a remembrance, if I could but have obtained as particular a knowledge of their affairs as I have done of these.

As to the rest, if any one can prove me to have been so far mistaken as to have praised in this little book any undeserving person, now for then I renounce to any praise I may be found to have given them. For that I only applaud and admire those who sensible of the dreadful vows they have poured forth before the altar in the presence of Almighty God and all the host of heaven, are careful and solicitous to live up steadily to them; not those who by contrary practices blot out of their minds such terrible obligations though so solemnly contracted in the face of heaven and earth: an invincible argument that they do not love Jesus Christ our dread God and good Lord, or else they would not fling off his sweet and light yoke; seeing the proof of his love he assures us to be the execution of his **sacred and amiable commands**. Wherefore what can be said to them but that at the hour of their death and (by consequence) of their judgment they will find it had been much better for them * that they had never heard or known of the ways of sanctity and justice than to turn their backs to the Sun of Justice † and Righteousness which hath risen to them to manifest to them the secrets of his dread glory, while in the depth of his terrible yet just judgments ‡ he permits so many others for a just punishment on their wicked deserts to see them without seeing them § till their wilful blindness unfold itself when seeing will nothing avail them, for that no more time ‖ will be left them to work in.

I have nothing further to say on this little book than that it must take patience in its silence of the just praises of the worthy and honourable Superior to whom it addresses itself, for that I dare not presume to attempt on your Very Reverend Paternity's known modesty and humility superior to all applause and admiration of inconstant mankind. Wherefore the reader must not expect to hear from me your incomparable moderation and meekness in the supreme power of the Congregation, your singular readiness and exact justice to afford satisfaction where reason craves it, your undaunted fidelity in the performance of your honourable charge which neither the vexations of the seas or the inconveniences or dangers of the armies on land have been able to hinder in its progress, your just regulations in your Visits which when exactly remembered and followed will ever prove a main support to that regularity and good order which is by the public expected in Religious houses, and which, if the Son of

---

* 2 Peter ii. 21. † Wisdom v. 6. ‡ Ps. cxlvii. 20.
§ Is. vi. 9, 10. ‖ John ix. 4.

God find not there, He will call them dens of thieves.* These things and many more on which I cannot reflect but with pleasure I must silence to respect your humble conduct and no longer tire your patience, presuming nothing further than to assure your Very Reverend Paternity that by the grace of God you will ever find me

    Very Reverend Father

      Your most humble Servant and dutiful subject

        Br. B. W.

   From the Convent of
St. Edmund's at Paris. May 25. 1709.

* Mat. xxi. 13.

NOTES

CONCERNING THE VENERABLE BODY OF BENEDICTINES IN ENGLAND WHICH SO MUCH ENDURED AND SMARTED WITH THE REST OF CATHOLIC RELIGION UNDER THE TYRANNICAL IMPIETY OF KING HENRY VIII.

CHAPTER THE FIRST.

THE MODERN BENEDICTINE REFORMATIONS.

It is remarkable that Saint Benedict, author of the Benedictine monks, as Saint Gregory the Great, a most illustrious ornament of the said Order witnesses in the admirable history he has left to the world of the actions of that great Patriarch of Western Monachism, that he having founded several monasteries, they held of him as of their common father, and he corrected in them what their Abbots informed him went amiss. This example of this glorious Patriarch does not appear in History to have been followed by his children after his triumphant exit out of this life, nor indeed could it be followed, the Order spreading into dominions subject to different sovereigns; but experience convincing the Church of the inestimable benefits that might redound from it to monachism, and that no way could be thought of so proper to conserve in its primitive purity and integrity that holy profession, the most vigilant universal pastor Innocent III in a council he held at the Lateran Palace (1215) issued out a Decree to oblige the Benedictines in each kingdom to unite into a Congregation, that is to resolve to hold assemblies from time to time, and agree on laws, and superiors who should take care they were put into due execution, that the holy Rule might be faithfully observed and equally practised by each house. But these happy delineations of an assured and stable reformation obtained not thoroughly and in good earnest their blessed effect till in these latter ages, when the Venerable Lewis Barbo, (who of a

Canon Regular of Saint George of Alga in Venice was made abbot of Saint Justina of Padua in 1408 by Pope Gregory XII and professed under the Rule of Saint Benedict February 3rd, 1409), at Ariminum was presently blessed Abbot; and blessed with the Spirit of Saint Benedict he resolved and effected the reform which bears now the title of Mount Cassin Congregation. Not long after sprang up that of Bursfeld in Germany which held its first Chapter on the Sunday *Vocem Jucunditatis* 1464, and Cisneros began that which is called of Valladolid in Spain about the year 1520. In 1596 began that of Saint Vanne in Lorraine from which have risen those of Saint Maur and Cluny in France besides those monasteries which in Flanders have embraced it.

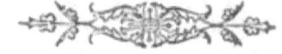

CHAPTER THE SECOND.

Providence of God to the Order of Saint Benedict in England especially.

But as the Order of Saint Benedict though everywhere in great request, yet, never flourished in any kingdom as it did in England, hence the English Benedictine Congregation hath very singular prerogatives, beyond all others confirmed unto it by the Holy See. For the understanding of which, it is necessary to take a view of Saint Austin's arrival in England, with the Gospel in one hand, as I may say, and the Rule of Saint Benedict in the other, under the banner of Christ our Saviour. And though it be not my present subject to entertain the reader with the greatness and eminence of the order of Saint Benedict for piety and learning in the Church and splendour in the world, (the former of which is as ungratefully by men passed by and forgotten, as the latter is gazed at with malignity and envy), yet I cannot but take notice of that particular regard Divine Providence has from time to time had of this Order, which ever since its first planting has grown up with the Church, becoming both her support and ornament, flourishing with her and sharing more than all others in her sufferings and vexations. Neither was the See of Rome (the Mother and Mistress of all Churches and particularly of England) ever since she shook off the yoke of secular oppression and enjoyed that liberty wherewith Jesus Christ endowed her, better administered than while

St. Benedict's disciples sat in that Chair, nor more generally venerated than while monks were her apostles, nor more safely guarded than when Benedictines were her champions.

And this singular favour of God to the Order does appear yet more evident in our nation, and to it also, if men are not dead to all sense of gratitude; for this religious Institute took root among the English as soon as Christianity itself, spread with the Faith and sank with it likewise; as if there were so close an alliance between it and orthodox profession, that that saving belief which was disseminated among us but by it, could not subsist without it. As long as monachism held up in England the Catholic Church had its fences and bulwarks, but that being cast down, the Church became the prey of the impiety of the times.

CHAPTER THE THIRD.

THE BENEDICTINE MONACHISM OF ST. AUGUSTINE, THE ITALIAN APOSTLE OF THE ENGLISH NATION.

I know that many and those not unlearned authors do drive up the conversion of our country much farther, many ages before St. Augustine and his companions entered the land. I know they attribute one conversion thereof to St. Joseph of Arimathea under King Arviragus, and a second to Pope Eleutherius' missioners under King Lucius: nay some stick not to challenge Simon the Chananean, others St. Paul, others St. Peter for our apostles: but without entering into a particular examen of these assertions (which want not probable grounds and powerful abettors) my reader is to know that not any of these blessings reached the English; the ancient Britons reaped them all. Neither was there among the English any footstep of Christianity before St. Augustine's landing, except in King Ethelbert's royal consort, and that in the kingdom of Kent only, and confined to a private chapel and some few domestics, and those too, externs. And that St. Augustine introduced and established the Rule of Saint Benedict, is as certain as that himself was a monk and had order from his Abbot and Pastor St. Gregory to admit no others to serve in the Matrice (or Mother) church of Canterbury. This I say, is certain; at least it was so to all former ages. For though this Order was ever attended by that blessing to be hated and detracted by the world, yet none of her most desperate adversaries ever dared attack her on that side which they saw so well guarded, and from whence they were sure to be beaten with shame and confusion. The first that ever made doubt thereof or would seem to do so, was a German, James Whipheling, who like the fellow that set on fire Diana's temple, was resolved to get himself a name though only for his impiety and impudence; but according to the ordinary fate of such obscure and temerarious writers, the work perished with the author after it had been learnedly confuted by Paulus Langius, though it deserved not so skilful an adversary, since it maintained that not only St. Gregory or St. Augustine, but that St. Bede also and Alcuin were no Benedictines, an untruth visible to all the world.

CHAPTER THE FOURTH.

Baronius excused and confuted.

THE attempts of Baronius, Galloni and Spondanus found better success, not only for the strength of their reasons, but for the great authority of the authors, yet the two latter discover too much earnestness and passion to be esteemed indifferent judges. And the eminent and holy Baronius gives us an emblem of human frailty, which many times betrays itself in smaller matters wherein the greatest persons are more subject to be less circumspect. Neither are we alone that wish more diligence and application in so laborious an historian. The French, the Spaniard, the German take notice of his mistakes in what concerns their particular history, yet the admirable service he hath done the whole Church, renders his lapses not only excusable but even necessary. For had he employed his time in turning the annals of so many different nations more exactly he would have spent that time much less profitably than in the general history of the Church. And how ill grounded were this Cardinal's suppositions is discovered by many learned Benedictines who presently took the alarm and fought invincibly for the glory of their Order, among which were the learned Abbot Cajetan in Italy, the Abbot Zieppe in the Low Countries; our learned Annalist Yepez in Spain, and for the English, the Fathers of the ancient Congregation in their *Apostolatus*, where they have demonstrated S. Gregory the Great and his disciples to have been of no other Order than theirs, and this from all sorts of topics.

First, from the common tradition and consent of the English nation, delivered from father to child and instilled into them together with the Catholic faith. And even when that faith St. Augustine preached began to be impugned so many ages after by Wiclef and after by protestant writers of our nation under King Edward VI, Queen Elizabeth &c, they were so far from questioning that he was a Benedictine Monk that from that supposition as certain on both sides, they found matter to calumniate him upon that account and charge him with ignorance and superstition as inseparable from his profession.

Secondly, from a just enumeration of all the Monasteries in England and Cathedral Churches which were inhabited by Religious, that they were in the hands of the Benedictines till the entrance of William the Conqueror all other Religious Orders that afterwards appeared in our Island were posterior to his Conquest nor seen before in our nation. And this verity is attested by all the authors, more ancient or contemporary with the said Prince, William Duke of Normandy; viz Ordericus Vitalis who lived under King Stephen and in his old age writ a history very faithful and free from all bias of parties or prejudice; William of Malmesbury who lived at the same time and is no less esteemed for his sincerity than for his eloquence; Eadmar a monk of Canterbury and the inseparable associate of his holy prelate S. Anselm in all his sufferings and exiles; and in a word, by many other historians of our nation who writ after S. Bede, and are published by the learned diligence of Mr. Cambden and Mr. Selden. Lastly in France none has more admirably digested and better gathered together all the proofs of the former writers to shew that St. Gregory the Great was a member of the Benedictine order than the most learned Benedictine antiquarian of the Mauritian Congregation, Dom John Mabillon of renowned memory in his 2nd tome of his Annalects where he unanswerably proves this assertion. And after that many other Religious Orders, which with their admirable variety adorned the Church in other countries were transplanted into the English soil, they were far from overshadowing the Benedictine Order which served as a cover and shelter to those younger sons that were coming up, and was regarded by them as their mother, and though in succeeding time that of the Canon Regulars and Cistercians spread very much and obtained great dignity and immunities, yet the honour and grandeur of St. Benedict's Order remained sacred and untouched, all the great Abbeys of the Nation were never possessed by any other, unless when themselves abandoned them by reason of persecution. They kept their eight Cathedral Churches where the Bishops were chosen out of the body by the suffrages of the Monks only; they had twenty six Abbots of their Order only who had their seat in Parliament; and to this point of greatness they held up, rivalled if not surpassed the (secular) clergy; overshadowed if not kept down all other Orders, till under the reign of Henry VIII it sank with the religion it supported, and fell from so high an elevation to so low a condition as we see it is in at present.

CHAPTER THE FIFTH.

THE ANTIQUITY OF THE ENGLISH BENEDICTINE CONGREGATION.

Now having, at least in passing, seen the Order take root grow strong and bring forth such seed as peopled the whole nation, we pass on to our subject, which is to see how the branches thereof were interwoven, what kind of union there was between the several houses, and whether the members of the same Order were also members of the same Congregation.

The authors and ancient writers of monastic discipline use these terms promiscuously for one and the same thing. St. Gregory often calls single convents by the name of Congregation, and in the Congregation of Cluny we see that of Order substituted as univocal, how sharply soever that body endeavour to prove they make an Order distinct, the whole Controversy is resolved into no more than that they limit the ancient signification of the word, and will needs understand it in their modern and stricter sense, which imports, according to the definition of each separately taken: that a Religious Order is a number of persons or monasteries that profess the same Rule, practise the same ceremonies and conspire in the same religious observations; but a Congregation superadds an association of several houses in laws, constitutions, Superiors, in a communication of temporals and spirituals towards the better establishment and conservation of discipline and regular observances and government. So that within the bosom of the same Order and under the profession of one and the same Institute there may be many Congregations, or none at all if each Monastery will frame a Republic by itself independent of any other. And to apply this explication to the subject I have now in hand : I may affirm not ungroundedly that the Benedictine Congregation is as ancient as the Order itself in England. Not that the form of a Congregation (the name taken in a stricter signification and that which the two or three last ages have confirmed it to) was introduced by St. Augustine, but because very many of those conditions and properties which are required in a Congregation strictly taken are to be found in our Order, even as soon as it took footing in England, though at all times not so discernible and stable ; as it happens in all political and human bodies which are subject to change and decay.

CHAPTER THE SIXTH.

Properties of a Congregation found in the primitive Benedictine Order in England.

Of which properties the first is one and the same nation or Province in which the English Order was comprised. For as that part of the Catholic Church is properly called the English Church which is comprehended within the limits of that nation and confined to the natives thereof, so by the same analogy or manner of speaking such a number of monasteries and Religious that live under the same Rule and according to the same rites and form of life, may not improperly be called the English Congregation.

The second is a closer alliance and bond of fraternal communication, namely in the Divine Office, in habit, ecclesiastical ceremonies, conventual acts, allowance of meat and drink, hours of refreshing according to the exigencies of the climate, or everywhere equal labours, which seems to be a tacit constitution and as it were civil law passed not so much by consults and votes as by common necessity and convenience equal to them all. For as law is the soul of civil bodies, and the soul is the form of the whole and one thing can have but one form: the same laws, the same rules, the same observances frame as it were the same city or congregation, and this especially if there be added thereto an agreement of the Governors and Superiors to lend a hand to one another towards the promoting or recovering monastic discipline, assisting their brethren in temporals, according to laws jointly to that end enacted and confirmed by lawful authority ; none of which requisites to constitute a Congregation were wanting in our Order from the very infancy of it in England as appears from St. Bede and other ancient monuments, but especially from the wholesome counsel St. Gregory gives his disciple and our first apostle, and which both he and his successors did without question strictly observe ; first that they should live together and apart from the clergy ; secondly, that they should imitate the simplicity and innocence of the first Christian Church and no one should call anything his own ; thirdly, that they should collect such rules as were proper for the circumstances they were in, not only from the Roman, but also Gallican or any other Church, and having done so guide themselves by them, which counsel had the force of precept, coming from their Abbot, supreme Pastor of the Church, and particularly their Father and only director, exhorting them not only not to relax anything of their own religious observances, but also to found their church as near as possible could be to the purity and method of the Church of Jerusalem. Now as that Church in its beginning was entirely religious and monastical, and very indifferent from the Churches of other Provinces (Alexandria excepted) so the monastical Order engrafted into the Cathedral Churches of England did constitute a certain peculiar Congregation very different from the Order of St. Benedict in other Provinces ; different I say, not so much in regular observances or manner of conversation, as in the end of religious observance raised to a higher point of dignity and charge ; for religious men made up the nobled and governing part of the clergy yet ceased not to be Religious nor to live like such, both in Community and other duties of their profession ; and over them besides their local Superior, St. Augustine was placed as their common Father or President General, whose paternal solicitude and daily instance extended itself no less to all Abbeys than to all Churches of the Kingdom, and had no less a dependence of him and himself no less responsible for their lives and conversation.

CHAPTER THE SEVENTH.

THE TITLE OF CONGREGATION IS AS DUE TO THE ENGLISH BENEDICTINES AS TO THE OTHER CONGREGATIONS AT THEIR BEGINNING.

But these which are in effect no more than the first lineaments and rudiments of our Congregation yet are able to merit that appellation since we see other such like confraternities did assume it as their due upon no other title. For in like manner the Cluny Congregation is said to have taken its beginning from St. Benno and St. Odo, notwithstanding that in their days the celebrating of General Chapters was not yet begun nor an entire union and communication of monasteries commenced nor Pontifical privileges nor Royal Patents granted for the confirmation and practice of such an union; for of these (so necessary for a complete form of a Congregation) there is no certain record before St. Mayolus.

And the Cistercian Congregation, nothing inferior to that of Cluny, is said to have its rise from St. Robert of Molesme, its increase from St. Bernard, yet it obtained not the form and regimen of a Congregation strictly taken, till the latter days of this holy Doctor, which he obtained from Eugenius III once his disciple, and yet there is no one that does not refer the beginning of these Congregations to St. Benno and St. Robert. The same may be said of the Italian, Spanish, German and French Congregations and others of posterior Orders, as that of the Discalced

Carmes, of the Recollects &c., though their origin be calculated from the first reform or coalition of houses, yet they arrived not to the perfect form of a Congregation but by tract of time and several degrees of perfection much after the manner of the body of a man, which first is an embryo, then an infant and through several stages of growth and increases, at length arrives to the perfect state of manhood and by a like decrease goes backward and approaches to old age and decay.

CHAPTER THE EIGHTH.

SEVERAL AGES OF THE CONGREGATION.

The first age therefore or rather infancy of the Congregation was under the government of St. Augustine and his successors, when that great Apostle and Doctor of our English Church effected what the great St. Augustine and Doctor of the Catholic Church attempted but unsuccessfully in Africa; that the greater and more dignified part of the ecclesiastics were monks of the Order of St. Benedict as they are still of St. Basil's Order in the Greek Church, though dismally rent by the unhappy Schism.

The second age was under St. Wilfrid, and especially St. Bennet Biscop, who was the master of Venerable Bede, and was raised up by Almighty God to recover monastic discipline, which by success of time and irruptions of pagans not yet converted was extremely decayed and almost extinguished. But by these two holy men's admirable life and vigilance, and by their frequent journeys into France and Italy, were collected the choicest flowers of regular observances which they met with in monasteries there, and transplanted into their native soil where they most happily flourished and brought forth those great men by whose sweat and blood all Germany &c, received the Faith and was peopled with holy religious. Of St. Bennet Biscop who died in the year 705, Baronius gives this eulogium: "Moreover by the "means of such a founder monachism was wonderfully spread in "England, insomuch that that island so watered by the Spirit of

CHAPTER THE EIGHTH.

"God became a heavenly Paradise, where while monastic disci-
"pline persisted entire, heresy could find no entry, but that
"dissolving and loosening, the fruitful land was turned into
"barrenness for the wickedness of them that dwelt therein;"
where it is to be observed that this great historian styles St. Bennet
Biscop the founder of Monachism in England not because he
first introduced or propagated Monastical Conversation in England, or because by his endeavours it was more largely extended
and improved, for Baronius could not be ignorant of the great
labours aud no less success of St. Wilfrid in that affair, or that
there were divers Benedictine Monasteries ancienter much than
either of these Saints: But he calls him *Founder* because St.
Bennet Biscop established several excellent reformations, regu-
lated with more exactness the Divine Service, increased the
solemnity and gravity of singing and ceremonies of the choir,
and, as it were, added the last hand towards the absolute
perfection of that Order, whereof himself formerly was a member, then a Reformer and improver, and since a Patron and Protector, which last title the English Benedictine Congregation
revived, and (after so great a wreck it suffered under Henry VIII)
at last united, gives the Saint out of a particular gratitude for his
solicitude and labours in that work.

But about a century afterwards the Danes having made that
dire incursion which laid almost all the country waste before
them, and monasteries having particularly felt the effects of their
rage and malice, the admirable St. Dunstan began to build up
the ruins of Jerusalem and reunite the stones of the Sanctuary
which lay scattered in the streets: so that in a short time there
were seen more than forty monasteries revived out of their ruins;
the piety of King Edgarus furnishing necessaries towards the
material houses of God, and the Abbey of Fleury in France,
seated on the great river Loire and blessed with the relics of the
great Patriarch and founder of our Order, together with the
famous Abbey of Gant in Flanders towards the spiritual. For
out of them in great repute for sanctity and learning, he borrowed
spiritual directors and masters, scribes learned in the law of their
profession, that brought forth out of their store both new and old

whatsoever might contribute towards the forming of their new disciples. And to establish a greater uniformity of discipline and form of Congregation in such his Monasteries, St. Dunstan himself though oppressed with the cares of his pastoral charge, found time to make a collection of such maxims as he desired might be universally observed, which he entitled his Constitutions (they are extant at the end of the *Apostolatus* ;) and they continued in vigour and observance till the Norman Conquest, though not without great difficulty and some delay, because of the frequent and almost daily piracy and inundation of the implacable Danes of whom the princes of those times were so often forced to buy their liberty till they pleased again to invade their dominions, and turned their arms particularly against sacred places and monasteries.

But after that the warlike Duke of Normandy had settled himself in his new conquest of England, and changed the municipal laws into Norman, Lanfranc Archbishop of Canterbury began a change likewise in the English monachism, or rather revived the observance of such wholesome institution as had been enacted long before him and were repealed now by new observance. He had herein, besides the royal permission, the assistance of two holy and learned men, his own nephew Paul, Abbot of St. Alban's, and his successor in his see, the learned Abbot of Bec, St. Anselm ; and in the model of this reformation (extant in the appendix of the *Apostolatus*) is very near expressed that of a Congregation, and it aims like St. Dunstan's forementioned concordat not only at reforming each monastery apart, but also uniting and joining them together into one continued body.

CHAPTER THE NINTH.

THE CONGREGATION RECEIVES ITS LAST PERFECTION.

YET we confess that this body received not its last perfection and property of a Congregation till the decree of the Council of Lateran (1215) in compliance with which decree, which extended itself to all kingdoms, the Order of St. Benedict divided itself in England into two Provinces, the one of Canterbury, and the other of York with obligation to keep a Chapter every three years, after the Innocentian form. But this form was afterwards changed or rather amplified and better adjusted in the year 1300 by Benedict XII, who revived the Decree of Innocent almost generally laid aside, excepting in England where it still held up in strict observance. Yet our ancestors who were always most obedient to the orders of the See Apostolic humbly submitted to Benedict's alterations, and united their two Innocentian Provinces into one, governed by two President Generals and a determinate number of Definitors and Visitors to be renewed every three years; which system continued unchangeable among all the revolutions of State, inviolable in the midst of civil wars and popular tumults, strengthening itself by excellent laws and constitutions (as are yet to be seen in the appendix to the *Apostolatus*) and guarding itself without by the singular odour of sanctity and exemplary virtue, until the unhappy schism of King Henry VIII, when desolation came upon it like a tempest, and the impiety and avarice of one man swept away the ransom of sinners, (the) donations and labours of the just, and drawed into his coffers these immense treasures which rendered him so poor in his life and at his death a beggar

CHAPTER THE **TENTH**.

ITS RECOVERY BEGAN BY THE **ITALIAN** AND **SPANISH** CONGREGATIONS.

From which miserable time, deplored even by Protestants, after a captivity of about seventy years there came (to England) English (monks) professed in the Congregations of Cassin in Italy and Valladolid in Spain of the Order of St. Benedict, who after the manner I shall now describe, revived the Congregation.

T'is known that after the death of the said king Henry VIII there ensued a consequence which naturally followed but which he did not foresee: that upon the ruin of religious Orders there must follow the ruin of religion itself. Whatsoever provision he made in his life by extirpating heresies and maintaining the Catholic religion in all points but those two of the supremacy of the Pope and Religious Profession, or, at his death by assigning in his testament (extant in the English Benedictine Archives at St. Gregory's in Doway) sixteen tutors to his son most of which were Catholics, he was by the just judgment of God crossed in both these his principal concerns. For in supporting the doctrine of the Church of Rome and razing monasteries which are her columns he plucked down with one hand what he built with the other; and desiring that his son should be educated in the Catholic Faith (supremacy excepted) and heresies suppressed, he was scarce cold in his bed before the contrary was settled; all religions connived at but the Catholic, a forged testament produced, where instead of sixteen governors (for the most part Catholics as abovesaid) during Edward VI's minority, one was set up under the title of Protector, and the Prince educated in that religion which the father most of all persecuted and abhorred, Zuinglianism.

But this infant King's reign being but short, the enemies of monasteries had not swing enough to wreak their spleen, nor time wholly to extirpate a profession that had taken such deep root in our country and was yet so numerous in her issue; wherefore she rather lay hid, than was wholly dead during the persecution of the reigning child. She lost her goodly and spreading branches, but the root lay underground concealing its life and vigour till the winter and storms were past; the wickedness of Edward and his councillors not permitting him to complete half his days.

CHAPTER THE ELEVENTH.

THE ENGLISH BENEDICTINES RE-ESTABLISHED BY QUEEN MARY.

THE pious and virtuous Mary had no sooner succeeded him, but her first care was to reduce her people to the obedience of the Church, her next to re-establish the dispersed and afflicted Benedictine Order as the best means to keep her subjects in the profession of the orthodox faith; as if no order was more proper and able to rebuild the church than that which first built it in that nation. To this effect she began with herself, and immediately resigned all tythes, first fruits, benefices, &c, that had been by her father and brother annexed to the crown, into the hands of the Pope's Legate, the eminent more for learning and sanctity than for birth and dignity, Cardinal Pole.

But the prudent conduct of the Legate was forced to mitigate her zeal, which otherwise certainly would have had no farther success. For most of the Abbey lands having been either usurped by or bestowed on noblemen of the kingdom, and so incorporated into their estates, that alone had been more than sufficient to make them averse from accepting of a religion that obliged to such restitutions, being men that had so small sense of piety (when Catholics) seeing how easily they abandoned the religion they had been bred up in; and so hardened in sin, that it was indiscreet to expect that fear of God now which they had not at the beginning. Wherefore the Legate most prudently removed that impediment in the name of Pope Julius III, whereby he absolved and exempted all such invaders and detainers of Church lands obtained in the Schism, from all ecclesiastical punishment and canonical censures whatsoever, and declared the possession of such lands secure and lawful (as to any pretentions of persons) for ever: the Church quitting her right and remitting the possessors to the judgment of God to whom belongs revenge, especially upon usurpations and sacrileges and such as invade the patrimony of Jesus Christ.

And not only he dispensed with this perverse generation as to the immovables of the Church but even to the movables too, yet desiring all to remember what befell Balthassar King of Babylon profaning the holy utensils his father had taken from the Temple of God. And all this was transacted by not only the free consent but also upon the petition of the immediate Lords and pretenders, the present clergy of the Province of Canterbury, convened according to their custom whilst the Parliament was sitting in the first and second years of Philip and Mary, and by the said Parliament accepted of, and in the third and fourth year of their reigns read in the Parliament of Ireland.

CHAPTER THE TWELFTH.

WESTMINSTER ABBEY RESTORED AND SOON AFTER DISSOLVED.

THIS condescendence of the Pope and Queen calmed the minds of the interested party, disposed more to religion and won their consent towards their restoring Westminster Abbey to its ancient possessors the monks, with exclusion of the College of secular Canons which her father had erected in their place.

This happy beginning and second birth (as it were) of the English Congregation was allowed by Act of Parliament the fourth year of Queen Mary's reign (1556) who nominated Abbot of Westminster Dr. John Feckenham, a learned and pious Monk of Evesham, whom Cranmer of detestable memory, by a dreadful judgment of God Archbishop of Canterbury, out of hatred to his constancy in the orthodox faith had imprisoned in the Tower and from whence her majesty presently after her coronation having taken him, had made him her chaplain and Dean of St. Paul's. He then now with fourteen monks on the Presentation of Our Lady, November the 21st. 1556, again appeared in Westminster Royal Monastery in his venerable Benedictine habit which the violence of the former wicked times had forced him to lay down. But pious Queen Mary dying not long after, her unworthy successor frustrated all these happy endeavours, most cruelly and ungratefully turning the Reverend Abbot Feckenham and his monks out of their monastery, notwithstanding the great services she had received from him in her troubles and the good turns and kindnesses he had done to her friends. Moreover so void she was of all humanity that she held the holy Abbot in divers prisons for the space of twenty three long years till he expired in that of Wisbeach Castle (an unwholesome place) in the year 1585. His eulogium in the *Apostolatus* is very remarkable for his noble and learned encounters in defence of the orthodox faith, for his charity to the poor and public, having set up a fountain or aqueduct at Holborn in London, (though then Queen Elizabeth's prisoner), and a cross at Wisbeach Castle.

CHAPTER THE THIRTEENTH.

THE BEGINNING OF MISSIONERS.

For the first ten years of this unhappy Princess' reign matters passed concerning religion with such doubtfulness, that Catholics, hoping still some change or toleration were very little industrious to preserve their religion against the spreading canker of the wickedness of those days, nay rather the Protestants gained more to their side by gently dealing with Catholics, than they got by rigorous persecution in thirty four years following. For then many Catholics, if not almost all, went to their churches, sermons and communions, whereby abundance of them became infected; who, upon better information from the mission, which upon this soon sprung in upon them, they withdrew from such dangerous practice. The chief author of this mission was one Dr. Allen, afterwards made Cardinal at the request of Philip II King of Spain.

In the beginning of Queen Elizabeth's reign the exaction of the oath of supremacy had driven him and many other remarkable men from the Universities of England. As he was a person of great parts he easily conceived great designs for the glory of God; wherefore when Vendivilius, then Doctor of the Faculty of Doway and Royal Professor there, afterwards made Bishop of Tournay, had wrought on him to take the degree of Doctor in that University and had procured him a pension from the said

King Philip II, he turned all his thoughts on the erection of a Seminary which might enable men to withstand the heresies he saw devouring the Kingdom.

Vendivilius lent to this design all the help he could, and Dr. Bristow seconding Dr. Allen, the new Seminary of Doway was begun in 1562. The Council of England informed of this, fell to persecuting it by all the ways they could devise, and therefore first endeavoured to set the Catholics in England against it, as a thing that would exasperate the State and hinder their peace in England; and afterwards by the rebels of Flanders they drove them out of Doway about the year 1577, upon which they fled to Rheims in France, and were there kindly entertained. This so enraged their adversaries that they had also worked them from thence; but Pope Gregory XIII of holy and incomparable memory for his almost incredible charities to even the antipodes and aliens from the orthodox faith, argued the case with Henry III of France; as also the Duke of Guise and the Cardinal his brother, on whom Rheims and its University depended, supplicated for them. But under Henry IV, Queen Elizabeth prevailed; and Doway being at quiet the Seminary returned thither again, and hath remained there ever since.

CHAPTER THE FOURTEENTH.

THE FIRST ENTRY OF JESUITS INTO ENGLAND.

The state of England instead of ruining them by such pursuit rather advanced their affairs, for at the suggestion of Dr Owen Lewis afterwards Bishop of Cassano (1588—1594) in Italy, solicited thereto by Dr. Allen, the said holy charitable Pope erected the English Roman Seminary in 1578. And the said Dr. Allen hearing the Jesuits had considerable English subjects amongst them, used the name of the English Catholics to obtain them of the Society for the English Mission in which they arrived in 1580, and were made very welcome by the Secular Clergy and matters passed very charitably and humbly between them, each party deferring honour to the other, and both parties seeking the common good and not what might be for their own advantage.

Mr. Pitts says that these Jesuits at their arrival found fourscore seminarists labouring in the mission, besides several of the ancient clergy of England who, by the grace of God, had abandoned the schism and some of the collegiates or seminarists had endured cruel deaths. Indeed, Queen Elizabeth, who for the excess of a gaudy court was called in foreign countries the Comedian Queen, gave them after the twentieth year of her reign occasion to augment the title of Comedian with that of Tragedian; for Christendom stood astonished at her frequent and cruel executions of poor Catholic Priests; so that Sir Richard

Baker one of her great admirers, is so confounded at this red part of her history that he seeks by apologetical excuses to lessen the height of its dreadful colour; and she herself finding how odious her name became abroad for such exorbitant cruelty, was glad to mitigate the fury of her state by ungutting her prisons of the Priests to send them by shiploads to Catholic countries. Of these doings, Stow and Baker, Protestant writers, are very unsuspected and remarkable witnesses.

The first who felt her cruelty of those Priests who were Seminarists was Mr. Cuthbert Mayn in 1577, upon refusing to acknowledge her supremacy, and the gentleman who harboured him, had his goods confiscated and his person adjudged to perpetual imprisonment,

But none were more hotly pursued by her state and council than the Jesuits at whose coming they were extremely offended, wherefore Father Campion after little more than a year, was taken, put to cruel torments and lastly to a cruel death, all which he endured with wonderful cheerfulness and a most undaunted courage. Father Parsons his Superior and companion, seeing no hopes of a calm and being violently pursued, having spent about two years in the mission, departed the land and never returned more, but applied himself to great persons for foundations of seminaries, and presently set up one at Eu in Normandy; which, though it be just on the sea shore enjoys a pleasant situation and an air wonderfully healthy. The Duke of Guise gave to it one hundred pounds a year which held till he was murdered at Blois in 1588; and then Father Parsons procured its erection at St. Omers, as also he procured the setting up of the seminaries and residences of Valladolid, Sevil and St. Lucar in Spain and Lisbon in Portugal and great alms to the old seminaries of Douay and Rome.

CHAPTER THE FIFTEENTH.

THE MISUNDERSTANDINGS OF THE SOCIETY AND CLERGY.

THE Society soon supplied these two places with Father Haywood and Father Holt, when unhappily the great amity and friendship which had been hitherto betwixt the Clergy and Society vanished into smoke and a dismal dissension arose betwixt them to the very great scandal of Catholic religion. That part of the clergy which relished not the Jesuits (for many kept to them against their brethren), began to repute the Jesuits politicians and thought they felt their politics in all their affairs. It grieved them that all the colleges or seminaries were either immediately in the hands of the Jesuits or such as were totally devoted to them; and they thought the Jesuits lorded it over them and would make them the drudges of the mission and prescribed them rules to draw all the credit of the good order of the English Clergy on the Society, of which the English afflicted Church, they said, had implored helpers and not masters, which they desired might be only such as the hierarchy of the Church only acknowledges, to wit Bishops; which desire failing, and an Archpriest with twelve assistants being appointed over them by the Holy See (for that the Cardinals of the Inquisition apprehended that a higher title might give too great an alarm to the State), the said English Clergy fell absolutely from the Jesuits, esteeming them to be the only persons that thwarted their desires and designs, to make all things depend on their secret orders and intentions. Upon this they wrote against the Jesuits, and the Jesuits and those that adhered to them against them again; which miserable doings much rejoiced the enemies of the Church and further contributed to their eternal ruin. And these miseries lasted all the rest of Queen Elizabeth's days and further. The chief plea of the clergy against this new form of Hierarchy was a law made in Catholic times with the free and full consent of all the Clergy and Temporality in such manner that upon admission of such a novelty as this of an Archpriest and his twelve assistants, the Sovereign could have taken a fair occasion of pursuing them very rigorously as in a manifest Premunire.

CHAPTER THE SIXTEENTH.

THE FIRST ENTRY OF THE STUDENTS OF THE ENGLISH SEMINARIES INTO THE ORDER OF SAINT BENEDICT.

The youths of the Seminaries likewise taking great distaste at the Jesuits, several of the Roman College became monks in the Congregation of Mount Cassin, and those who were in Spain and had an inclination to the Order of St. Benedict, after some difficulty and delays were very kindly admitted into the Congregation of Valladolid; (1588—1600) but all of them intending the English Mission with leave of their Superiors. And what is worthy of observation these young men had nothing to do with the aforesaid dissensions and heats. They were all of them who first entered the Italian Congregation Priests, and engaged in the Order as follows:

Firstly, R. F. Gregory Sayr at Mount Cassin itself in 1588. In the world he was called Robert Sayr and brought up at Cambridge where he began his Philosophy, but broke it off out of a desire of becoming a Roman Catholic and so began it again at Rheims from whence he went for divinity to Rome, and after he was become a monk taught divinity in his Monastery and in 1602, October 30th died in Saint George's Monastery in Venice; a man who for the integrity of his life, the sweetness of his manners and his singular modesty in conversation was grateful to God and all good men, and one who by the benefits of his solid wit constant judgment and happy memory arrived at a great height of learning as his books sufficiently witness: of which Mr. Pitts in his ingenious work of the illustrious English writers has published a Catalogue.

Secondly, R. F. Thomas Preston from the same College, (became a monk) after he had heard his course of divinity under Vasquez then reader at Rome. He was known to be learned, of a good sober life, very much admired for the elegance of his style and rare skill in Canon Law, though employed upon an unfortunate subject and wherewith he maintained a bad cause too well, which upon better considerations he afterwards detested.

Thirdly, about the same time R. F. Beech known by the name of Dom Anselm of Manchester went to St. Justina's at Padua and there became an egregious Benedictine monk, and

Fourthly, R. F. Austin Smith at Mount Cassin, where he was so esteemed especially for his skill in the Canon Law that they made him their Vicar to discharge the episcopal jurisdiction that blessed and renowned Sanctuary enjoyeth in its territory.

Fifthly, Dom Raphael in those times also entered the same Congregation yet never took to the mission, but became at Rome the agent and procurator of the missioners and died in that employment after many years of a Monastical life.

Sixthly, at Cave in Italy R. F. Antony Martin known in religion by the name of Dom Athanasius; to whom Cardinal Allen writ the following remarkable letter:

"Most dear Brother and Child,

"I have received two letters from you since you
"have withdrawn into those holy places both of them elegantly
"and lovingly, but what is above all, religiously written. To
"the first I answered by some about me, but to the last, having
"got a little leisure, I resolved to write myself. First, that you
"might not by other persons' words only see how much I affec-
"tion you, but also by my own. Next, that you might know
"how much I esteem your progress in that most holy state of
"life, for which much more now in the Lord than ever in the
"world, (though your remarkable talents ever rendered you very
"dear to me,) I love and embrace you. Lastly, that I might
"communicate unto you the joy I have conceived of this most

"happy state of life to which I apply the words of the Apostle: "'I have no greater joy than to hear that my children walk in "'the Truth.'* Wherefore I most highly congratulate your "contempt of human affairs and fervour in pursuit of those of "heaven; and that having escaped and overcome the most cruel "and most turbulent movements of a worldly and secular life, "you model and form yourself in such holy discipline; pru- "dently preferring to the most turbulent businesses of the world "the most holy leisures of a most ancient and most glorious "religious state of life. For this most solid good and most "saving advantage I congratulate with you from the bottom of "my heart, neither is there anything more for you or me to "crave from Christ our Sovereign Good who inspired you this, "than that He will please of His infinite piety and goodness to "assist you to the end of the work of your salvation which he "has so happily begun; which he will not fail, if that since you "have put your hand to the plough of the Lord you do not look "back, but advance forward to the utmost you may be able, if "you are diligent in the hard yet sweet labours of religion, if "courageously and stoutly you shake off temptations, if you cast "out of your mind what for your trial you have suffered in the "world either from heretics or bad Catholics or rivals and envious, "and also pray for your persecutors which all the Saints in "heaven do whose life and charity you have taken on you to "express on earth by a lively imitation of them.

"Let others think and say what they list of this your most holy "state of life, I would have you persuaded I most heartily espouse "your affairs and mightily like this resolution you have taken of "engaging in religion, and hope that you are taken from this "wicked world to contribute to the restoration of this most holy "Order which formerly so flourished in our country, and your "pen and genius will render you an ornament thereof; and "therefore, so much the more profit you make in that most "holy discipline so much the more I shall love you and you will "have no occasion to repent you of this resolution.

* *II St. John*, 4.

"If a letter would allow it or that I had time I could expose to your piety out of the histories of our nation many things concerning the sanctity and greatness of this Order in England. For St. Austin himself and all the other disciples of St. Gregory who converted our nation to the faith were all of this Order, and all the first monasteries (of which venerable Bede), as likewise he himself, were of this venerable Institute; and all the Cathedral Chapters which were afterwards held by secular Canons were at their beginning in the hands of Benedictine Monks. So was Canterbury Church in the time of Lanfrank, Anselm, Thomas the Martyr, who themselves were monks of the self same Order; that I may say nothing of the most noble monasteries of Westminster, St. Alban's, St. Edmund's, Glastonbury, whose Abbots and many other more proved glorious martyrs under Henry the 8th. These examples, my child, are able to encourage you and the rest of our countrymen to strive after the solid glory of Christ and his Church: for my part I mightily delight at the sole thought of such great men; which thought and the remembrance of our old affairs has made me longer than I would have been, but not to the distaste of either you or me, for I talk freely with you. Wherefore remember me in your prayers and Sacrifices and salute from me the Superiors of your House and Order very affectuously in the Lord, who will abundantly recompense this most Christian charity which they thus exercise on our fellow pilgrims and exiled. Adieu my dear child. From our mansion at Rome the 12th of the Kalends of February, 1594. With my own hand

     Thine in Christ
      "William Cardinal Allen."

This was but a little before the good Cardinal's death, for he died the 16th of October following, however it shows how much he coveted the restoration of St. Benedict's Order in England, and contributed towards it what he could; for besides this he recommended Don Anselmo to St. Justina of Padua and credibly others elsewhere. Moreover Mr. Fitzherbert, one of his domestics was so active and jealous for it that to help it on he left at his death all he had to the English thus engaged in this Congregation at Mount Cassin; nor was less active in this pious design the already mentioned Dr. Owen Lewis. And so strictly were these English Priests held to monastical discipline, that as Father Thomas related of himself to R. F. Austin Baker, though he entered the Monastery as a Priest of a middle or mature age, and was esteemed by his Novice-Master as a learned and virtuous man, yet would not the said Master allow or permit him to say Mass in the space of three whole years that he spent under his conduct according to the practice of that Congregation save only out of a special favour on some principal Feasts, as Christmas, Easter, &c, telling him to this effect : " You are not " come hither to exercise your priestly function that hath dignity " or honour in it, but to become recollected, to know and hum- " ble yourself and cleanse your soul."

As to those who entered the Spanish Congregation, though he neither lived nor was clothed in any monastery, as Father Baker affirms, Mr. Mark Barkworth alias Lambert challenges the first place.

1°. Because he was a great furtherer and concurrer with those who engaged amongst the Spanish monks, which the Fathers of the Society took very ill, fearing lest thereby the mission would be ruined.

2°. In 1601 after frequent occasions and even provocation to make an escape, after nine several examens before several tribunals, endowed, as R. F. Sadler attests, with the gift of miracles besides many dowries of mind, being condemned for his faith to be put to death, to make the nation remember how it received the said holy faith and manifest the secrets of his heart and intentions in regard of the Benedictine Order, he chose to be drawn to Tyburn in the Benedictine habit which by some means he had provided or gotten, and had his tonsure accordingly made ; confounding by that silent rhetoric the hideous insensible impiety of his adversaries, who yet glorying in the name of Christians while they reject unity of faith with the Church of Christ, stick not to be so cruel to such, to whom the English monarch Ethelbert when he knew neither Christ nor his Church, was yet so kind as St. Bede has recorded to posterity; and though absorbed in the darkness of idolatry, yet so rationally weighed their lives and words that convinced of their candour and sincerity, became a son of that light to which their descendants now turn their backs. God grant them to turn their faces again to the same that they may not be for ever confounded.

CHAPTER THE SEVENTEENTH.

THE MODERN BENEDICTINE MISSION OF ENGLAND.

But of those who formally took the habit in the monasteries, the first was Father Austin White, alias Bradshaw, who according to the practice of monachism in those countries left his surname to take that of a Saint, and so was called Father Austin of St. John.

The next was Father John Mervin alias Roberts and after him is counted Father Maurus Scot &c. And the same year Mr. Barkworth was put to death (1601) a petition of some noblemen of England was presented to Pope Clement VIII by the Most Illustrious and Most Reverend Lord, Frederick Cardinal Borromeo, upon which his holiness gave leave by word of mouth for the English professed in the Congregation of Mount Cassin to go into England in Mission for the further advancement of the faith, the execution of which grant, because of the disturbances that were then in England betwixt the Clergy and Society was delayed to the year following, and then decreed on the 5th. of December in the Sacred Congregation of the Holy Inquisition. During this time died R. F. Gregory Sayr the intended prime star or sun of the English Italian Benedictine Mission, in this like the first Benedictine Mission from Italy to England, that as that was headed by an illustrious Gregory who was hindered in his purpose in the thought he had of personally labouring in it, so was also this likewise headed by an illustrious Gregory, who was also frustrated of his purpose and intention, which was executed by his two brethren R. F. Thomas Preston and R. F. Anselm Beach (alias of Manchester) who landed at Yarmouth in the year 1603 where he spent that winter, and at Mr. Francis Woodhouse of Cisson near Wendlam found the Reverend Dom Sigebert Buckley, the only monk left of the old monks of Westminster whom King James a few months before had ordered to be freed from his prison at Fromegham (Framlingham). From which time he and F. Thomas Preston took care of the old man till his happy exit from this world.

The English Spanish Benedictines did not tarry long after, but forth came to open the way to the rest, R. F. Austin Bradshaw and R. F. John Mervin. And Mr. George Blackwell was ordered by his Holiness Clement VIII (Pontificatus sui anno 11, 5° Octobris) not to think of extending the jurisdiction of his Archpriesthood over these new missioners or other regulars, but solely to watch over the Priests who had been brought up in the Seminaries.

Their faculties were enriched with several important privileges added to those which before had been granted to the Jesuits and at this time particularly conferred on the Bishop of Vasoniensis who this year took his way for Scotland, and afterwards by Urban VIII to F. Edmund Gavel of the Order of Saint Francis, and to Thomas, Archbishop elect of Cassel in Ireland, which I took notice of to show that those ample privileges which other orders enjoy for the English Missions were almost all posterior to those granted to the monks of the Italian and Spanish Congregation.

They had not been long in the mission when they found they should, whether they would or no, be a continual impediment to each other, unless they were united into one body; for that they saw their concord being no better than that of confederates, could not be of any durance, except they did conspire into a union, not only of persons, but much more of laws and superiors. For where the heads are different the members must necessarily be divided, and where different laws which draw different or perhaps contrary ways are in force, no uniform

government can be built upon them. Wherefore after they had for a long time deliberated upon it, and could not come to a resolution, at last that Wisdom which reaches from end to end and makes both one, inspired them to raise up children to their brethren and to lay down whatsoever power else they had separate, to receive a joint and larger authority from the ancient English Congregation, which still survived in the person of the Rev. F. Sigebert Buckley upon whom was devolved and in whom preserved inviolate all the privileges of the old English Benedictine Congregation. And to this they were mightily urged by R. F. Austin Baker, native of Abergavenny in Wales, a most egregious legist as any of his times, and who thereby might have risen to the higher preferments of the Kingdom, but one day "returning home from a journey, his servant that attended
"him left him out of sight and he being in some profound
"thoughts and not marking the way instead of going on forward
"to a ford by which an impetuous river might be safely passed,
"he suffered his horse to conduct him by a narrow beaten path,
"which at last brought him to the middle of a wooden foot
"bridge, large enough at the first entrance but growing still
"more and more narrow and of an extraordinary height above
"the water. He perceived not his danger till the horse by stop-
"ping suddenly and trembling awaked his rider who soon became
"sensible of the mortal danger into which he was engaged. It
"was impossible for him to go forward or return back; and to
"leap into the river which being narrower there was both
"extreme deep and violent in its course, (besides the greatness of
"the precipice) seemed to him (who could not swim), all one as
"to leap into his grave. In this extreme danger, out of which
"neither human prudence nor any natural causes could rescue
"him, necessity forced him to raise his thoughts to some helper
"above nature, whereupon he framed in his mind such an inter-
"nal resolution as this. 'If ever I escape this danger, I will
"'believe there is a God who hath more care of my life and
"'safety than I have had of his love and worship.' Thus he
"thought: and immediately thereupon he found that his horse's
"head was turned round and both horse and man out of all dan-

"ger. This he plainly saw, but by what means this was "brought to pass he never could imagine. However he never "had any doubt but that his deliverance was supernatural."*
Upon this he sought God in good earnest, was reconciled to the Church and became a monk at St. Justina at Padua in 1605, but wanting health the fathers dismissed him with a very liberal viaticum, and testimony of his religious behaviour, and offered him a permission to be professed in any of their monasteries, or recommendation to any other Congregation. All along the way a secret blind impulse vehemently urged him home, at which he often wondered not being able to give any reasonable account of it; and it was so strong, that against his settled resolution of going leisurely home that he might curiously survey the nature and fashion of the countries through which he was to pass, he never ceased posting till he came to London, where at his arrival he was entertained with the sad news that his father lay sick of an infirmity from which he was never like to recover. Then he perceived that the abovesaid secret impulse was sent by God as a messenger to hasten him that he might assist his father at his death, as he did to his great joy and comfort, easily obtaining the old man's consent to quit the heresy wherein he had lived. Having buried his father and settled his affairs, he was professed by the English Italian monks in the Mission.

* *R. F. Serenus Cressy in the preface he designed to the abridgment he made of this Father Baker's works and printed under the title of "Sancta Sophia."*

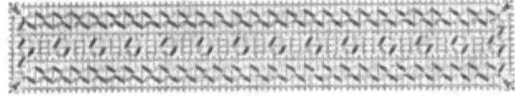

CHAPTER THE EIGHTEENTH.

RENOVATION OF THE OLD BENEDICTINE CONGREGATION OF ENGLAND.

FATHER BAKER being then commissioned by them to treat with F. Buckley about this business of aggregation, which he had demonstrated both by ancient and more modern laws and **Canons** was a thing which might be done, made it his principal care that nothing illegal should pass in it; so that if anything was done ignorantly or not so legally (which notwithstanding was afterwards supplied by his Holiness in his Bulls and other Rescripts) that was done without or against F. Baker's counsel. And the day of the aggregation was the 21st of November, 1607, and mightily he sought to know from the venerable old man the way of living of both the elder and the later monasteries of England, but he could tell nothing of older times of his own experience and as for what passed in Westminster in Queen Mary's days as the house was but resettling it had scarce received the first tracts or delineations of monastic discipline. They rose at midnight, eat flesh, and sat in the refectory face to face on both sides the table, four to every mess, as they do in the Inns of Court. At supper first came a dish of cold sliced powdered beef, and next after a shoulder of mutton roasted; which seemed strange diet to rise with at midnight, when Father Baker called to mind that the Italian monks rising at midnight eat no flesh.

G

CHAPTER THE NINETEENTH.

THE CHIEF BENEDICTINE MONASTERIES OF ENGLAND.

AND now because some miserable troublesome men have pretended there was no other Congregation in England of Black Benedictine monks than that of Cluny it will be much to the purpose to particularize here the houses of both the Congregations with the rates at which they were undervalued at their suppression, that the poor public weal might not be sensible of the illustrious Charities it was then most sacrilegiously robbed of; to all which estates the monks have renounced (their claims) as shall be shown, how and when and where in the continuation of these notes.

The chief monasteries and houses only of the old Benedictine Congregation of England.

I. The renowned Abbey of St. Alban's in Hertfordshire which had yearly £2510 sterling; which had eleven Priories subject to it as follows:

1. Beaulieu in Bedfordshire.
2. Belvere or Belvoir in Lincolnshire; its yearly income £135 sterling.
3. Bingham in Norfolkshire consisting of 16 monks, £160 per annum.
4. Hatfield Peverel in Essex, £83 sterling yearly.
5. St. James' in Hertford, £88 sterling.

6. Pembroke or Monkton in Wales.
7. Redburn in Hertfordshire.
8. St. Trinity of Wallingford, Berks.
9. Tynemouth Priory, Northumberland.
10. The **Nunnery** of Berkgate, Bedfordshire, **and**
11. Our **Lady of** Sopewell, (a nunnery) founded in Hertford by Godfrey Abbot of St. Albans, £68 sterling. St. Alban's Abbey had also two hospitals standing just by the Abbey.

II. Our Lady of Abingdon in Berkshire £2042 sterling yearly. Its Priory of our Lady of Coln in Essex £175 sterling, with a cell at Edwardeston. It had also St. Frideswide's nunnery at Oxford which was given to this Abbey and not much regarded, lastly fell to the Canons Regular.

III. The famous Abbey of St. Austin at Canterbury £1412 sterling yearly.

IV. St. **Martin of Battle** in Sussex, £987 sterling. It had two Priories, the first of St. John the Evangelist, at Brecon, the other of St. Nicholas at Exeter which had £154 sterling.

V. St. Oswald **of Bardney** in Lincolnshire £429 Sterling.

VI. St. John **of Colchester**, with cells at Barrow in Essex, and Wickham Skeyth and Snapes in Suffolk.

VII. St. Guthlac of Crowland in Lincolnshire £1217 sterling. With **Priories at** Freston, **and Holland,** Lincolnshire, **and** at Cambridge.

VIII. Our **Lady and St. Edburg of** Evesham in Worcestershire £1268 sterling. **With Priories at** Penwortham, Lancashire and Alcester, Warwickshire.

IX. Our Lady **of York,** £2085 sterling yearly. It had nine Priories.

1. St. Bees in Cumberland, £149 sterling.
2. Neddrum in Ireland.
3. St. Mary Magdalen at Lincoln.
4. St. Trinity of Wetherall in Cumberland.
5. Sandtoft and Haines in Lincolnshire.
6. Warmington in Northumberland.
7. Marsh, in Nottinghamshire.
8. Romburgh, in Suffolk.

9. St Martin's at Richmond in Yorkshire.

X. The renowned Abbey of St. Edmund, King of the East Angles and Martyr, in Suffolk £2336 sterling.

And its nunnery of Thetford in the same Shire founded by its Abbots £50 sterling yearly.

XI. The egregious sanctuary of our Lady of Glastonbury in Somersetshire £3508 sterling. It had cells at Bristol; Basselech, Monmouthshire; Lammana in Cornwall, and at Kilcumin and Ocymild in Ireland.

XII. St. Peter of Gloucester £1550 sterling. It had these cells:

1. St. Michael and St Nicholas at Ewyas Harold, Herefordshire.
2. St. Guthlac in Hereford.
3. Broomfield in Shropshire.
4. Kilpeck, Herefordshire.
5. Ewenny, Glamorganshire.
6. St. Leonard at Stanley in Gloucestershire.

XIII. SS. Peter and Paul of Hyde in Hampshire near Winchester £865 sterling.

XIV. St. Bennet of Hulm in Norfolk £677 sterling.

XV. St. Aldhelm of Malmesbury in Wiltshire, £803 sterling. It had two Priories; St. Michael of the Mount in Devonshire and our Lady of Pilton in the same Shire, which had £56 sterling.

XVI. Peterborough in Northamptonshire £1972 sterling.

XVII. St. James of Reading in Berkshire £2116 sterling, which had the Priories of:
St. James of Leominister in Herefordshire, May and Rindelgros in Scotland.

XVIII. The glorious Abbey of Our Lady and St. Benedict of Ramsey in Huntingdon, which had yearly £1983 sterling, and in the same Shire the Priories of St. Ive and Modney.

XIX. SS. Peter and Paul of Shrewsbury £615 sterling, with the Priory of St. Gregory at Morfield in Shropshire.

XX. St. German's of Selby in Yorkshire £819 sterling, with a cell at Snaith in the same county.

CHAPTER THE NINETEENTH.

XXI. Our Lady of Tavestock in Devonshire £702 sterling. It had Priories at
1. Cowick near Exeter.
2. Modbury, and
3. St. Nicholas, at Trescaw in Scilly.

XXII. Our Lady of Thorney in Cambridgeshire £508 sterling. with a cell at Deping, Lincolnshire.

XXIII. St. Peter of Westminster in Middlesex near London £3977 sterling. It had two Priories:
1. Our Lady of Hurley in Berks £134 sterling.
2. St. Bartholomew of Sudbury in Suffolk £122 sterling.

XXIV. Our Lady of Winchelcomb in Gloucestershire, £759 sterling.

All the Abbots of these Abbeys had their places in the House of Lords or Parliament as Barons and Peers of the Realm. Those of the Abbeys which follow were also counted among the Spiritual Barons and Peers of the Realm but had not the prerogative of seat in Parliament.

I. S. Peter of Abbotsbury in Dorsetshire £485 sterling.

II. Our Lady and St. John Baptist of Alchester in Warwickshire £101 sterling; afterwards made a Priory under Evesham.

III. Athelny in Somersetshire £209 sterling.

IV. Our Lady and St. Modwen of Burton-on-Trent £356 sterling.

V. SS. Mary, Peter and Benedict of Cerne in Dorsetshire £623 sterling.

VI. St. Peter of Chertsey in Surrey £744 sterling. It had a Priory at Cardigan in Wales £13 sterling.

VII. Our Lady and St. Eadburg of Eynsham in Oxfordshire £421 sterling.

VIII. St. Saviour of Feversham in Kent £286 sterling.

IX. Our Lady and St. Michael of Middleton in Dorsetshire £720 sterling.

X. St. Peter of Muchelney in Somersetshire £498 sterling.

XI. Our Lady of Pershore in Worcestershire £666 sterling.

XII. Our Lady of Sherbourne in Dorsetshire £682 sterling.

It had two Priories:
1. Kidwelly in Carmarthenshire £29 sterling.
2. Horton in Dorsetshire.

XIII. Our Lady of Tewkesbury in Gloucestershire £1598 sterling. It had these Priories:
1. St. James' at Bristol.
2. Cranburn in Dorsetshire,
3. Derehurst in Gloucestershire.
4. Goldcliff in Monmouthshire.
5. Cardiff in Glamorganshire.

XIV. Whitby, otherwise St. Hilda of Strenshall in Yorkshire, £805 sterling. It had these Priories in Yorkshire:
1. Hackness.
2. Middlesborough.
3. Gotheland, and
4. All Saints at York.

XV. St. James of Walden in Essex £406 sterling.
XVI. St. Wereburg in the City of Chester £1073 sterling.
XVII. Wymundham in Norfolk.
XVIII. Our Lady and St. Peter at Humbersteyn in Lincolnshire.

Now follow the Cathedral Priories whose Abbots were their Bishops, there being at those Cathedrals none but Benedictine monks to compose their Chapters as Canons do now-a-days in other places.

I. The Archiepiscopal Priory of the Primate and Mother Church of all England, St. Saviour of Canterbury £2489 sterling. It had three Priories depending on it:
1. Risbury (Bucks) of 14 monks.   (?)
2. at Dover £232 sterling.
3. Canterbury College, Oxford. It had also other Priories.

II. Coventry whose Prior was a Baron and Peer of the Realm and had place in Parliament.

III. Durham, £1615 sterling, and its College at Oxford £115 sterling. It had moreover these Priories or Cells.
1. Coldingham in Scotland.
2. Finchall £146 sterling.

CHAPTER THE NINETEENTH.

    3. Lindisfarne £60 sterling.
    4. St. Leonard's of Stamford in Lincolnshire £36 sterling.
    5 & 6. St. Peter at Wearmouth and St. Paul at Jarrow, which had been the monasteries of St. Bennet Biscop and the School of Venerable Bede, Doctor of the English Church; the first rated at only £26 sterling a year, the other at £40 sterling.
    7. Lynch, and
    8. Warkworth in Northumberland.
  IV. Ely in Cambridgeshire £1301 sterling.
  V. Norwich £1041 sterling. It had these Priories:
    1. St. Leonard's by Norwich.
    2. Aldeby.
    3. Lynn.
    4. Yarmouth.
    5. North Eltham, in **Norfolk**, and
    6. Hoxne, in Suffolk.
  VI. Rochester in Kent £486 sterling. It had a Priory at Felixstowe in Suffolk.
  VII. Worcester £1386 sterling.
  VIII. Winchester £1507 sterling.
  IX. Bath in Somersetshire £695 sterling. It had these Priories or **Cells**:
    1. Dunster in Somersetshire, and
    2. Waterford, Cork, Legan and Youghal in Ireland.

And here I take notice that the Schism has made or erected Bishoprics in three of the former Abbeys, viz, Peterborough, Gloucester and Chester. Now follow the chief Priories of this Congregation which were immediate by themselves not subject to any Abbeys or **Cathedrals**.

  I. Our Lady **of Bradwell** in Buckinghamshire.
  II. Birkenhead in Cheshire £102 sterling.
  III. Howland in **Lancashire** £65 sterling.
  IV. Our Lady of Hatfield Brodoke or Bradstock in Wiltshire £170 sterling.
  V. Our Lady of Luffield in Buckinghamshire.
  VI. St. Mary Magdalen of Monk Bretton in Yorkshire £322 sterling.

VII. Our Lady of Great Malvern in Worcestershire £375 sterling. It had a cell at Avecot in Warwickshire.

VIII. Lesser Malvern in the same Shire £102 sterling.

IX. Pill in Pembrokeshire which had belonged to the famous Benedictine reform of Tyrone in France £52 sterling.

X. Sneshal in Buckinghamshire £24 sterling.

XI. St. Nicholas of Spalding in Lincolnshire, which had belonged to St. Nicholas of Angers in France £878 sterling.

XII. Sandwell in Buckinghamshire £38 sterling.

XIII. Candwell or Caldwell in Bedfordshire, (which Speed through a mistake assigns to Black Canons) £148 sterling.

The most remarkable nunneries (for the others are omitted) which were not only visited by the Bishops but also by the Visitors chosen at the General Chapter of the Congregation.

I. St. Eadburg of Barking in Essex. £1684 sterling.

II. St. Trinity of Ellenstow in Berkshire £325 sterling.

III. Godstow near Oxford £319 sterling.

IV. Rumsey in Hampshire £528 sterling.

V. Holiwell at London £347 sterling.

VI. Our Lady in Clerkenwell £282 sterling.

VII. Sheppy in Kent £129 sterling.

VIII. The noble nunnery of Shaftesbury £1329 sterling.

Moreover the Congregation had a famous College at Oxford now known by the name of Gloucester Hall (Worcester College) and another at Cambridge called Monks' College and Buckingham College (St. Peter's) because the Duke of Buckingham had been a great benefactor to it. These Colleges were common to those houses of the Congregation which had not places of study in those Universities.

The Congregation frequented for its General Chapters chiefly St. Andrew of Northampton because it standing in the middle of the kingdom was of easier access to the Congregation, and Bermondsey in Southwark in London, because there the Fathers were out of the noise of the Court which stood on the other side of the river at Westminster. Both these houses belonged to the Congregation of Cluny which signified nothing to this Congregation which regarded solely its conveniency in election of place. These Cluny Monks were brought in by William Earl of Warren, son-in-law to King William I, about the year 1077 and enjoyed there no other monasteries than (these) which follow and were but Priories.

CHAPTER THE TWENTIETH.

THE MONASTERIES OF THE CLUNIAC CONGREGATION IN ENGLAND.

I. St. Pancras of Lewes in Sussex of which the yearly value was £1091 sterling.
II. St. Saviour of Bermondsey above mentioned £548 st.
III. St. Andrew of Thetford in Norfolk £418 sterling.
IV. St. Andrew of Northampton £334 sterling.
V. Our Lady in the fields at Northampton, a nunnery, £119 sterling.
VI. St. John the Evangelist of Pontefract in Yorkshire £472 sterling.
VII. St. Milburg of Wenlock in Shropshire £434 sterling.
VIII. St. Trinity of Lenton in Nottinghamshire £417 sterling.
IX. Farley in Wiltshire £217 sterling.
X. SS. Peter and Paul of Montague in Herefordshire £524 sterling.
XI. Castleacre in Norfolk £324 sterling.
XII. Our Lady and all Saints in Westacre £308 sterling.
XIII. Messingham.
XIV. St. James near Exeter in Devon.
XV. St. James in Derbyshire.
XVI. Stangate in Essex. £43 sterling.
XVII. Dudley in Staffordshire.

XVIII.   Kirby Beller, £178 sterling.
XIX.   Mendham in Bucks, £23 sterling.
XX.   St. Helen in the Island of White.
XXI.   St. Maur of Clifford in Herefordshire, £65 sterling.
XXII.   Carswel in Dorchester.
XXIII.   Horksley in Essex, £27 sterling.
XXIV.   Hagham in Lincolnshire.
XXV.   St. Clare of Malpasse in Wales, £14 sterling.
XXVI.   Normansbery.
XXVII.   Aldermanshave.   ?
XXVIII.   Cockersand in Lancashire, £218 sterling.
XXIX.   Tivardreath in Cornwall, £151 sterling.
XXX.   Pritwell in Essex, £194 sterling.
XXXI.   Newton Longville in Norfolk.
XXXII.   St. Mary of Wangford in Suffolk £30 sterling.
XXXIII.   Our Lady of the Rock in Wilts, £278 sterling.
XXXIV.   St. Sepulchre of Bromholme in Norfolk, £144 st.
XXXV.   St. Mary Magdalen in Barnstaple Devon, £129 st.
XXXVI.   St. John Evangelist of Horton, £111 sterling.
XXXVII.   Tekeford in Bucks, £126 sterling.
XXXVIII.   St. Austin of Daventry in Northamptonshire, £238 sterling.

The Abbey of Cluny itself had two Manors, Ledcombe and Offord, and moreover the Cluny Monks had three hospitals at London : St. Giles by Cripplegate, another by Aldgate, and the third in the suburbs of Holborn. Cluny had nothing more in England, and upon the Wars of Henry V with France they were not suffered to have any communication with their brethren out of England; upon which several of them took new Titles of Foundation and joined themselves to the Congregation here exposed in these notes particularly, as Lenton and Daventry had done long before.

Ingenious Mr. Pitts, the learned Jesuit Possevin and the laborious Benedictine Wion have made great mistakes in ascribing to the Cluny monks in the Province of England, both men and monasteries which never belonged to them. The ground or cause of their mistake was that they found houses styled of Cluny and modelled of Cluny reformation because they had taken on them that sort of reform; but they never incorporated in the Congregation or Order of Cluny. And of this the famous Abbey of St. James at Reading is an illustrious example as the *Apostolatus* evidences (p. 152 Tract. 2) and the same book gives other examples (p. 101, ibid) of monasteries taking on them certain reforms without incorporating in them.

But now concerning the aggregation to the old Benedictine Congregation of England. He (F. Sigebert Buckley) aggregated but two at first, to which he afterwards added as I find no less than ten more. The first person aggregated the said 21st of November was the V. R. Father Vincent Sadler (called also Robert Walter or Faustus Sadleir or Sadler) born in Warwickshire at a place called Collier's Oak in the parish of Fillongley (Hillongley) who forsaking his office under Sir Walter Mildmay then Secretary of State to Queen Elizabeth and going a pilgrimage to Rome was there after he had studied for some years ordained Priest by Pope Paul V. and by him sent into the English Mission, where he joined himself to the English Italian monks and became a member of their Congregation, and was now incorporated into the old Benedictine body of England and made a monk of Westminster. (Nov. 21st 1607.)

The second was R. F. Edward Maihew or May (he shews them to be the same names in his *Trophies* speaking of St. Osmund,) of Dinton in Wiltshire not far from Salisbury, who after twelve years spent in the mission there took the habit of St. Benedict at the hands of Dom Anselm of Manchester, and at the end of his Noviceship was the said 21st of November (1607) professed by Father Buckley at that time through I know not what occasion detained in the Gatehouse prison at Westminster. He mightily admires the day of the aggregation because it proved to be the same with that of the restoration of the Abbey by D. Feckenham in the time of Queen Mary on which circumstance none of them thought or reflected till all the ceremony and business was over. Moreover he protests that the good old Father Sigebert, though almost consumed with misery and age yet enjoyed his sight to the end of his holy work, which done, he became quite blind; "I write" saith he "what I know for certain, for that day at my profession he helped to put on me my religious habit."

This aggregation was entertained by His Holiness Pope Paul V. and approved as the first dawning of a full and entire union. And in effect it was so happy a beginning that a union without it could never have found place amongst men of such different bodies and pretentions that they scarce ever would have found where to lay the corner stone. But before they could arrive at the wished for union, many difficulties were to be waded through which could be cleared but by little and little.

CHAPTER THE TWENTY-FIRST.

THE BEGINNING OF DOUAY CONVENT.

The land was sorely disposed in regard of Catholics when the new monastic missioners arrived, and the effusion of Priests' blood which cruel Queen Elizabeth had began still continued; but after that in 1605 the execrable attempt of Gunpowder Treason was broken out the condition of Catholics became very sad and unsafe; (and hence it is very credible happened Father Buckley's present imprisonment,) that affair having been the design of a few seduced Catholics decayed in their temporal estates, and therefore apt for any desperate chance, but imputed to the whole body of Catholics by those who probably contrived the business for that purpose. Wherefore F. Austin Bradshaw, Vicar General of the English Spanish Benedictine Missioners seeing such a dismal storm found himself in a necessity of withdrawing out of the land; and fearing the violent cruelties in force would soon bereave his mission of a continued succession unless they could procure some refuge both to shelter themselves in when such violent storms broke out, and a nursery for the education of such as the Spirit of God should dispose to such a vocation, for both which purposes Spain was too remote, he went to Douay where he obtained a Dormitory in Anchin College. Thither he called some of the English Fathers of that Congregation who were intended and designed immediately for England, he gave order likewise to such of his Obedience that were there already to send over some youths to be educated in this new obtained place. (End of November 1605).

A year or two after finding this habitation too straight and incommodious for his much larger designs he removed from thence into a quarter, near and belonging to the Trinitarians, and which he rented of those Fathers, which they found proper enough, and themselves sufficiently numerous (but five with a lay brother) to venture upon Conventual duties; kept choir and took novices. In this house Brother Peter was clothed and merited by his fortunate labours the favour of the town and the first considerable charity they did them. The tenant of the house before (they took it) was accused of stamping and counterfeiting money; his process was made before Magistrates, he was found guilty, condemned and put to death. His friends to vindicate his and their own honour appealed to the Court of Mechlin, pleaded the party's innocence, charged the magistrates (with) either misinformation or malice, called for a review of the accusation and justice upon his judges. In fine, the magistrates found themselves so pressed and the evidence so imperfect, that they expected every day a nulling of their own sentence and a severe amend upon themselves; when Brother Peter digging in the garden made a discovery (very advantageous to them and a manifest justification of their proceeding) of forges, moulds and other instruments that coiners use; in acknowledgment of which good service, the town in 1607 released them (from payment of) the maltot till it was recalled in 1645.

Some years they lived in this low and obscure condition, still practising austerities greater than their necessity before they were taken notice of or so much as known to Philip Cavarel Abbot of St. Vaast. This charitable Abbot and munificent prelate was busy at this time in building a College for the Jesuits in Arras. As he went one day to see how the building advanced, he met there an old Welshman, John Ishel, chaplain of our Lady's, who was very seriously gazing upon the work. The Abbot asked him what he thought of it. The Chaplain replied that it was a stately fabric and not misapplied, yet it was his opinion that his Lordship would do better to begin his charity towards his own Order, and that there were at Douay a considerable number of English Benedictines that had not a house to put their heads in, or wherewithal to subsist. This news made some impression on the Abbot's mind, who besides a natural tendency to do good to all, had a singular tenderness for the Order of which he was so considerable a member and ornament.

A fortnight afterwards, F. Bradshaw not knowing what had passed went over from Douay to present a petition to him in behalf of his distressed brethren. The Abbot entertained him very coldly, not so much as admitting him to his table, and despatched him the next day with an inconsiderable alms.

CHAPTER THE TWENTY-SECOND.

THE BEGINNING OF DIEULWART CONVENT.

YET during these miseries and hardships this F. Bradshaw obtained a place for a Convent in Lorraine; for the better understanding of which affair we must trace the business a little higher. In 1602 a Primatial Church was erected at Nancy in Lorraine by the authority of Pope Clement VIII, to which the Canons of a Collegiate Church in a place called Dieulwart, situated on the Moselle in the territory of the Bishop of Verdun, and in the diocese of the Bishop of Tulle (both Princes of the Sacred Empire) were transferred together with all their revenues. Sometime after F. Bradshaw upon notice of the vacancy of this old Collegiate Church, made all the interest he could to obtain it. The gift of it was in the Cardinal Prince Charles of Lorraine (now Primate of the new erected Primatial Church at Nancy,) the Venerable Dean and Canons thereof as also of Prince Eric of Lorraine, Bishop of Verdun and of the Very Reverend John Mallaneus à Procellettis, Bishop of Tulle.

The chief person in obtaining this grant was one Mr. Arthur Pitts, an English clergyman who was very powerful with his said Eminence, and was then Canon and Theologal of the noble Abbey of Remiremont, and wonderfully zealous for the English Benedictine Mission. He then obtained it *(the old Collegiate Church of St. Laurence at Dieulwart)* of the Cardinal (and) the Dean and Canons of Nancy for Father Bradshaw in behalf of the

I

English Benedictines. The grant bears date the 2nd of December 1606, and Father Bradshaw being at Verdun got the grant confirmed by the Bishop of that City, with his orders to the officers of Dieulwart for to take legal possession of it December 5th. 1606; and immediately that very day gave a *procuration* before a notary in due form from Verdun to the said Mr. Arthur Pitts, by virtue of which, with the solemnity used on such occasions he was put into possession of the said Church and all that was granted with it, by the officers of the town of Dieulwart, for and in behalf of the English Benedictines, 26th. of December 1606. Now it is to be noted that though those countries were then subject to the crown of France subdued by King Henry II yet this donation needed no confirmation from France, for that Dieulwart had been part of an estate of a Prince of the house of Lorraine, who taking to the Church, gave to the Cathedral of Verdun of which he became Bishop, the little territory of Dieulwart; and though long before the country was become subject to France as I said, yet when this Collegiate Church was thus given to these Fathers, the laws of France did not speak law there. Their force in those parts is of later date than the English Benedictine establishment at Dieulwart. This I have here noted because Louis the Great in 1707 questioned their establishment as not having had his royal approbation according to an order he put out many years before about building and founding new monasteries.

But to return to the donation. The Bishop of Tulle confirmed it April the 18th in 1609. The original of these acts are kept in the archives of Dieulwart. The two Congregations of Italy and Spain were excluded from the benefit of this gift as appears by many acts, which for a testimony of the zeal of those who by this sought the reconversion of England and the re-establishment of the Order of Saint Benedict in the said kingdom, still remain in the said archives. And Mr. Pitts in his acts adds that the Very Reverend FF. Austin Bradshaw and Leander of St. Martin had promised him in their letters to him, (the better to move his charity in this affair,) that Dieulwart should be the head of the English Congregation and the chief residence

CHAPTER THE TWENTY-SECOND.

of the President General thereof, an article agreed to by the said two RR. Fathers upon several other occasions as their letters still extant at Dieulwart make appear.

And the Spanish Congregation upon information of the necessities of their English Brethren obtained letters in their behalf from the King of Spain to Albert Archduke of Austria and Governor of the Low Countries, to whom also the Most Reverend General Perez writ, as likewise the English Benedictines in Spain; the Archduke in 1606 recommended them to Abbot Cavarel as to the common Father of his country and particularly of the afflicted. Also the Archbishop of Damascus, His Holiness' Nuncius at Brussels writ to the same effect. And the magistrates of Douay gave an ample testimony dated 1607 of the English Fathers' good behaviour and religious conversation. The *Magnificus Rector* in a paper signed by him (Marontus Comes) said no more than that such persons had been admitted to live quietly in the University.

After this the Abbot seriously took them into his protection, bought a little house for them and ground about it sufficient to build a more convenient habitation; and while he was laying the designs and providing materials, the Fathers now grown more in esteem found means to get lessons in Marchin College, an habitation and maintenance of several English pensioners, and sent for more of their brethren out of Spain and took novices at home; and no small encouragement to the Abbot of Arras in his designs for the distressed Community was the following letter of Cardinal Montalt, Protector of the Congregations of Mount Cassin and Valladolid.

Admodum Reverende Pater,

Ad protectionis munus quod Congregationis tum Cassinensis tum Vallisoletanæ sustineo, attinere videtur ut omnia veræ charitatis officia quibus R.P.V. earundem Congregationum Monachos Anglos in Belgio, ac præsertim pro monasterio in civitate Duacensi ædificando conficiendoque prosequitur grata acceptaque habeam, in id certe incubiturus ut nullam unquam prætermittam occasionem qua illis rebusque suis esse adjumento queam. Quandoquidem vero ipsos monachos apud Paternitatem vestram haudquaquam nova commendatione indigere certus sum, tantum hisce adjiciam, quicquid eorum commodis accessum fuerit mihimetipsi æque ac si proprium esset perpetuo fore jucundissimum. Ceterum illam benevalere et a Deo prospera omnia consequi desidero.

   Romæ die X Maii. MDCVIII.
     Paternitatis vestræ
       uti Frater Card. Montaltus.

Which for those who are strangers to Latin I have thus Englished :

   Very Reverend Father,
     It seems to belong to the charge of Protectorship which I exercise in regard of the Congregations of Mount Cassin and Valladolid that I gratefully accept all your charitable offices to the English Monks of the said Congregations in Flanders and particularly in rearing them a monastery at Douay. I shall let no occasion escape in which I may ever be able to render you any service in your affairs ; and as I am certain those said Monks need no new commendation to your Paternity I shall only add that whatever kindnesses are done to them I shall take as done to myself. As to the rest I wish your Paternity perfect health and all prosperity from God.

   From Rome on the 10th of May 1608,
     Your Paternity's Brother
       Cardinal Montalt.

CHAPTER THE TWENTY-THIRD.

THE FIRST NOVICES OF DOUAY.

THEIR first Novice was R. F. Joseph Haworth (à Sancta Maria) a Lancastrian who made an oblation of himself to the Order on the 18th of July 1607, and by a solemn oath vowed to R. F. Bradshaw that he would take the holy habit which he faithfully performed. And as in 1608 Dieulwart took the form of a convent by the monks who began that year to live there conventually and Douay was but a-hatching he was professed for Dieulwart; and in 1624 on the 24th of June died at St. Malo's not without the opinion and signs of great sanctity. For many diseased and infirm persons visiting his sepulchre in the chapel of Clermont where he lay buried, obtained their desired health, whereof they gave a public testimony under their hands and seals.

The second was Nicholas Fitzjames of Redlinch in Somersetshire, a secular Priest, May 12th 1607, professed in 1608 on the 15th of May for the convent of Dieulwart of which for some years he was afterwards Prior. He was also Novice-Master in which office he had the honour of having Dr. Gifford Dean of Lisle and afterwards Archbishop of Rheims for one of his novices, who then took the name of Gabriel of St. Mary, which he kept to his dying day even in his Archiepiscopal dignity; however in these notes I shall use the name of Gifford. Though he may be esteemed a Founder of Dieulwart for that his money gave it the form of a Convent, he was past fifty when he became a monk and had been Theologal to nothing less than the holy Cardinal St. Charles Borromeus Archbishop of Milan which is one of the first Sees in Christendom, yet Father Nicholas with his undaunted spirit in a diminutive body was so zealous in the exact practice of the Holy Rule which is so particular about trying of spirits, that when the Doctor returning from a sermon he had been sent to preach did not reach home time enough and therefore went into a garden to excuse himself to his master who was there at recreation with the community, he ordered him to prostrate though the ground was covered with snow, and bidding him rise said aloud, "There lay the print of a Doctor;" all which the venerable Doctor took with that spirit which St. Benedict requires in those which profess his discipline when he desires they may be learned in suffering affronts and injuries that they may enjoy the happiness in sharing in the opprobrium of the Cross of Christ. As to Father Nicholas, after many years of very commendable behaviour in the Mission he died at Stourton, the 16th of May, 1652, aged 92.

The third was R. F. Boniface Wilford of London who was professed the 8th of September, 1609, and died (on) the 12th of March. 1646, on the Solemnity of his house *(St. Gregory's)* in the prison of Newgate at London where he lay condemned for the truth of the Orthodox Faith expecting every day to be executed at the age of fourscore and ten.

The 4th on their Register is F. Columban Malon of Lancashire who was clothed by the R. F. Leander of Saint Martin the 2nd of September 1608 at the great monastery of St. Remigius at Rheims, where the said Father Leander had in charge the novices and young Religious of that great house to form them in piety, so wonderfully were the monks of that place charmed with his great abilities and capacity. Moreover they gave him leave to bring up as we here see English youths with theirs for his own Congregation. This Father Columban is the first that I can find downright positively of the house of Douay, and was professed 13th. of September 1609 ; a person of a most innocent life and of great example in all kinds of virtues, an exact observer of regular discipline, a constant practiser of rigorous penance and severe mortification, and yet of a most pleasing and pleasant conversation. He passed from the offices of Professor of Philosophy, Sub-Prior of Douay, Secretary of the President &c., to be Prior of Dieulwart, where in the second year of his government he saintlike slept in our Lord on the feast of All Saints 1623.

Next follows Mark Crowder of Shropshire professed in 1609 who after he had lived long in holy conversation at Douay and Dieulwart was sent into England where he endured half a year's imprisonment for the faith, and afterwards died at Lambspring in Germany.

Then Father Thomas Monnington of Herefordshire professed in 1610, and with him (*Brother*) Peter Huitson of Ashburn in Derbyshire after two years noviceship which delays commonly happen when their temporal estates and concerns are hard to be settled, or friends won't assent to a profession. F. Thomas was a very learned, pious and devout man and a good preacher, who after he had laudably executed the offices of Master of Novices, Definitor, &c, died most holily in the Mission on the 12th of June, 1642.

After these the same year professed Father Gregory Hungate of Yorkshire, who after he had well employed his time in sacred studies was sent into the mission where he successfully laboured till his dying day.

Lastly Father Anselm Crowder of Montgomeryshire clothed the 15th. April 1609, and professed the 3rd. of July 1611. He was brother to the above named F. Mark Crowder and the last that I find on their records before they were placed in Abbot Cavarel's foundation.

CHAPTER THE TWENTY-FOURTH.

CRUEL OPPOSITION TO THE ESTABLISHMENT OF ST. GREGORY'S CONVENT AT DOUAY.

Now those enemies, or some others of the same spirit who so vigourously opposed the fathers' first taking the Habit of St. Benedict in Spain, and about this time the first appearance between them of a union at Rome, were no less diligent to obstruct their settling and growth at Douay. To which end they spared neither them nor themselves, neither their credit nor their own conscience, painting them out for vagabonds, dangerous men and counterfeit monks; and seeing all this artifice did not succeed according to their desire they got a surreptitious Bull from Rome directed to the Archduke and nuncio Bentivoglio, to break up their conventicle and expel them the University under pain of excommunication if they obeyed not within twenty four hours after the intimation, and then to employ the assistance of the secular arm and compulsion.

The Nuncio (1610) cited Fr. Bradshaw the Superior to Brussels; he upon advice of Abbot Cavarel did not appear. Second orders came which were not regarded. At last came a formal precept full of threats. Father Bradshaw made report thereof to the Abbot of Arras and demanded again his advice. The Abbot answered that he saw their enemies were too strong for them, and that it was impossible for them to fix at Douay; told them it was indifferent to him where he placed them, and called for his book of maps to seek for a convenient place in some other town. While he was turning the book Father Leander entered with a letter from Rome directed to the Superior, or in his absence, to the most ancient of the English Fathers in Douay. It was from a Benedictine Cardinal; the only one that then was, (Annas d'Escars, O. S. B. Cardinal Archbishop of Metz) to inform them that such a Bull had been surreptitiously obtained much to their prejudice. Out of love to his Order and justice, he gave them notice of it; and upon any question about it they should if need were, produce his letter.

The Abbot much rejoiced at this, and looking upon it as a singular providence, (as indeed it was), commanded Fr. Bradshaw and Fr. Leander to make presently to Brussels, and without permitting them to return (*to Douay*) himself furnished their expenses.

As soon as they arrived there and presented themselves before the Nuncio, he expostulated with them in very high terms for their demurs and disobedience to his orders. They pleaded (and justly) indigence and want of money to make such a journey. "Well" replied he "to be short you must disperse and quit "Douay. Such is His Holiness' pleasure." Father Leander who by the Abbot's orders was *Dux verbi* (he that spoke) begged the favour of his Lordship to see the date of the Bull. "Do you take me then for an impostor," answered the Nuncio in great indignation, "this shall not serve your turn." (Then he) commanded the original to be brought. Father Leander having seen the date and compared it with the Cardinal's letter, begged pardon for asking a question in appearance so uncivil but withal so important, produced his letter of a later date, which maintained that the Bull was surreptitious, and asked the Nuncio if he knew the hand. "Yes" says he "and the persons too", (and) read the letter much surprised: and told them he saw they had been injured and himself abused; bade them return home and be secure that he would never trouble them with any summons till he had better warrant for them, and had first heard what the Fathers of Douay could say for themselves.

They came home in triumph without any opposition from

CHAPTER THE TWENTY-FOURTH.

the town or University. But this storm was scarce blown over before another no less furious began to rise against them. Their adversaries seeing their malicious designs frustrated on this side, applied themselves to the Archduke, produced their pretended Bull, begged his assistance towards the ejection of a company of vagabonds who under the mask of a religious habit machinated disturbance in the State and Academy.

The Duke tired with their importunities and not suspecting so much as that they were the same persons whom he had formerly recommended to the Abbot of Arras, gave order to an Hussar of Mechlin to expel them the town without possibility of returning. The Officer presently prepared for his journey and was ready to take horse, but knowing that the Abbot of Arras, his benefactor, was at Brussels, went first to receive his commands for those parts. The Abbot asked him the occasion of his journey; and having heard it, desired him to stay an hour or two till he writ some letters. He went to Court, had audience of his Highness, asked the reason why his Highness had issued out such a commission against men of an unblameable life whom he had formerly commended, and for whose behaviour himself (the Abbot) was ready to answer. The Duke replied that they were not the same persons whom he had heretofore recommended to the Abbot's charity, "Those were members of the Spanish Con-"gregation, these wanderers and no Benedictines." But being disabused and better informed by the Abbot he promised they should live unmolested for the future, encouraged the Abbot to build for them, gave his consent for their establishment with an obligation of an anniversary Mass for himself and the Archdukes for ever.

After things thus settled abroad Abbot Cavarel began to lay the foundation of his noble Gregorian Convent and College.

And during these difficult beginnings at Douay in 1608, R. F. George Gervase born of noble and Catholic parents at Bosham in Sussex, and who had taken the habit of St. Benedict privily at the hands of R. F. Austin Bradshaw when he came out of the English Seminary at Douay to go missioner for England, preferring the confusion of the Cross before the lustre of his birth,

CHAPTER THE TWENTY-FOURTH.

and despising all those advantages of education and learning as dust to gain Christ and win to him an acceptable people, the followers of good works, became a victim of the true Faith giving up his life for the same with an undaunted courage at London (April 11th, 1608).

The year after, to wit in 1609 on the 14th of April died in Lancashire R. F. Andrew Sherley a monk of Najar in Spain, a missioner of rare zeal and modesty.

The same year (1609) April the 23rd, (*as we learn from a decree*) in the archives of St. Gregory at Douay, Pope Paul V decreed for the English Benedictines, against whom the Jesuits had demanded sentence of excommunication if they exhorted the youths of the Seminaries to embrace their Order; that as the Jesuits should not under pain of excommunication hinder by dissuading the said youths from entering into the Order or any other that was approved, so the Benedictines under the same penalty should not dissuade any of their youths from entering into the Society or any other approved Religion.

CHAPTER THE TWENTY-FIFTH.

THE DEATH OF THE V. R. F. SIGEBERT BUCKLEY AND THE MARTYRDOM OF F. ROBERTS.

ON the 22nd of February 1610, at the age of 93, died R. F. Sigebert Buckley, and because the heretics would not let him be buried in the Churchyard, F. Anselm of Manchester and Father Thomas Preston buried him in an old Chapel or country hermitage near Ponshall the seat of Mr. Norton in Surrey or Sussex. They much wished that his body might be placed more honourably for that they did not doubt but that he was a very good old man and of great merit who had endured for the Catholic Faith forty years persecution, always shut up in some prison or other.

The same year (1610) December 10th. S. V. suffered the Reverend Father John Mervin alias Roberts. He entered the Congregation of Valladolid in 1598 say his printed Acts (R. F. Baker on the Mission says in 1599, in the company of F. Bradshaw who entered with the order of Priesthood) and by order of his Superiors was made Priest in 1600 and the same year sent to the Mission. But I think this a mistake for that all that I have hitherto been able to see excepting this, maintain the Congregation of Mount Cassin first entered the Mission, and we have seen it was not before 1603. But to return to Father Mervin. He was of Merionethshire in Wales, a man of admirable zeal, courage and constancy, the first who out of a monastery after the suppression of Monasteries in England attacked the Gate of Hell and provoked the prince of darkness in his usurped kingdom which he overcame like his great Master the pattern of Martyrs by losing his life in the conflict. Neither the raging fury of the plague that happened a little before could make him quit the flock, nor his own pestilent adversaries whose souls were worse infected than others bodies, **could** hinder him entering **again** though often banished, **till he had** lost his life where he **had** saved the souls **of** so many. They would have saved **his life if** he would but have taken the oath of allegiance.

His quarters were thrown into a pit under **the** gallows of Tyburn, and sixteen malefactors there executed **at** the same time were cast **in** upon them ; yet two nights after one of his brethren **with** some Catholics got them out at midnight with **those of Mr.** Wilson a secular Priest who for the same cause suffered with him. But by break **of** day by London, the watch of the town being in the way, one of these pious thieves that he might more certainly escape let fall a leg and thigh of Father Mervin which was carried to cruel George Abbot, titular Bishop of London who stood with great vehemency against Father Mervin at his trial, animating the judge against him ; he ordered them to be buried in the Church of St. Saviour *(St. Mary Overy, near London Bridge)* to hinder the Catholics from recovering them. The rest were carried off to Douay and into Spain, one bone (*being*) given to his intimate friend, the famous Spanish Benedictine Annalist the most Reverend Abbot Yepez, and one of his arms carried to St. Martin's at Compostella where he had been professed, as the said Abbot testifies in his Annals, speaking very honourably of F. Mervin (Tom. IV. p. 70 in the French version of them printed at Tull 1649.)

Bucelin a German Benedictine relating in the Benedictine *Menologe* (Veldtkirchii anno 1665), on the 10th of December the glorious triumph of this zealous missioner, assures that Pope Gregory XIII of blessed memory, so respected the relics of such as suffered thus in England for the Orthodox Faith, that he declared that they might be made use of in the consecration of

Altars. Behold the words of Bucelin: "Qui et aliis plures "Angliæ Martyres etsi nondum sint canonizati tamen iisdem "Gregorium XIII felicis recordationis Pontificem Maximum con- "stat detulisse ut declaraverit illorum Reliquias in consecrandis "altaribus adhiberi posse loco Reliquorum sanctorum canoniza- "torum cujusque declarationis mentio fit ab Episcopo Tarrasone "in Hist. Mart. Angl."

Also the same year under James 1st. Nicholas Sadler and Nicholas Hutton both Benedictine Monks suffered, as attests F. Sadler quoting John Molanus, Corcag and Menardus for witnesses, but where and for what he says he cannot find.

The Gregorian Convent of Douay was so far advanced in 1611 that F. Bradshaw presented an address to the Chapter of the Cathedral of Arras (that See being then without a Bishop) to have leave to transfer their altar from the Trinitarians, tenement to their new Convent. The place was visited by the Dean of Douay (deputed by the Archdeacon) and found convenient and decent upon which they were licensed to celebrate the Divine Office publicly, erect Altars, ring their bells, &c.

CHAPTER THE TWENTY-SIXTH.

THE BEGINNING OF ST. MALO'S CONVENT.

AND this said year 1611 Father Bradshaw having sent F. Gabriel of St. Mary (formerly Dr. Gifford Dean of Lisle) to Spain to obtain help from the Spanish Congregation, his community of Dieulwart being become very numerous without having wherewithal to live, and he tarrying at St. Malo's, with Father John Barnes expecting the opportunity of shipping, an English gentleman then free citizen of St. Malo entertained them, and the wind standing contrary held them there some time, in which visiting the Bishop the Reverend Lord William Le Governeur, he became so charmed with their learning and piety that he began to persuade them to let the thoughts of Spain alone and remain there. Several of the chief citizens expressed the same desire, delighted with Dr. Gifford's sermons; who hereupon writ to Fr. Bradshaw. He presently sent them many able men who arrived there the same year in the months of August and September, of whom I shall here give an account as they were the first beginners of the Convent.

1. R. F. Placid Hilton alias Musgrave, who earnestly and courageously promoted this affair; and going from hence afterwards into the mission he was present (October the 24th. on Friday, 1623) at the unfortunate fall of an upper chamber at Hunsdon House in the Black Friars' at London, where a great number of Catholics were assembled (Sir Richard Baker sayeth

about 300 men and women), when about the middle of the sermon a great part of the floor broke and fell down with such violence that it broke down the next floor under it. The preacher and almost one hundred of his auditory perished in the fall and about as many more were hurt. Father Hilton came to no harm and was a most compassionate helper and comforter of these poor distressed Catholics, whom the protestants hereupon with much bitter foolishness frivolously insulted as if it were an argument that the Catholic Religion was reproved by God, because, according to the Scriptures, by this affliction he was pleased to try the piety and patience of his servants. This gave occasion to the Catholics to exercise the press with writings on the manifold ways by which God tries his elect. As to the rest, Father Hilton was a zealous and excellent preacher and ended his days in Middlesex on the 20th. of February 1626. He was professed at Dieulwart.

2. Father Mellitus Babthorpe afterwards an industrious Missioner, in which function he died in the North. He was Brother to Father Thomas Babthorpe of the Society.

3. Father Thomas Green, Monk of St. Benedict's in Valladolid, Licentiate in Divinity; who having profitably spent many years in teaching his Brethren, was sent into the Mission, where after long imprisonments and many hardships endured for the Truth he preached, he ended his days in peace in 1624. He made a formal recantation of what he had written in defence of the Oath.

4. Father Boniface Kemp otherwise Kipton, professed of Montserrat, who with F. Ildephonse Hesketh in 1644 in the civil wars of England were taken by Parliament soldiers and driven on foot before them in the heats of summer, by which cruel and outrageous usage they were so heated and spent, that they either forthwith or soon after died. (July 26th. 1643.)

5. F. Columban Malon of whom we have spoken.

6. F. Bennet D'Orgain then a brother (entituled à Sancto Johanne) a noble Lorrainer who leaving all to follow Christ became a monk of Dieulwart; a truly apostolical man, most zealously preaching about the villages and by his powerful doctrine and example bringing many to embrace piety and

virtue; a most punctual observer of the holy Rule which he endeavoured to practise to the rigour of the letter. He writ several devout books for the use of the poorer sort of people in French. At last to avoid the wars, with leave of his Superiors he went forth of his monastery and came to the great Abbey of Cluny, where he died not without the opinion of sanctity. His dead body being according to the ancient custom of that holy place stretched forth upon ashes, shined with an extraordinary brightness and whiteness to the eyes of the admiring spectators, who there buried him with much honour; the Abbot saying and writing back to his Superiors of Dieulwart that Providence had guided him thither that his bones might lie by them of their many Saints. He died on the feast of St. Mayolus, Abbot of Cluny (which is the 11th. of May,) 1636.

Such were the beginners of St Malo's English Benedictine Convent. They were placed in the house of the Theologal, which dignity the Bishop conferred on Dr. Gifford, and on Father Hilton the Preceptorial which was to teach the children of the town. This was done with great contentment to all that were concerned therein, as the Dean, Chapter and people of St. Malo. Now as Mr. Towtin about the same time had given them his house and chapel of Clermont, a place out of the town on the Continent, part of them followed duty there, while the others remained at the Theologal's to help the citizens; wherefore by the said Bishop's appointment, Father Barnes taught Casuistry in the Cathedral, and the others sweated in the Confessionals and pulpits; and as it began in drudgery so it continued on, for the city of St. Malo's was scant of Religious and needed such helps, the Cathedral itself was but a poor business; and the English Benedictine Monks formed two Benedictine nunneries in the city besides, at the request of the Bishop.

CHAPTER THE TWENTY-SEVENTH.

OF THE GLORIOUS MARTYRDOM OF FATHER MAURUS SCOT, AND OF THE DIVINE VENGEANCE ON A HETERODOX ENEMY OF THE CONGREGATION.

ANNO 1612 suffered Father Maurus alias William Scot nobly born, bred up to the Civil law in Trinity Hall at Cambridge and converted to the Catholic Faith by Catholic books. He became a monk of Saint Benedict's at Sahagun in Spain from whence returning to the Mission, at his arrival at London he beheld the Priest who had reconciled him hurried away to death for the Faith, and he himself three days after was cast into prison for the same and there held a year. After this he was banished and so went to Douay, from whence returning again to England, he was soon taken and pursued to death by the aforementioned George Abbot, titular Bishop of London, to whom he was carried to be examined.

The chief proof of his priesthood urged against him was that as he came by water from Graves End, that he might not be discovered he flung into the Thames a little bag where his Breviary, faculties, medals and crosses were, which a fisherman catching in his net, carried to George Abbot, Titular Bishop of London (*now become*) Titular Archbishop of Canterbury.

As soon as Father Maurus heard the fatal sentence, he answered with a loud voice "Thanks be to God, never any news "did I ever more wish for, nor were there ever any so welcome to "me." Then turning to the people: "I have not yet confessed "myself a Priest, that the laws might go on of course, and that "it might appear whether the judges would offer to condemn "me upon such mere presumption and conjectures which you "see they have done. Wherefore to the glory of God and all "the Saints in Heaven I confess I am a monk of the Order "of Saint Benedict and Priest of the Roman Catholic Church. "But be you all witness I pray you, that I have committed "no crime against his Majesty or the Country: I am only "accused of Priesthood and for Priesthood condemned." This said he returned to his prison as unconcerned as if nothing had been done against him, whereas the said Titular Bishop George Abbot, who had sat with the Judges to hear him condemned, withdrew from the company like a man possessed with Orestes' furies.

R. F. Maurus gave up his life on Whitsun Eve on the 9th. of June (1612) very courageously with Mr Newport a Secular Priest. And George Abbot his persecutor hunting afterwards in a park and shooting at a deer, his arrow by mischance glanced and killed a man, upon which fact, sayeth Sir Richard Baker, it was much debated "whether by it he "were not become irregular, and ought to be deprived of his "archiepiscopal function, as having hands imbrued (though "against his will) in blood. But Andrewes Bishop of Win- "chester standing much in his defence, as likewise Sir Henry "Martin the King's advocate gave such reasons in mitigation of "the fact, that he was cleared of all imputation of crime and "thereupon adjudged regular and in state to continue his archi- "episcopal charge; yet himself out of a religious tenderness of "mind kept the day of the year in which the mischance "happened with a solemn fast all his life after."

However he afterwards fell entirely into the disgrace of Charles the Ist who succeeded James the Ist, and so endured involuntary pain for the voluntary butchery of Priests while he voluntarily afflicted himself for the involuntary murder of a man. And though he may pretend his disgrace at Court was on good account, his bloody barbarity is easily answered. Had he been a harmless, innocent soul such sufferings might have brought him a crown of justice; but to him an alien from the Church, and shedding the blood of the Priests of the Church, his vexations were the just punishments in part of his guilt, the rest being reserved to the last moments, when due penance is not rightly performed but in the union of the Church. The Eternal Wisdom of God by many ways scourges sinners with rods of their own making while he leaves them in their wilful blindness, and they persuade themselves vainly that they act with God and for God when in the end they will see they have basely deluded themselves and their part will be with those to whom he will say "I know you not." Though they tell him they have done wonders in his name, they will hear "Go ye accursed into everlasting "fire." But to return to our Chronological Notes.

CHAPTER THE TWENTY-EIGHTH.

FURTHER TROUBLES AND OPPOSITION AGAINST THE
CONVENT OF ST. GREGORY AT DOUAY.

The license of celebrating publicly Divine Service given by the Chapter of Arras to the new Convent of St. Gregory at Douay was confirmed afterwards by John Richardot who was promoted to that See, and being from thence translated to Cambray he gave a testification hereof on the 30th of March, 1613, his successor making some difficulty about it. Upon this unquestionable testimony of his metropolitan and so eminent a prelate, he on the 22nd of April following continued the said license to the first of July ensuing, before which term he ordered the Fathers should evidence to him their canonical and lawful reception and admission unto that Diocese.

Whereby it seems to appear that their enemies whoever they were, after they had missed of their aim in circumventing the Pope's Nuncio and (the) Archduke, endeavoured to fix their imposture on their Bishop and engage the Ordinary to prosecute their uncharitable designs. For unless he had been prejudiced by misinformation, how should he be inclined to call into question their admittance which had been consented to by the University, approved by the Magistrates, confirmed by the Archduke, and even desired by his Catholic Majesty? So that their enemies made use of a graduation contrary to that which is observed in other appeals, which are ordinarily from a lower court to an higher.

But it seems the Bishop too, received satisfaction, especially after the king of Spain's letters were produced which perhaps arrived not before, dated March 21st, 1613, directed to the Archduke Albert, and Cardinal Bentivoglio writ to the Bishop in their behalf.

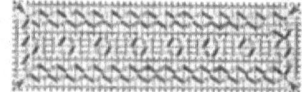

CHAPTER THE TWENTY-NINTH.

OF THE EDIFICATION GIVEN BY THE ENGLISH MONKS IN THE LOW COUNTRIES.

What edification they gave in the Low Countries appears from the following writing (in the archives of St. Gregory in Douay) of the Rev. Abbot of Marchin, Jean de Foucquoi, signed with his own hand and dated October 4th, 1614.

"Ego infrascriptus testor et fidem facio mihi certo constare, tum ex personarum fide dignissimarum frequenti relatione tum etiam ex authenticis testimoniis et instrumentis mihi sæpe exhibitis sub regimine Reverendissimi et venerabilis Patris, Fratris Leandri de Sancto Martino in Sacra Theologia Magistri et Superioris Collegii S. Gregorii Duaceni fundati a Reverendissimo Domino, Domno Philippo de Cavarell, Benedictinorum Anglorum Professorum Vicarii Generalis in Congregatione Hispanica et actu viventium sub obedientia illius, octoginta plus minus monachos Deo famulari summa cum pietate erga Deum, qui utilitatem Reipublicæ litterariæ et Ecclesiæ Catholicæ haud vulgarem quotidie afferunt et litterarum professione et religiosissima conversatione et particulatim mihi constat ex prædicto numero monachorum quam plures esse Doctores in Sacra Theologia et Artibus et Licentiatos; nonnullos scriptis utilissimis et doctissimis hereticos exagitasse, quorum libros non sine gaudio legisse testor et ob experientiam summæ illorum Religionis recepi in Collegium meum Marchianense octo, qui summa omnium satisfactione et laude aut versantur in professione philosophica aut continuis studiis se disponunt ad illas. In Collegio item S. Gregorii multi sunt monachi quorum alii professione Theologicæ egregie vacant, alii omnes aut Theologivè auditores sunt aut Philosophicis studiis intenti. Denique certo constat omnes ex supradicto numero, aut sacerdotes esse, aut sacerdotio initiandos; studiorum theologicorum et philosophicorum curriculo perfunctos, aut illi insudantes esse; quique ut honestius sese alant et pro Anglicana messe sese præparent continuis confessionibus, prædicationibus et piis exemplis jugiter exercentur in locis ubi degunt, iisque quibus præsunt mirifice prosunt. Fratres vero qui in Angliam prædicandi Evangelii ergo migrarunt fructus fecisse non vulgares in conversione animarum bonorum omnium constantissima fama nobis persuasissimum est. Novem carceribus mancipati, aliqui crudelitate hæreticorum in custodiis absumpti, quatuor glorioso martyrio pro Fide Catholica perfuncti, concursus piissimorum Catholicorum Anglorum pro spirituali ope et solatio, quid aliud possunt persuadere nisi quod Angli Benedictini professionis Hispanicæ Sedis Apostolicæ auctoritatem et Fidem Catholicam in Anglia mirabiliter fulcient."

The same in English for those who are not accustomed to Latin.

I (the) under written witness and assure that I know for certain as well from the frequent relation of persons most worthy of credit, as from authentic testimonies and instruments often shown me, that under the government of the most Reverend and Venerable Father, Brother Leander of Saint Martin, master in Divinity and Superior of the College of Saint Gregory at Douay (founded by the most Reverend Lord, Lord Philip Cavarel,) and Vicar General of the English Benedictines professed in the Congregation of Spain, who actually live under his obedience. There live in the service of God about fourscore monks most piously affectioned towards God, who not at a common rate advance learning and the cause of the Church of God, by their religious conversation and profession of letters. And I certainly know that out of the said number of monks there are several of them Doctors in Divinity and arts, and Licentiates. Some of them have much vexed the heretics by most useful and learned writings, whose books I have read with joy; and for the experience I have had of their extraordinary religious comportment I have received eight of them into my College of Marchin, who either by their continual studies prepare themselves to teach Philosophy or actually do teach it, to the very great satisfaction of all and their own commendation. Likewise in the College of Saint Gregory there are many of the monks of whom some are egregious professors of Divinity, the others learn it or Philosophy. In fine, it is certain that all of the said number are either Priests, or to be ordained such, have done their studies of Philosophy or Divinity or are actually in them; and the better to maintain themselves and prepare themselves for the English Mission exercise themselves continually in hearing confessions, preaching and pious examples in the places where they live, and are wonderfully profitable to those who are under their care. By the constant relation of all good men, we are entirely persuaded that those who have been sent to preach the Gospel in England have done much good in the conversion of souls; nine have been imprisoned, and some of them through the cruelty of heretics have died in prison; four have died glorious martyrs for the Faith. The concourse of the most pious English Catholics for spiritual help and comfort, what can it else persuade but that the English Benedictines of the Spanish Congregation wonderfully maintain the authority of the See Apostolic, and the Catholic Faith in England." Thus the said Abbot.

The first who taught in his Marchin College was F. Torquatus Latham who read six courses, F. Barnes who read three, to him succeeded F. Anselm Crowder; F. Leander had the Catechistical lesson &c, and they continued in this employment with great applause till the Abbot of Marchienne became so enamoured of the Jesuits that he put out his English Brethren and took away his own Monks, and totally abandoned to the Society the said College, about the same time that the English Monks began to teach publicly in the College of St. Vaast where Abbot Cavarel placed those the Abbot of Marchienne had put off. Here F. Clement Rayner was the first, with F. Rudesind and F. Leander.

CHAPTER THE THIRTIETH.

THE ENGLISH BENEDICTINES OF THE SPANISH OBEDIENCE BROUGHT TO PARIS A. D. 1615.

ANNO 1615 the English Monks of the Spanish obedience thus reached Paris: Dom Bernard, Prior of Cluny College at Paris, much esteemed in that great city for his learned and pious sermons, hearing of the wonderful abstemious life of the Monks of Dieulwart recommended them to the Abbess of the royal nunnery at Chelles near Paris. Then few Religious houses of St. Benedict's Order in France were reformed, and Her Highness (for she was a Princess of the house of Lorraine) being totally bent upon the reformation of her nunnery knew not where to find men to help her in such a work, but directed as is said, (*by the Prior of Cluny College*) Father Francis Walgrave, clothed at Dieulwart in 1608 and professed the year following by Father Bradshaw, was by him in 1611 sent to Her Highness with several other monks of the same Spanish Obedience to be Confessor to her community and perform the duties she should desire of them: for her nunnery like the other great nunneries of France, used to have a little community of Monks for its service. In 1612 F. Bradshaw himself followed him thither to help him and they admitted some English youths to the Habit. And the Abbess was so pleased with their religious behaviour that she resolved to procure them a settlement in Paris, where, having finished their studies, they might either be sent into the English mission or live at Chelles in the ministry of her community.

This year then (1615) she obtained from Dieulwart six monks for Paris; namely

1. Father Clement Reyner descended of an ancient family in Yorkshire. He became a monk at Dieulwart, did his studies at Douay, taught there as hath been said, and passed Doctor; was the Procurator of the Congregation in Germany and twice its President General. Half a year he was Superior of Rintelen in Germany, where he had a famous dispute with Dr. Stechman, Superintendent of Hesse, a man esteemed by his Calvinists very learned; he was so confounded that he died for grief a few days after, crying to his last moment "O Clement thou hast killed me." Nor was less extraordinary his second dispute there with Dr. Gisenius, Superintendent of the Lutherans of Brunswick; it lasted three days together, and the heresiarch was just a-going to be covered with as much confusion as the former, when the city was taken by Gustavus Adolphus' army, which spoiled the dispute, and the monks had but time to save themselves across the river (the Weser) and so escaped. The soldiery pursued them but could not get over the river after them. R. F. Townson who has writ the history of Lambspring says the mitre of the great monastery of St. Peter de Monte Blandinio just by Ghent, worth 80,000 imperialists, was offered him; which he refused and returned to Germany and set up Lambspring of which he was the first Abbot. He was indeed so dear to them at Ghent whom he reformed, that I have seen a letter whereby it appears the Fathers of this Congregation seriously and in great earnest were in great concern how to get that Abbey to let him return freely home to his Congregation which had never intended more than to lend them his help, but would not abandon the right they had to him themselves. He lived very much considered in Germany and died at Hildesheim, 27th. of March 1651 S. N, from whence his bones were brought to Lambspring in 1692 and there buried in the body of the Church.

2. F. Nicholas Curre who after many labours in the mission happily ended his life at Weston in Warwickshire in 1649 (Aug. 5th).

3. Father George Sayer.

4. F. Alban Roe nobly born, who after a long practice of religious virtues in the Monastery, many labours and persecutions in the Mission, gave up his life for the Faith with an undaunted courage at Tyburn in the 60th. year of his age, (January 21st.) 1642, after 17 years imprisonment. His execution is printed in the *Année Benedictine &c.*

5. Brother Placid Gascoign, son to a Baronet, professed at Dieulwart before he was sixteen (the term fixed for religious profession by the holy Council of Trent;) informed of the mistake he renewed his profession, and profited so in studies at Paris that he passed the examen for Doctor and was admitted, but the disputes that were then on foot betwixt the Regulars and the Bishop of Chacedon hindered him of the honour of the Doctoral bonnet. He spent sixteen years in the mission very profitably and advantageously to the Church, in great danger of his life in a violent persecution. After which he governed the Congregation four years (as) President General, and from thence totally betook himself to the government of his Abbey of Lambspring giving great examples of humility, patience and sweetness. He was very exact in that part of his Rule which commands the Abbot to first practise himself what he commands others to do, and show by his actions what is not to be done. From the beginning of his abbatial dignity, he cast the care of the temporals of his Abbey on R. F. Joseph Sherwood whom he obtained for his co-adjutor; and spending all his time in holy exercises, he died in 1681 (July 24th.) at the age of 83, professed 66, Priested 57, of his abbatial dignity 31; and lies buried in his Abbey Church.

6. Brother Dunstan Pettinger, surnamed afterwards Captain Bold and White, a painful labourer and zealous preacher for a long time in the mission, wherein he died at London in Drury lane, as it was supposed of the plague in 1665 (at the age of 79), the 15th. of August.

These were all professed of the house of Dieulwart. The Abbess placed them in the suburbs of St. James, in the hotel of St. Andrew, where afterwards the Union was agreed on, and where now the Visitation nuns are established. The rent came to

£60 sterling a year to which for their subsistence she further gave every year £100 sterling and besides sent them from Chelles frequently provisions of bread, wine and meat. This residence totally depended on Father Walgrave whom the Reverend General of Spain had appointed Superior over the Religious at Chelles in 1614 where they were six or seven; and F. Bradshaw was Superior of it till the next year, namely 1616, in which he was called to reform Longueville in Normandy where he died.

Anno 1616 September 29th. in the General Congregation of the Holy Inquisition, Pope Paul V very favourably assented to the humble request of the Spanish Congregation declaring that the English of that Congregation having finished the time of study set down in Clement VIII's Brief might take the degrees of Doctor with leave of the Cardinal Protector *pro tempore* and their Superiors only, when they have studied more in their cloisters than in the Seminaries in which case there would be no need of the leave of the Rectors of the Seminaries.

Father Parsons the Jesuit had obtained of Clement VIII a Brief which commanded that no Englishman should pass Doctor in Divinity till after a course of four years in the study of Divinity, and four years added to that again to perfect them therein and render them thorough Divines.

CHAPTER THE THIRTY-FIRST.

The Union.

But it is now time to consider the progress made towards the so much desired union of the English monks of the three Congregations, to wit, Mount Cassin, Valladolid, and the English; (for Father Sadler and Father Mayhew aggregated by Father Buckley, had professed several persons,) in order to have but one Benedictine Congregation in England which should be the old English Congregation renewed; which was found very hard to be effected. Many meetings there had been about it, many articles conceived and proposed about the manner, and great expenses there had been in journeys upon this account. And these treaties and doings had continued many years, and notwithstanding all this seemed every day farther off than before.

Some of the monks were in prison, as F. Thomas Preston, Superior of the Italian mission; others beyond sea, as F. Bradshaw Superior and Vicar General of the Spanish, laying the foundation of Douay and Dieulwart, and the rest scattered in England as sheep without pastors, lying in covert from the fury of the persecution.

But it happened by a secret conduct then not well understood, but soon after discovered, that Fr. Bradshaw diverted to Rheims to confer with Dr. Gifford then Rector of the University of Rheims, and with Fr. Leander of St. Martin, then at the royal Monastery of St. Remigius, concerning the new foundations and of the present state of their Order in England. It was soon agreed amongst them that it was impossible to regulate the mission well unless they entered upon a stricter alliance between the members of the Congregations; and while they were deliberating upon the means how to bring it to pass, Father Thomas Preston came in; and so came in, that while one of them said he wished Father Thomas Preston were there, he that was wished for being exiled out of England, knocked at the door to enquire for them. His coming so unexpected and so seasonable was regarded by them all as a certain sign of the Divine Will, and no light argument that the union they were meditating was acceptable and pleasing to Him whose Providence so happily brought them together, and whose honour they zealed.

It was hard to please the Spanish Congregation which expected to give the law in this affair as having many more Missioners in England than the Congregation of Mount Cassin which yet liked to have carried it, when after much for and against the Union, F. Anselm of Manchester compiled several articles which the Pope ratified, and presently they were despatched to the Pope's Nuncios at Paris and Brussels, who without delay intimated them to all the monks in Flanders, France and Lorraine, and strictly commanded them to be put in execution. But as they were found grounded on a mistake, Dr. Gifford, Prior of St. Malo's and Preacher then at Paris, obtained space to communicate (on) the affair with the Spanish Vicar, Father Leander of St. Martin, who acquainted his Reverend General with what had passed. The General commanded him in virtue of Holy Obedience to go to Rome himself or send an intelligent person to rescind the contract and break off the Union. Father Leander had no sooner received this command but he was cited to Brussels by the Legate, then Archbishop of Rhodes, afterwards Cardinal Bentivoglio, to intimate to him His Holiness' orders to publish the Union. He humbly desired to be heard, for his General had charged him with an express command to that end. His reasons were found such that Father Bennet of St. Facundus was sent with them to Rome as Procurator to dissolve the Union and reduce such of their Spanish subjects in

France who under pretence of this Union had withdrawn from the obedience of their former Superiors.

The English Congregation sent Fr. Sigebert the younger to plead their right and stop the attempt of the adversary. He joined in commission with Father Anselm Beech of Manchester whose power in Rome and experience in such affairs was no small advantage to his side, (and) vigourously pursued the union both by opposing Fr. Bennet and presenting frequent informations to the Congregation of Cardinals.

This Father Anselm of Manchester after he had been four years in the mission, was sent to Rome, as Father Baker observes (in his Treatise of the Mission) "there to negotiate the affairs "of the mission for his Congregation, and there remained "for a great many years and never returned to England, but "growing to be extreme old went thence to the Monastery of St. "Justina (*at Padua*) where he had taken the habit and professed, "and there after two or three years died and made a good end. "I never knew any man in Mission," continues Father Baker, "whom for my part I should have judged fitter for the Mission "than he was, all qualities considered, nor do I know any man "that succeeded better for the good of others for the time he "was there."

And besides these opponents *(of the Spanish party)*, on this side the Alps the monks of Chelles, who were all English of the Spanish Obedience, were as zealous to maintain the said union as they were willing to accept it; and their Superior, Father Walgrave, relying on the protection and favour of the illustrious Abbess of Chelles, obtained letters of divers persons of the highest quality in the Kingdom in behalf of his cause. But for all this so unbiassed were the judgments of that supreme Court of Rome, and so unregarding of persons and interests, that the reasons of the Spanish Vicar prevailed and a decree was made for the suspending the execution of the articles, and for commanding such as had accepted them to return to their former obedience, and order given that they should be benignly received by their former Superiors.

This Decree was drawn Feria V, 15th. of January, 1615, in

CHAPTER THE THIRTY-FIRST.

the General Congregation of the Holy Inquisition, and the promulgation of this Decree was particularly pressed upon those of Chelles (who seemed the most likely to fall out) with threats of having recourse to more efficacious remedies if they would not submit. And to reduce the said Father Walgrave and his subjects to their former obedience, there were sent from Douay by the Vicar General, Father John Barnes his assistant and Father Paul Grineus. Yet they were excusable in that they rendered obedience to the Superior of the English Congregation only upon the Pope's command, and refused to withdraw it till they had acquainted the said Superior with the business and represented (to) His Holiness their reasons; and to this, obtained a letter from the Nuncio at Paris, [Episcopus erat Politianus] dated the 1st. of July, 1615.

But though this form of Union did not please his Holiness yet he saw a great necessity of the Union itself, and he laid it to heart so much and judged it so necessary for the conversion of our country that he directed a command to Father Leander by his Nuncio, either to send up another Procurator or send to him that was there a new commission to treat of a more solid union according as his Holiness should find most convenient.

But those who were in England aggregated by Fr. Buckley to the English Congregation, seeing that this commotion was chiefly raised upon their account, namely towards the uniting the rest to that Congregation whereof they as yet were the whole, thought themselves obliged by charity to their brethren and by duty to our Holy Father the Pope, to ease them both from further solicitude by proposing an accommodation more agreeable to all sides; wherefore the same year (1615) on the 11th of June they present a request to his Holiness humbly showing that the underwritten having by many evident proofs experienced the great zeal of his Holiness for the good of our country and conversion of souls and paternal solicitude for our mission and a Union betwen the religious of the Order of St. Benedict destined by their Superiors to that end, over which his Holiness watched as a common and to them as a particular Pastor and Father, and having maturely pondered what advantage or disadvantage may arise if the manner of the union be convenient and by all equally approved, or inconvenient and only acceptable by some few as the last method presented to his Holiness (for all desire a union as to the substance but differ upon the manner), they most humbly desire his Holiness not to take any new measures till he had strictly and under censures, commanded all the fathers of the three Congregations to choose by plurality of suffrages nine Definitors without regard to Congregation but promiscuously as the votes should run out of all three or any two or one of them, which Definitors meeting together should also by plurality of suffrages agree upon the nature and form of the Union and present it to his Holiness to be approved, and after the approbation thereof should proceed by the same Apostolic authority to constitute the regimen and laws of the united Congregation.

A proposition so rational and moderate as this, and coming from such as had an equal interest, yet no party hitherto in the differences which shaked the rest, could not be excepted against by any side unless they would declare themselves abettors of dissension; it was also well received in the court and congregation of Cardinals of the Inquisition as appears by Cardinal Bellarmine's letter to Father Leander (22nd of May, 1616); though writ after Father Sigebert's arrival at Rome, wherein the holy Cardinal assures him that all things had a very good appearance and face of peace and union. He feared only some opposition on Father Anselm's side, which nevertheless he thought would not be of any great effect; and if that he and his body would not conspire to promote the common concern of the Mission, it was the Cardinal's judgment that it imported not much if the Cassin Congregation were utterly excluded as being so far from England, and the other Cardinals were of his opinion.

The Spanish Vicar confirmed Father Bennet in his procuratorship and sent him a new and more ample commission with instructions for his behaviour in the affair; and this with the unanimous consent of the Religious in France of the Spanish Obedience.

And Father Anselm was continued by the Italian Congregation both Superior and Procurator of the English Congregation which hitherto lay in covert under the **shadow** of the Cassin Congregation and as yet was in its minority, negotiating nothing but by the Cassins' hands; yet now it sent as its Procurator apart Father Sigebert (whose surname was Bagshaw), and **as he** was intituled to Westminster Abbey, to distinguish him from Father **Buckley** he is often in writings called Father Sigebert or Father **Sebert the** younger. This was by commission and **even invitation of Father** Anselm in his letter to them assembled at Dieulwart, **dated the** 7th of May, **1616; for** Dieulwart was properly **the** house of the English Congregation, for not only Mr. Pitts **got it for that end** as hath been said, but also he **was the** person who **proposed the** Reverend FF. Sadler and Mayhew for the **aggregation who soon** after were associated and appropriated **to the house of Dieulwart, from** which two that place laid **its claim to Westminster and** expect it **yet** if ever it be restored; **though this Congregation as I** shall say in its place hath renounced **the lands and estates of the** Abbeys, &c. But to return to the affair **of our Union.** These things being thus far advanced, the **Procurators met at Rome** made a joint protestation that they would **sincerely and what in** them lay efficaciously treat of and procure **the desired union ;** setting chiefly before their eyes the **conversion of our country by** the labours of the Apostolical **Mission, and (in) the next place the recovering and re-establishing the ancient English Benedictine** Congregation.

His Holiness expedited **a Brief, the 19th** of May, **1616, wherein** he commands nine Definitors to be chosen out of the whole body of the English Benedictine Mission without **any respect of Congregations**, but such only as shall be judged by **the electors to be** in sanctity, virtue, prudence, and religious practice, **more remarkable and fit.** In the election all should have **a vote that were** professed, and that person should *ipso facto* **be chosen who had** more suffrages according to the manner and form the Nuncio of France should prescribe ; **that the Definitors elect should have power** to constitute and enact such ordinances and rules as they **should** judge proper for the present and future state of the mission, habit, office, ceremonies, &c, to nominate officers and **Superiors to their Communities ; that such** laws as they should pass should be sent to the City, and presented to the Congregation of the Inquisition, and that the said laws should not be in execution till they were corroborated by the Apostolic approbation.

The publication of this Brief was imposed on the Nuncio of France Cardinal Ubaldin who intimated it the 4th of August following and communicated copies to the persons concerned; requiring moreover that the suffrages of each person should be secret, according to conscience, unbiassed by interest or persuasion, and that they should be sent to him as scrutator within three months, and that such nine as he should collect out of plurality of suffrages he declares Definitors and that he would appoint the time and place where they should meet that they might agree on what should be judged necessary for the perfection of the Mission and Union of the Congregations.

As soon therefore as the Superiors of the Spanish and English Congregations had received the Brief, on their part they communicated copies to all their subjects and others of the English Mission within and out of England; and the Cardinal Bentivoglio succeeding Ubaldin in the Nunciature of France, there were sent to him all the suffrages of the monks of the Spanish and English Congregations excepting at the most five or six who either would not vote or their votes miscarried in the way as it may easily happen at such a distance and in such difficulties of times, and 'tis more strange that more did not than that so few did miscarry.

After his Eminence had compared the suffrages according to the orders given by His Holiness to Cardinal Ubaldin, he pronounced Definitors the nine that had most suffrages, who were as follows:

1. R. F. Leander of St. Martin, Vicar General of the Spanish Congregation. His surname was Jones descended of the noble family of the Scudamores of Kentchurch in Herefordshire. At scarce a year old he was carried from Wales where he was born into England to suck in the language together with his nurse's milk. After some time spent in some country schools he was committed to that famous one of Westminster at London, where giving extraordinary token of a great genius, he was sent to the

College of St. John's **at Oxford.** Here he gave himself chiefly to the study of the Civil Law and made such progress that it exposed him to the envy of his companions, as on the other side his steadiness in the Catholic faith exposed him to the fury of Calvin's followers; wherefore to avoid the consequences thereof he was forced to return to London. There he found his family afflicted with the plague, so that his parents **and brethren** died all of them a few days after his arrival. Upon this he went to the English College of Valladolid the better to instruct himself in his religion and learn divinity. After some years thus spent he entered into the Order of St. Benedict in the Monastery of St. Martin at Compostella in Spain; and from thence, to form him in all sorts of learning that might any ways help him against the Sectaries of England, he **was sent up and down to many of the** monasteries of Spain, and lastly was sent to the Mission. But as he took his journey through France, **at the** great monastery of St. Remigius at Rheims they most earnestly entreated him to lend them his company for a few months to form in learning and piety their novices, which he did to their very great satisfaction. From hence his brethren called him to rather help them who most needed him in their new settlements; wherefore he went to Douay and afterwards to Dieulwart, charming all the monasteries wherever he came with the great renown of his learning and piety. From Lorraine where he taught Divinity he **was** called to be Prior of Douay; afterwards he was constituted President General of the English monks of the Spanish Congregation residing out of Spain. He spent in the University of Douay almost twenty four years in teaching Divinity and the Hebrew tongue, of which he was a public professor before he passed Doctor of Divinity, nor did he give it over till his dying day. During the said twenty four years he corrected many books and caused them to be printed very exactly and with all this was so modest and humble that he suppressed many very fine things both in prose and verse of his own doing and would never but against his will let them be known for his. He was so skilled in all the oriental languages that few were superior to him in those sciences, and enjoyed so prodigious a memory that in a short time he could learn any of them in perfection if he did but once fix his resolution to set itself after it; an accomplished rhetorician, poet, grecian and latinist. Twice was he Prior of Douay and twice President of the Congregation after the Union, which offices he performed most nobly and worthily, and was by the Congregation designed Abbot of Cismar. He rendered the Catholic cause great services when upon the marriage of Charles I with Henrietta of France there appeared an aurora of England's conversion, the Queen being Catholic and attended with a Chapel splendidly served by a great retinue of Priests both Secular and Regular; the King inclining and the famous Dr. Laud, that renowned protestant archbishop of Canterbury (the best of them who have occupied that See since error hath prevailed in England), steering his course directly to the old and only Faith, guided and directed by his dear friend and old intimate acquaintance the R. F. Leander, to whom he gave a College in Kent. They had been colleagues together at Oxford, and not only this Reverend Father was so highly prized by Dr. Laud but also by others of that heterodox misery, so that more than once in most desperate times he had a special Royal grant or leave to go into England. The last time he went he was called by the aforesaid good friend Dr. Laud who wanted to confer with him about some points of controversy. But he had not been long in England when he fell sick and died the 27th of December 1635, and made a good end, saith Father Baker, having had a good warning and assurance of his death near at hand in his last sickness that was long and made him keep his bed. He died about the 70th year of his age and was much lamented and very nobly attended by many great persons to his grave which was the first made at Somerset Palace in the Queen's chapel, consecrated but four days before. I should have specified amongst other his church dignities, that of his being Cathedral Prior of Canterbury; and yet nothing of all this could alter or change or disturb his incomparable meekness and affability.

2. Reverend Father Vincent Sadler, President of the English Congregation, whose story hath been related.

3. Dr. Gifford, Prior of St. Malo's. Both Father Mayhew

and Mr. Pitts (de Scriptoribus) agree his extraction was very illustrious and splendid, descended by his father of the old noble Giffords of Normandy, and by his mother of the most illustrious Throckmortons. He was born in 1555, and during his childhood a person gave a cross to his mother, advising her to keep it for her son William (for that was his name in Baptism) he being destined to an high dignity in the Church. His father dying while he was in the flower of his youth, his most pious mother kept him four years at the University of Oxford, from whence to enjoy the freedom of Catholic religion he went with his Tutor to Louvain. Here he passed Doctor of Arts and spent four years in Divinity, for the most part under the learned Fr. Bellarmine (who was afterwards Cardinal Bellarmine) and passed Bachelor in Divinity. Louvain becoming almost abandoned through the civil wars in Flanders, he went to Paris to continue his Divinity, and not long after William Allen, President of the English College at Rheims and in process of time Cardinal, called him to him to Rheims, and sent him to finish his studies at the English College at Rome, at the end of which he called him again to Rheims and placed him Professor of Divinity at the English College. And that he might acquit himself thereof with greater authority he sent him to Pont-a Mousson in Lorraine, no contemptible University, and there he passed Doctor in Divinity, the 14th. of November 1584, with great applause, and returning to Rheims he there taught Divinity with as great commendation for the space of eleven years during which time he had many for his scholars who afterwards shed their blood for the Faith at the gibbets of England.

Hence it came that the government of England bore him such hatred that he could never return hither but very privately, whereby he lost his inheritance which God even then began to repay him; for he raised him great friends in the persons of Henry Duke of Guise and Governor of Champaign and Lewis his brother, Archbishop of Rheims and Cardinal, who gave him yearly as long as they lived an honourable pension of 200 pieces of gold (Ducentos aureos); but they perishing at Blois and France beginning to flame with civil war, Dr Gifford went again to Rome. I find he voyaged thrice into Italy, and in one of them he had the honour and blessing of living in the family of that incomparable prelate of Milan St. Charles Borromeus, as his Theologal. In his last voyage to Italy he adhered and kept to his good old friend Cardinal Allen in the same quality of Theologal, and the Deanery of Lisle in Flanders by Pope Clement VIII was conferred upon him through the means of the said Cardinal Allen. He held this considerable benefice very honourably for the space of ten years, keeping open house to virtue, especially when banished for religion sake. But as his inclinations were altogether French and no ways Spanish, he was forced to quit his Deanery of Lisle then in the Spanish Dominions and return to Rheims again where he became Rector of that University, and acquitted himself of the charge with great applause. Then leaving all and becoming a monk at Dieulwart, after his profession he taught his brethren and was Preacher to the Duke of Lorraine, very exact to all religious duties and austerities, and so humble notwithstanding his great parts and abilities that it soon exalted him to the first place of the house, where he stayed not long, when he was sent as hath been said to Saint Malo's. Here his fame so spread that he became Visitor of the most famous and noble Abbey of Fontevrault, which great charge he performed egregiously for some years; and his affairs obliging him to resort to Paris, he was there so followed for his sermons, that though an Englishman he was honoured with the chief pulpits of that renowned city, and so esteemed one of its best preachers that the most Christian King Louis the XIII and the chief of the court and many other great men were frequently of his auditory. He was very expert in that useful faculty having often made Latin orations before many Princes; as at Lisle at the inauguration of Albert and Isabella, Soveréign Princes of the Low Countries, and at Rheims before the Cardinals of Bourbon, Vendôme, Guise, Vaudmont, and the Dukes of Guise, D'Aumale &c. In all he spent fourteen years in preaching at Paris, so universally applauded that he acquired to himself through the excellency of his merits, the name of Le Père

Bénédictin, the Benedictine Father. Of this preaching a pleasant thing is assured which deserves mention. His practice was not only loyal, but his public discourses tended altogether to inspire the same virtue into the public which then was somewhat off the hinges. Notice was given him to take heed or else he would be pistolled; but he persisting intrepidly in his duty, one day a coach stopped at the door where the Fathers lived, and an unknown person demanding him, gave him a bag full of gold pistoles, praying him to continue on his lessons of loyalty. Coming upstairs he told his brethren he was pistolled, but to ease them of their grief he presently showed how. The Abbess of Chelles made such account of him that to contribute to his credit and to give credit to the house she had begun at Paris for the English Fathers, she would needs have him to be Superior of it while his sermons held him in town.

In the misunderstandings which happened, as I have above related, betwixt the Secular Clergy and Society in England, the Jesuits were mightily offended with this Dr. Gifford, insomuch that they obliged him to appear before the Pope's Nuncio in the Low Countries, where they learnt to have a better opinion of him; for the Nuncio declared him wronged; and they were forced to ask his pardon for yielding so much to their suspicions as to persuade themselves that he was the hinges in part on which those disturbances turned.

In 1608 being Rector of the university of Rheims he took the habit on the 11th. of July from the hands of R. F. Leander of St. Martin, in the great Abbey of St. Remi at Rheims, for the house of Dieulwart, where in 1609 on the 11th. of July he was privately professed in the Chapter house in presence of Father Nicholas, and gave to the house a great number of books and much household stuff.

4. R. F. Robert Haddock, Superior in England of the Spanish Mission. His other name was Benson. After a long time spent with great success in the Mission, he died full of years in Staffordshire in 1650. (Feb. 8th.)

5. R. F. Rudesind Barlow, Prior of St. Gregory's at Douay. He was descended of an ancient and noble family in Lancashire,

and coming as I have said from Spain to Douay, became there another Gamaliel in regard of the Low Countries. For he taught there, (as) first Professor of Divinity so long at the College of St. Vaast with the applause and admiration of all, that he formed almost all the Bishops, Abbots, and Professors that flourished in those parts for some time after. He was esteemed the first or chief of the Scholastic Divines or Casuists of his time and in knowledge of the Canon Law inferior to no one of his time or the age before. Hence it came that he was consulted like an oracle out of all the provinces of the Christian commonweal, even by such as were esteemed the greatest Divines of the world at that time. The dignity of Abbot and Bishop his egregious humility rejected more than once; and it was thought he would have refused that of Cardinal which was said to have been a-preparing for him. This is certian, he was most highly acceptable and even dear to the Cardinals Bellarmine, Bentivoglio and Ubaldin, and others of that illustrious purple senate, and even to the Pope himself: witness that when after the death of the Catholic Bishop who governed the Catholics of England under the title of Chalcedon, the English clergy much coveting another under the same title, the Pope ordered F. Rudesind to propose in the name of himself and his brethren that person whom he thought most proper to preside over the English Catholic Church. This is so very certain that the Protestants themselves knew the whole detail of this business; witness that virulent book called " The Popish Royall Favourite" printed at London in 1643, which has the letter Father Rudesind writ to the Cardinals *de Propaganda* to obtain that Episcopal dignity for Dr. Smith; and when he was so unworthy after this as to rise against the monks who had set the mitre on his head, F. Rudesind with as great courage exerted the force of his pen against him, and the Pope and the senate of the Church maintaining him, the said Prelate was forced to desist from his attempts and pretended jurisdiction of ordinary of Great Britain, which caused such distractions in England that protestant historians of those times take notice of them.

On the death of this renowned monk, a Bishop sent to the Fathers of Douay to offer them an Establishment if they would but make him a present of the said Father's writings. But in vain they were sought for, for they were destroyed by an enemy. St. Austin sayeth that as he never knew better men than good monks so he never knew worse than bad monks. And that now and then there be found some bad ones ought not to scandalize any one, seeing how our Lord and Saviour Jesus Christ declared that among his twelve Apostles one of them was a devil, meaning Judas. For therefore the bad are many times among the good either to purify them by patience from the dross of their imperfections, or to become purified themselves by a serious return from their wickedness to the goodness of God. But to return to Father Rudesind; he lies buried in the Choir of St. Gregory's at Douay before his stall with this epitaph :

"Sub hoc lapide recondita jacent ossa R. A. P. Rudesindi Barloe, Ecclesiæ Christi Cantuariensis totius Angliæ Matricis Prioris Cathedralis, sacræ Theologiæ Doctoris ejusdemque per quadraginta annos professoris eximii; qui postquam 39 an. vel totius Congregationis Præsidis vel Definitoris aut hujus conventus Prioris officiis laudabiliter perfunctus, tandem in senectute bona 19 Sep. Anno Dni. 1656 mortuus est, ætatis suæ 72, conversionis monasticæ 51, Sacerdotii 48. Requiescat in sancta pace."

Englished thus : "Under this stone lie buried the bones of the Very Reverend Father Rudesind Barloe, Cathedral Prior of the Church of Christ at Canterbury, the Mother Church of all England, Doctor of Divinity and an egregious professor of the same for forty years together : who after thirty nine years laudably spent in discharging either the duty of President-General or of Definitor of the Congregation or of Prior of this Convent (of Douay) died in a good old age, Sep 19, 1656 ; the 72nd year of his age, the 51st of his Monachism, and 48th of his Priesthood. May he rest in holy peace."

6. Reverend F. Edward Maihew, whose history we in short already delivered. (page 60.)

7. R. F. Bennet Jones, assistant of the Spanish Vicar in England: he was otherwise named William Price, and died Cathedral Prior of Winchester at London, October 19 (S. V.)

1639, after he had commendably performed the offices of Procurator at Rome and Superior in the mission. He was one time chosen President General but did not cross the seas to execute the charge, and when he died he was designed the Vice President in England. He contributed much to the beginning of the English Benedictine Nunnery at Cambray; and, tried by imprisonments for his Faith, was found just. He was professed of St. Facundus' in Spain.

8. R. F. Torquatus Latham, Professor of Philosophy at Douay, where he died December 19th, 1624.

9. R. F. Sigebert Bagshaw, monk of the English Congregation. He was a man of singular zeal and industry, who after he had most laudably and successfully performed the offices of Procurator in the Roman Court, of Prior of Paris, and lastly, of President of the Congregation, departed this life at Douay during the time of General Chapter, anno 1633.

These were the nine Definitors all men of great esteem for their learning, piety and experience in the affairs of the English mission, and seemed to be picked out not without a particular providence, considering that in so great a number of votes there were some that were averse from all manner of Union, others too much wedded to their interests or Congregation; but they placed their votes so judiciously and faithfully as if they had been men without passion or bias and no difference had ever been among them, and were of one heart and mind as of Order and Profession.

The Nuncio was much rejoiced at the election, and for the place of the Definitory made choice of the house they had at Paris, St. Andrew's in the Suburb of St. James. He appointed their meeting on the first day of June, 1617 and cited them according to form to appear at the place and time.

They obeyed, met, entered the Definitory and were several times visited by the Cardinal while they were upon the matter, where after invocation, and, as we piously confide, particular assistance of the Holy Ghost, the Pope's Decree and the Cardinal's citation were publicly read; after which the Fathers as acting by a delegated authority from the See Apostolic (to whose censure and correction they preliminarily submit all their resolutions), and as representing the whole body of the English Benedictine Mission, (by whose common suffrages they were chosen), unanimously and as one man they enacted and framed an entire body of laws and Constitutions which are extant in R. F. Leander's own hand, whose pen they made use of. 'Twould be an unnecessary labour to give an account of them, since they are, as to the gross, still in force and re-established by the last compilation An. 1661. But I will not deny my reader the satisfaction, nor this reverend assembly the honour due to their zeal and prudence in pronouncing against the takers and abettors of the oath of allegiance or any suspected or pernicious doctrine. Thus they speak, Chap. I. Art. 1 and 2.

"Since the Benedictine monks of several Congregations who by the authority of the See Apostolic labour in the Mission, have hitherto exercised their functions independent of one another, it seems necessary to us all that those of the Spanish Congregation from this time forward be united into one body or Congregation, that their endeavours towards the conversion of souls may be more faithful and that they may fight the battle of our Lord orderly. And because this Union is principally intended that the Catholic and Roman Faith may be propagated and rooted in the kingdom of England, as far as it shall please God to make use of our labours; therefore it is our will, that this Union be not agreed upon in any other manner than that all and every one of such as are to be united, do conform themselves to the doctrine of the Holy Roman Church; as well generally in all matters that concern either belief or manners, as specially and in particular, in accepting and submitting to the Decrees of our Holy Father Pope Paul V touching the oath of allegiance, and authority and jurisdiction of the Church and holy Apostolic See. But with others (if there be any such) who dissent from those articles or Decrees, we do by no means intend to strike up an Union or hold communion, unless within six months after a sufficient admonition thereof by their Superiors, they purge themselves from such imputation and give sufficient satisfaction to the said Superiors of this Congregation.

"If any President, Provincial, Definitor, Prior, Counsellor or any other Superior, Capitular person of this Congregation do turn heretic, as God forbid, or schismatic, or commit any great or public scandal to Catholic religion, he shall by this constitution be judged deposed from and deprived of his office and Capitular dignity. But if any one teach, disperse or defend any temerarious or dangerous doctrine, or that sounds ill, or is offensive to pious ears, either against Faith or against good manners, or against the Apostolic See, or any sentiment or opinion prohibited or branded by the said See; or is a manifest and voluntary contemner and prevaricator of the Rule of our Holy Father Saint Benedict as it is explicated by our Constitutions approved by the See Apostolic, or be found so remiss and negligent in correcting such offenders, that such his prevarication and negligence is prudently judged to tend towards the destruction of the Congregation and dissolution of regular observance, let him be admonished even to the fourth time to correct himself, by the President, Provincials or Judges of Causes respectively; and if he does not amend after such admonition, let him be admonished to lay down his office. If he refuse, his faults being proved against him, let him be deposed by sentence of the President or Judges of causes respectively, if he be their inferior; or by sentence of all the Definitors if he be President; or by sentence of the President and the rest of the Definitors if he be one of them, and another chosen in his place."

This is the basis and pillar upon which the English Benedictine Congregation renewed is a-new built and by which it is supported 'tis its *murus* and *antemurale*, its walls and its bulwark by which it is defended against all the impressions of its enemies; and like a castle built upon a rock, the winds and the waves may beat upon it, but cannot subvert it, for it is founded on that rock which has a promise from Truth itself that the gates of Hell (which are errors in Faith and manners) shall never prevail against it. And the modern successors to the authority and virtues of this wise and holy assembly so faithfully obey the Prophet's advice (Isaias 51. 1.) in "attending to the rock from which they are hewn and on " which they are founded," since in their General Chapter in 1681 they set before their own and their subjects' eyes (at which time

CHAPTER THE THIRTY-FIRST.

the Nation was desperately inflamed against Catholics) this Constitution and in effect renew it; depriving *ipso facto* of their missionary faculties any and all such as shall any way abet and favour this oath that has nothing of allegiance but the name, which it deserves as ill as those deserve the name of Catholic that take it. We conceive there are other forms of expressing our allegiance to a Christian prince than by such a one as endangers our Christianity; and for those that press it upon us we have no other answer than that of the Apostles (Acts. v. 29). "We ought to obey "God rather than men;" nor for those that endeavour to allure us to it by mitigating interpretations than that of the Doctor of the Gentiles and not improbably the first Apostle of Great Britain, "Walk cautiously and do not give credit to every spirit." (Eph. v. 15.).

Thirdly, they oblige all and every one of the members of this Congregation under the severest punishments to be inflicted by the President, that no one design or counsel, speak or write anything which may savour of sedition, contempt, or injury against the Kingdom, state, or civil magistrates, or concern himself in politic affairs or whatsoever may concern the states; but that all tread the plain and apostolic way, and that though they converse among heretics they are to remember they are sent "like sheep amongst wolves." (St. Matth. x. 16.) Let them therefore have a care that they do not set upon their adversaries like wolves, and let them be convinced of the truth of that admirable doctrine of St. Chrysostom, "As long as we "are sheep we shall overcome. Though a thousand wolves "surround us we surmount them, and the victory is ours, "whereas if we become wolves we shall be vanquished, for "then we become destitute of the help of our Pastor, who "feeds lambs not wolves."

They decree that the Constitution of this Congregation is to be governed by one President, who during the Schism is to reside beyond sea, and by two Provincials immediately in England, and by the Priors of Convents out of it. Also by five Definitors till the growth of the Congregation require more, the number of which cannot exceed nine: of which the three chief are to be the judges of causes and grievances, to whom the Religious may appeal from sentence of the President ; and from them only to the General Chapter.

They subject this Congregation to the Spanish General no further than to give him the title of General of both Congregations ; that is, he might style himself General of the English Congregation as he did that of Spain. Likewise they allowed he might visit any convent of the English Congregation seated within the Spanish dominions (proceeding according to the tenor of the English Constitutions,) as also they left to him to give license to the members of this English Congregation to receive degrees of Doctorship in Universities, and to make choice of which he pleased of the two whom the English Congregation presented to him for their President.

For what concerns elections, the power of the President, Vacancy and successions, appeals, regular discipline, visits, the Divine Office &c, I refer the reader to the acts themselves which were laid together and digested by the R. R. Fathers Leander of St. Martin, Edward Maihew and Sigebert Bagshaw deputed by the rest for that end, and for the most part were extracted out of the Constitutions of Valladolid, printed at Madrid in 1612.

They conclude with a declaration, that this Definitory of theirs had (the) full power and force of a General Chapter, and that the laws and constitutions therein compiled are no less obligatory than Definitions passed in such Chapters; whereto they subjoin an humble supplication to His Holiness to confirm the same by his Supreme authority, to supply all defects Juris et facti ; and that immediately after such approbation, should ensue the election of the President and other officers of the Congregation.

To the offices respectively were nominated :

R. F. Gabriel Gifford, President.
R. F. Leander of St. Martin, second-elect President.
R. F. Gregory Grange, Provincial of Canterbury.
R. F. Vincent Sadler, Provincial of York.
R. F. Francis Atrobos, Prior of Douay.
R. F. Jocelin Elmer, Prior of Dieulwart.

R. F. Paulin Greenwood, Prior of St. Malo's.
R. F. Thomas Monington, Prior of Paris.
R. F. Sigebert Bagshaw, Procurator at Rome.
R. F. Columban Malon, Secretary to R. F. President.

And here I can't but take notice of the singular blessings that have come to this body from the holy Apostle St. Andrew, which ought to endear very much his holy memory to them.

1. Under the banner and Cross of our Lord and Saviour Jesus Christ, St. Austin brought to the English nation from his Monastery of St. Andrew at Rome, the holy Gospel of Jesus Christ our God and Lord, together with the holy Rule of his servant Saint Benedict of Nursia.

2. The life of St. Wilfrid, the great Bishop of York, shows how by the intercession of this holy Apostle, his dulness and backwardness in learning was transformed into such a capacity and vivacity that he proved to be a most singular ornament of both the English nation and Benedictine Order.

3. St. Boniface the Apostle of Germany, that splendid astre of the English Benedictine firmament, on St. Andrew's solemnity darted his glorious rays amongst the higher orbs of the Church, through the Episcopal consecration he received that day.

4. The life of St. Dunstan, Archbishop of Canterbury and glorious pillar and support of Benedictine monachism in England, exposes the great favours he received from St. Andrew.

5. On this solemnity Cardinal Pool broke the Schism of England by reconciling it to the Holy See again, and therefore ordered it to be kept as one of the greatest in the year. This reconciliation reconciled the English Nation to the Order of its first Apostle St. Austin, and again the Benedictine habit was seen in Westminster Abbey under the worthy Dr. John Fecknam, after its long eclipses under the cruel tyrannical dotage of Henry VIII. and the childish reign of his son Edward VI.

6. And now for the further advancement of the Catholic Church, in a house under the protection of St. Andrew at Paris, like an eagle the English Benedictine body totally renewed itself, in the union of St. Andrew's Cross, to preach and testify the orthodox faith of Christ, till the two great witnesses come, (as is

piously to be hoped,) who are to prepare the world for its last catastrophe and final conclusion.

The news of this Union so long desired and at last concluded between the Fathers of the English Mission, was joyfully received by all their friends both in England and in France; but especially by their worthy patron the Archbishop of Rhodes, who with open arms accepted of the Constitutions, praised them, and sent them up to Rome whither himself soon after went, and gave a great lustre to them by his authority. The Definitors and even the Nuncio himself gave an account to the Spanish General of their proceedings and begged his consent, and the ratification of their Mother the illustrious Congregation (of Valladolid).

The most Reverend Father General, Maestro Antonio de Castro, having communicated the affair with the Definitors and Fathers of that body, rendered an answer October following, and (which is a most ample approbation and confirmation of all the acts of the Definitors), at the same time despatched letters to his Procurator at Rome to use all diligence and all the power he had in the court, to procure the reception thereof and his Holiness' final confirmation.

But the expected issue at Rome was not so soon obtained. The Union had only appeased all civil tumults within themselves, and laid asleep those differences which had so long rent the mission and much obstructed its fruits; but it no ways qualified their enemies without: such angry spirits as appear well pleased with the tempest themselves have raised, and (men) that, like soldiers who grow insolent when they see they are something feared, will admit of no articles but such as themselves propose and for themselves, with very little regard of the suffering party.

The Definitory yet sitting had voted that Father Bagshaw who had before been so vigilant and successful in promoting the Union, should go again to Rome to labour as faithfully for the conclusion of it. To Rome he was no sooner come but he found the whole Cassin Congregation united against this Union and conspiring to break it, either judging it prejudicial to their body or suprised into such a design by some misinformation given them by some one or more of their own members who preferred their private liberty and independence before the public good. Yet there appeared a much more formidable party in France itself where this Union was framed, who had gained the French ambassador at Rome to interpose in his master's name and protest against the Acts and Constitutions which he was informed did contain points contrary to the Laws and prejudicial to the Gallican State.

Moreover the agent of Philip Cavarel, Abbot of St. Vaast in Arras, President of the exempt Abbeys of the Low Countries, and Pay-master General of the Spanish Forces in the Netherlands, the most worthy patron and founder of the College or Convent of St. Gregory in Douay, publicly appeared against this Union, and even stood out after the Brief was given in behalf thereof; using all means to make it be recalled as derogatory and prejudicial to such ultramarine Abbeys as had formerly possessions in England. So that amidst the greatest appearance of a calm and in sight of the harbour, there arises of a sudden the most violent tempest and commotion that ever shook the Congregation and almost split it when it seemed the nearest its quiet and security. Three of the most powerful bodies of the West, the whole Benedictine Order in Italy, the civil State of France, the whole power of the Low Countries which was in Abbot Cavarel's hands, as in the common Father's of the Country, leagued against an infant and inconsiderable body, whose pretensions lay far off in another nation, and which each of them severally might be able to crush even when arrived at its greatest height. But the Providence of God who often chooses the weak and contemptible things of this world to confound the strong, and perfects His praise out of the lips of infants, checked the winds and the storms, and there followed a great tranquillity such as even the enemies that opposed it were forced to admire. For Father Bagshaw aquitted his office with such dexterity and vigour that the adversaries soon dispersed, and after two years' conflict and resistance a free field was left him to prosecute his pretensions. The Cassin Congregation pleaded nothing that he did not fully satisfy, offering them an equal share in the Union and fruits thereof if they would come in.

The French Ambassador, having no particular orders from the State or better informed, surceased.

Abbot Cavarel commanded his agent silence, and was satisfied with the last clause of the Brief which professes that by concession thereof it does not intend that any prejudice should arise to any other Congregation.

In a word, His Holiness and the Congregation of Cardinals were confirmed in their former judgment and the Brief found clear from all just and grounded exceptions, and delivered to the English Procurator and by him sent to those that employed him.

When the Brief came to their hands, they, out of peculiar respect or thinking themselves not wholly mancipated from the Spanish Obedience, thought fit before they published it, to send it to the Reverend General of Spain that it might be done with his consent and benediction, and themselves discharged of that part of their duty. The Very Reverend General with his Definitors consulted upon it some days and then remitted it with full license and authority to accept of it and publish it, and to incorporate into this thus erected Congregation all such missioners as depended on the Spanish Congregation if they would consent thereunto; and nevertheless, such as refused he subjected them to R. F. Leander as his Vicar General. This was in 1619, R. F. Leander being President, having succeeded in 1618 to the first elect R. F. Gabriel Gifford who was then seated amongst the Princes of the Church, consecrated the 17th. of September Bishop of Archidal (Archidapolitanus) and made Suffragan of Rheims.

There was nothing wanting now to the entire perfection of this great work, but the publication of the laws and Constitutions on which it was built, and the Supreme Pastor of the Church's confirmation thereof. And it was the first business of the President to issue out his orders to that effect, which he did the third of September following; and out of his subjects he chose persons eminent for learning and fidelity and created them Apostolic Notaries according to the privileges and practices of other Religious, in order to the publication of such acts and writings as concern their Orders. This was solemnly performed, first at Douay in St. Gregory's Convent and in Marchin College, next at Paris, Chelles, St. Malo's, (and) Dieulwart, according to the form prescribed by the R. Fr. President which was

That in Chapter where all the Religious then residing were to be present

1st. Should be read the writing of the Rev. General of Spain whereby he approved of the form of the Union and the acts of the Definitors in Paris.

2ndly. His command for publishing the Apostolical Brief and the said General's orders to accept of it.

3rdly. The decree of the said General and also the consent of the Definitors and deputies to accept of the Union.

4thly. The Apostolical Brief itself.

5thly. The election of the five Definitors and the oath of some of them made before their respective communities.

6thly. The election of himself, R. F. Leander, to the office of President to the English Congregation, and his confirmation from the Rev. General of Spain.

7thly, And lastly, the Superior of the community should record the day of the promulgation and the names of all the Fathers that accepted of and submitted themselves to the said Union, that accordingly they might be able to proceed to the election of conventual Superiors; for the Rev. Father promises all kindness and good usage to such conventuals or others that excuse themselves from accepting the Union yet he decrees that the elections are not to be made but of them that accept it, as to the rest, each one enjoying all the rights and privileges that he ever used to do or could pretend to.

All of this side the sea subscribed excepting three; and these orders having been executed in all the Convents and the Mission, the execution, signed and authenticated by Apostolic Notaries, was sent to the President and Definitors convened at Douay, as it was before agreed upon in the Definitory at St. Andrew's; and with (the) subscription, the suffrages also for the election of Conventual Priors. The original acts of this Regimen, are subscribed with the President's and Definitors' own hands and contain four articles :

1. That as soon as ever sufficient privileges are obtained of the Pope, especially exemption from the Ordinaries, the Union shall be published and the laws thereof introduced.

2. That the Ceremonies, subscribed with the President's and Definitors' names, together with the Calendar of Saints, should be received.

3. That whosoever of the Definitors could not be present at the election of conventual Priors, should signify their will by letters, upon which letters those that were present might validly proceed.

4. That nunc pro tunc was chosen Secretary to the President Father Paul Greenwood, and after the publication of the Bull and other writings above named, the Regimen proceeded to the elections related.

So that the decrees of the Union were almost four years a-putting in execution; two years their affairs were in suspense at Rome; the next and some part of the latter was taken up in settling the affairs of the Residences and making the Visits; and towards the middle of 1620 the President despatched his letters patent to England, France, and Lorraine to appoint the following Chapter and inform those that were to be convened at Douay the 2nd of July 1621, a little before which he received an advantageous declaration of the General Chapter of Spain whereby that renowned body did approve of these Fathers' proceedings and the conduct of the General in all the said affairs.

Thus then this great and important work, which was as zealously embraced by his Holiness, promoted by the Court of Rome, desired by the whole Western Church, and as maliciously impugned by the enemy of mankind (and some others who had more zeal than knowledge), as if thereon depended the conversion of England and the restoring three kingdoms to the Catholic Church, was at length brought to its last perfection; and the Divine Hand which was the chief architect thereof, fenced it in on all sides, established it in the beauty of peace, gave it rest from its neighbours round about; nor was there anything of wicked or adverse to rise against it. The Convents flourished with regular discipline and eminent practices of the contemplative life; the missions abounded with the fruitful labours and sufferings of the active; and when any storm arose 'twas only to revive their spirits and give the world more manifest arguments of their courage.

What access was made to the Catholic Church by those painful missioners in converting of souls, what wonderful edification and example given to the ancient Catholics by the unwearied patience and long imprisonment of others of them; what a fruitful harvest promised her by the seed which others of them sowed in their country and which never fails to bring forth a hundred fold, which is the blood of martyrs, we may more fully learn from men than books. The increase and succession of the English Catholics till this day are so many witnesses of their zeal, trophies of their victories, and fruits of their planting. Not that we deny much less envy, the labours and success of other members both of the Regular and Secular Clergy which we joyfully see and congratulate, but only that the Benedictine Order which had a double share in the pains, may at least reap an equal one in the glory.

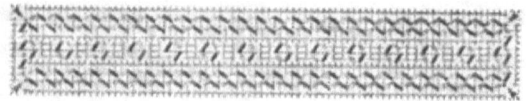

CHAPTER THE THIRTY-SECOND.

CONTAINING NOTICES OF SEVERAL FATHERS OF THE CONGREGATION WHO DIED ABOUT THIS TIME.

The said year of the Union on the 12th of July (1617) at Harding in Flintshire, R. F. Thomas Minshall admitted to the habit in the mission, a man very diligent in the performance of his apostolical duty and highly charitable towards his neighbour, ended his labours by a happy death.

The next year at Longueville in Normandy died Fr. Bradshaw, where Fr. Walgrave put the ensuing epitaph on his grave.

D. O. M. S.

"Venerandæ memoriæ viro, Domno Johanni Bradshaw, dicto Fratri Augustino de Sancto Johanne, Wigorniensi Anglo, S. Martini Compostellæ in Hispania monacho primo gentis Anglorum a schismate post S. Augustinum ejusdem Ordinis Apostolo, invictissimo Hæreseon protagonistæ, vigilantissimo Monachorum Patriarchæ, augustissimo missionis Benedictinæ in Angliam auspici, fausto felicique disciplinæ monasticæ apud Anglos instauratori, sex eorum in Gallia, Belgio et Lotharingia Collegiis et Conventibus institutis, qui quatuor monachorum suorum in Anglia martyrum, quinquaginta et amplius confessorum, decennio quo Missione præfuit coronis insignitus, huic tandem loco, sæculi injuria ruderibus suis obruto, planeque sepulto disciplinæ regularis neglectu, obsoleto prorsus ac squalido a clarissimo Domino de Bellieure

CHAPTER THE THIRTY-SECOND.

ejusdem Priore commendatorio expetitus, dum ille mœnium hic de morum restitutione satagunt, carus suis et patriæ ob insignem pietatem, clarus sibi et Ordini ob præclara facinora, Deo atque Sanctis carissimus ob eximiam sanctitudinem, suis, eheu! præpropere ad luctum, sibi ter feliciter ad coronam, vix biennio subprioris functus officio, de hac luce raptus est IV Nonas Maii, 1618, ætatis sui 42 ; nutu, necnon sumptibus præfati cl. domini, pietatis atque gratitudinis ergo, ponendum curavit Frater Franciscus a Walgravio, pii patris humilis ex habitu conversionis filius, indignus in officio successor."

Englished :

"Sacred to God, most Good, most Great.

To the Venerable Memory of Mr. John Bradshaw, called Br. Austin of St. John, native of Worcester in England, monk of St. Martin of Compostella in Spain, the first apostle in England after St. Austin, monk of the same Order, since the Schism ; a most invincible champion against heresy, a most vigilant monastic patriarch, the most august guide of the Benedictine mission into England, the happy and prosperous repairer of Monastic discipline amongst the English, having in France, Flanders and Lorraine instituted for them six colleges or Convents; during the ten years he governed the English mission ennobled with the martyrial crowns of four of his monks and the confessorial of about fifty others ; the most illustrious Monsieur de Bellieur commendatory Prior of this place besought him to succour it almost buried in its ruins through the injuries of time, and become ugly and abandoned through neglect of regular discipline ; and while he was busy to repair its walls and Father Austin to repair its manners, the said Father was snatched out of this light on the 4th of May, 1618, to his own great happiness, but alas ! over speedily for his monks ; dear to his Congregation and country for his great piety, illustrious in his Order for his egregious deeds, highly acceptable to God and his Saints for his sanctity of life, he had scarce performed the office of Sub-prior two years, being but forty two years of age ; with the good-liking and at the cost of the said illustrious Commendatory Prior, Brother Francis Walgrave out of piety and gratitude to him who had clothed him in religion, and to whom though unworthy he succeeded in the office, took care to place this monument."

This Fr. Austin became known to old Cecil of Salisbury and so allayed his fury against Catholic religion that he resolved for as much as he could hinder, a Benedictine should never more be put to death in England for the Roman Faith.

The same year on the 30th of October R. F. Nicholas Becket a monk of Onia in Spain, having laudably performed the offices of Novice-master at Dieulwart and of Prior at Douay, and done the duty of an apostolical man in the mission, left this life at Cank in Staffordshire.

In 1619, April 18th died in the mission, R. F. Gregory Grange, monk of St. Martin in Gallicia, a man very well versed in divine and human learning and full of religious virtue and piety, the first Provincial of England after the Union, wherefore by his death R. Fr. Vincent Sadler became first Provincial *(i.e. of Canterbury)*, and Father Bede (Helme) of Mountserrat succeeded in the place of Fr. Sadler for the Province of York.

Anno 1621 died Pope Paul V. who was as the second parent of this English Benedictine Congregation and most loving nurse; a Pontiff of most incorruptible manners who so carefully tendered the Church, that she spread her branches from sea to sea, and from Tyber to the end of the earth. In India he erected several bishoprics; in Great Britain he enlarged the mission and resuscitated the old Venerable Benedictine Order in the persons of this Congregation. He sat fifteen years and nine months.

The same year died Philip III, king of Spain ætat. 43, regni 23, who recommended the Fathers of Douay to the Arch-Duke Albert, who also died the same year æt. 62, much lamented by the Flemings. How much the Congregation is indebted to his piety for the establishment of Douay Convent is already said.

Likewise went off from the stage of this mortality in Barbican in London, through a cruel fit of the stone, the V. R. Fr. Vincent Sadler(21st of June, 1621) as he was intending to retire to his monastery at Dieulwart in Lorraine, with his nephew Mr. Thomas Vincent Sadler, the last of his many converts, but the first and only one of his own family and blood, leaving behind him a great opinion of his sanctity, as he was a person of a most exemplary life and wonderful industry, governing the English Congregation before the Union in quality of President. Mr. Arthur Pitts was the person who proposed him and Fr. Maihew for the aggregation.

CHAPTER THE THIRTY-THIRD.

THE SECOND GENERAL CHAPTER, 1621.

The second General Chapter, (for the Union with reason passes for the first since the renovation of the old Benedictine body of England), began also this same year on the 2nd of July at Douay.

The way of their sitting in Chapter was then after this manner:
The President in the middle.
On each side of his Reverence, the Definitors as in a Choir; after them in like manner the ex-Presidents.
Then on the right
The Provincial who was eldest in the habit.
The Vicar of France.
The Cathedral Prior of Winchester.
The Prior of Douay who claimed St. Alban's
The Prior of St. Malo who claimed Glastonbury.
A Magister Generalis whose task is to read in the Convents Philosophy, Divinity, &c.
The Secretary of the President.
One of the Procurators of England.
The Procurator of Rome.
on the left
The other Provincial.
The Cathedral Prior of Canterbury.
The Prior of Dieulwart who claimed Westminster.

CHAPTER THE THIRTY-THIRD.

The Prior of Paris who claimed St. Edmund's.

A Predicator Generalis, that is such a one who is licensed by the Congregation to preach publicly.

The other Procurator of England; these were Procurators of the Provinces of Canterbury and York.

The Vicar or Confessarius of the Nuns.

The Secretary of the Chapter.

But in the last review of the Constitutions this order was established.

        Rev. Father President;   And on the right

The actual Definitors.

Abbots.

Ex-Presidents; the Provincial of Canterbury.

The Cathedral Prior of Canterbury,

The Cathedral Prior of Durham.

The Prior of Douay.

The Prior of St. Malo's.

Ex-Definitors.

Magistri Generales.

The Procurator of Rome.

One of the Procurators of England.

The Vicar of the Nuns.

              On the left.

The actual Definitors.

Abbots.

Ex-Presidents.

The other Provincial.

The Cathedral Prior of Winchester.

Cathedral Priors.

The Prior of Dieulwart.

The Prior of Paris.

Ex-Definitors.

Predicatores Generales.

The Secretary of the President.

The other Procurators of England.

Next, if any prelate be deposed from his office, or his deputy, and the Secretary of the Chapter in the middle.

CHAPTER THE THIRTY-THIRD.

In this Chapter of 1621 R. F. Rudesind Barlo was chosen President.

R. F. Thomas Torquatus Latham, second elected President who succeeds when the first fails within the Quadriennium, for the General Chapters of this Congregation are held every four years; which I specify for those who are not acquainted with such things.

Provincial of Canterbury, R. F. Joseph Prater.
Provincial of York, R. F. Robert Haddock.
Vicar of France, R. F. Bernard Berington.
Prior of St. Gregory's, R. F. Leander of St. Martin.
Prior of Dieulwart, R. F. Columban Malon, who dying within the quadriennium R. F. Laurence Reyner succeeded.
Prior of St. Malo's, R. F. Paulin Greenwood.
Prior of Paris, R. F. Sigebert Bagshaw.
Procurator at Rome, R. F. Robert Sherwood.
Secretary to the Rev. President, R. F. Clement Reyner.

The 17th of September following (1621) died the famous Cardinal Bellarmine, æt. 79, who espoused the interest of the Union, and had taught formerly the Bishop of Archidal, R. F. Gabriel Gifford.

CHAPTER THE THIRTY-FOURTH.

THE DIFFICULTIES ATTENDING THE FOUNDATION OF THE MONASTERY OF ST. BENEDICT AT ST. MALO; REFORMS IN FRANCE; THE ROMAN COLLEGE OF SAINT GREGORY.

But now St. Malo's affairs call us to them. The Fathers had not seen the end of 1616, but the Cathedral Chapter was grown jealous of them and resolved to force them out of the town, thinking the rising Convent so much taken off from their necessitous circumstances. But the good Bishop and the citizens stood by those they had called in, and who spared no pains to serve them. Wherefore that same year (Nov. 16) Father Gifford in the name of himself and his Brethren bought a house and garden in the town, and transferred his little yet laborious Community from the Theologal mansion to the new acquisition, which he sought by such unwearied industry to render yet more convenient by means of alms given, that he justly deserves the title and honour of being Founder of that Monastery.

The Canons again in 1617, sought anew to disturb them, but in vain; and they again in 1618 added another house and garden to what they had already bought. This so exasperated the Canons that to appease them R. F. Gifford, now consecrated Bishop and constituted Suffragan of Rheims, came in great haste from thence; but he was no sooner returned when he saw his journey had been to no purpose, Upon which in the name of himself and his Brethren, he petitioned the Bishop to favour them as he had hitherto done, and permit them to have a house in which they might live conventually, and a chapel in which they might celebrate Mass and the Divine Office, hear Confessions, catechise, and bury their own ; all which the good Bishop most easily and freely granted. Yet the said Canons were very troublesome. Notwithstanding all which oppositions, this year 1621, November the 21st. (a memorable day to the English Benedictine Congregation), the Fathers reared up on the ground they had got together, a wooden cross in token of possession taken, and that that ground was consecrated to God in honour of St. Benedict, and presently built a little chapel with boards, and on the solemnity of St. Thomas of Canterbury, the 29th of December following, honoured it for the first time with the Holy Sacrifice of the Mass.

This same year (1621) Pope Gregory XV gave power to the Cardinal of Rochefoucault to reform the Order of St. Benedict in France, with the Congregations of Cluny and Citeaux, and the Order of St. Austin. He had seen the happy success under his immediate predecessor Pope Paul V, of the renewed English Benedictine Congregation, which in those days when the reformers of France were not risen, made a great figure. Living strictly to the Rule, and bringing to France the novelty of a reformed education, it drew after it the eyes of the better sort where they lived in France and Flanders. We have seen how the Bishop of St. Malo's coveted their establishment in his city, Fr. Bradshaw reforming Longue-Ville in Normandy, (a house founded by the ancestors of his Grace R. F. Gabriel Gifford, Bishop of Archidal), and R. F. Reyner occupied in reforming the great Abbey at Ghent; and other places upon that account the Fathers might have had but they excused themselves, for that their vocation was the English Mission not the reformation of foreign Monasteries.

Likewise this year (1621) the said Pope Gregory XV having begun at Rome at the instance of the famous Sicilian Abbot Cajetan, a college for the whole universal Order of St. Benedict, by the means of the said Abbot the English Benedictine Congregation was in for its share with the rest; and as the said Abbot while he lived had always some of the English Fathers with him, he at last devolved this college on them, and at his death bequeathed to them his Library which is said to be very copious. But the greatest favour of this liberal Pope was in 1622, when recalling all the grants that had been made by his predecessors by word of mouth only, he excepted those which the Cardinals had ascertained to have been so; as if on purpose he had sought that no damage might arrive to the English Congregation from such revocation, seeing the coalition of it was built on several gratious grants delivered to Cardinals only by word of mouth from Pope Paul V of happy memory. And moreover he gave this same year to the renewed Congregation of the Order of St. Benedict in England by the mediation of the Cardinal Du Sourdis, all the indulgences and privileges which to that day were enjoyed by the two Congregations of Italy and Spain.

And to the great grief of all, Regulars especially, this good Pope died in 1623 after he had sat but two years and three months; to whom succeeded Urban VIII.

And the same year died Dom Didier De la Cour, author of the reformed Congregation of St. Van (SS. Vitonis et Hydulphi) in Lorraine, November 14th. æt. 72.

Anno 1624, April 13th. (S. V.) died William Bishop the first Titular Bishop of Chalcedon given by the Holy See to the Catholics of England, where he behaved himself with such moderation and discretion that he was by all both Clergymen and Regulars most dearly beloved and honoured; and after imprisonments, banishments and all sorts of afflictions patiently tolerated for the true religion, he expired near London; and his memory is justly recorded here by reason of the singular affection he bore to the English Congregation. He was of a noble family in Warwickshire and brought up at Oxford, but out of love to Catholic religion he left his parents and despised the hopes of a large estate and became a Priest at Rome. Betwixt this Bishop and the Catholic Bishops of England, I find but two Arch-priests; the first, Mr. Blackwel, who though very cautious and very courageous in danger, yet taken by the king's officers yielded to them in what they demanded of him concerning the Oath of Fidelity and drew many Priests and Lay-men into the same misery along with him; a terrible example of human frailty.*

The other is Mr. William Harrison who the 23rd of July, 1615, obtained such faculties and privileges as were granted to the first English Benedictine Missioners coming from Mount Cassin and Spain in 1603, and which were afterwards granted to the Dominicans in 1627.

The charitable compassion of the great Abbot of Arras, Cavarel, was such to the English nation, that besides what he did for it in the foundation of St. Gregory's at Douay, he lent to the English Clergy the College of his Monastery which stood at Paris near St. Victor's gate. To Dr. William Bishop, Dr. Anthony Champney, Dr. William Smith and Dr. William Reyner the first concession was made in 1613 only for three years; that term expired it was renewed, in 1616; and again in 1623 extended till 1631.

The said year 1624, Br. Epiphanius Rhodadelphus Stapylton, sub-deacon, monk of Douay, died on the 25th of July in a village not far from Perone in France as he was on his journey to Paris. He was clothed on the 17th of April 1616, but not professed till the 5th of May 1620 for want of age.

---

* *The History and antiquities of Oxford say that Mr. George Birket succeeded to Mr. Blackwell in the dignity of Arch-priest, An. 1608.*
Mr. Blackwell had been a Socius of Trinity College. [*Note in original.*]

CHAPTER THE THIRTY-FIFTH.

THE EXTRAVAGANCES OF F. BARNES AND F. WALGRAVE.

AT this time also the clamors of Fr. John Barnes and Fr. Francis Walgrave being grown very loud against the Union, (which Fr. Walgrave could not now relish at all), they denied that there ever was so much as an English Congregation heretofore, and affirmed that the late one was chimerical, and the Bull of confirmation surreptitious. The Fathers of Douay (as the chief ministers and members of the new united body), soon took the alarm, and replied with such strength of reason and eloquence, that the adversary was forced to fly to his usual arms of calumny and libels, which had no further effect than to awaken the zeal of all good Christians to appear for, and give testimony to justice: and particularly the worthy Abbot, founder of Saint Gregory's, in a public writing set out this 1624, gave a full account of his own proceeding and the motives he had to found them a house at Douay; of the good service they had done the Church of God by their exemplary life and singular learning; that the Union had been promoted by himself as well as by other respective Superiors of the English Monks, and that no means were used to circumvent the See of Rome, but that his Holiness after a faithful information, and great deliberation had imposed the last hand to that great work.

CHAPTER THE THIRTY-FIFTH.

The Bishop of Archidal, now Archbishop of Rheims, gave in 1625 the following declaration on those affairs in Latin, which I only relate in English, but from the original.

"Gabriel of St. Mary, by the grace of God and the Apostolic See, Archbishop and Duke of Rheims and first Peer of France, to all the faithful Christians of the Catholic Church, happiness in the Author of all happiness, Christ our Lord.

'Tis the proper office and charge of our dignity and vocation to bear witness to Truth, especially for the domestics of our Faith, against all such as calumniate and attack the said truth. For to that end Christ has placed us in the watch tower of his Church, as faithful daily watchmen diligently and carefully to announce to his faithful obedient servants, our fellow servants, when any danger arises from false doctors and the enemies of sincere truth and religious piety. Wherefore whereas the English Benedictine Congregation (over which we once presided as President, and at whose establishment not only we were present with the other Definitors, but even governed when its Constitutions and laws were agreed on, and upon Paul V's apostolical command promulgated by his most illustrious Nuncios, now Cardinals of the Holy Roman Church, the most excellent prelates Ubaldin and Bentivoglio), is resisted by some few monks, men of no certain obedience, by books put out which the Church has condemned, and in which books those said men have unworthily usurped our authority in some respects; we have thought it belonging to the dignity of our charge to make known to all pious persons that we were taken out of the bosom of this Congregation to this high state of ecclesiastical authority, and that not only we honoured its Constitutions and laws with our consent, but also dictated them, and that even now we approve them; and that of many years we have known the Superiors and monks of the said Congregation for religious, pious, learned, grave men, earnest desirers of quiet and union, observers of regularity. Moreover, we testify that we have seen and read many mandates and letters patents of the Generals of the Spanish Congregation, and of the General Chapter of the said Congregation several acts, by which all things were approved and confirmed that had been done by these monks of the English Mission in concluding the erection of the said English Congregation, and the monks of the mission commanded to be obedient to its laws. We also testify that we know for certain, for that we were there present, that the Definitors assembled by the Pope's orders in the first Chapter, no ways built on the pretended antiquity of the English Congregation of Wearmouth as the adversaries suppose, but that all (excepting only one man) rejected that antiquity, and all unanimously adhered to the antiquity derived from Pope Innocent III's Constitution which is in the body of the Canon Law, Chapter *In singulis*; and that they did not offer to the Pope any titles and merits of the old Congregation thereby to move His Holiness to confirm their proceedings, but simply offered the Holy See, as it had commanded, the acts and constitutions made in the Definitory to obtain their approbation, and asked that the Union they agreed on (after the manner and form contained in the said laws and which they called the English Congregation) might be confirmed, and that name given to the said Union, and the same power which is allowed to other Congregations, and all the privileges hitherto granted to the Spanish Congregation and to the old English Congregation however and whatever it was; and that in this their union, that said old English Congregation might be restored and, if need were, new erected. To this narrative we testify that the Brief of Pope Paul answers, and that therefore as 'tis the opinion of all Doctors, according to this narrative or petition, to which we also subscribed, proofs may and ought to be exacted; and that against this signify nothing the objections of some under the name of John Andrew, or "Examination of the trophies of the English Congregation," or "Grammatopœia" or "Syllabus," whether they be in Latin or French, we know and declare; as also we testify this to be our sentiment concerning these debates, by these our letters to all who shall read them; and which we publish not out of hatred or favour but out of zeal of truth and justice and the conservation of religious discipline, as becomes Archiepiscopal authority, which though undeserving, we desire no longer to enjoy than we employ our power to defend and maintain truth and piety.

CHAPTER THE THIRTY-FIFTH.

Given at Rheims in our archiepiscopal palace, under our lesser seal, on the 10th. of April 1625.

Gabriel Archbishop and Duke of Rheims.

The place of the seal.

Here it is necessary to give some account of this Father Barnes for of Fr. Walgrave we have spoken and have yet further to say.

CHAPTER THE THIRTY-SIXTH.

THE TROUBLES CAUSED BY FR. BARNES. THE BEGINNING OF ST. EDMUND'S CONVENT AT PARIS. THE LITERARY LABOURS OF FATHER AUGUSTINE BAKER.

FATHER BARNES was clothed in St. Benedict's of Valladolid on the 12th of March, 1604, and professed the next year on the 21st of March and made Priest on the 20th of September 1608, and presently placed by his Reverend General in a curateship or some such like business which depended on that Congregation. We have seen him in the beginnings of Douay and St. Malo; and in 1613 in the General Chapter in Spain he was assigned first assistant of the English Mission. Now after the Union and consecration of Father Gifford, upon his departure from Paris to Rheims, the Abbess of Chelles and the monks there signified to those of Paris that they desired they would leave St. Andrew's and go to another place more convenient to establish a convent and bought expressly for them. But because they did not so presently comply they were complained of to R. Father Leander (become President by the elevation of R. Father Gifford), upon which Father Leander sent them an order to obey. They exposed the just exceptions they had reason to make against the new house, so he recalled his order (April 9th, 1619) being then at Rheims with the said Lord Bishop Gifford, and appoints R. F. Berington to succeed R. F. Matthew Sandeford in the superiority of the Paris house on the 15th of May, 1619; Father Matthew being to attend his Grace as he did, living with him at Rheims.

The worthy Bishop who had now wherewithal, having upon all occasions continually sought the good and advantage of his brethren, so now, thinking it derogatory to the prosperity of the Union to have the monks who had engaged in it at Paris to depend any longer on Fr. Walgrave and his at Chelles, he at his own expense placed them in another house, and the Abbess she withdrew her pension and spent it on those she had at Chelles. This was the beginning of the Convent at Paris which is now entitled to St Edmund, King of the East Angles and Martyr; and Father Walgrave fretting and vexed that he could not make things ply to his humour, incorporated himself in the said year 1619 into the Congregation of Cluny without leave of his superiors. This caused many disputes before the Abbot of Cluny and Parliament of Paris, &c, during all which time he and his adherents did all they could to bring the English Congregation under the Congregation of Cluny or force the English monks from Paris. And Father Barnes in 1622 being got to him at Chelles they united their malice to attack with all the vigour they could the quiet of their brethren, and take upon them, in virtue of titles worn out of date, and for certain absolutely extinguished and abolished by the Union, to excommunicate the English Benedictine Community at Paris which did not depend on them. I can't find exactly the time of this criminal attempt but if I may conjecture, R. F. Rudesind's letter to Father Berington dated the 3rd of November 1623 argues it to have been about that time. In which letter that Venerable Father tells the other that the excommunication of those men was of as much force as that of the Protestants when they excommunicated Sixtus V, and their scandalous impudence forces him to lay them forth. "The reason," sayeth he, "why these Fathers proceed so irreligiously "and inhumanly is because it is necessary that they should "always be a-brawling and a-scolding. Who can say that Father "Francis ever lived quietly? When he was in Spain did he not "behave himself so seditiously that he was expelled the Colleges? "At Dieulwart was he not burdenous to all his brethren? Have

"not all sorts of men, religious, clergy and seculars experienced
"his rudeness since he has been at Chelles? But what wonder
"when he came to religion that he might not starve in the world.
"He seeks the world here and like a worldling despises religious
"men. As to the other, Father John (Barnes), he is never well
"than when upon some rash act or other; for from the time that
"he first apostatized (i e. *from the Order*) and like an apostate was
"received in Chapter, his arms naked and crossed, holding his
"hands full of rods, he seems to have hated both religious and
"claustral life. God grant him a sound brain, for many think
"him out of his wits, otherwise he could never do as he does, 1º
"apostatizing; 2ndly, living a worldling nine years; 3rdly, writing
"famous libels against his brethren for filthy lucre's sake; 4thly,
"apostatizing again; 5thly, returning to the Congregation he left
"without saying anything to the Superiors; 6thly, feigning causes
"against his conscience to excommunicate his Superior. Do not
"these things argue madness and furiousness? I could say more
"upon this thing but I am forced to break off here abruptly.
"Adieu.
   "The 3rd. of November 1623.
     Your Brother
      "Rudesind."

 This Father Barnes also engaged in the Congregation of Cluny without leave, and the Reverend General of Spain writ to them both on the 15th of February, 1624, a severe letter where after greeting he adds "et spiritum obedientiæ" (and the spirit of obedience); and R. F. Rudesind the same year on the 21st. of June commissioned R. F. Bernard Berington and R. F. Sigebert Bagshaw to proceed against Father Barnes.

 Father Barnes thus vigourously pursued by all Superiors both Spanish and English, thought to have sheltered himself at Saint Martin's of Pontoise near Paris; but Monsieur Duval a most famous, holy, orthodox Doctor and professor of Sorbonne routed him thence, letting the commendatory Abbot know that a certain author whose books had been condemned and censured by the Pope was withdrawn thither; whereupon he strictly commanded the community and his officers to expel him thence. Yet at last the Rev. General of Spain writ a long but very fine letter laying forth the extravagant conduct of these men, blaming their libels which he specifies, and declares the excommunication they had so ridiculously darted to deserve nothing but contempt, and commands them back to their duty, to which summons if they yield, he remits them all punishment and disgrace.

What they did upon this, I cannot find; what follows, evidences Fr. Barnes persisted in his criminal condition; and Fr. Walgrave either got leave to remain in the Congregation of Cluny or did the same, for we shall see him relieved by that said Congregation after he was driven from Chelles. But to end with Fr. Barnes: I have gathered many letters which show him to have tampered much with the State of England to become its pensioner, to mince the Catholic truths that the Protestants might digest them without choking, and so likewise to prepare the Protestant errors that Catholic stomachs might not loathe them. He was hard at work in the prosecution of this admirable project in the years 1625 and 1626.

He took upon him in a letter to a nobleman of England, which is without date of year or month, to maintain out of true divinity the separation of England from the court of Rome as things then stood, and the oath of fidelity of the English Communion, to be lawful and just according to the writers of the Roman Church. And he says at the beginning of this wonderful letter, that he had been about eight years at work to get an opportunity of insinuating himself into His Majesty's knowledge.

And the fine letters that were writ to him from England upon such happy dispositions (when his mooncalfship was seeking to make the world the same sport the mountain did when it brought forth a ridiculous mouse) were directed to Fr. Barnes at the lodgings of my Lord the Prince of Portugal near the Cordeliers at Paris. These are of the date of 1626.

The English Fathers having patience no longer with a conduct grown so criminal and which so directly thwarted the very foundations of the renewed Congregation which I have specified in the article of the Union, where they declare they will never have to do with men who are not sound in their faith, they acquainted His Holiness with these extravagances, and such order was taken that Fr. Barnes was seized on and sent up to Rome to the Inquisition; but acting moderately with the wretch and not letting things run to that extremity they might have done, he was only imprisoned there to his dying day, which happened in August 1661. "If he was in his wits," (writ R. F. Leander Norminton from thence) "he was a heretic; but they gave him Christian burial because they accounted him rather a madman."

Dr. Leyburn in his encyclical answer to an encyclical epistle sent to the clergy of England, which he printed at Douay the year this Father died, proposes him as an example for to teach men to beware of novellism. "Besides," saith he, "Dr. Ellis is not ignorant of our English Benedictines' zealous proceeding unto securing and punishing of that learned man of their Order Fr. John Barnes as soon as they were fully acquainted with his wicked designs to broach dangerous tenets to the destroying of souls. And indeed that famous man of their Order Fr. Rudesind Barlo himself told me that the securing of the said Fr. John Barnes cost the Order £300 sterling."

Now while these miserable men thus sought the destruction of the Congregation by disparaging it, they procured it one of the greatest advantages that ever yet befell it. For Father Baker fell to searching the antiquities of England to invincibly prove how the old English Benedictine Congregation of which we have said so much, never depended on that of Cluny. The learned antiquary Mr. Selden, a Protestant to whom he communicated the absurd proposition, accounted it a pretension so groundless and withal so dishonourable to England (namely that so many royal monasteries as were in England should owe subjection to a foreign Congregation), that he intended to write a confutation of such absurdities, himself having been entreated thereto by the then Lord Treasurer, and had really done it if Father Baker had not told him that some of the English Benedictine monks were already employed about it.

The places which afforded Father Baker the best proofs were the Tower of London and the famous Library of Sir Robert Cotton; many journeys likewise he made into several counties where he could hear of any ancient records; so that with incredible pains and the expenses of almost two hundred pounds sterling out of his maintenance, (which he freely gave to serve his Congregation in such affairs), he furnished all or most of the remarkable instruments and writings which render the book entitled "Apostolatus Benedictinorum in Anglia" so esteemed both at home and abroad. At the same time he prepared memorials for a universal history of the Church of England, all which extracts of the old manuscripts &c, which were taken from the monasteries at their suppression, now enrich the archives of St. Gregory's at Douay.

Moreover he was not content to send such things, but he also shewed the advantages that several passages of the said records presented to prove the truth of the English Congregation and likewise to demonstrate that St. Gregory the Great and the monks sent by him to convert England were all of the Order of St. Benedict. So that his collections and discourses alone were sufficient for the compilation of that work of which indeed he may be well esteemed the principal author, having had the chief hand in it, and next to him the V. R. Father Leander of St. Martin who put it into Latin and polished it, though they left it to come out under the name of R. F. Clement Reyner. And Father Leander being in England during the said searchings refused not to be the scrivener; and often afterwards admired not only Fr. Baker's solid judgment, but also his good memory; for one day leaving off in the midst of a sentence or a period, when two or three days after Father Leander with his papers returned to him again, Father Baker continued on where he had left off, as if he had but just then given over. This will appear much more wonderful if one consider the high intellectual contemplation he was happily endowed with, and how during all the time of these searches he was in a continual exercise, after a more particular manner than ordinary, of this said intellectual affective contemplation. And yet this occupation caused him no distractions, though he applied himself to it as to his only affair, as likewise at the same time to his recollection as if he had attended to nothing else: an example so rare that it can scarce be paralleled.

And though it may seem not appertaining to my affair here, yet because nothing ought to be prized by men like truth, for the instruction of posterity I shall here add a passage of which he was both eye and ear witness when he was gathering these things, as the writers of his life assure, at Sir Robert Cotton's Library; the which was, says Father Cressy " that he " heard a discourse between the said knight and Mr. Cambden " about a chest of papers which had belonged to Sir Francis " Walsingham, Secretary of State to Queen Elizabeth, containing " most of the principal business of state during his secretaryship. " These had been lately bought for a small sum by Sir Robert " who told Mr. Cambden, and made it good by the same papers, " that he had had very false information of many passages in his " history of Queen Elizabeth; and particularly from the same " letters (it) appeared that the insurrection in the North under " the Earl of Westmoreland &c, had been contrived by the said " Secretary of State; whereupon Mr. Cambden exclaimed ear-" nestly and loudly against his false informers and wished that " that history had never been written."

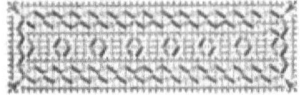

CHAPTER THE THIRTY-SEVENTH.

THE FOUNDATION OF THE MONASTERY OF OUR LADY OF CONSOLATION FOR THE ENGLISH BENEDICTINE DAMES AT CAMBRAY.

IN the year 1625 on the first of January, nine young English gentlewomen, (brought to Cambray by the Fathers to begin there an English Nunnery of the Order under the care of the Congregation,) made their solemn profession ; namely

1. Dame Gertrude, otherwise Hellen More, daughter to Mr. Crisacre More, little grandson in direct line to the famous Sir Thomas More, High Chancellor of England ; for he was son to Thomas, who was son to John the only son and heir of the said most worthy Lord Chancellor of most glorious memory.

2. Dame Lucy, otherwise Margaret Vavasour, daughter to Mr. William Vavasour of Hazlewood in Yorkshire.

3. Dame Benedicta, otherwise Anne Morgan, sister to Mr. Thomas Morgan of Weston in Warwickshire.

4. Dame Catherine Gascoign, daughter to Sir John Gascoign of Barnlow in Yorkshire, one of those that are called Scotch Baronets.

5. Dame Agnes, otherwise Grace More, and

6. Dame Ann More, near Cousins to Dame Gertrude, descended also from Sir Thomas More by younger brothers of the same family.

CHAPTER THE THIRTY-SEVENTH. 143

7. Dame Mary, otherwise Frances Watson daughter of Mr. Richard Watson of Parke in Bedfordshire.

8. Sister Mary Hoskins, and

9. Sister Martha otherwise Jane Martin. These two were for the services of the Community, and the others for the duty of the choir.

They had been altogether solemnly and publicly vested the year before (1624) on the 31st of December, Sunday, by the renowned Archbishop of Cambray Vander Burgh, who very freely and generously exempted this new rising Nunnery from himself and his successors and committed it to the English Fathers through whose industry it began. R. F. Rudesind Barlo assisted at their Clothing.

Their house was the refuge of the Abbey of Femy of the Order of St. Benedict, a monastery not far from Cambray which was begun by English but then lay utterly ruined through the wars; nor was the said refuge in a much better condition, for there was only four walls standing, without any partitions, and the walls cleft open from top to bottom in several places, so that before they could make it a dwelling-house it cost them five hundred pounds sterling.

At first it was only lent them and they were according to agreement to leave it at six months' warning and the money paid for the reparations to be reimbursed to them when they should be warned out of the house which the workmen said could not stand past thirty years; yet it has stood above these fourscore years by the help of other buildings joined to it. In 1638 Anthony of Monmorency, Abbot of St. Andrew's (to which monastery Femy was then annexed,) consented that the said refuge should be given to the English Dames for ever; which Pope Urban VIII. approved by a Bull granted the 18th of January the same year. And further in 1639 the Abbot confirmed and approved the said donation to the English Dames by an act dated the 27th of January. And in 1640 the abovesaid worthy Archbishop confirmed it upon condition that when regular discipline should be established at Femy, the Dames should pay to the house of Femy three thousand five hundred florins money of Flanders.

Since their establishment there they have purchased houses and gardens to the value of one thousand pounds English to enlarge their enclosure; they have disbursed for buildings and reparations above three thousand eight hundred pounds sterling at several times; and it's esteemed that they have lost at several times in England and in Flanders by several misfortunes occasioned by war &c, above eight thousand pounds sterling, most of it money for the portions of several of the religious. By these losses the house hath been reduced at divers times to great poverty and many thought they must disperse during the unhappy civil wars of England, but the English Fathers who have ever been very tender of them, relieved them and put them into a method (when Rev. Fr. Benedict Stapylton was President, who mightily took to heart the prosperity of this house) of putting out the value of £200 sterling upon every head professed in the Convent by which means the yearly income increases; and another help is the taking of pensioners; yet this would not prove sufficient to support the house if the Divine bounty did not now and then cast them in alms, through whose merciful Providence they live without the affliction of being anyways indebted to any one, decently provided of all necessaries as well in sickness as in health out of the common purse; so that the use of particular pensions or anything savouring of propriety is unknown in the monastery where all is in common and at the disposal of the Superior as the Rule and Constitutions ordain. They have always said Matins at midnight and do so still, and observe the holy Rule of St. Benedict as it is moderated by the Constitutions written, approved, and delivered to them by the RR. Fathers of the Congregation in General Chapter.

They entered this place on the 24th of December (Sunday) 1623 and the worthy Archbishop Vander Burgh honoured their entry with his presence and opened their chapel with saying the first Mass that ever was said there. They called their said house "Our Lady of Comfort" of which they keep a particular feast on the 4th of July. The Fathers had provided them of three virtuous English Dames of the Order of St. Benedict from Brussels, namely Dame Frances Gawen who became first Abbess of this place; (for though the Superioress be elective every four years, yet she is styled Abbess):

Dame Potentiana Deacons and Dame Viviana Yaxley. These were to form them in religion, and soon after good Fr. Rudesind gave them an excellent interior director the R. F. Augustine Baker who founded them so admirably into an interior sort of life that the aforesaid Archbishop took some of them to reform a nunnery in Cambray, which had very good success and highly contented that noble prelate, who from the first day he knew them to his last moment continued them the honour and favour of his friendship. Some of them have lived in such eminent sanctity that their lives have been written.

CHAPTER THE THIRTY-EIGHTH.

THE THIRD GENERAL CHAPTER, 1625.   THE SEMINARY OATH.

The third General Chapter on the 2nd of July 1625 was held at Douay, where neither the first elected President R. F. Justus Edner nor the 2nd elected R. F. John Harper would take the charge on them. Wherefore R. F. Rudesind was continued in the office with the title of President administrator, not with that of President absolutely.

I cant get to know the names of the Provincials of Canterbury and York.

The Vicar of France was again R. F. Bernard Berington of St. Peter.

The Prior of St. Gregory at Douay, R. F. Rudesind Barlo.

The Prior of St. Laurence at Dieulwart, R. F. Laurence Reyner.

The Prior of St. Benedict's at St. Malo's, R. F. Jocelin Elmer.

The Prior of Paris, R. F. Sigebert Bagshaw.

The Abbess of Cambray, Dame Frances Gawen.

The Procurator at Rome, R. F. Austin Hungate.

Secretary to the President, R. F. Clement Reyner.

On the 14th of September following died at Cambray the Vicar of the Nuns, R. F. Edward Maihew, and lies buried in the parish Church of St. Vaast. Besides his "Trophies," he hath written a book entituled "The grounds of the new and old religion."

CHAPTER THE THIRTY-EIGHTH.

And this year 1625 by order of the Pope as 'twas said, the Cardinals de Propaganda published an oath to be taken by all Seminarists at the age of fourteen years old, that they will not enter any Monastery till they have spent three years in the mission. This oath hath been since extended to all their life time, all the world standing astonished, even the learned, at the tenor of such a strange oath. This was because many of them became monks; and the other Priests and Jesuits who tutored the Seminaries, maintained it was unreasonable that they who had been brought up at the cost of the Church left her service to hide themselves in cloisters; and yet the English Congregation stands bound to the mission as much as they, but with this difference; that the monks do not send so hastily as the Seminaries, taking more time to perfect those they design for so great a work.

Anno 1626, March 4th, S. V. full of days and good works died at London R. F. John Richardson a pious and industrious man, obliging all he could with his civilities and benefits. He became a monk in the mission and patiently there endured several imprisonments and persecutions.

And His Holiness on the 23rd of May stopped the mouths of those who calumniated the Congregation, declaring by the Cardinals interpreters of the Council of Trent that there had been formerly in England and was then, an English Benedictine Congregation, notwithstanding whatever any could chatter to the contrary; and that the Brief of Pope Paul V of the 23rd of August, 1607 ascertained the same. Moreover a little while after because the adversary party would have made it pass for surreptitious, he declared that assertion false, and renewed it and gave another confirming the Union agreed on in the Definitory of Paris.

And by his confirmation of the foundation at Douay Convent we will take a final view of that affair.

CHAPTER THE THIRTY-NINTH.

A FINAL ACCOUNT OF THE FOUNDATION OF ST. GREGORY'S MONASTERY AT DOUAY. THE DEVOTION OF THE BONDAGE OF THE B. VIRGIN.

It doth not appear that the commendation of the King of Spain procured to them any more from the Archduke than his recommendation to Abbot Cavarel, besides a *mortissement* of the ground whereon the house stands, and privileges that other Colleges of the University enjoy. And this was sufficient; for the charitable Abbot upon the first petition presented to him by the Fathers Rudesind Barlo, Leander of St. Martin and Bennet of St. Facundus on the 14th of September, 1616, in order to obtaining a stable foundation (for his first allowance was not settled and came to only five pounds English a quarter in money and such a quantity of corn at first, afterwards something increased), bestowed on them 2000 florins a year of perpetual rent. And because the Fathers in the petition had offered to take upon them great rigour of discipline, choir, abstinence, &c, the Abbot took occasion to deliver their Constitutions.

The next year, 1617, was the long desired Union, and as R. F. Leander was one of the deputies that compiled the Constitutions, and that with Father Rudesind he was one of the nine Definitors, they had occasion to strengthen what the Abbot had ordained to their satisfaction and obtain an address to him to change what they disliked. Wherefore soon after their return they fell again to petitioning their foundation which they prudently judged was not so strongly bottomed and so well laid as it ought to be, because the consent of the Convent (of St. Vedast at Arras) had not yet been obtained nor so much as asked by the Abbot. The Convent consenting very freely and joyfully, he resolved to try for one year what 1200 florins would do, and the next year added to that sum 200 florins more.

The term of the allowance being expired with the year another petition was to be presented which they did on the 27th. of September 1619 with so much more earnestness and entreaties for a perpetual rent as they perceived every year this way more burthensome and unsecured (as depending on the Abbots or mutability of a man's mind), and with more confidence as they had already gained the grand Prior M. Nizar and the Sub-prior's good liking; who assured them there was no difficulty in the thing, and to whom particularly the Abbot had commended the considering of it.

And accordingly this wise prelate seeing that important affair concluded, in expectation of which perhaps he deferred so long to make the settlement which he had designed from the beginning; viz, the confirmation of the Union and Constitutions, and, which he no less desired and the rest of his convent, an entire exemption from all ordinaries whatsoever, the Abbot presently proceeded, with consent and approbation of his Chapter, to a foundation more ample than the former and such as comprehended all the additions and expunged whatsoever the Definitory of Paris and the Fathers of Douay did desire.

For this munificent and liberal foundation, in the name of the whole Convent (*of Douay*) and Congregation, thanks were given by a public instrument drawn and signed by R. F. Leander, President, whereby he accepted thereof with all its conditions &c, which we will specify by and bye from the Bull which confirmed the transaction.

But there was a very ticklish clause inserted in the foundation, that every new Prior at his entry should ask of the Abbot of Arras or his Convent the continuation of their College or habitation; a condition not only very burthensome, but also such an one as obliged only the petitioner and not the convent of St. Vaast or Abbot thereof to grant such petition. Wherefore the Abbot upon redress made to him by Father Leander, explained it by a codicil added to the letters of Foundation, having first communicated and deliberated on the point with the councillors, of his Abbey, and declared that as the Prior was to ask the said continuation, so it was to be granted always as long as the English monks kept to the conditions of the foundation according to what a sincere, prudent, and pious judge might determine they did.

The year after, which was 1620, the Abbot published a writing of this his foundation and its accceptance, and declared the revenue was to rise from the money himself had formerly put out upon the states of Artois to be paid at two terms and received by M. Le Mercier and his successors, regents of the new College of St. Vaast (at Douay).

Not long after, (it was, namely, in 1621) the Abbot of Marchin put out of the College of Marchin his own religious and the English Fathers, where they had so long supported the honour of their Nation and Order, as being inferior in learning to none in the whole university; and their ejection (not for any demerits, but to make way for the Jesuits to whom the Abbot would give that place) had been much lamented had it not been so timed by Providence that the new College of St. Vaast was ready to receive them with open arms, whither they returned by the Abbot Cavarel's orders and drew a great number of their scholars after them though the schools of St. Vaast were not opened without great resistance of the University. The whole process, the Abbot's and the English Fathers' replies, with the Arch-duke's patents, are all on record in the College of St. Vaast.

But upon occasion of this proceeding of the Abbot of Marchin, V. R. Father President thought he had a happy opportunity of discovering what he had long concealed in his breast and was in appearance disgustful to the founders but necessary to the founded.

Wherefore another petition was drawn wherein he humbly proposed to his Lordship's consideration and fatherly providence, that in succeeding times such might be found as would be willing to make it a question whether they fulfilled the conditions of the foundation, and therefore desired the said articles might be razed out. The Abbot who was always ready to condescend to R. F. President's desires, yet not to disoblige his Brethren who had purposely inserted such restringent clauses to make the English Fathers' dependence on them the greater and closer, remitted the petition to the perusal and sentiment of M. Nizart then Sub-Prior of St. Vaast, and reader of Scripture in their College at Douay, and to M. Mercier, Regent of the said College; and having heard their opinion and that of the other principal officers of his Abbey (who as may be seen above were earnest promoters of the foundation) which was favourable to the supplicant, he added another codicil to the foundation, dated 5th of November, 1622, wherein he declares that it neither was nor never has been his intention that the religious or convent should be deprived of their dwelling at the free will and pleasure of himself and his successors as long as they satisfied the conditions &c; that clause was only inserted to oblige the said religious to remember the respect and friendship due from them to those of Arras and that there might be for ever a right understanding betwixt them, with love of regular discipline and learning, especially a serious study of philosophy and divinity.

There remained nothing now but that our Holy Father the Pope, who had made ample provision for the establishment of the Congregation in general, should be inclined to extend his fatherly care to St. Gregory's College in particular, and ratify by apostolic authority the charitable and prudent institution thereof by the worthy founder. Therefore in 1625 a petition was drawn by consent and approbation of the Abbot, who finding it not penned in the style of that Court, gave order it should be sent to the Procurator at Rome together with a transcript of the letters of the foundation, whose business should be to see it worded and framed better, and if he found it difficult to connect and express all the articles of the foundation, that he should insert the said letters of foundation word for word; and this so much the rather because such information would fall under *motu proprio*, or *ex certa cognitione*, a style that carries with it more authority than a simple confirmation; which was accordingly and faithfully performed by R. F. Paulin Greenwood, then Procurator of the English Congregation, and by the Abbot's agent as appears by the exact and entire enumeration of all the material clauses, ordinations and articles of the letters of foundation mentioned and comprised in the Bull gratiously accorded by Urban VIII on the 3rd of June 1626, in the third year of his Pontificate.

The Fathers finding the building too great for their use, obtained it might be divided, and offered half of it to the Founder, which with some other buildings constituted the College of Arras; and they upon this have obliged themselves to all reparations of the whole fabric and Church of which they have likewise the use, but do not keep choir in it but in the day time on Sundays and holidays with the English Fathers. Wherefore the Bull after the delineation of the division of the house tells us the Abbot's foundation is only for twelve Monks of the English Nation.* And for their expenses and necessaries he allows them

---

Though Abbot Cavarel's foundation was for twelve monks the actual Community was always in excess of that number. The following figures may be of interest to our readers.

The Community of St. Gregory's Monastery at Douay.

Gen. Chapter.	Priests.	Choir-religious.	Lay-brothers.	Total.
1621	13	14	2	29
1625	15	23	2	40
1629	22	10	2	34
1633	19	5	1	25
1639	11	8	1	20
1641	14	3	1	18
1645	17	8	1	26
1649	13	6	1	20
1653	14	8	1	23
1657	18	5	1	24
1661	14	7	1	22
1666	13	2		15
1669	10	5		15
1673	11	8		19
1677	16	5		21
1681	12	6		18
1685	14	10	2	26
1689	13	14	3	30
1693	15	7	3	25
1697	15	5	4	25
1701	12	10	5	27
1705	11	11	5	27
1710	13	5	5	23

CHAPTER THE THIRTY-NINTH.

a yearly revenue of 2000 florins to be paid at four times in the year quarterly.

In token that the Abbot and Convent of St. Vaast are absolute lords of this rent and dwelling, and likewise in token of gratitude, the President of the Congregation or the Prior of Douay on the appointed day and at the appointed place, with declaration that they do it by way of thanks, are to offer or present a white wax candle.

Likewise all new Priors are to acknowledge as much in writing in presenting a petition to the Abbot and his successors to desire the confirmation and renewing of this favour, and testify that could they have it otherwise from some other power, that yet they would not take it, and their petition is to be granted.

They are to add to their vows of religion a fourth Vow of the English mission.

The Abbot takes on him the ordering the solemnity (and such like) of the Divine Office, their victuals, abstinence, fasts, studies &c, and they are to have always some able to teach philosophy, divinity and even the lesser Schools. These are to be totally at the devotion of the Abbot and his successors who may place them and displace them as they please; and they are none of them to be sent anywhither unless there be others whom the Abbot and his successors shall judge as capable, and none are to take degrees in the University but with the Abbot's leave. And if it be the fault of the Convent that it hath not such men, there may be taken from it out of the annual rent, fifty florins for each regent or teacher so wanting, but no more and never upon any other account.

The Convent is to be governed by the Prior and his Counsellors, but the Regent of the College of St. Vaast or the Abbot's deputy is to take place of him out of his conventual acts.

The Priests of St. Vaast in choir are to take place of the English Fathers, and so the brothers of the brothers of the English Convent.

The suffrages for the election of a Prior are to be presented to the Abbot and his successors; out of them he chooses three, one of which the English General Chapter is to choose and constitute Prior, or else they are to present him three chosen by the Convent and he pronounces ; and he can make use of either of these ways as he pleases.

When any of the twelve places are vacant, the persons to be admitted must be presented by the Prior to the Abbot ; and if the Prior has a mind to take others beyond that number he must be sure that each man he will so admit has at least a pension of thirty ducats yearly ; and so with the leave and conseut of the Abbot he may take them whether they be English or Flemings ; likewise he may take other Religious as boarders or guests with a pension or without, desiring to study, but so that every one of them so admitted shall take his oath before whom the Abbot shall depute for that purpose, that he will maintain the honour of the said Abbot, and that he will not by any means seek to extort upon the accompt of the said foundation anything from him or his monastery further than what is established. Moreover he must promise not to disturb the peace of the Convent or seek to change to worse the Laws of it, or seek absolution from the said oath or take it if offered ; and that if he offend in any of these, he will undergo the penalty enjoined or to be enjoined, all liberty left of appeals to the Holy See, or his Nuncio having the powers of Legate a Latere.

Of the said twelve there are never to be fewer in the convent than ten or nine to perform rightly the Divine Office.

The Prior cannot dispose of the Religious in other cases without the Abbot and his successors' knowledge; and as for those the Abbot has chosen to teach, they must not be disposed of without his consent, besides what is said of their place being supplied.

During his life only as Founder, they were subject to his Visits and correction; and he could send to live amongst them, paying a pension, any of his Religious of St. Vaast, either by way of penance, or for recollection, or for any other cause.

Every week the Procurator is to give his accounts to the Prior of the house, and the Prior every year to the Abbot and his successors. If it become indebted, neither the Monastery of Arras, nor the said revenue it has from the Abbey, become any

CHAPTER THE THIRTY-NINTH.

ways concerned in the solution of the debts.

Whatever accessions or augmentations happen from Benefactors of that Province, or through the portions of Novices of that said Province, they are all to be counted in the Foundation. But whatever the English bring out of England during the Schism or otherwise add, are to be united after the same manner; but when they restore the place (for they can't hold it when Catholic religion is restored in England), they may take back to England what they have brought; all things else, goods and persons, remaining in the power of the Abbot and his successors.

Lastly whatever is here said of the Abbot, in case that Abbey became commendatory or that abbatial seat vacant, was to be understood of the Prior and Convent of St. Vaast.

Moreover the Religious are to say a certain number of Masses for the Abbot and his successors; and when it shall please God to make England Catholic again, they are to receive at Oxford whom the Abbot and his successors shall send from the Abbey of Saint Vaast.

And now I end this mention of Douay with the liberal Founder's tacking another appendix to the Charter of Foundation, wherein he bestowed on his Gregorian Community a country house conveniently situated at Esquerchin, a village about a league out of Douay, with a large garden adjoining, enclosed on one side with the river Escerbien and on the other with a wall: which place he designed for a retreat for the Religious upon occasion of sickness, divertissement or recollection; and that the said mansion and fruits thereof should be proper and peculiar to the English, yet without exclusion of the Religious of St. Vaast when they had a mind to return thither; and that the said Manor and inheritance should be annexed unalienably to the foundation and with it return to the Abbey of St. Vaast when the English parted with it. The house was plucked down and timber brought away by the then Prior of St. Gregory (R. F. Joseph Frere) in the great consternation and apprehension the country was in when the French took Arras. (1640.)

On the 10th of June (1626) died R. F. Francis Atrobos, professed of Onia in Spain, a man of a most meek and gentle disposition who had laudably executed the offices of greatest concern in the Congregation and had suffered imprisonment and exiles for the Faith, and was waxed white in the apostolical labours of the Mission.

On the 3rd of August the illustrious Francis Vander Burgh, Archbishop of Cambray, approved the devotion called "the Bondage of the Blessed Virgin," (Mancipium B. Virginis Mariæ). Also Paul Boudot, a Doctor of Sorbonne and Bishop of Arras approved the same, and some canonized Saints not weighing how far the term of bondage struck, have been taken up with the thoughts of this devotion.* Wherefore no wonder if the R.R. Benedictines Anselm Crowder and Thomas Vincent Sadler have in their devotions to our Lady given in to the same thing. But the Bishop of Tournay (Gilbert Choiseul) in a choice pastoral letter (of June 7th, 1674, and printed anew at Lisle 1689), declares that by the decree of the Congregation of the Holy Office, approved by the Holy See, 'tis severely condemned and whatever has any *rapport* to it. Behold the words of the decree.

"Ut ritum et quodcumque aliud ad mancipatum ejusmodi pertinens statim rejiciant.

Ut novus hic Beatæ Virginis mancipatus omnino aboleatur contrariis quibuscumque non obstantibus."

We are not properly to call ourselves the slaves of any creature not even of the most glorious Mother of God, in taking that word it its natural sense; for that a slave (according to the notion that men have formed to themselves of the thing they understand by the word slavery), is so in the power of his master that he depends on him without any restriction, which belongs to God alone, who by the rights of creation and redemption can dispose of us as a potter the vessel he hath made, as St. Paul saith in the 9th Chapter of the Romans.

Anno 1627, His Holiness gave leave to the President of the English Benedictine Congregation to give power to his Religious to read forbidden books and absolve the cases in the Bulla Cœnæ.

---

* *George Colvenerius, to: Kalend. Mariani.*

CHAPTER THE FORTIETH.

THE LIBERALITY OF THE CONGREGATION OF BURSFELD TO THE ENGLISH CONGREGATION.

The Emperor (Ferdinand II.) having recovered a great tract of ground from the heretics, on which stood many monasteries of the Order of St. Benedict, the English Fathers knowing the Bursfeldian Congregation to want monks to put into them, petitioned them to consider fraternally the case of their affliction and exile, and charitably to stretch their arm to help them. The worthy Abbot of Arras, Philip Cavarel, writ to the same effect to the prelates of the German Congregation of Bursfeld, who on the 18th of May 1628, gave them the Abbey of Cismar in the Diocese of Lubeck and Dukedom of Holsace with all its goods, rights and privileges upon these conditions.

1. That they should get it at their own cost.
2. That they should swear fidelity and dependency on the Union of Bursfeld according to what is here expressed.
3. That when they had recovered the monastery they should contribute with the other monasteries to the supporting of the burthens of the Union; but this demand they mitigated afterwards.
4. That they should give assurances that when England returned to the Faith they would restore the monastery to the Union, with all that it might then be worth.
5. That they will do nothing to its prejudice by sales, alienation &c, without the consent of the President of the Union or the annual Chapter.

6. That they should specify which of the English monasteries they expected, which when they had obtained, they would let Cismar go back to the Union of Bursfeld. To this article was answered Canterbury Cathedral and St. Alban's Abbey.

7. Then they exacted that they should send to the next annual Chapter an exact account of the income of the house.

8. Lastly, that they should give assurances and swear they would not act against these conditions, and that if they did, ipso facto they should forfeit all right to the monastery, &c.

These were the conditions for this and others which they afterwards thus lent to the English Congregation of their Order, of all which the Fathers have been able to retain but one called Lambspring and that with great difficulty, of which we shall have occasion to say more hereafter.

The Emperor not only liked of this and confirmed this donation on the 22nd of April, 1629, but he also consented that the neighbouring prelates and others might confer more on the English Congregation.

November 10th (S. V.) 1628 died most piously of an hectic fever at London, Father Amandus Venner alias Farmer, born in Devonshire, monk of Dieulwart, a sedulous missioner and great sufferer in long imprisonments and other persecutions patiently endured for the faith.

And that same year of 1628 (October 21st) at the famous Abbey of Chelles by Paris, died R. F. George Brown, a man of great piety and adorned with all sorts of religious manners and virtues; a diligent promoter of the residences newly begun in France and Flanders.

And at Dieulwart in opinion of sanctity after many years spent there in the condition of a lay-brother, died John alias Oliver Towtall (or Toudelle) a Lancashire man, of a truly humble and obedient spirit, and who had in a high degree that virtue called the simplicity of Saints. (January 28, 1626.)

CHAPTER THE FORTY-FIRST.

THE DECEASE OF ARCHBISHOP GIFFORD. DEATH OF BR. HERBERT CROFT, FR. CELESTINE TREMBY &c.

ANNO 1629, on the 10th of April, died the Reverend Father in God, Gabriel of St. Mary (otherwise William Gifford,) Archbishop and Duke of Rheims, first Peer of France and Legate born of the Holy Apostolic See.

His condition of Bishop of Archidal and Suffragan of Rheims upon the death in 1621 of the Cardinal Archbishop of Rheims was changed to that of Archbishop of Rheims. He behaved himself in his episcopal functions like an apostle, visiting the diocese, preaching and catechizing in the villages, sometimes too, no less than seven or eight times a day notwithstanding that he was then much indisposed and in a declining age. A world of people he confirmed, consecrated churches, and in a word, proved himself a real pastor (says his panegyrist an Augustinian Abbot,) amidst a people in great necessity of such help that it had scarce ever seen or heard speak of a Bishop; pastoral duty in those parts had been so neglected.

And of himself the said Abbot relates as follows: "I remember, Messieurs, that being sent a boy to begin my studies in the Low Countries, I heard a very considerable Englishman (under whom I had the honour to be brought up and who once did our Divinity School of St. Denis the honour of teaching there) say that Mr. Gabriel Gifford (for so he named him whom since we have called our Archbishop) was, it may be, the greatest divine that hath been since St. Thomas of Aquin that great Master of the Schools. The sole testimony of so great a man is worth a thousand others; yet it was seconded by the universal consent of all the learned. And in Paris the most curious, who often hear sermons only to censure them, used to say of *Le Père Bénédictin* that they must needs ingenuously own that he was a prodigy of learning; yet with all this he was of a wonderful humble and affable carriage and behaviour, familiarly conversing with the most ignorant to render them capable of his doctrine. "In a word," continues the said Abbot, "the fame of his great deserts spreading far and near, the most Christian King Louis the Just made him Archbishop of Rheims." The Abbot is very eloquently diffusive to expose that nothing but his great virtue and worth drew on him this honour which no days altered his manners.

The more he advanced in age the more infirm he became yet his fervour no ways slackened thereby, and he still continued, as much as possibly his decrepit age would permit him, his pastoral fatigues, and in his episcopal state held to his monastical condition, wearing constantly his religious habit, keeping to the regular fasts of his Congregation, rising in the night to pray and using such severe disciplines that those who were most about him thought it piety to hide those instruments of penance from him, which solely was capable of altering the calmness of his temper, for then he would be angry till they were given him again. Besides in those great feasts to which his condition obliged him to lend his presence, he found means to practise great mortifications.

At his advancement to this Archiepiscopal See, the Abbey of St. Remigius of Rheims was annexed by consent of the Pope and the King of France to the Archbishop mense (that is to help him out in his maintenance and table). But the royal great and apostolical consent had not been verified in Parliament wherefore the Duke of Guise (who died at Florence) craved of the King that that Abbey might be given to his son then called M. L'Abbé de S. Denis; but the king by the mouth of Fr. Segran his confessor signified to Bishop Gifford that his intent was to give him the Abbey so annexed to his Archiepiscopal See, and therefore he would not give it without his consent to M. l'Abbé de St. Denis. As the worthy prelate had great obligations to that family, at the first word of the Duchess of Guise to him upon the affair, he gave his consent and thereby deprived himself of 40,000 livres a year ; so that his revenue considering his dignity could not be very considerable ; yet of his little he was very charitable, particularly to the poor of his city who were ashamed to ask alms publicly, and he has been known to have given at once for an alms one hundred crowns and even two hundred crowns, nay as far as a thousand livres, and besides this made rich presents to churches and employed much of his revenue in works of piety ; and if in the streets any of the poor asked an alms, he would make his coach stop and give it with his own hands.

He knew not how to do ill to any one, but delighted to do good to all even to his very enemies ; naturally inclined to forget injuries he easily pardoned them. And when his charge obliged him to punish any one, it drew tears from his eyes. A person of great account used to say, if he were to blame in anything, it was because he did not punish enough those who deserved it.

Yet this lamb was a lion against the enemies of the orthodox Faith, against whom he writ notably and set others a-writing. For all his lifetime he had but little leisure himself for composing of books. Calvin out of contempt he used to call Maître Jean : and used to weep for joy when news was brought him of the King's victories over that detestable man's rebellious offsprings.

He had so perfect an intelligence of the Holy Scriptures, that he knew the better part of them by heart, and would recite whole passages without so much as opening the Bible.

From his tender years he bore a particular affection to the Passion of our Saviour and much coveted to die on a Good Friday. Though he had not entirely his design in that, yet he had it in part, for he died in Holy Week. He was also very devout to our Lady, insomuch that 'tis thought she favoured him with some assurance of assisting him at his death : for addressing himself to her a little before he died, he thrice repeated with great courage these words: " Adjuva me, quia tu promisisti mihi," " Help me because you promised me."

Two days before he expired he was absolutely insensible to all things but what immediately regarded his salvation ; so that when he was spoken to of God, our Lady or Eternity, he would as 'twere revive again, strike his breast and lift his hands to heaven. To say all in one word, he died the death of the just. " Mortua est anima ejus morte justorum, et facta sunt novissima " ejus horum similia."

He lies buried in his Cathedral behind the High Altar under a holy water pot, without inscription or epitaph. His heart was carried in great ceremony to a famous nunnery of his Order at Rheims entitled to St. Peter and laid in their choir before the altar of Our Lady, with this inscription without date of the year or month:

" Hic jacet cor Virgini sacrum Illustrissimi et Reverendissimi D. D. Gulielmi Gifford, Benedictini Angli, Archiepiscopi Ducis Rhemensis &c, ; non potuit uno totus condi sepulchro, dividi debuit mortuus qui vixit utilis ubique, quod restat unicum, unice et integre consecrat tibi, Virgo integerrima. Jacuit ad pedes tuos quod stetit semper humana supra. Admitte munus Religio D. Benedicto sacra tuas enim ante infularem dignitatem cordi inserverat regulas Dignus tanti Patris filius, cor cordi reddit dum suum tibi donat."

Which may be Englished thus :

" Here lies consecrated to the Blessed Virgin, the heart of the most illustrious and reverend Lord William Gifford taken from the English Benedictines to be Archbishop and Duke of Rheims &c. He could not be shut up under one tomb, and therefore it was just he should be divided dead, by whom all profited so much wherever he lived. What alone remains is solely and entirely consecrated to thee, O most entire Virgin, for it lay at thy feet while it evermore stood superior to all human affairs. Embrace this gift, O holy religion of St. Benedict, for before the honour of the mitre his heart had deeply imbibed your Rules, a worthy son of so great a Father. He returns heart to heart when he gives you his."

At this ceremony of his heart his panegyric was made by Messieur de Maupas, Abbot of St. Denis at Rheims, from whom I have much of what I have here written. There is also a very honourable account of him in Mr. Pitt's (De illustribus Angliæ Scriptoribus) and in R. F. Maihew's *Trophies* which are dedicated to his Lordship, and in his book of *English Benedictine Writers*. His Grace before his monachism was very intime with William Reginald or Reinald, a person reputed a prodigy of learning, whom he piously assisted at his death, and finished and published his *Calvino Turcismus* which he had left imperfect. His other works I forbear seeing they are to be found in the above mentioned authors. I only add that he was also with St. Francis de Sales very intime ; and as that glorious Saint much honoured the English Fathers with his company when he was at Paris, one day as one of them was to sing the first Vespers of his first High Mass, to do him honour that holy apostolical Bishop of Geneva stood on one side of him and R. F. Gabriel Gifford then Archbishop and Duke of Rheims stood on the other, as a very venerable exemplary old Father who knew the said monk assured me.

The Mauritians who have St. Malo's keep Bishop Gifford's anniversary as Founder of that house, on the 23rd of April, though an English monk of that place assures us in notes he writ for the history of the house that he died on the 11th of April. At the library of the King of France in Paris he is said to have been sent into England as an Envoy from a Prince, but the rest of what is there noted of him is false, as also what the Messieurs of St. Martha relate of him in their *Christian France* (a book so entitled). His original picture is kept in the English Benedictine monastery of St. Edmund's in Paris and at the monastery of Rheims, because that the Archbishop of Rheims (brother of Mr. Louvoy), ill informed of his merit put it out of the gallery of the Archiepiscopal palace at Rheims; neither did he abuse him alone but likewise other great men whose pictures were there, upon no other account than that they had been monks. For though he hath done great things in his archiepiscopal administration, yet there will remain for ever in his scutcheon the blot of having been preposterously prevented and prejudiced against monks, as the miseries of the times go, though he was a great admirer and promoter of the famous Benedictine Mauritian Antiquary Dom John Mabillon who died at St. German's Abbey at Paris on the 27th. of December, 1707, æt. 76.

The same year Bishop Gifford died, but on the 10th of April at Douay died Sir Herbert Croft who retiring to St. Gregory's in a decrepit age, spent the rest of his days in devotion, and before his death was admitted to the confraternity of the Order.

The "Antiquities of Oxford" thus relate his history and epitaph, speaking of Christ College.

"Herbertus Croft familia cognomini perantiqua apud Castrum Croftorum in Agro Herefordiensi oriundus, in Collegio isto commensalis annos aliquot egit, et in ætate matura constitutus argumenti polemici librum in 12mo typis mandatum composuit, quem tamen videre nondum contigit, ipsius etiam inscriptionis proinde sum ignarus. De authore isto nihil habeo quod addam præter quam quæ ex epitaphio ejus in monasterio Anglicano (S. Gregorii Magni) Duacensi (ante altare S. Benedicti) comparente innotescant; id autem sic se habet.

Hic jacet corpus Herberti Croft, equitis aurati, Angli, de comitatu Herefordiæ, viri prudentis, fortis, nobilis, Patriæ libertatis amantissimi, qui in hoc monasterio in paupere cella tanquam monachus aliquot annos devote vixit et pie efflavit, secutus exemplum primogenitoris sui Dom: Bernardi Croft qui ante sexcentos annos, relicta militari gloria, monachus in Cœnobio Benedictino defunctus est. Obiit 10 Aprilis, 1622.

In pace requiescat.

Alia porro quædam scripsisse dicitur licet facta mihi haud dum sit eorum copia. "Hæc Anton. a Wood Hist. et Antiq. Oxonii, 1674."

[We may here imitate our author and *English* what Wood says, "for the benefit of those who are not familiar with latin."]

"Herbert Croft born of the very ancient family of that name of Croft Castle in Herefordshire, spent some years as a boarder at this (Christ Church) College; and at a mature age committed to the press a duodecimo controversial work which he had written, but which I have not yet seen; hence I am ignorant of its very title. I have nothing more to add of the author besides what I gather from the epitaph on his grave in front of St. Benedict's altar in the English monastery of St. Gregory at Douay; it is as follows:

Here lies the body of Sir Herbert Croft, Knight, born in England in the County of Hereford, a prudent, able and high souled man, and a great lover of his Country's freedom who devoutly spent several years in a poor cell in this monastery, and here died; imitating herein the example of his ancestor Sir Bernard Croft who six hundred years before had abandoned the renown of military fame to die a monk in a Benedictine monastery. He died on the 10th of April, 1622.

May he rest in peace.

And at St. Malo's died the RR. Fathers Celestine, otherwise John Tremby, and Rupert Guillet, a Breton, at the plague house where their great charity had placed them to assist the infected. (25th. and 28th. October, 1629).

But before their exit the fourth General Chapter was held at Douay on the 2nd. of July.

CHAPTER THE FORTY-SECOND.

The Fourth General Chapter 1629. Notice of several members of the Congregation who died about this time.

Rev. F. Bennet Jones, elected President, not coming out of England in due time for his installation, Rev. F. Sigebert Bagshaw, 2nd elected, took the place as the laws of the Congregation require; a man of prodigious success against contradiction; witness what we have seen in the affair of the Union and the disputes which rose at the beginning of this quadriennium betwixt those of this renewed Congregation and those of Mount Cassin, and some who would not yet embrace the Union. But they were not able to hold the field against this President; for he produced the Pope's letters, those of the Reverend General of Spain, with the decrees of the Spanish Chapter, and compelled to peace by his patience and doctrine those who hated peace.

The Provincial of Canterbury, R. F. Claude White.
The Provincial of York, R. F. John Hutton.
The Vicar of France, R. F. Bernard Berington.
The Prior of St. Gregory's, R. F. Leander of St. Martin.
The Prior of St. Laurence's, R. F. Jocelin Elmer.
The Prior of St. Benedict's, R. F. Adeodatus L'Angevin, Vice Prior.
The Prior of (*St. Edmund's*) Paris, R. F. Placid Gascoign.
The Vicar of the Nuns at Cambray, R. F. Francis Hull.

CHAPTER THE FORTY-SECOND.

Secretary to Rev. Father President, R. F. Anthony Batt.

And this 1629, on the 29th of August, the Bursfeld Congregation gave to the English Fathers the monastery of Rintelen in the county or Earldom of Scawenburg or Schaumberg and Diocese of Minden, and for the Nuns of this Congregation they gave them the monastery of Stoterlingburgh in the Diocese of Halberstad.

Anno 1630, June 25, in his palace at S. Malo's died the Rev. Father in God, William Le Gouverneur, who persuaded the English Fathers to fix there and continued the same friendship to them to his last moment.

September 30. S. V. Father Thomas Emmerson professed of S. Facundus in Spain died in England. He was Doctor in Divinity and famous for his sufferings of imprisonments and banishments having endured the heat of a smart persecution.

Also this year the Pope suppressed a rising order of Jesuitesses which certain learned English gentlewomen mightily skilled in the Hebrew and Greek tongues were a-beginning at Cologne, Liege &c. The Bishop of Troy was ordered to break up their houses. The Pope apprehended lest this institute might degenerate into great evil seeing they were to keep no inclosure, but follow the same course of life as the Jesuits, teaching girls as they teach boys, and voyaging up and down as if they had been men.

Anno 1631, May the 25th. died R. F. Joseph Prater, a man of great piety and much beloved and admired by his brethren, professed of Valladolid in Spain and twice elected Provincial of Canterbury, laudably discharged that important duty.

June 4th (1631) at Stafford Castle, died R. F. Francis Foster, own brother to the Countess of Stafford, admitted to the habit in the Mission, renowned for his imprisonments and banishments very particularly addicted to deeds of Charity both spiritual and corporal in which he gave away all that he had.

August 30th, the Pope having heard the Cardinals who have care of the affairs of the Regulars, gave out a Brief whereby he declared he would maintain the authority of the English Benedictine Congregation, and therefore commanded its superiors and those of the Spanish Congregation to make Father Walgrave return to the Congregation in which he had made his profession, which was that of Spain.

The next year he sent a Brief to the most Christian King to whom the Legate who gave it supplicated in the name of His Holiness for a certain and fixed house for the English Benedictine monks, but he did not obtain any such thing.

Anno 1632, May 8th, Placid Frier, a most worthy, witty, and hopeful young man, and (for his time) an excellent scholar, being newly made Priest and having sung his first Mass, died to the great grief of all his brethren, at Rintelen in Westphalia. This is remarkable, that he being an excellent violist, and having a bass viol hanging in his cell, the great string thereof brake asunder whilst he was in his agony and his brethren reciting the Litanies by his bed-side. And soon after he expired.

July 6th (1632), Placid Muttleberry, born in Somersetshire, changing the mission for a monk's habit, came to Dieulwart, where full of pleasing qualities which rendered him highly grateful to all his brethren, in a good old age he happily ended his life.

November the 9th, died Father Michael Blackeston of the Bishopric of Durham, a great musician and esteemed very pious; and on the 17th of November, Father Jerome Porter who writ "The Flowers of the English Saints." They both returning home to Douay from a journey, fell into a continual fever which carried them off.

Anno 1633, January 14th, died at Douay whither he was sent to perfect his studies, Brother Celestine de Landres, a young noble Lorrainer, who left a barony to become a monk at Dieulwart.

CHAPTER THE FORTY-THIRD.

THE FIFTH GENERAL CHAPTER, 1633.   DEATH OF FR. SIGEBERT BAGSHAW AND FR. LAURENCE LODWICK.

On the first of August 1633, was held at Douay the Fifth General Chapter.

First elected President, R. F. Leander of St. Martin.
Second elected President, R. F. Clement Reyner.
The Provincial of Canterbury, R. F. Robert Sherwood.
The Provincial of York, R. F. Augustine Hungate.
The Vicar of France, R. F. Bernard Berington.
The Prior of St. Gregory's, R. F. Joseph Frere.
The Prior of St. Laurence's, R. F. Jocelin Elmer.
The Prior of St. Benedict's, R. F. Adeodatus L'Angevin.
The Prior of Paris, R. F. Gabriel Brett.
The Prior of Rintelin, Rr F. Clement Reyner.
The Abbess of Cambray, Dame Catherine Gascoign.
The Procurator at Rome, R. F. Wilfrid Selby.
The Vicar of the Nuns, R. F. John Meutisse.
Secretary to the President, R. F. Christian Govaerdt, to whom succeeded R. F. John Worsley.

During this Chapter, R. F. Sigebert Bagshaw fell sick at Douay, and obtained the day before he died (Aug. 18th), that for the future all Presidents at their decease should be prayed for as if they had died conventuals of every Convent in the Congregation. He lies buried in the middle of the Church of St. Gregory's with a short account of who he was and when he died.

At Stoke in Gloucestershire, October 13th, died Fr. Laurence Lodwick professed of Dieulwart, a man of a weak constitution but of a strong faith, and greatly industrious and charitable in helping his neighbours.   x

CHAPTER THE FORTY-FOURTH.

HOW LA CELLE WAS GIVEN TO THE HOUSE OF PARIS. FR. WALGRAVE MAKES HIS SUBMISSION; NOTICES OF R. F. GABRIEL LATHAM, FELIX THOMPSON, GEORGE GAIRE &c.

AND now we must show how La Celle belongs to Paris. The inconsiderate, rash, violent, passionate conduct of Fr. Walgrave with his associate Fr. Barnes so lost him at Cheiles, that in the Holy Week of 1627, the Abbess who had taken him in, caused him to be routed out thence, though she had devolved the Abbey on another. And he and his monks were used with great severity and ignominy, God punishing his insolences to his brethren at Paris, as hath been related. In this distress after a great stir to no purpose, he exposed his affair to Cardinal Richelieu; but he got nothing more than to be handed over with his religious to the College of Marmoutier at Paris, which, with the great Abbey from whence it has its name, was subject to the Congregation of Cluny, and the Cardinal was head of that great body. The old monks grew weary of them at the College, and therefore began to seek to get handsomely quit of them, but could find no better expedient than to put them at an old venerable monastery of above a thousand years' standing, called La Celle, about a good English mile from the renowned nunnery of Faremoutier in Brie. It had been an Abbey by itself, but by a Council held at Meaux it was subjected to Marmoutier that it might be reformed; and now it was in a lamentable condition and scarcely deserved the name of a monastery, attended but by three or four monks. The conditions on which it was given to F. Walgrave on the

CHAPTER THE FORTY-FOURTH.

28th of October 1633 were that it should remain subject to them as to the proprietors of it; so that they would visit it and know when any more were taken in, and when any died in order to pray for them. And F. Walgrave was to make good all the rights &c, of the place and let nothing of them fall or perish.

Father Walgrave at his entry into it had a very troublesome time of it from the commendatory Prior, who was vexed that these new comers hindered him from doing there what he pleased, and compelled him by law to so many things, that the benefice was not worth to him so much as it used to be. This enraged his worldly humour so far, that at last after some extravagancies, he ended in breaking in upon Father Walgrave and his Religious and their two domestics, and imprisoned them in holes there at La Celle.

Father Walgrave grew now advanced in years and was quite broken with endless vexations that continually broke out on him from on all sides since his rebellion against his lawful superiors; wherefore now he sought for peace from them, and therefore would deliver to the house of Paris upon certain conditions, this business of La Celle. But how he made his peace with them, I could never yet find, yet certainly he did about this time, for I find that he had for his procurator here, the first professed monk of Paris, (1622) R. F. Gabriel Latham, a Lancastrian, who in 1634 (or 1635) endeavouring to pass a boat over a certain dam there at La Celle, perished in the stream. Others say he was drowned in endeavouring to save a poor boy that was fallen into a deep hole which is at the corner of the Abbot's garden and looks towards Guerard.

The said year 1634 April 2nd (S. V.), died Rev. Fr. Felix Thompson, illustrious for his imprisonments and banishments wonderfully obliging to all and charitable to the poor; he himself being very poor in spirit, to whom of right, according to the word of the Son of God, the kingdom of heaven appertains. He was a monk of St. Malo's.

November 21st, R. F. George Gaire, a monk of Dieulwart, also famous for his enduring of imprisonments and several afflictions for his faith, died in the mission.

This same year the President of the Congregation was empowered from Rome to give all the faculties for missioners that used to be given to the subjects of the King of Great Britain, and to lessen and augment them as he saw convenient. Also all Benedictine monks whatever who laboured in the mission of England were to labour under his Presidentship excepting those of Mount Cassin.

At St. Malo's died R. F. Romuald D'Anvers (August 15th. 1634). He had been a minister and richly beneficed, which he left for his conscience, or rather was deprived of it for professing the Catholic Faith; and being cast into into prison, was with others banished and became a Priest of the Seminary of Douay, which he left to become a monk at St Gregory's in the same town, where he professed on the 24th of June 1620. In which Convent this 1634 on St. Gregory's solemnity there were three novices professed who were brothers, namely Gregory, Maurus, and Placid Scroggs of the Diocese of Chichester in the county of Sussex.

And at Madrid died R. F. Boniface of St. Facundus, a man of singular piety and a most religious conversation, who for many years was procurator of the Congregation of England in Spain, in which he continued so long that he was become as a native of the country. (March 22nd. 1634).

Anno 1635, April 13. S. V. in Oxfordshire, died suddenly Rev. Fr. Justus Rigg otherwise Edner, professed of Valladolid, a person of great learning and talents, who let fall the charge of Presidentship as I have already said.

In the same Shire likewise died R. F. Maurus, otherwise John Curr (June 20th, 1635) a painful missioner, who, banished by the King's edict yet returned again.

Anno 1636, (January 8th.) Father Anselm Williams and Brother Leander Nevill, both professed of Dieulwart, being sent by their Superiors to charitably assist a lady of quality in Lorraine, were met by certain soldiers belonging to the heretical army of Saxon Waymar, near S. Miel and there by them cruelly murdered and, (as may be supposed), in hatred of their religion, hanged on a tree in the wood in their religious habit.

This year swept off several very exemplary Religious at

Dieulwart, the plague raging there at this time; R. Fr. Jocelin Elmer, a very holy and worthy Superior, strengthened them with the holy Sacraments of the Church and his pious exhortations.

Also this year died R. F. Bennet of the Most Holy Trinity, otherwise Edward Smith, a man of a most religious conversation. He was sent to Chelles, thence into England, where he was made tutor and governor of A. Brown, the son and heir of the Lord Viscount Montacute, with whom he travelled &c, and lastly ended his earthly pilgrimage at Madrid in Spain, doing the office of Procurator for the Congregation (July 21st.).

CHAPTER THE FORTY-FIFTH.

THE DEATH OF ABBOT CAVAREL, CUTHBERT FURSDEN &c. THE ROMAN COLLEGE OF ST. GREGORY.

AND now behold we are arrived at the exit of the great Abbot of Arras, the singular patron of this Congregation. The last ten years and remainder of this excellent prelate's life were spent by him in perfecting the building of the new College of St. Vaast, settling the schools and discipline, and defending it from the frequent attempts of the University, which by endeavouring to exclude it from the number of her members, for many years impugned her own felicity. Within this term also he founded a convenient house for the Austin Friars at Bassec, largely contributed towards the setting up the English Franciscan Friars at Douay, and support of other communities elsewhere, and amidst such charitable works (to which he prefixed neither number nor limit) having at length arrived to the desired period to his personal life (for that of his good actions is as endless as the felicities they have merited for him), and that period too, being to give a fuller course to his munificence, being procrastinated to a very old age, his last breath was full of blessings in a particular manner to his beloved convent of St. Gregory. His testament was a new foundation to it, and his last will as liberal as if he then first had begun to provide for it. He gave Almighty God thanks that Divine Providence had pleased to make use of him as an instrument to so great a work so much to the honour of his Creator and ornament and benefits of his blessed Mother the holy Roman Church; he humbly begs of the same goodness to continue the blessing hitherto so plentifully bestowed on it, and as a pledge of his sincere and unalterable affection, he bestows on the Convent a double legacy; the one of a thousand florins of perpetual rent to be added to the Foundation of six hundred florins a year, to the Church of St. Gregory exemption from all expenses upon the fabric, charging the College (of St. Vaast) with all reparations; the other of his heart which he desired might be interred among the Fathers where it had dwelt so many years; and that it might find a place among them after its death which had given them a place where to live. And as having now completed the number of his merits, sent before him to Heaven an unperishable treasure, (and) secure of an eternal mansion in lieu of all those he left on earth to pious uses, he calmly breathed forth his soul into the hands of his Creator in the 84th year of his age, two hours after he had signed the forementioned writing. (December 1st, 1636).

He was a person in whom the perfections of the body and soul seemed to dispute which should outvie each other, on whom nature had conferred such excellent parts, that an addition could not be but supernatural, and which he enjoyed in an eminent degree. His stature was of the middle size, fitted for any condition, neither distinguishing him from others by too large a port in a private life, nor causing disrespect if Providence placed him in a higher station. His countenance was such as spoke him a gentleman; his tongue an orator; his complexion full, without burthen or repletion; his comportment affable, free, accessible, such as begot both love and respect before acquaintance and familiarity. His soul was endowed with moral virtues as a proper foundation for supernatural, all of which seemed to have an equal share in him, but charity predominant. 'Tis hard to say whether he was a better subject or superior, religious or statesman. And as in his conduct he verified the maxim that no one knows well how to govern that has not first learned to obey, so he gave an ample proof that a politician may be a Christian. The civil powers reposed in his hands did not make him forget he was an Abbot, nor command that he was a father, nor confidence with the prince that he was a subject. The settling of the States of Artois whereof he was President did not obstruct his pastoral solicitude of the Abbey, the most beautiful part whereof he built from the ground; and the riches which flowed into his coffers, hindered not the growth of monastic discipline nor the observance of poverty. He reaped nothing but what his own hands had sown, and that with the sweat of his brows; where he found not one penny, he left thousands, and yet gave as liberally as if he had intended to leave nothing. He found that promise literally verified upon himself, that what we leave for God in renouncing the world we shall receive an hundredfold even in this world. The millions he expended upon others did not at all impoverish his family of Religious, to whom he was as much a second founder as he was a first to externs.

His largesses were not at any man's cost but his own; and what he spared out of many embassies, deputations, employments &c, was the only method he used in fulfilling the Evangelical precept, giving alms of what was superfluous, as himself professes in his last testament, and the chapter of that royal Abbey ingenuously confesses. As Abbot he was a great example at home and abroad that superiors ought to command more by actions than by word; as President of the exempt Abbeys of the Low Countries he was a true law-giver, beginning the execution of the excellent statutes he framed from the forming his own household and domestics. As President of the States he was the father of his country and right hand of his Prince. He managed business with as much success as prudence and honesty, and such counsels were held suspected which were not approved by Cavarel. His wisdom very much contributed towards the peace with Holland, and at last concluded it in quality of Plenipotentiary. To perform so considerable a work and bear so illustrious an office, he refused to do heresy that respect, that injury to himself, as to meet it in disguise and without his habit as the rebels did desire before they saw him. But when he arrived the habit and person so became each other that they both forced a veneration from the spectator; while it was hard to determine whether the person made the habit respected or the habit the person. He was the husband of widows, the **father of orphans, a refuge** of the afflicted and shelter of exiles. Such as he patronized he richly founded either by a settled **subsistence, or no less secure** protection. He was one of those admirable **prophets sent by** God, not to pluck **down and** destroy **but to build and establish;** one of those more **than** ordinary Saints who **did wonders in his** life not **by curing the deaf,** the **dumb, and the blind in the** literal sense, **but in the spiritual, which is certainly as more eminent a gift of miracles as the effects are nobler; as spiritual cures surpass the** corporal and **more resemble the Divine nature and savour of his** operation. **In a word, his whole life seems to have been only one** continual act **of charity as that of the Blessed, (and among them, as we** piously confide) **is in heaven; and if the effect did not every where appear 'twas only by defect of an object of his compassion: as we experience the sun doth warm more or less or not at all according as there is body to reflect his light; and in this exercise his Great Master found him, when by death he cited him to give an account of his stewardship, and though men do not know what passed in that rigorous calcule, we are** abundantly **certain that blessed is the servant whom his Master finds thus** doing.

His **body was interred on the left side of the High Altar of his Abbey, within the Sanctuary; his bowels at the English Recollects of Douay, his heart was carried in** great ceremony **to** Saint Gregory's **of Douay and there lies** buried **before the** High Altar under **a great brass plate on which** is engravened a heart held up by **a monk of St. Vaast and an English** Benedictine **monk, with a** label **containing these words:** *"Cor meum jungatur vobis."* **(Let my heart be joined to you). And round** the **four sides of the** plate this inscription: **" Rmi D. D. Philippi Cavarel Antistitis S.** Vedasti Atrebatens: **Fundatoris hujus ædis sacræ, Conventus Gregoriani Collegiique Vedastini, quæ sui monasterii** sumptibus a fundamentis excitavit. **Cor hic conditum est, anno** 1636, 19 Decembris. Obierat Calendis **ejusdem mensis.** Requiescat in pace." **That is: "Here lies, reposed on the 19th of December, 1636, the heart of the most Reverend Lord, Philip Cavarel, Abbot of St. Vaast at Arras, founder of this Church and Convent of St.**

Y

Gregory and of the College of St. Vaast, which he reared up from the very foundations at the cost of his Monastery, and died on the first of December of the year abovesaid."

Anno 1637, February 8th, died the Emperor Ferdinand II, who mightily favoured the Congregation in Germany, where besides Cismar and Rintelin, it obtained Dobran in the Dukedom of Mekelbourg, Scharnabeck in the Dukedom of Lunebourg, Weine in the territory of Brunswick, and Lambspring in the territory of Hildesheim. The original letter of this Emperor dated the 12th of March, 1630, to R. F. Sigebert Bagshaw, then President, is yet extant, wherein he lets him know he had confirmed Rintelin and Scharnabeck, aud that Fr. Clement Reyner had informed him that his paternity intended to set up a Seminary at Rintelin for the instruction of youth, and to employ in that design the revenue of Scharnabeck till, according to the Pope's promise he could meet with a more commodious place; all which his Imperial Majesty does him the honour to approve and applaud.

Anno 1638, February 2nd, died at London R. F. Cuthbert alias John Fursden, noted for a very worthy religious and regular man in his Convent and as charitable in the Mission. He was the happy instrument in the conversion of the noble family of the Faulkland's and many others. The example of Fr. Austin Baker's great piety together with his instructions were the cause of his becoming a monk, though he were his father's eldest son. Douay he chose for his monastery and proved a faithful imitator of his ghostly father, pursuing the conversion of souls more by good example and by prayer than by disputing.

The same year at Paris died Father William Gourdan a Scot. (September 14, 1638).

And the famous Sicilian Benedictine Abbot, Dom Constantine Cajetan aggregated the English Benedictine Congregation to the possession, rights &c, of his Roman College, which only brought great expenses upon the Congregation, it being a huge building which requires much repairing; and so proving of small account, a General Chapter made it be disposed of afterwards. As for the good Abbot, after he had very zealously and very opportunely much bestirred himself for the glory of the Benedictine Order, he pied in the 73rd. year of his age in the year 1641.

CHAPTER THE FORTY-SIXTH.

THE GENERAL CHAPTER OF 1639. NOTICE OF THOSE WHO DIED DURING THE ENSUING TWO YEARS.

ANNO 1639, the seventh General Chapter met at Douay; it was to have been held in 1637; but the Christian Commonweal was in such heat of war, that those who were in office obtained a dispensation to delay the time till now, when R. F. Clement Reyner, who as second elect President had succeeded to R. F. Leander of St. Martin (who had died Dec. 27, 1635), called all by Encyclical letters to Douay for the 9th of August. When they met they decreed superiors should continue, for not to break the constant course of four years, and two years after the Chapter should be held according to its custom. At this the President and Conventual Priors were uneasy and begged to be discharged of their offices, but the fathers would not yield to them. And as for the President, they commanded him in virtue of Holy Obedience to continue on his charge. And because he pleaded his detention at the famous Abbey of St. Peter at Ghent, they allowed him a Vice-President in England like to that of France, to all which with extraordinary humility and modesty he replied nothing but " God's Will and yours be done." And though this Chapter was out of the common course, yet it was such a notable assembly that a curious reader can in nothing better behold the countenance of the Congregation than in the acts of this meeting which are very remarkable and deserve special attention. And here at this time was authenticated their great Bull " Plantata in agro

Dominico," a thing of that consequence to the Congregation as nothing can be more, which gives it all its grandeur and decorum and puts it upon equal terms with all the religious Congregations that ever were or will be.

And Father Francis Walgrave upon humble suit obtained an amnesty for all his past misdemeanours, and strict order was given that none of the Religious should reproach him with anything of what he had done, but that all every where should use him civilly and respectfully.

My Lord Windsor was received into the Confraternity of the Congregation; and humble thanks with a civil refusal were returned to his highness the Abbot of Corvey, who desired the Father's help to begin a University he designed in a place depending on him.

At London died R. F. John Harper who let fall the charge of Presidentship, a man of excellent parts and perfections, and of a rare temper of composition and manners. Imprisonments and banishments hindered him not from consummating his course in the mission. He was a monk of St. Æmilian in Spain. (December 1st, 1639).

Likewise died R. F. Bernard Berington at Paris, the Vice-President of France, a grave reverend monk, also professed in Spain (November 2nd, 1639).

Anno 1640 March 21st. S. V. died in Sussex, R. F. Austin Lee otherwise Johnson, who had vowed to become a monk in Spain sixteen years before he actually became one; a zealous preacher and promoter of the Catholic faith and of a most unblemished life and conversation.

In the prison of the Clink at London died (April 3rd, 1640) R. F. Thomas Preston. There are many books written concerning the oath of allegiance under the name of Widdrington and attributed to him, but he ever more disowned them. The V. R. Father in God Angelus de Nuce, Abbot of Mount Cassin and consecrated (afterwards) Archbishop of Rossano in Calabria, in his notes to the Chronicles of Mount Cassin, magnifies R. F. Gregory Sayr for his great sanctity of life and learning, and next extols this Fr. Preston, calling him first a most learned Divine, then admires his

CHAPTER THE FORTY-SIXTH.

great constancy in having defended the Roman Catholic faith in England for the space of fifty years, whose theological commentaries he had seen in manuscript. See concerning this father the 40th page of these Notes where I have noted some particulars deserving remembrance, as also page 46.

Likewise died the worthy and pious Dame Frances Gawen, first Abbess of Cambray as hath been said (May 7th, 1640).

And Fr. Swithbert Latham, brother to the Fathers Thomas Torquatus Latham, and Joseph Latham. He was a person of singular virtue who gave great edification both in his monastery and in the mission, where after he had laudably executed the office of Provincial in the North, he ended his earthly pilgrimage at Mosborrow(Dec. 15th 1640).

About this time also died full of holiness in the monastery of St. Gislen in Flanders, R. F. Henry Styles who compiled a pithy history of the Martyrs of the Order of St. Benedict who suffered under King Henry VIII. (January 13th. 1640).

Anno 1641 (July 20th) R. F. Laurence Mabbs a courageous professor of the orthodox faith, died in chains for the same in the prison of Newgate at London.

CHAPTER THE FORTY-SEVENTH.

THE EIGHTH GENERAL CHAPTER, 1641: WITH NOTICE OF FATHER AMBROSE BARLO, FR. THOMAS HILL &c.

On the 9th of August began the 8th General Chapter (held at Douay) 1641. R. F. Jocelin Elmer was chosen President, a most exact observer of claustral discipline famous for his sermons, renowned for his skill in physic, and remarkable for his knowledge of chymistry; in a word, a saint of a man by all the memorials that I have been able to meet with concerning him, who in time of the plague administered at Dieulwart the Sacraments with his own hands to his dying Religious.

The Provincial of Canterbury, R. F. Paulinus Greenwood.
Vicar or Vice-President of France and second elect President General, R. F. Francis Hull.

The Prior of St. Gregory's, R. F. John Meutisse.
The Prior of St. Laurence's, R. F. Cuthbert Horsley.
The Prior of St. Benedict's, R. F. Gabriel Brett.
The Prior of Paris, R. F. Francis Cape of St. Joseph.
The Abbess of Cambray, Dame Christina Brent.
The Procurator at Rome, R. F. John Wilfrid who was also named Read and Selby.
The Vicar of the Nuns, R. F. Austin Kinder.
Secretary R. F. Bernard Ribertier, to whom succeeded R. F. Andrew Whitfield.

CHAPTER THE FORTY-SEVENTH.

On the 19th of August S. V. æt. 69, at London died of the plague R. F. Austin Baker. He lies buried at St. Andrew's in Holbrun (Holborn); he belonged to Dieulwart (1641).

On the 10th of September, S. V., R. F. Ambrose, otherwise Edward Barlo, Cathedral Prior of Coventry, (brother to the renowned Fr. Rudesind who professed him at Douay for St. Malo's,) by a cruel death for the orthodox faith, made a glorious and triumphant exit out of this world as may be seen in the Année Bénédictine &c, (1641 Sep.)

Anno 1643, May 14, died Louis XIII surnamed the Just, most Christian king of France, and a most Christian patron of the Congregation by several favours he royally conferred upon it.

Anno 1644, July 29th, died Pope Urban VIII also a singular Patron of the Congregation. He was succeeded by Innocent X.

On the 7th of August died (1644) R. F. Thomas of Saint Gregory otherwise Thomas Hill, who being a Priest in England received the habit by commission from R. F. Leander of St. Martin whilst he was in prison for the faith and condemned to die in 1612; but being afterwards freed he gave great example in the mission as he was a person of singular zeal and piety. He first detected the error of the Illuminati who expected the incarnation of the Holy Ghost from a certain young Virgin. And he died at Douay, æt: 84, of his priesthood 53, of religious profession 33, of his labours in the apostolical mission 50. He was Doctor in Divinity and writ a very devout book entituled "the Plain Pathway to Heaven."

Likewise this year in a good old age in the mission, died R. F. Placid Hartburn (otherwise Foorde) of St. John, there received and professed by order of R. F. Rudesind Barlo. He laboured at least forty years in the mission with great zeal and fruit, exceeding charitable and laborious, and often imprisoned (Sep. 29, 1644).

On the 7th of September at Rome, æt. 65 died the singular patron of the Congregation, the renowned Cardinal Guido Bentivoglio.

CHAPTER THE FORTY-EIGHTH.

SOME ACCOUNT OF FR. WILFRID SELBY, WHO WAS CHOSEN PRESIDENT AT THE CHAPTER 1645; THE DONATION OF LAMBSPRING TO THE CONGREGATION. VARIOUS DEATHS.

ANNO 1645, the 9th General Chapter was held at Douay. Rev. Father Selby was chosen President, who in the world was called Richard, in religion Wilfrid of St. Michael. He died of the plague in Rome 1657. He had writ from Rome to beg of the Fathers not to put him in any office; wherefore R. F. Paul Robinson, upon publication of the election, stood up and in his name renounced the office, producing for so doing a commission of Father Selby; which the Fathers would not admit of. His great learning and piety appears in his works; besides he helped the Reverend Abbot Constantine Cajetan in his edition of St. Peter Damian's works. He lived in high esteem at Rome; by all the great persons of that quick sighted court reputed a saint while his own thought him a courtier; wonderful ready to serve any one who needed his assistance; in a word, a man not born for himself but for the good of all mankind; so humble, that though he was a most accomplished and perfect Divine, yet he obtained that he might not take the degree of Doctor, which the Fathers were forced patiently to bear away with, because of the earnestness with which he sued to them for that freedom; and when upon the death of R. F. Clement Reyner (Abbot of Lambspring) he was chosen to succeed, he refused it; and obtained a Brief of the Pope that R. F. Placid Gascoigne might take on him that Abbatial dignity and continue on his Presidentship to the end of the Quadriennium. But of all the favours he obtained at Rome,

CHAPTER THE FORTY-EIGHTH.   185

none is comparable to (the Bull) "Plantata in agro Dominico."
   The Provincial of Canterbury, R. F. Claud White.
   The Vicar of France, R. F. Paul Robinson.
   The Abbot of Lambspring, the V. R. F. Clement Reyner.
   The Prior of St. Gregory's, R. F. John Meutisse.
   The Prior of St. Laurence's, R. F. Cuthbert Horsley.
   The Prior of St. Benedict's, R. F. Gabriel Brett.
   The Prior of St. Edmund's of Paris, R. F. Francis Cape.
   Abbess of the Nuns at Cambray, Dame Catherine Gascoigne.
   The Procurator at Rome, R. F. Austin Conyers.
   The Vicar of the Nuns at Cambray, R. F. Gregory Mallet.
   Secretary, R. F. Christopher Anderton.
   Confessor to the Nuns at Brussels, R. F. Bernard Palmes.

   At this Chapter, Lambspring, an old German Benedictine Nunnery given (or rather lent, as hath been said) to the Congregation for nuns, was now incorporated to the Congregation for an Abbey of men; because the Elector of Cologne who then held Hildesheim, and therefore was Lord in chief of this territory, would have it so. And because of its dignity, the first place in the Congregation after the Rev. President, is every where given by this Chapter to the Abbot of Lambspring.

   At this place they have a bell which they found there, which proves of wonderful efficacy against thunder when it is rung in time of tempests.

   After great sufferings in the Civil Wars, died this year (1645, August 27th), at Harding Castle in Flintshire R. Father James Anderton, a painful and pious missioner, brother to Christopher, Thomas and Robert Anderton, all monks of the Congregation.

   Item, R. F. Paulin Greenwood of Brentwood in Essex, who was the first professed in the new house of St. Gregory's at Douay on the 10th of January, 1612; the Convent having till then resided at the Trinitarian tenement. After he had laudably executed several offices at home, he was sent into the mission, where he suffered a long imprisonment for the Catholic Faith in the Gatehouse; from whence being at last freed and returning to his monastery, he was appointed Secretary of the Congregation, then Prior of St. Malo's; and finally going back into England

z

he was made Provincial of Canterbury, in which office he died at Oxford on the 27th of November (1645). He was a man of singular moderation and who every where gave most singular satisfaction to all that had to do with him.

At St. Malo's died R. F. Francis Hull, a most devout man and author of several pious books; but mistaking the spiritual conduct of R. F. Austin, caused him very great troubles of which he sorely repented himself on his death-bed. He was the first person buried in the Church of St. Benedict at St. Malo's, and because he was a Prædicator Generalis, they laid him by the pulpit. December 31st (1645).

Anno 1646 (May 22nd), at Worcester died Father John Moundeford, a rare cantor, and companion to Brother Richard Hodgson of St. John in his voyage to St. Martin's monastery at Compostella where he died not without great signs of sanctity. (February 29th, 1626).

On the 10th of July S. N. most gloriously triumphed over civil war and heresy by a cruel death for the holy faith, R. F. Philip Powel, otherwise Morgan, publicly executed at London; though those who condemned him were so taken with his modesty that they became earnest supplicants to obtain his life, and the executioner abhorring to drive the cart away (whereby the person to be executed falls down half strangled) hid himself and the Sheriff could scarce get a man to do so odious an office. He was a monk of Douay, brought up from his childhood by Rev. Fr. Austin Baker.

At St. Malo's died the Lord Bishop thereof, Achilles de Harlay, a great alms giver, who empowered the English monks of his city to sing the office and bury in their Church.

Anno 1648, January 24, died Fr. Francis Gicou, a Breton, professed at Paris for the house of St. Malo under the English obedience. He augmented the library with books, the sacristy with ornaments and plate, very much helped on the building of the Church, spent twenty five years in hearing confessions and such like charitable works of a christian and religious life, and governed for above three years very quietly, that house in very turbulent times.

CHAPTER THE FORTY-NINTH.

THE ELECTIONS AT THE GENERAL CHAPTER OF 1649. BRIEF NOTICES OF SOME OF THE FATHERS WHO DIED IN THE SUCCEEDING QUADRIENNIUM.

Anno 1649, the 10th General Chapter (was) held at Douay.
1st Chosen President, R. F. Placid Gascoigne.
2nd Elect President, R. F. Laurence Reyner.
The Provincial of Canterbury R. F. Claud White.
The Provincial of York, R. F. Laurence Reyner.
The Vicar of France, R. F. Jocelin Elmer.
The Prior of St. Gregory's, R. F. John Meutisse.
The Prior of St. Laurence's, R. F. Cuthbert Horsley.
The Prior of St. Benedict's, R. F. Jocelin Elmer.
The Prior of St. Edmund's, R. F. Francis Cape.
The Abbess of Cambray, Dame Catherine Gascoigne.
The Procurator at Rome, R. F. Austin Conyers.
The Vicar (of the Nuns) at Cambray, R. F. Gregory Mallet.
The Secretary, R. F. Placid Cary, to whom succeeded Rev. F. Hilarion Wake.

Anno 1650, February 8th, S. N. died R. F. Robert Haddock otherwise Benson, one of the first Benedictine missioners who came from Spain and had laboured till now with great fruit in the mission.

Item, May 23rd died R. F. Bennet Cox in the prison of the Clink in London. He was a condemned person and had long endured the imprisonment.

Likewise about this time R. F. Francis Blakestone, brother to F. Michael Blakestone, in the time of the long Parliamentary rebellion, assisting such Catholic soldiers as adventured their lives for their king, ended his days in the employment, (March 6th 1650); as did in attending His Majesty Charles II in Jersey, R. F. Dunstan Everard on the 10th of February (1650), illustrious for his ingenuity, piety and learning, loyalty to his King, love to his country and zeal for the orthodox faith for which he had suffered imprisonments and banishments, and disputing often with the most famous heretics had converted many, amongst which was my Lady Faulkland, illustrious consort to Henry Cary, Viscount Faulkland and Viceroy of Ireland.

As King Charles II much honoured him with his favour, and had taken a wonderful liking to him, his body was brought with great honour from Jersey to St. Malo's the house of his profession and there interred.

Anno 1651, Jan. 12th, died Rev. F. Anthony Batt, monk of Dieulwart, a great promoter and practiser of regular discipline, a famous translator of many pious books into English. He writ a most curious hand and spent much of his time at La Celle where there is a catechism of a large size which he composed at the instance of some of the Fathers in the mission.

On the 1st of July, 1651, died R. F. Jocelin Elmer, famous for his holy and severe life by which he gave a great edification every where. He lies interred at St. Malo's.

And in September King Charles II losing the battle of Worcester was preserved by R. F. John Huddlestone &c, as it is at large written in the ingenious history of Boscobel.

CHAPTER THE FIFTIETH.

THE ELEVENTH GENERAL CHAPTER WAS HELD AT PARIS. THE DEATH OF V. R. CLAUD WHITE AND OTHERS. SOME ACCOUNT OF THE CONVERSION OF KING CHARLES II.

ANNO 1653 in July, Brother John Barter, a novice, son to John Barter (who both coming to Douay there changed their secular warfare to that of religion) dying of the plague (July 1st) and Fr. Christopher Anderton being swept away in the same month by the same infection (July 11th), the President &c, ordered the Chapter to be kept at Paris which was accordingly done, and R. F. Claud White chosen President.

The second elect President, R. F. Laurence Reyner.
The Provincial of Canterbury, R. F. Anselm Crowder.
The Provincial of York, R. F. Gregory Hungate.
The Vicar of France, R. F. John Meutisse.
The Abbot of Lambspring, R. F. Placid Gascoigne.
The Prior of St. Gregory's, R. F. Bernard Palmes.
The Prior of St. Laurence's, R. F. Laurence Reyner.
The Prior of St. Benedict's, R. F. Ildefonse Cliffe was chosen, but at the petition of that Convent R. F. John Meutisse was placed there, though he was chosen Prior of St. Edmund's; whereupon this was placed in his place R. F. Austin Latham, but soon giving it up R. F. Bennet Nelson succeeded.
The Abbess of Cambray, Dame Catherine Gascoigne.
The Prioress of the English Nuns at Paris Dame Brigit More.

CHAPTER THE FIFTIETH.

The Procurator at Rome, R. F. Bernard Palmes.
The Vicar of the Nuns at Cambray, R. F. William Walgrave.
The Vicar of the Nuns at Paris, R. F. Dunstan Pettinger.
Secretary, R. F. Hilarion Wake, who being taken away by the plague (February 20th, 1657), he was succeeded by R. F. Austin Constable.

Anno 1654 January 6 (S. N.), died at London in Drury Lane, R. F. John Owen a man of a flourishing and facetious wit but somewhat scrupulous, having done good service to God and his country in the mission.

Anno 1655 January 7th, died Pope Innocent X to whom succeeded Alexander VII.

October 14th, (1655) at St. Edmund's at Paris died the Rev. F. President, Claud otherwise Bennet White æt. 72, of Priesthood 46, of religious profession 50, having spent 36 years in the mission where he endured miserable imprisonments; often Definitor, often Provincial and twice President General with great applause; a person of rare integrity and of an apostolical spirit, powerful in word and example. He lived in England with my Lord Windsor and afterwards at Weston with Mr. Sheldon. His body was caried to the Royal Benedictine Abbey of St. Germain's at Paris and there honourably interred in the Chapel of St. Margaret; the Rev. General of the Congregation of St. Maur celebrating the funeral, Dom John Darel by name.

And now upon R. F. Laurence Reyner's becoming President, R. F. Cuthbert Horsley became Prior of Dieulwart again.

At Longwood in Hampshire died R. F. William Palmer, professed in Italy, a man of great learning and rare perfection and of long and faithful labours in the mission (May 31st, 1555).

On the 26th of November S. N. died Rev. F. Richard Huddlestone æt. 72, of whom thus his nephew Rev. F. John Huddleston, publishing in 1688 his "Short and plain way to the Faith and Church," in his preface to the reader:

"Please to know the book was long since composed for the medicinal instruction of a private friend by my uncle Mr. Richard Huddleston, the youngest son of Andrew Huddleston of Farington Hall in Lancashire. He was born towards the end of the reign of Queen Elizabeth ; when he arrived at years of maturity for studies he was sent to Rhemes in France where he became an exquisite proficient in poetry and rhetoric ; from Rhemes **he** went to Rome where he passed his schools of philosophy and divinity with an improvement proportionable to his great wit and industry. **These studies** completed, that he might effectually advance as **well** in piety as learning, he **entered** into **a religious** state and was professed **at famous** Mount Cassin, ye chief monastery founded by the H. Patriarch St. Bennet in Italy. In this H. Place he spent divers years in solitude, Prayer, Reading ye Scriptures, Councils, Fathers, &c, in which theory having attained to an eminent degree of perfection, **at length thoroughly qualifyed for an** apostolick missioner **he returned into England.** Here like another St. Austin endued with **an Evangelical spirit he** exercised his talents in Preaching, teaching, Disputing and reducing his stray'd countrymen to the sheepfold of Christ. And it pleased ye Divine goodness to bless his endeavours and second his words with extraordinary successe. In all as well publick debates as private Conferences he still came off a conqueror in **so much yt many chiefe families as those of ye Irelands,** Watertons, **Middletons, Traps's, Thimbelby's** &c, **in Yorkshire; Those** of ye **Prestons,** Andertons, Downs, Straffords, **Sherbourns, Inglebys** &c, **in Lancashire** with **numberles others of all states and** conditions, **owe** next to God their Respective Reconciliacions to this Worthy Benedictine. But I do not pretend to frame here a Panegyrick, it may suffice in short to averr; That ye **Purity** of his life bore equal measures **with ye** Candour of his **Doctrine,** both unblemish'd: and yt after **thirty years of faithful labours in Christ's Vineyard,** he rested in **Peace,** leaving behind him a sweet odour of vertue to all Posterity. He writ on several occurrences several Treatises of which one is **this small but fortunate** Book **we now** publish, **Fortunate I say for that, God so ordaining, it** became an occasional **instrument towards the Conversion of our Late** Soveraign King Charles **II to ye faith and** unity of ye Catholic Church.

To explain myself in this matter; the malignity of the times and ye disasters ensuing thereupon for above these 40 years have been too pernicious to be soon forgotten. There are none so

CHAPTER THE FIFTIETH.

ignorant who have not heard of the defeat of his late Majesty's army by the Rebels of Worcester on ye 3rd Sept: 1651, and of ye then Preservation of his sacred life and Person by the care and fidelity of his Catholic subjects, of whom I acknowledge myself the most unworthy. In this sad Conjecture it was that the Desolate King after having been harass'd to and fro, night and Day in Continual Fatigues and Perils, from Wednesday the day of ye Battle till Sunday following (ye particulars of which are out of the sphere of my present design to enlarge upon), at last found an assylum and Refuge at Mr. Whitgrave's house at Mosely, whither Divine Providence not long before brought me, and where I had first ye honour of attending upon him. During this Retreat, whilst Mr Whitgrave's Lady and Mother (who alone of all ye family were Privy to ye secret) were often busy in watching and other discharges of their Duty toward his accomodacion and safeguard, His majesty was pleased to entertain himselfe for the most part with me in my chamber, by perusing several of my Books, amongst others he took up this present Treatise then a manuscript lying on the Table of a closet adjacent to my chamber. He read it. He seriously consider'd it and after mature deliberacion pronounc'd this sentence upon it (Vizt), I have not seen any thing more plain and cleare upon this subject, the arguments here drawn from succession are so conclusive I do not conceive how they can be denied. Now that this was not any sudden mocion or superficial complement of his Majesty but ye product of a real and solid Conviction is Manifest by the Tenor and Gravity of ye words themselves; by the Papers found in his Closet after his Decease under his own hand, which seem even to the Very manner of expression to Breathe the same spirit and Genius with yt of ye Book; and lastly, by those truely christian Catholic Resolutions he took (albeit thro' frailty late) in disposeing himselfe for an happy departure out of this world by an Entire Reconcilement to God and the Church."

Anno 1657 (April 25th), died F. James Shirburn of Little Milton near Whally in Lancashire. The second time he was sent into England he was taken at his landing and cast into prison where he confuted some ministers who came to dispute with him.

CHAPTER THE FIFTIETH.

On the 31st of July (1657) at Rouen in Normandy died Fr. Maurus (otherwise Nicholas Pritchard) as he was on his journey for Paris where the General Chapter was to meet; he was a monk of Douay.

In August (the 21st) died Fr. Peter Warnford, who being a Secular Priest in the Mission, received the holy habit in England; and together with himself bequeathed to us, says Rev. F. Sadler, that inestimable relic of the Holy Thorn, which is now carefully kept by the Dean of the Rosary in London.

This relic belonged to the famous Abbey of Glastonbury before the suppression of Catholic religion in England.

In the Parliamentary rebellion some papers of affairs regarding the Secular Catholic clergy of England were taken and printed at London anno 1643, where in a letter to the Bishop of Chalcedon are these words: "I must not omit to certify your Lordship that I have inserted Mr. Peter Warnford's name amongst those who are suggested here to be made Canons; and I should humbly desire he may be made such for one main reason above others that I have a probable hope hereby to secure the Chapter of the Holy Thorn after his decease: and that is a Jewel which I am sure your Lordship values at a high rate, as do all others that know thereof."

As to the Chapter here mentioned, 'tis but an imagined business, first devised by Dr. Bishop, Titular Bishop of Chalcedon and continued by his successor Dr. Smith, but could never get to be confirmed at Rome, as Dr. Leyburn declares openly in his Encyclical answer in 1661.

CHAPTER THE FIFTY-FIRST.

THE ELECTIONS AT THE GENERAL CHAPTER OF 1657. DEATH OF F. MICHAEL GASCOIGNE, &c.

THE twelfth General Chapter (1657) was kept at Paris where R. F. Paul Robinson was chosen President.
The Provincial of Canterbury, R. F. Anselm Crowder.
The Provincial of York, R. F. Augustine Hungate.
The Prior of St. Gregory's, R. F. Bennet Stapylton.
The Prior of St. Laurence's, R. F. Cuthbert Horsley.
The Prior of St. Benedict's, R. F. Gabriel Brett.
The Prior of St. Edmund's, R. F. Francis Cape.
The Abbess of Cambray, Dame Catherine Gascoigne.
The Procurator at Rome, R. F. Bernard Palmes.
The Vicar of the Nuns, at Cambray, R. F. Leander Normington.
Secretary R. F. Austin Constable to whom succeeded R. F. Bernard Millington.

At this Chapter Abbot Cajetan's Roman College cost the Congregation £600 sterling, to make up which sum each residence, namely Lambspring, Douay, Dieulwart, St. Malo, and Paris gave one hundred pounds.

In October (17th, 1657) F. Michael Gascoigne, brother to the Abbot of Lambspring, a painful missioner, died in the North, in his return from York homewards.

At St. Malo's died (August 20th, 1657) F. Maurus Roe, brother to F. Alban Roe who suffered for the faith at London; among other good qualities, he was an excellent cantor.

CHAPTER THE FIFTY-FIRST.

In the North again died **Fr. Robert Hungate, a zealous missioner,** professed in Spain, brother to R. F. Austin **Hungate, who was** afterwards President (Oct. 18th, 1657).

Anno 1659, R. F. Paul Robinson laid down **his charge of Presidentship,** finding the charge too troublesome, which the Fathers at the next Chapter took very ill. R. F. **Cuthbert Horsley, second-elect** President, succeeded in the charge.

The same year (May 25th, 1659) died **Father Constance** [Nathal alias Mathews], who suffered very much for the **orthodox faith,** and being prisoner in **London was** wonderfully **delivered out of** his restraint after his fervent prayer. He was a painful Missioner in Norfolk.

CHAPTER THE FIFTY-SECOND.

THE 13TH GENERAL CHAPTER OF 1661 WHEN THE DEPENDENCE ON SPAIN WAS BROKEN.

ANNO 1661 the thirteenth General Chapter was kept at Douay where R. F. Austin Hungate was chosen President.

Second elect President R. F. Bennet Stapylton.

The Provincial of Canterbury, R. F. Anselm Crowder.

The Provincial of York, R. F. Bede Taylard.

In the residences no change happened but at St. Malo's where R. F. Thomas Anderton became Prior.

The Procurator at Rome, R. F. Leander Normington.

The Vicar of Cambray, (upon the refusal of R. F. John Barter), R. F. Leander Pritchard.

Secretary, R. F. Laurence Appleton.

King Charles II ordered the Fathers to nominate to him so many of their body whom he was resolved to maintain at London at the chapel of his Queen. In this affair R. F. Paul Robinson was very active and wonderfully acceptable to his Majesty, whom he had the honour of visiting during his royal exile in the company of R. F. Dunstan Everard.

The Fathers hitherto had been very rigid in exacting of the Presidents that they should neither be installed in England nor live there during the time of their office, but on the Continent either in Flanders, France, Lorraine or Germany. The first with whom they dispensed with in this point was R. F. Claud White in 1653, but now not only the President but even the Definitors were left free to live in England or out of England.

Moreover the Fathers finding it an excessive trouble to the Congregation to expect every General Chapter's election of a President to be confirmed by the General of Spain before he could be installed, upon diligent review and consideration of their great Bull "Plantata in Agro Dominico," they found this Spanish dependency abrogated. And as they had acquainted the Spanish General with the inconveniences the Congregation endured thereupon, they resolved for the future to embrace the freedom the Pope had conferred on them and not compliment away the happiness and prosperity of the Congregation, especially since this dependence was nothing more than respectful civility in regard of the Spaniards, while at the same time it proved to the English Congregation and mission very nocivous and perniciously inconvenient; such a grievance, through Spain being so far off, that it was enough to ruin all. Wherefore the Fathers having maturely weighed all things, they took those resolutions which they published in the General Chapter of 1661, namely that the English Benedictine Congregation no longer depended on that of Spain.

Likewise they strictly forbade their religious to concern themselves with the odious fooleries of Blacklo (alias Thomas White) and will allow no one to read his detestable books but with the express leave of R. F. President, under pain of privation of active and passive voice &c; they command them never to maintain such execrable opinions, and with great constancy the Congregation hath ever since very laudably kept steady to this judgment.

Furthermore, the house of St. Malo through the admission of French, being become a greater trouble to the Congregation than it could manage in a foreign country where the Fathers were unknown and had no friends to support them, they resolved to put it off the best way they could. The Royal Council of France was alarmed at the establishment of Englishmen bred up in Spain fixed in such a seaport town in France; and the Parliament of Brittany was so contrary to them on the said account that when Louis XIII had piously given his royal consent that the Fathers might have the Abbey of St. Jacut in the said province, (the Abbot and convent having agreed to it) they would never verify the agreement or transaction whereby it had no effect.

And at this Chapter Rev. F. John Huddleston was made Cathedral Prior of Worcester.

Anno 1662 (May 11th.) at Paris, died F. Basil Cheriton, one who had a natural aversion to all manner of flesh meats.

CHAPTER THE FIFTY-THIRD.

THE ESTABLISHMENT OF THE ENGLISH BENEDICTINE DAMES AT PARIS, 1662. THE CASE OF F. TRESHAM. VARIOUS DEATHS.

TIME hath now brought us to the settlement of the pious swarm of our Cambray bees at Paris. The Convent of Cambray was fallen into sad circumstances through losses it endured in England under the usurpation of Oliver Cromwell; wherefore after many thoughts of what might be most expedient, (the Fathers tendered them like the apple of their eye, and so had stretched to the utmost they were able to help them), nothing was found so much to the purpose as to try to begin a new house at Paris. In order to this, some worthy Dames they sent to Paris, the chief of which was the honoured Dame Clementia Cary, daughter to Viscount Faulkland, Viceroy of Ireland in the reign of king Charles I, a lady of great virtue and example, as she was dear to the Queen-Mother Henrietta of France, the royal consort of the said king, while she abided in her Court. Her Majesty conserving the said kind affection to her, very charitably favoured the attempt and inclined thereto the two Queens of France Anne of Austria and Marie Thérèse; but the times were then dreadful even to the highest conditions. Also the honourable Dames of the great Parisian convent of Mount Carmel and those of Port Royal with their directors, were very charitable to them. To make short, after the ordinary inconvenience of beginnings, in change of lodgings &c, M. de

Touche on the solemnity of St. Gregory the Great, 1664, bestowed a house on them in Lark fields where they have continued ever since; and because the Archbishop would not consent to their establishment unless they were totally subject to his authority, the Fathers let go their right &c, and yet gave them letters whereby they are still considered as Sisters of the Congregation; and ordered the Convent of St. Edmund's (as the nearest to them) to treat them as such, and they were to have the same considerations for the Congregation which hath been so kind as to give them out of its bosom those for their Confessors whom they have most desired, though necessary elsewhere.

And now I turn to obits again. As last year at Little Stoke in Oxfordshire æt. 66, died Father George Bacon (brother to Judge Bacon and to an Ignatian of that name), a learned and prudent man and an excellent preacher: (April 4th, 1663).

Item, F. William Johnson otherwise Chambers, æt: 80 and more, in my Lord Dorset's house in Charter-house yard at London, an ancient professed of Spain and a famous missioner. (October 28th, 1663):

And Father Bernard Palmes upon his return to Rome at Gratz in Styria, in a monastery of the Order, where he was very honourably interred (Christmas day, 1663):

So likewise this 1664, on the 8th of April died R. F. Laurence Reyner, the elder brother of R. F. Clement Reyner, who after he had laudably executed the chief offices of the Congregation was in his old age sent into the Mission, in which he died in the North upon Good Friday, æt. 82. He was wonderfully zealous in gaining souls to heaven, a patient sufferer of many persecutions and long imprisonments, and a great promoter of regular discipline.

On the 19th of May 1664, Ascension Day, at Hereford, æt. 88, died blind, R. F. George Berington a laborious missioner, brother to R. F. Bernard Berington the continual Vice-President of France.

July 2nd (S. N.) Fr. Richard King otherwise Scott died suddenly at Sir Francis Dorington's house in Somersetshire in his return from Wells to his residence at Leighland.

CHAPTER THE FIFTY-THIRD.

August 13th. died Br. Peter Huitson, the first lay-brother of Douay, almost one hundred years old.

In September Sir Henry Gifford was interred at St. Edmund's at Paris with this epitaph which stands in the Church:

D. O. M.

In Spem Resurrectionis
Hic jacet Henricus Gifford de Burstall
In Comitatu Leicestriæ in Anglia Baronettus
Vir cui laudes addere est mortuum lædere
Quia laudari se vivum nunquam permisit.
Laudarunt tamen cuncti et amarunt
Quippe qui tum fide tum moribus vere Catholicus
Vitiis dum vivebat moriebatur
Adeoque cœlo maturus inter preces Benedictinorum quos adamavit
Mortuus est
Parisiis die XXVII Septembris, anno Domini M.D.C.LXIV
Ætat. suæ XXXI

*Vivit tamen prole quam Maria Vaughan de Ruerden in comitatu Glocester
Illi peperit, viamque morte ad vitam stravit.
Peperit quidem cœlu tres, Marian, Henricum, et alium Henricum:
Annam et Elizabetham Deo et Sancto Benedicto.
Johannem non tam bonorum hæredem, Patriæ et pauperibus.
Qui marmor hoc mœrens posuit
Requiescat in Pace.*

Englished. To God, most great, most good.

In hopes of rising again here lies Henry Gifford of Burstall in Leicestershire in England, Knight, Baronet. To praise him would be an injury to him since when living he would never suffer it, though every one loved him and praised him, for that as to faith and manners he was a true Catholic and died to vice whilst he lived, wherefore ripe for Heaven he expired amidst the prayers of Benedictines whom he had always loved, aged 31, in the year 1664 at Paris on the 27th of September. Yet he lives in his issue by Mary Vaughan of Ruerden in Gloucestershire who died before him and so showed him the way to Heaven by her example. Their three first children, namely Mary, Henry, and another Henry died in their innocency, Anne and Elizabeth became Benedictine Nuns, and John, whom he did not leave so much to inherit his estate as to serve his native soil and befriend the poor; who in his sorrow erected this monument. Requiescat in Pace.

Anno 1665, R. F. Robert Sherwood famous for his piety and learning having discreetly managed the chief offices of the Congregation died in the mission at Kiddington in Oxfordshire, æt. 77 (Jan. 17, 1665).

R. F. William Walgrave died suddenly at Flixton in Suffolk (January 21st) by falling down from a pair of stairs, æt 77; he was a very charitable man and did much to help up the house of Cambray.

Item (September 8th), R. F. Leander Normington or Norminton who of a Cambridge scholar, became not only a convert but a monk of Douay; esteemed a clear wit and solid judgment, well learned and an excellent poet both in English and Latin.

Item R. F. Gabriel Brett, æt: 66, who had behaved himself in many offices of the Congregation and the mission very worthily as became his birth. He was son of Sir Alexander le Brett of White Stanton and Somersetshire and became a monk of St. Malo's under his uncle R. F. Gabriel Gifford, who gave him his name of Gabriel whereas otherwise his name was Robert. (Aug. 12, 1665).

Likewise at London (Aug. 15) died R. F. Dunstan Pettinger, a painful labourer and zealous preacher for a long time in the Mission.

Anno 1666, January 20, died Anne of Austria, Queen mother of France in the 65th year of her age.

"Et Soror et conjux et mater, nataque regum
"Nulla unquam tanto sanguine digna fuit."

The Convent of St. Edmund's at Paris is highly indebted for ever to her charity and piety for that she obtained them such a great grant that the Chancellor of France thinking it too much for strangers, would not seal it; and frequently she did them the honour of visiting their poor Chapel (which was then a miserable spectacle), especially when her son Louis the Great used to come and fetch her Majesty from her holy retreats at her royal nunnery of Val de Grace.

On the 5th of May (1666) æt. 78, died at London in the Old Bailey, R. F. Anselm Crowder (or Crowther) who was singularly devoted to the Blessed Virgin, to whose honour he set up a noble confraternity of the Rosary at London; the Altar was in honour of our Blessed Lady of Power and it became a powerful object of devotion and was as powerfully maintained, for Robert, Earl of Cardigan was Prefect of the Sodality.

The same year (May 5th 1666) died R. F. John Meutisse, after some time laudably spent in the Mission and several offices well executed in the Congregation; who very much helped the good Nuns of Cambray in their beginnings.

While he (F. Meutisse) was Prior of Douay, Father Francis Tresham, a Definitor of the Congregation and Cathedral Prior of Gloucester, without leave of his Superiors became an English Recollect at Douay; whereupon Fr. Meutisse pursued the Guardian for having so received him; and the Provincial of the Franciscans the learned Marchantius, ordered Father Tresham to put on his Benedictine habit and present himself before the Fathers assembled in their General Chapter in 1649, to obtain their leave for his change of habit and life.

CHAPTER THE FIFTY-FOURTH.

THE GENERAL CHAPTER OF 1666. BRIEF ACCOUNTS OF SOME OF THE FATHERS WHO DIED DURING THE ENSUING YEARS.

THE fourteenth General Chapter which last year should have been held at Douay was put off till now, because the plague was very strong at Douay; and it began at the old Bailey at London at the first of May, where the Fathers continued President R. F. Austin Hungate and likewise the second elect President, and those who were at that time Provincials.

    The Prior of St. Gregory's, R. F. Austin Coniers.
    The Prior of St. Laurence's, R. F. Cuthbert Horsley.
    The Prior of St. Benedict's, R. F. Bennet Nelson.
    The Prior of St. Edmund's, R. F. Michael Cape.
    At Cambray, the Abbess and Vicar continued.
    Secretary, R. F. William Hitchcock.
    At Lambspring died (Dec. 11th, 1666) Dr. Bennet otherwise Robert Meering. At 60 years of his age he became a monk and lasted to the 70th year of his age. He had attended the famous Sir Walter Raleigh in his sea-voyages.

    Anno 1667 died Pope Alexander VII, to whom succeeded Clement IX.

    Father George, otherwise Bernard Millington, who succeeded Mr. King or Scott in his western employment in the Mission, likewise died suddenly in his return from Taunton to his residence at Leighland, aged about 40. He was professed of Dieulwart (April 9th, 1667).

R. F. Francis Crathorne professed of Douay, an excellent poet and humanist, died at the three Sister Cumberford's house in Warwickshire, aged about 69. (April 19th. 1667).

Father Swinburn, likewise professed of Douay, a very devout and good religious man, there ended his days, aged about sixty (June 23rd 1667). He once petitioned the General Chapter that he might live a hermit at the hermitage of St. Blandin which belongs to La Celle.

At Longwood in Hampshire, aged 66, on the 6th of August, died R. F. Paul otherwise Robert Robinson, descended of a noble family, a famous lawyer before he came to religion, a finely spoken man and very polite in all respects. In applying himself to religion (and) to holy studies, he became a famous preacher, passed Doctor in Divinity, was made Cathedral Prior of Ely, chosen President, (and was) designed by King Charles II for one of those who were to have accompanied him if Sir George Booth's undertaking had succeeded.

Father John Barter, who of a stout soldier becoming a monk (together with his son) after his wife's death, was, from the Convent of Douay, the place of his profession, sent into the mission where he laudably behaved himself and died by a fall from his horse not far from Guildford, (August 11th, 1667), aged 68.

Likewise died R. F. Godrick Blount of Falley in Berkshire, Prior of Douay, who was very charitable to the Nuns of Cambray. This triennium (for the Chapter being held a year later than ordinary, made it no more) Douay saw three Priors, (Sep. 12th. 1667).

Anno 1668, at London, æt: 70, died of a dead palsy R. F. Austin Stoker, (or Stocker) commonly called Dr. Stoker by reason of his great skill and practice in physic for which he had leave, (April 18th).

At Paris within a day of each other died the RR. Fathers Francis Cape, professed of Douay (Jan 30), and Michael Cape professed of Dieulwart, (Jan 29th, 1668). F. Francis was about the age of 66 a very regular, abstemious and exemplary man, who through many quadrienniums was Superior of Paris. Father Michael was his younger brother and about the age of 58, very zealous in his duty and had been also Prior of Paris.

At Dieulwart died R. F. Placid Johnson who acquitted himself with great industry of the office of Cellerarius of that convent and was lamented by all his brethren who lost very much in being deprived of his assistance (November 3rd, 1668).

CHAPTER THE FIFTY-FIFTH.

THE 15TH. GENERAL CHAPTER IS HELD AT ST. JAMES', LONDON. EVENTS IN THE SUCCEEDING QUADRIENNIUM.

ANNO 1667, the 15th General Chapter was held at St. James' London, where R. F. Bennet Stapylton was chosen President.

The second-elect President and Provincial of Canterbury R. F. Gregory Mallet.

The Prior of St. Gregory's, R. F. William Hitchcock.

The Prior of St. Laurence's, R. F. Cuthbert Horsley.

The Prior of St. Edmund's, R. F. Thomas Anderton but upon his refusal, R. F. Joseph Sherburne.

The Priory of St. Malo's was now in the hands of the monks of St. Maur.

The Abbess of Cambray, Dame Catherine Gascoigne again.

Their Vicar R. F. Alexius Caryll.

The Secretary, R. F. Placid Bettenson.

R. F. Francis Morgan, nobly born (sometimes I note this and sometimes I have not minded, for that true nobility is solid virtue) at Weston in Warwickshire, a diligent labourer and great sufferer in the Mission, died in Hampshire about the age of sixty-seven (Sep. 8th, 1669).

And at Dieulwart Father Maur Flucot, (or Flutot) a Lorrainer, yet professed of that house, after a long and tedious infirmity of the stone patiently endured. It is an argument his exemplarity was very remarkable, R. F. Bennet Nelson coveting his help at St. Malo's, (Oct. 2, 1669).

CHAPTER THE FIFTY-FIFTH.

Near Paris died Maria Henrietta of France, Queen mother of England who on all occasions showed her royal favour to the Congregation.

Anno 1670 died Pope Clement IX to whom succeeded Clement X.

Anno 1671 (April 26th) died Dame Clementia Cary who led a most holy life and may justly be esteemed the beginner of the English Benedictine Nuns at Paris.

In England at Sir Francis Hungate's in Yorkshire, near upon the age of sixty soon after his coming into the Mission, died R. F. Thomas Anderton (Oct. 9th. 1671), who everywhere gave very extraordinary example, one while Superior at Paris, another while at St. Malo's a very charitable missioner; but in his Convent, through I know not what scruple, refused entirely the mitigation and kept perpetual abstinence.

In Herefordshire died R. F. Anselm Cassy after he had for a long time laboured fruitfully in the Mission. (October 28th, 1671).

At London R. F. Gregory Scroggs, after a long time spent in the Mission was seized on by a sudden apoplexy, as is supposed, and fell down in the street and immediately expired, aged about fifty-six (November 3rd, 1671).

Anno 1672 January 2nd, died R. F. Austin Hungate professed at Mount Serrat in Spain, who was very much liked in Presidentship, and caused the Convent of St. Malo's to be put altogether into the hands of the French Benedictines of the Congregation of St. Maur, for a certain rent to be yearly paid of two hundred pistoles to the English Congregation. And having given singular example of piety and virtue to all with whom he conversed, he ended his earthly pilgrimage in Yorkshire at the house of the Lady Fairfax his niece in the venerable old age of eighty-eight.

And Father John Martin, soon after his ordination sent to give his old father a visit, fell sick of the small pox in his way thither, and before he could reach home, died at Wells happily assisted by a very able Father of his own Congregation, and having sent for and seen his said father before his death. (April 30, 1672).

CHAPTER THE FIFTY-SIXTH.

THE GENERAL CHAPTER OF 1673; DEATH OF RR. FF. SERENUS CRESSY, PETER SALVIN AND OTHERS.

ANNO 1673, the 16th General Chapter was kept at Douay, where Dr. Stapylton was again chosen President General.

Second-Elect President, R. F. Austin Conyers.

The Provincial of Canterbury, R. F. Gregory Mallet.

The Provincial of York, R. F. Bede Taylard.

The Prior of St. Gregory's, R. F. William Hitchcock.

The Prior of St. Laurence's, R. F. Gregory Hesketh.

The Prior of St. Edmund's, R. F. Austin Latham, upon whose refusal R. F. Joseph Shirburn was again Prior.

Abbess of Cambray, Dame Maura Hall.

Their Vicar, R. F. Placid Shafto.

The Procurator at Rome, R. F. Austin Latham.

Secretary, R. F. Francis Fenwick.

Anno 1674 (January 12th) æt. 30, died R. F. Mellitus Hesketh in the mission, *re et nomine* Mellitus, and therefore much bewailed by all that knew him, whom he had exceedingly obliged by all offices of charity and civility.

At East Grinsted Sussex (Aug. 10th, 1674), died R. F. Serenus otherwise Hugh Cressy of Thorpe Salvin in Yorkshire, who with four others professed at Douay on the 22nd of August 1649. His true name is Hugh Paulin de Cressy. He was a protestant Doctor in Divinity, Prebend of Windsor, and Dean of Leighlin in Ireland. R. F. Cuthbert Fursden contributed to his conversion by his pious conversation. Fr. Cressy has left written several pieces of controversy and a remarkable Church history of Great Britain. He died very piously, carried off with the stone accompanied with a fever in the 68th year of his age.

Anno 1675 R. F. Peter Salvin of Thornton in the Diocese of Durham, after he had painfully and profitably laboured for a long time in the Mission, being withdrawn in his old age to Dieulwart and there charitably assisting certain of the English diseased soldiers who were quartered in the neighbourhood, he fell sick of a fever and died aged about seventy, a most wonderful candid, sincere soul, and a very devout man (January 22nd,).

In Northumberland died Father Roland Dunn (Aug. 20th 1675) a Scotch monk of Wirtzburg in Germany, aggregated to this Congregation as have been several others from divers places, as Lorrainers, Flemings, Irish, Scotch, French and Portuguese; yet sparingly, for that such subjects are not the affair of this Congregation which might still have retained St. Malo's if French had never been taken in there.

Anno 1676 (February 21,) Father Austin Kinder an ancient Missioner and a virtuous exemplary man died in Herefordshire, aged about eighty; and F. Eleyson Thomas another missioner in Berkshire aged about sixty-six (January 25).

And to Pope Clement X succeeded Innocent XI.

On the 20th of March in the Nunnery of Cambray died Mrs. Hall of High Meadow. She retired thither two years before her death; her life was very pious which she concluded with a happy end. She was a good friend and benefactress to that Nunnery and lies buried amongst them near to her daughter and granddaughter who had both been exemplary religious there; and her youngest daughter who was Abbess when she died, lies buried in the same grave with her with this following epitaph:

M. S.

Ornatissimæ Matronæ Domnæ Annæ Hall Angliæ,
Illustri Marchionum Wigornensium
In Anglia stemmate oriundæ
et

D. Benedicti Hall de High Meadow
In agro Glocestriensi Toparchæ
Conjugi et viduæ
quæ
Ultima pœne senectute Patriæ simul
Et sæculo renuntians ut sibi
Vacaret et Deo, ex hoc
Monasterio in cœlum
Migravit Mart. 20
An. Salutis. 1676
Æt. suæ 79

What follows is on the same stone.

In spem resurrectionis
Hic dormit

R. A. D. Catharina Hall hujus Monasterii quondam Abbatissa. Fuit insigni patientia, pietate et prudentia ornata, suavitate morum multum amabilis, immortalem animam Patri Creatori sanctissime reddidit, mortale quod a creatura habuit matri in hoc tumulo jacenti, pia gratitudine restituit die 17 Martii An. 1692.

Requiescant in pace.

Englished. To the memory of the most accomplished matron Mrs. Ann Hall by birth an Englishwoman descended from the illustrious Marquesses of Worcester in England, and consort and widow of Mr. Bennet Hall, Lord of High Meadow in Gloucestershire; who in the extremity of her age renouncing her native soil and the world that she might attend to God and herself, from this Monastery departed to Heaven on the 20th of March in the year of salvation 1676 and the 79th of her age.

In the hope of rising again here sleeps the most Reverend Dame Catharine Hall formerly Abbess of this Monastery, endowed with egregious patience, adorned with piety and prudence, very amiable for the sweetness of her manners, she gave up most piously her immortal soul to the Father Creator; what she had of a mortal from a creature she restored out of pious gratitude to her mother resting in this tomb, 17th of March in the year 1692. May they rest in peace.

The same year died Dame Catharine Gascoigne honoured with this epitaph:

Here lies our venerable mother M. Catherine Gascoigne Abbess forty years of this Convent of our B. Lady of Consolation of the holy Order of St. Benedict and English Congregation, being one of the nine first that began this house. She professed the first day of the Holy year 1625, was made Abbess 1629 at twenty eight by dispensation from Rome, renewed nine times, twice more generally desired. In her first cessation from the Abbeyship 1643 she reformed the monastery of St. Lazarus. In her last 1673, she kept her Jubilee with that of the honse, suffered with remarkable patience grievous infirmities and died piously the 21st of May, 1676, the 76th year of her age and the 53rd of her entry into religion. She was born of Catholic and pious parents, descended from the Lord Chief Justice Gascoigne who imprisoned Harry V when he was Prince. She was a most worthy Superior ever seeking to establish religious observance by efficacious exhortations and edifying example: most especially labouring to plant and conserve the spirit of true internal prayer and tendance to God, the faithful and humble pursuit of which she inculcated as well by her own most assiduous practice, as incessant recommendation living and dying.

Requiescat in pace.

During the time of this Lady Abbess in 1633 on the 18th of August died Dame Gertrude More: amidst the disciples of R. F. Austin Baker she was singularly memorable for her holiness of life.

CHAPTER THE FIFTY SEVENTH.

SOME EVENTS CONNECTED WITH THE MONASTERY OF ST. EDMUND THE KING AT PARIS. THE BENEFACTIONS OF KING LOUIS THE GREAT TO THE SAME CONVENT.

Anno 1677 February 28, Shrove Sunday M. L'Abbé Noailles (now Archbishop of Paris and Cardinal) blessed the new Church of St. Edmund's at Paris. The first stone of it was laid on the 29th of May 1674 by the Princess Mary Louise, Daughter of Philip, Duke of Orleans and brother to Louis the Great, King of France. Her mother was Henrietta of England, sister to the Kings Charles II and James II. In 1679 she became Queen of Spain and died on the 12th of February 1689, ætat: 27, after only three days sickness having received the last Sacraments with exemplary piety, making an end worthy of the religion and wisdom the gravity of Spain had admired in her green age. At her laying the said first stone, M. L'Abbé Mountaigu, first almoner to the Queen of England, officiated. Louis the Great her uncle in consideration of Henrietta of France, her grandmother and his aunt, granted the English Benedictines letters of establishment at Paris in October 1650 at Bordeaux, on condition of a solemn Mass at the feast of St. Louis for the health and prosperity of his Majesty and his royal successors for ever.

And at Versailles on the 9th of September, 1674, he granted to those who were professed of the house of Paris the grace of naturalization, giving them power and right to enjoy the benefices of their Order in his kingdom as if they had been born his subjects, and extended the said favour to the rest of the houses of the Congregation, if being within his dominions their Superiors send them to the Convent of Paris and that they there go on with their studies as far as Master of Arts. He enlarged this favour and confirmed it at the camp of Nydrecassel the 10th of June 1676. Moreover his majesty gave to help their new building at Paris seven thousand livres; and hath given for a long time about twenty-five pounds English a year to the Convents of their Congregation at Douay, Dieulwart, Paris and Cambray, which has only ceased this 1709. And to Dieulwart he gives them their salt free; a great charity considering their country *ménages*. Douay Convent (as I have been told by one of that place) esteems his royal favour worth to them about one hundred pounds English a year. So his royal predecessors, Pepin and Charles the Great cherished and protected the English Benedictines of their times.

CHAPTER THE FIFTY-EIGHTH.

THE GENERAL CHAPTER OF 1677. BRIEF NOTICES OF RR. FATHERS AUSTIN LATHAM, CUTHBERT HORSLEY, LIONEL SHELDON; OF BR. WILFRID REEVES. THE OUTBREAK OF OATES PLOT, WHICH CAUSED THE DEATH OF BR. THOMAS PICKERING AND ARCHBISHOP PLUNKET.

AT the 17th General Chapter held at Douay (1677) R. F. Stapylton was continued President.
Second elect President R. F. Austin Latham.
The Provincial of Canterbury, R. F. Gregory Mallet.
The Provincial of York, R. F. Francis Lawson.
The Prior of St. Gregory's, R. F. Austin Howard.
The Prior of St. Laurence's, R. F. John Girlington.
The Prior of St. Edmund's, R. F. Austin Latham.
The Abbess of Cambray, Dame Christina Brent.
Their Vicar R. F. Placid Shafto.
The Secretray R. F. Bede Tatham.

Rev. F. Austin Latham died on the 13th of November following, to the great grief of his house and Congregation, about the age of fity-six. He had been chosen one of the Queen's Chaplains and performed the duty of the place with great edification till by the persecution he was forced to retire into France. What money he had been able to spare from his allowance at the Royal Chapel he left to his house,(St. Edmund's, Paris)which at this time was in a low condition; and which, if he had lived, he would have put into a very flourishing state both as to temporals and spirituals. He was the second person interred in the new burying place at Paris; the first was one Adrian Coppens, who in quality of tailor had served the house no less than thirty years and died the 16th of October 1676.

At Dieulwart died R. F. Cuthbert Horsley on the 21st of December (1677) and R. F. Thomas Fursden on the 23rd following, both very famous for their exact claustral observance. R. F. Cuthbert was aged about eighty, whereof he had spent about fifty in regular duty without ever quitting to go to the Mission; and of this fifty he spent almost thirty in governing that house as Prior, of which he had a sad time; for the country being involved in dismal wars his house fared ill, which he bore like a Job with a pleasant and gay countenance; and God gave him such grace before the Generals and commanders of the soldiers that though not a monastery in the country was more alarmed than Dieulwart yet not one suffered less. All the time he had to spare after the Divine Office and from his domestic affairs, he spent in holy meditations and writing them in a most delicate hand. His government was eminently in the spirit of meekness. As for R. F. Thomas he had spent above sixty years at Dieulwart in religious duty without ever desiring to return into Englnad; and died about the age of ninety two.

Anno 1678, February 2nd. at Paris died Sir Francis Anderton, a great benefactor to St. Edmund's which repays his kindness with a solemn anniversary, &c. He is interred in the cave and has this epitaph in the Church :

D. O. M.

In spem Resurrectionis
Hic quiescit vir omni nomine clarissimus,
Franciscus Andertonus Baronettus Lostochii &c Dominus.
Nobilitas ejus major quam quæ eferri indigeat
Antiquiorque quam possit
Crevit tamen conjuge Somerseta
Atque inde privato stemmàti Decus Regium accessit

CHAPTER THE FIFTY-EIGHTH. 217

Hic bello domique strenuus
Pietate in Deum, beneficentia in pauperes, summa in adversis con-
Enituit [stantia
Sic fide integer & christianis virtutibus jam cœlo maturus
Cum Benedictinæ huic familiæ cui conjunctissimus vixerat
Æternum amoris pignus corpus reliquisset
Obiit Parisiis IV Nonas Februarii
An. Domini M.D.C.LXXVIII ætatis LI
Hoc marmor Elizabetha Somerseta Francisci relicta
Mœrens posuit
Requiescat in pace.

Englished. To God, most good, most great.

In hopes of the resurrection here rests a man in all respects illustrious, to wit, Sir Francis Anderton, Knight, Baronet, Lord of Lostock &c ; whose nobility is greater than needs to be laid forth and more ancient than can be unfolded, which yet was increased by his consort Somerset who was a royal honour to his pedigree, valiant in war and peace, famous for his piety towards God, liberality to the poor and egregious constancy in adversity; thus through integrity in faith and Christian Virtues ripe for heaven, after he had left to this Benedictine family (which he had much affected living) his body an eternal pledge of his love, he died at Paris on the 2nd of February 1678, æt. 51. This marble monument, Elizabeth Somerset his relict, in her mourning placed here. Requiescat in pace.

On the 13th of October of a pestiferous sickness got through charitably assisting the English soldiers at Brussels, died at that town R. F. Lionel Sheldon, professed of Douay, where with applause he taught philosophy four years and was Definitor of the Congregation, and being sent into England was Master of Ceremonies to her Majesty in her Chapel, and afterwards for three years Chief Almoner to the Duchess of York (now Queen mother of England); lastly banished for the orthodox faith, died as was said in the 45th year of his age, the 25th of his profession and 21st of his priesthood.

After the Restoration of King Charles II the estates of the rebels in Ireland were given to the Duke of York. Now it happened unluckily that these estates had been taken from the poor Catholics and given to those rogues. Of this R. F. Lionel gave the Duke notice, but his Highness answered him again that he was but a young man and of no great experience in such matters, for others thought he might lawfully take them. These who were of this opinion endeavoured to justify his keeping those estates by the common parity of one's buying goods that have been recovered of pirates without the right owner's being able to lay claim to them; a comparison too far stretched in this case as has since appeared in the executive sentence of the Supreme Judge of all, who when he was pleased to converse in mortality on earth, admonished mortals to take especial care of just dealings with one another, for that they should have the same measure returned them again. This is what his own flesh and blood have done to him, keeping from him his royal inheritance out of which they have forced him, and by authority of the parliament in 1689 took the moneys which his Majesty was known to have in different companies of merchants to give to the protestants who were flown out of Ireland into England for fear of being ill used by the Catholics who there stood for his Majesty. God punishes in time that he may spare in eternity.

This 1678 began the confusions and miseries of Oates' plot in which many of the Religious were hideously calumniated by detestable miscreant accusers, among which thus falsely accused was Mr. Reeves who of a famous Oxford scholar became a Catholic and a Benedictine monk at Douay where he was known by the name of Brother Wilfrid Reeves. Living at La Celle, a venerable Canon of Faremoutier one day read to him the following verses made on the Revocation of the Edict of Nantes in 1685:

"Calvin outré de l'Edit qu'on publie
La larme à l'œil vint dire à Lucifer
Ah! c'en est fait ma secte est abolie
Il faut songer à rétrécir l'enfer

Il ne faut pas que cela vous chagrine,

CHAPTER THE FIFTY-EIGHTH.

> Luy répondit cet horrible démon,
> Le mal n'est pas si grand qu'on s'imagine,
> Tous ces gens là n'ont changé que de nom."

He presently without any further ado, thus echoed them in Latin.

> Cum fama Edicti Calvini venit ad aures
> Dæmona mox plorans et furibundus adit
> Heu! actum est pater, inquit, ego et mea secta perimus
> Ilicet! inferni contrahe claustra tui.
>
> Subridens Dæmon, Nate! inquit, pone dolorem
> Pone metum, non est hic ita grande malum;
> Nempe fugat cœnam jam missa, Ecclesia templum,
> Esto, omnes mutant nomina, nemo fidem.

The pious Canon acquainting the renowned Bishop of Meaux, M. Bossuet with this passage, his Grace so admired the verses that he would needs see the Author, and thereupon caused his coach to roll down from Faremoutier to La Celle and took great satisfaction in Br. Reeves' company and made very great account of him. He never took Orders because of his lameness and died in England in the year 1693 (Oct. 31st).

There are some pieces of his ingenuity extant, as his Megalesia Sacra on the Assumption, printed in 1677, and a panegyric to Cardinal Howard printed in 1675, both pieces of poetry.

Another person injured in these false accusations and with whom it went so far that he was tried for his life, was R. Father Corker whom the judge cleared of treason and condemned to death for his sacred Order of Priesthood; but he escaped that anger by the coming to the crown of James II, till which time he lay in prison where he reconciled to the Church above a thousand persons and was afterwards twice blessed Abbot, first of Cismar then of Lambspring the house of his profession.

But with Brother (Thomas) Pickering (a Lay brother of Douay), it went harder, for he was irremissibly executed, a poor harmless soul, whom those miscreants wickedly impeached of having designed the King's death, which the King himself openly declared he was convinced was false. But so violent were those times, that he himself was constrained for a time to connive at their wickedness (May 9, 1679).

Anno 1679 on the first of March, Mr. Penrodock died at Paris and was burried at the Cave of St. Edmund's with this epitaph on his grave:

Hic jacet Carolus Penrodock
Ex antiqua et nobili Familia
Brittannorum
Stirpe Progenitus
Pietate in Deum
Munificentia in pauperes
Comitate in omnes
Fuit insignis
Obiit Parisiis I Martii 1679
Ætatis suæ 28.
Requiescat in pace.

Englished: Here lies Charles Penrodock descended of a noble and ancient family of the old Britons, very remarkable for his piety towards God, his liberality to the poor and affability to all. He died at Paris the first of March 1679, æt. 28.

Requiescat in Pace.

CHAPTER THE FIFTY-NINTH.

THE DEATH OF FATHER BENEDICT STAPYLTON.

Anno 1680 (August 4) died R. F. Bennet Stapylton at Dieuwart where he lies buried with this epitaph:

M. S.
R. A. P. Patris Benedicti Stapylton
Ecclesiæ Metropolitanæ
Cantuariensis
Prioris Cathedralis
Congregationisque Anglo Benedictinæ
Præsidis Generalis
Qui
In Monasterio S. Gregorii Magni Duaci professus
Ejusdem bis Prior fuit
Et in eadem Academia
S. Theologiæ Doctoratum
Et Cathedram adeptus est.
Deinde
In Apostolica Angliæ Missione
XX Annos impendit
Augustissimæ Angliæ Reginæ
Sacellanus Domesticus
Denique
In dictæ Congregationis Generalem

CHAPTER THE FIFTY-NINTH.

   Ter successive electus
  Quod munus post quam per XI annos
   Feliciter administrasset
  Suos moriendo destituens
   Ingens sui desiderium
  Et ingentem suis luctum
    Reliquit
  Obiit in hoc monasterio
  Pridie nonas Augusti
   An. Dom. 1680.
    Æt. suæ 58.
   Professionis 38.
   Sacerdotii 34.
  Requiescat in Pace.

 Englished : Sacred to the memory of the most Reverend Fr. Bennet Stapylton, Cathedral Prior of the Metropolitan Church of Canterbury and President General of the English Benedictine Congregation, who was twice Prior of St. Gregory at Douay whereof he was professed, also Doctor and Professor of that city's University. Twenty years he spent in the apostolic Mission of England and was Domestic chaplain to the Queen. Thrice chosen General of the Congregation, he performed the office eleven years very happily, and dying was very much wished for and lamented of his religious. He died in this monastery on the 4th of August 1680, æt. 58. Professed 38, Priested 34.
    Requiescat in Pace.

 He was of a noble family and the eldest son and left all to become a monk; indeed he rather not knew the world than left it; prevented with the blessings of goodness he had the happiness of a gentle soul which abhorred vice and adhered to virtue, very exact in regularity and very diligent in his studies, very ready in all exercises of humility and of a most sweet and charming conversation, venerable for his sanctity of life and wonderful for the sharpness and solidity of his wit, beloved of God and men. He taught philosophy and divinity at the College of St. Vaast sixteen years together, applauded by all, and with great satisfaction and profit to his auditory. But what is most wonderful and the argument most invincible that can be, of a very holy man and of a very great genius, was that, when he was made Prior of Douay he acquitted himself of it as if he had nothing else to do, and yet prosecuted his studies as if he had nothing else but them to mind, reaching from one end to another, as 'tis said in the Book of Wisdom, and sweetly ordering all things. He resolved to deserve the honour of Doctorship before he would wear the badges of it, most egregiously and prudently thinking that title to appertain not so much to the Degree as to the desert of the Degree. Charles II upon recovery of his British Empire called him over and made him Second Almoner to his Royal Consort, and her First Chaplain (Protocapellanus) and even Prefect of her Chapel. Lastly chosen President he proved in all respects an egregious Superior, not sparing his life to do his duty, when Dieulwart being uneasy within itself, to restore it to its former peace and quietness he went thither to visit it in the hottest season of the year, whereupon he fell sick and died.

And the second elect President being dead and Father Sheldon the first Definitor likewise, and F. John Worsley the second Definitor refusing to take on him the charge of President, it fell to the third Definitor, R. F. Corker, who the year following was, after God, the entire sole help and spiritual director of the Most Reverend Father in God, Oliver Plunket, Lord Archbishop of Armagh and Primate of Ireland, cruelly put to death through false accusations in the sham plot of execrable Oates. They were then both in the same prison (Newgate). The Bishop's quarters were conveyed to Lambspring, where R. F. Corker in 1693 shut them up in the crypt with this inscription:

Reliquiæ S. memoriæ Oliveri Plunket Archiepiscopi Archmachani, totius Hiberniæ Primatis, qui in odium Catholicæ Fidei laqueo suspensus, extractis visceribus et in ignem projectis celebris Martyr occubuit Londini 1° die Julii an. Salutis 1681. S. V."

Englished. The relics of Oliver Plunket, Archbishop of Armagh and Primate of all Ireland, of holy memory, who in hatred of the Catholic Faith was hanged, and having his bowels torn out and flung into the fire died a most glorious Martyr on the first of July (S. V.) in the year of Salvation 1681.

CHAPTER THE FIFTY-NINTH.

About the beginning of this sham plot, a monk of Saint Edmund's R. F. Placid Adelham much addicted to the reading of St. Austin, and who had formerly been a protestant minister, was laid in chains also at Newgate and died in them for the same cause; a person highly valued by all that knew him (January 17th. 1680).

CHAPTER THE SIXTIETH.

THE ELECTIONS AT THE EIGHTEENTH GENERAL CHAPTER. A MONASTERY ESTABLISHED IN LONDON.

In 1681 the eighteenth General Chapter was held at Paris where R. F. Joseph Shirburne was chosen President.

Second elect President, R. F. Austin Constable.

The Provincial of Canterbury, R. F. Gregory Mallet.

The Provincial of York, R. F. Francis Lawson.

The Abbot of Lambspring, R. F. Joseph Sherwood.

The Prior of Douay, R. F. Jerome Hesketh.

The Prior of Dieulwart, R. F. Austin Mather; but he refusing R. F. Gregson was chosen Prior, but being called to the Royal Chapel at London, R. F. James Mather succeeded.

The Prior of Paris was R. F. Bennet Nelson.

The Abbess of Cambray, Dame Marina Appleton.

Their Vicar, R. F. Anselm Carter; but he refusing, R. F. Placid Bruning became their Vicar.

Secretary, R. F. Cuthbert Parker.

Anno 1683 (December 11th) Father Bennet Constable died at Durham in prison, into which for the Faith he was cast a month after his arrival in England.

Anno 1685, February 5th (S.V.) R. F. John Huddleston, who had contributed so much to the saving of his Majesty Charles II after Worcester battle, reconciled him to the Church, administered to him the last Sacraments and helped him in his last extremity to make a most Christain, Catholic end, which happened the next day.

And King James II presently upon his coming to the crown, formed a convent of Benedictine Monks in his Palace of St. James', placing them at the Chapel of his royal Consort, their Majesties often resorting thither. Wherefore in 1685 the 19th General Chapter was held here at which R. F. Joseph Shirburn was continued President.

CHAPTER THE SIXTY-FIRST.

THE 19TH GENERAL CHAPTER. CONFIRMATION OF THE BULL "PLANTATA." JAMES II's ALLOCUTION TO THE BISHOP AND REGULARS.

The 19th General Chapter was held at St. James', where R. F. Joseph Shirburn was continued President.
Second elect President, likewise continued.
Provincial of Canterbury, R. F. Austin Llewellin.
Provincial of York, R. F. Robert Killingbeck.
The Prior of St. Gregory's, R. F. William Hitchcock.
The Prior of St. Laurence's, R. F. Bernard Gregson.
The Prior of St. Edmund's, R. F. James Nelson.
The Abbess of Cambray, Dame Marina Appleton.
Their Vicar, R. F. Francis Muttlebury.
The Procurator at Rome, R. F. Corker.
Secretary, R. F. Cuthbert Parker.

And now the Secular Catholic Clergy having had leisure to see the inconveniency of the Bishop of Chalcedon's claim to the title of Ordinary of Great Britain, had obtained from Rome that of Vicar Apostolic and now began to urge it on the monks. This caused some disputes which ended not of some years, for that the Benedictines in virtue of old rights &c, were totally independent of them, but of this ample title came to have some sort of dependence on them, which did them no hurt but good ; for their great Bull of *Plantata* being questioned, it was proved an authentic Bull, declared such and maintained as such by the Cardinals in 1695.

Anno 1686 January 1st, S. V. the Bishop and Superiors of the Regulars in England were ordered to attend his Majesty at nine o'clock, who made them all a most admirable speech to persuade them to love and unity amongst themselves as being all concerned for the public good; assuring them that for his part he would do as much as lay in him and as he could do by law, to propagate the Catholic Faith, and that he would be a most obedient child of his mother Church and desired their advice and counsel from time to time as to what might be most expedient to be done; desiring their conversation might be such as might give no ill example to the enemies of the Church, not only in their manners but doctrine. For, said he, there are some who out of ambition to be counted great and learned hold erroneous principles contrary to the Catholic Faith, and have had many followers, and this by name Mr. Blacklow; and advised them not to admit of his principles. And in doing other things, he said with much freedom, begging their prayers that he might prosper in his designs, his only aim and design being the honour and glory of God and advancing Catholic religion.

This same year at Lambspring amidst the prayers of the Religious died Sir Thomas Gascoign, Knight, Baronet æt. 93; a person of great piety who in his younger days visited the Holy Sepulchre at Jerusalem; and flung into the sham plot of Oates by two of his servants was imprisoned and in danger of his life. But by the goodness of God being delivered from these troubles (contrary to all human expectation) and the Abbot of Lambspring being his brother, he withdrew thither and spent the remainder of his life (which was about five or six years) in devotion, admitted to the Confraternity of the Congregation, and lies interred with his brother in the same grave.

CHAPTER THE SIXTY-SECOND.

THE CONGREGATION RENOUNCES ALL CLAIM TO ITS FORMER ESTATES IN ENGLAND. VARIOUS EVENTS CONNECTED WITH THE CONVENT AT ST. JAMES'. THE FATHERS ARE DISPERSED BY THE REVOLUTION.

But the most remarkable thing of this year was the sermon of Bishop Ellis, (then Father Ellis), on the Feast of All Saints of the Order of St. Benedict on the 13th of November, which was afterwards published by his Majesty's command, printed at London by his printer Henry Hills that same year, in which are these words to set at ease the hearts of such as were jealous of their Church lands and apprehensive of losing them.

"But this posterity of theirs, which by a special providence of God continues by an uninterrupted succession to this very day, through all the revolutions and changes which have swallowed up so many other Ecclesiastical bodies and laid them in the dust, does willingly and freely renounce all titles and rights which might possibly be inherent in the ancient and the present English Congregation of monks who acknowledge by my mouth that the alienation of their lands, how unjust soever in the beginning and ensuing confirmation of it, is now fixed by so full and incontrollable authority both of Church and State that they can by no law, ecclesiastical or civil be wrested out of the hands of their present possessors or their heirs. The Church and in her name the Supreme Pastor, **hath quitted all** pretentions **and prays that what she hath loosed upon** earth may be loosed in heaven ; and that everyone concerned may enjoy as quiet a conscience, as they do and shall to the end of the world enjoy an undisturbed possession. The Supreme Civil Magistrate and the highest Court in this realm have even with her consent passed it into a law, which nothing but the same power that made it can repeal. As for the monks themselves, they, ever obedient to the spiritual and temporal powers and tender of the consciences of their fellow Christians, not only willingly and without reserve submit to this double injunction, but also add a separate renunciation of their own. They suppose no judicious person will question their power to do it more than a conscientious person will question their sincerity that they have actually done it. That ecclesiastical as well as secular corporations and communities can alienate, is certain. And lest it should be doubted whether they have made use of their power in a case prudence and charity and even self preservation so much require, they again solemnly protest they desire nothing should be restored but their reputation and to be thought by their countrymen neither pernicious nor useless members to their country. And when I have in view the apostles of religion in this kingdom, the planters, the propagators and preservers of it, a Sigebert, an Alfred and an Ethelred and many others once powerful monarchs in this island who postponed the purple to the cowl; when I contemplate a St. Erminburga, a St. Eanfleda, an Editha, an Elianora, with many others once glorious Queens in this island who preferred the humility of a monastic habit and obscurity of a cell to the pomp and spendour of a court; when I behold I say, so many royal advocates appearing in behalf of their Order, I will suppose so just a cause is gained, so reasonable a request is granted." This was in the King's presence.

This same year also Dada the Pope's Nuncio was consecrated Archbishop of Amasia in presence of the said King and the two Queens, Mary Beatrix of Modena, Queen of England, and Catherine of Portugal, Queen Dowager of England, at the Chapel of St. James' (May 1st, 1687).

At Paris in 1688 (February 12th.) died R. F. Hugh Starkey

confessor to the English Benedictine Nuns, who in England lived with my Lord Bellasis; a very venerable and reverend Missioner.

At St. James' Chapel after Easter (May 6th, 1688) R. F. Philip Ellis one of the monks of that royal Benedictine Convent was consecrated Bishop of Aureliopolis. He was professed at Douay.

And on the 25th of October the baptismal ceremony of the Prince of Wales was there also performed; for as to the Sacrament it was administered to him the next day after his birth.

In December following, the Orangian Revolution bereaved the Fathers of their royal Chapel and Convent and the house was profaned by the wickedness which, in the depths of God's judgments, was then permitted to prevail.

Anno 1689 died Pope Innocent XI to whom succeeded Alexander the VIII.

CHAPTER THE SIXTY-THIRD.

THE TWENTIETH GENERAL CHAPTER IS HELD AT PARIS. DEATH OF FATHER MAURUS NELSON AND ABBOT SHERWOOD; THE BUILDING OF LAMBSPRING CHURCH.

THE twentieth General Chapter was kept at Paris (1689) in which R. F. Shirburn was again continued President.

Second elect President, R. F. Maurus Corker.

The same Provincials again.

The Prior of St. Gregory's, R. F. William Hitchcock.

The Prior of St. Laurence's R. F. James Mather.

The Prior of St. Edmund's, R. F. Francis Fenwick.

The Abbess of Cambray, Dame Marina Appleton.

Their Vicar, R. F. Wolstan Crosby.

Secretary. R. F. Bede More.

Anno 1690 (May 17th), at the English Benedictine nuns at Paris died an egregious pattern and rare example of virtue, Dame Justina Gascoigne, daughter to the above named Sir Thomas Gascoigne. She was professed of Cambray.

On the 3rd of May died R. F. Maurus Nelson Sub-prior, Novice-Master and Procurator of St. Edmund's, Licentiate in Divinity; wherefore all the Licentiates of Sorbonne came to St. Edmund's and sang a very solemn Requiem for him a little while after his interment. He was a great example of exact regularity and his death a great loss to his house of Paris.

And the 26th of June at Hildesheim died Rev. Fr. Joseph

Sherwood, Abbot of Lambspring, and was brought to this Abbey the same day; a most industrious, indefatigable, and successful man in the temporals of that house which owes its present welfare to his pious cares; for he looked after all things for a great while under Abbot Gascoigne who at last took him for his coadjutor. He was very acceptable to the princes of the country; namely: the elector of Cologne, the Prince of Neuberg, and the Bishop of Munster, who employed him in England when he was even only Prior of Lambspring, sometimes as their agent, sometimes as their envoy to King Charles II. He was a great lover of learning and spared nothing to promote and encourage it in his religious; much given to hospitality and notwithstanding his great expenses about the great new-built Church and repairing other buildings, he left fewer debts when he died than he found when he was chosen Abbot.

Anno 1691 died Pope Alexander VIII to whom succeeded Innocent the XII.

On the 26th of May, 1670 (Feast of St. Augustine of England), the English Fathers laid the first stone of their noble Church of Lambspring (which has eight or nine Altars and an organ of forty eight voices), and on the 26th of May this 1691, it was solemnly dedicated; and on the 8th of November following, the town of Lambspring took fire at four of the clock in the morning and was quite consumed in the space of six hours; by a singular providence of God the Abbey with its new Church escaped. I shall not here trouble my reader with the particularities of the corporal charities of the Fathers to the poor town folks in such exigences. But I can't omit relating and that without exaggeration, that when the English Monks began to live there, there was scarce above two or three Catholics, and in 1696 they counted at Lambspring about three hundred Catholics, if not more.

CHAPTER THE SIXTY-FOURTH.

The General Chapter of 1693 and the chief events during the Quadriennium.

Anno 1693, at the 21st General Chapter, held at Douay R. F. Joseph Shirburn was continued President.
Second elect President, R. F. Austin Howard.
The Provincial of Canterbury, R. F. Austin Constable.
The Provincial of York, R. F. Michael Pullein.
The Abbot of Lambspring R. F. Maurus Corker.
The Prior of St. Gregory's, R. F. John Phillipson.
The Prior of St. Laurence's, R. F. Laurence Champney.
The Prior of St. Edmund's, R. F. Placid Nelson.
The Abbess of Cambray, Dame Marina Appleton.
Their Vicar.   ?
Secretary, R. F. Bede Moore.

At this chapter La Celle was declared to make but one and the same house with that of Paris, whereas before it had carried itself like as if it had been a convent by itself.

Anno 1694, January 10, died R. F. Joseph Frere aged ninety six, and the 80th year of his religious profession. The Venerable Father was more spent than they were aware of who were about him, when the most Holy Sacrament of the Altar was given him, for his Viaticum; wherefore being troubled with phlegm and going to evacuate it, contrary to his expectation the Holy Eucharist came along with it on the floor; and R. F. William Hitchcock, a devout old monk (who by many notable things has highly deserved of his Congregation), with an heroical courage, a lively faith, and flaming charity most reverently took it up and overcoming all repugnancy swallowed it spittle and all; a glorious and venerable example worthy of eternal memory.

On the 29th of January (1694) died the Reverend Mother Marina Appleton, æt: 74, professed 51; of a convert of considerable parentage she became a nun at Cambray and gave great example of piety and religion not only in her private condition but also in the dignity of Abbess; of which function she most admirably acquitted herself for the space of thirteen years together, having been four times chosen to it.

In Holy Week his Majesty James II made a spiritual retreat at St. Edmund's at Paris, extremely satisfied with his accommodation though the house is but little.

On the 10th of April 1695 (Holy Saturday) died R. F. Bede (Foster) otherwise William Thornton, the last professed of the house of St. Malo.

October 22nd 1694 at Paris died R. F. Thomas Hesketh, Doctor of Sorbonne, aged 30; and on the 30th at Rome R. F. Francis Fenwick, Doctor of Sorbonne, a very fine preacher, in great repute with King James II who sent him to Rome to act for him at that Court. These Doctors were both professed at St. Edmund's.

This year (25 Maii) for the first time, the monks of St. Edmund's appeared upon public duty of the town, going in rocession, like the other convents, to the Cathedral and to the Church of St. Genovefa.

Anno 1695, my Lord Lauderdale dying at Paris, was according to his desire buried in the cave of St. Edmund's; but no one has laid stone on his grave or set up a monument in the Church.

Anno 1696, R. F. Corker on the 27th of July (S. V.) gave up the Abbey of Lambspring in which dignity succeeded Father Maurus, otherwise John Knightley whose promotion was the work of the Germans, whereby great trouble rose in that Abbey which could not be ended of some years; the country maintaining him, and the monks not liking to be imposed on. Woe unto the world because of offences; for it must need be that offences come, but woe to that man by whom the offence cometh. Avarice captivated Judas though in the company of the twelve Apostles guided and governed by nothing less than Christ himself. So no wonder if in a monastery an unhappy man be hurled away sometimes by ambition. Of such unhappy falls not only the earth but even the heavens themselves give us a strange example, to let us see that in truth there is nothing for us to take scandal at in such accidents. What ruined the first angel in heaven but ambition? But to return to R. F. Corker. In the time of King James he found means to rear up a very pretty Convent somewhere towards Clerkenwell at London which the mob pulled to pieces at the arrival of the Prince of Orange.

In September this same year 1696, King James II of happy memory made another spiritual retreat at St. Edmund's. The ancient histories of England shew a great connection betwixt the English purple and the Benedictine Cowl, which Divine Providence has been pleased to renew in these latter ages; for besides what I have already said of King Charles II, his said majesty in 1659, September 4, R. F. Gabriel Brett being Prior of St. Malo's, came privately to Clermont (a place on the continent belonging to the Convent of St. Malo's and making part of it), and stayed there with the monks eight days; upon which over their Guestroom they put these Verses:

> Augustæ paupertatem ne spreveris aulæ
> Hospitium Rex hic repperit atque fidem.
> Ce lieu quoique petit et pauvre ne t'offense
> Puisqu'un Roy y a pris son gît en assurance.

CHAPTER THE SIXTY FIFTH.

THE DECEASE OF R. F. SHIRBURN AT ST. EDMUND'S.

Anno 1697 April 9th, R. F. Joseph Shirburn died in the Convent of St. Edmund's the house of his profession in the 69th year and 46th of his monachism. Though one part of his body directly from his head to his toe was struck with a dead palsy, yet he held with great example to the austerity of the diet of the convent. He industriously reared up the new Church and dormitory of St. Edmund's and adorned the sacristy with church plate and ornaments, got his benefice of Choisy annexed to the house as a perpetual rent and procured that the Religious might be capable of benefices; by which means and the charitable piety of the faithful the said convent of Paris subsists. He was so acceptable to the late King James II of glorious memory, that by his Majesty's means he once brought Cardinal Bovillon into favour again with his most Christian Majesty, whose displeasure his Eminency had then for something or other very much incurred, so that he lived far from Court.

To R. F. Shirburn succeeded in the office R. F. Austin Howard, the second elect President.

CHAPTER THE SIXTY-SIXTH.

THE GENERAL CHAPTER OF 1697, ELECTIONS, DEATHS &c.

THE 22nd General Chapter was held at London (1697) in which R. F. Bernard Gregson was chosen President.

Second elect President, again R. F. Austin Howard.

The Provincial of Canterbury, R. F. Austin Howard.

The Provincial of York, R. F. Michael Pullein.

The Prior of St. Gregory's, R. F. John Phillipson.

The Prior of St. Laurence's, R. F. Laurence Champney.

The Prior of St. Edmund's, R. F. Joseph Johnston who giving up his office R. F. William Hitchcock was Prior of Paris.

The Abbess of Cambray, Dame Scholastica Houghton.

Their Vicar, R. F. Cuthbert Tatham.

Secretary, R. F. Laurence Fenwick.

Anno 1698 (September 22nd) æt: 90, at London in Somerset house died R. F. John Huddleston who was so instrumental in saving King Charles II &c, as hath been said.

Anno 1699, August the 25th on the Feast of St. Louis, the English Benedictine Bishop, the Reverend Father in God Philip Ellis sung the High Mass in the French Church at Rome before many Cardinals invited and received by the Cardinal of Bouillon; the Prince of Monacho ambassador of France, being then incognito assisted in a tribune.

On the third of September in the 81st year of his age and 59th of religion died R. F. Bennet Nelson. He was very zealous all his life time for exact regularity of which he was a great example. By order of the R. F. President Austin Hungate he put off the house of St. Malo's to the monks of St. Maur; but what fatigue he underwent before he could so happily conclude that affair is almost past relation. R. F. Hungate was so satisfied with him for this piece of service that he mighty kindly invited him into England to live with his nephew a baronet of whom he had formerly taken care; but he desired to be excused, dreading the Mission to be a work that might surpass him, wherefore he was left to his freedom and never quitted his Cloister but became a constant confessarius at the great Convent of the Carmelite nuns over against his Monastery.

In 1700, March 4th, Mr. Francis Stafford, son to Viscount Stafford (who in his decrepit old age was most barbarously and wickedly sworn out of his life by the miscreants of his days) died at St. Edmund's and lies buried in their cave. James II sent him thither that he might be better able to prepare himself for death.

On the 20th of May, the Solemnity of the Ascension, James, Prince of Wales, did them the honour of visiting them for the first time.

Anno 1701, June 9th, died Philip of France, Duke of Orleans, who in his time had much honoured the English monks of St. Edmund's; who repaid him with a Solemn Requiem for the rest of his soul.

CHAPTER THE FIFTY SEVENTH.

THE 23RD GENERAL CHAPTER ANNO, 1701.

The twenty-third General Chapter was held at Douay in 1701 in which Father Austin Howard was chosen President.

Second elect President, R. F. Augustine Constable.

The Provincial of Canterbury, R. F. Bernard Gregson.

The Provincial of York, R. F. Augustine Tempest.

The Prior of St. Gregory's, R. F. Michael Pullein.

The Prior of St. Laurence's, R. F. James Mather, upon whose refusal it fell at last to R. F. Watmough.

The Prior of St. Edmund's, R. F. Anthony Turberville.

The Abbess of Cambray, Dame Margaret Swinburn.

Their Vicar, R. F. Joseph Berriman.

Secretary, R. F. Francis Rookwood.

In the foregoing General Chapter in 1698, the RR. Fathers decreed that no President, Provincial, Conventual Prior and Abbess should be chosen immediately again to the same office.

CHAPTER THE SIXTY-EIGHTH.

THE DECEASE OF KING JAMES II; HIS OBSEQUIES AT ST. EDMUND'S MONASTERY AT PARIS.

On the 16th of September (N. S.) at St. Germans en Lay died King James II of most glorious memory. The next night his body was brought to St. Edmund's and laid in my Lord Cardigan's Chapel. The Benedictines of France of the Congregation of St. Maur, invited by their English brethren, performed the royal services the next day; Dom Charles Petey, Prior of St. German's Abbey, had the honour of singing the royal Requiem, and his subprior on the thirtieth day. In the meantime till the fortieth day, besides the office of the Mass, a Requiem never failed to be sung every day for the King; and during all that time, such being the rites of royal funerals in France, the royal corpse was attended night and day by a monk employed in praying for his soul, though it was thought needless: all the world esteeming his injuries on earth to have stood him instead of a purgatory. But before I go any further, for the satisfaction of the reader I think it may be to the purpose to insert the speeches made when his royal corpse was brought to the Church. Dr. Ingleby, one of the King's Chaplains, being then "in week", at the reposing of the royal corpse in the middle of the Church, addressed himself to R. F. Prior and the Convent in these words:

"Tristi, Reverende Pater, et lugubri admodum fungor ministerio, non verbis sed fletibus potius peragendo, dum offero tibi corpus potentissimi, excellentissimi, clementissimi Domini mei Jacobi secundi, Regis Magni Britanniæ. Laudibus illum celebrare non aggredior; lugerem potius ac dicerem cum sapientissimo illo regum: Laudent eum in portis opera ejus. Infirma enim sunt oratorum eloquia, fragiles etiam marmoreæ illæ tabulæ quibus perituri servantur tituli, et in pulverem sicut illi quos memorant, cito resolventur. Opera autem sanctorum sequuntur illos et in æternum permanent.

Laudabit ergo piissimum hunc Principem quamdiu stabit, ecclesia; eumque religionis non tantum defensorem ac Propagatorem, sed et victimam prædicabit. Laudabunt illum tot victoriarum suarum monumenta et invictissima illa animi fortitudo, seu quâ hostes victor toties debellavit, seu quâ hostibus victus ignovit. Minus enim miror, Reverende Pater, Regem de hostibus triumphantem, quam Regem crudelissimis hostibus veniam donantem. Minus illum miror in solio sedentem, quam propter amorem Christi ac defensionem ecclesiæ e solio descendentem. Laudabunt et ad cœlum pertingent tot gemitus pauperum atque exulum qui parentem suum æque ac regem lugent; sed et laudabunt tandem ipsa ingrata atque infausta illa regna, quæ ad pedes Agni instar regum Apocalypseos deposuit ut fidem servaret. Fidem servavit, et hæc erit victoria qua vicit mundum, Fides Christi. Utque omnia uno verbo ecclesiæ complectar, effecit fides illius ut prospera hujus mundi despiceret et nulla ejus adversa formidaret. Regnavit quippe in illo pietas; hocque veluti firmissimo propugnaculo per mundi illecebras et ærumnas æquo animo pertransiit. Prævalebat quidem exterius in diebus hisce nubis et caliginis, prævalebat ad tempus perduellionis ac tyrannidis furor, sed stetit semper interius ac triumphavit inconcussum illud regnum charitatis, quo, ut ait S. Augustinus, persecutor pervenire non potest ubi habitat Deus meus.

Est ergo, Reverendi Patres, cur vobis, imo et toti Galliæ gratulemur, cui pretiosissimas has reliquias custodiri concessum est. Benedixit olim Obededom et omni domui ejus, quia Arca Domini in eo habitavit. Det Deus ut domus et Imperium Ludovici Magni, Regum optimi et gloriosissimi benedicatur, ac cœlestibus æternisque donis cumuletur, qui illustrissimum hunc Principem, cujus reliquias veneramur, **viventem ac morientem cumulavit beneficiis.**

Nos autem, Reverendi Patres, dum Ecclesiæ triumphantis cœtus, atque angelici chori gloriam **defuncti Principis ac triumphum** celebrant, **sermonem in nosmetipsos ac luctum totum convertamus.** Liceat mihi **verba illa** usurpare, quæ **audire videor :** "**Nolite** flere super me, sed super vos ipsos flete." **Nostra enim est,** quanta quanta sit, illa jactura, nullis fletibus redimenda : **illi vero,** ut sæpius insinuare solebat, **et** vivere **Christus erat et mori lucrum.**

Verumtamen, si mortem subiisti temporalem, vivis tamen, O ! meritissime, piissime, clementissime princeps, vivis et regnas ante thronum Dei, ubi coronam tandem, non temporalem sed æternam comparasti. Vivis etiam in illustrissimo filio, vero meritorum tuorum non minus quam imperii hærede. Illius fama ac virtus a sæculo inaudita, nomen tuum ac gloriam in omne ævum prorogabit.

Sed et vivis semper in intimis animorum nostrorum affectibus. Quot sunt fidelium corda, tot tibi erunt viva perennis gloriæ ac memoriæ monumenta."

Reverend Father Prior replied :

"Lugubris hac pompa, Sapientissime Domine, gemitus et lacrymas magis quam verba exigere videtur : siquidem deponitis apud Benedictinam hanc familiam serenissimi Jacobi II, Regis Angliæ, Congregationis nostræ patroni præcipui, tristes exuvias ; imo potius, lætas reliquias sanctissimi confessoris, ne dicam inclyti martyris. Quid enim tot et tantæ ejus dum viveret virtutes, quid pia mors, nisi sanctissimum confessorem ? Quid tot ærumnæ, tot injuriæ ob Christi nomen patientissime toleratæ ? Quid tria florentissima regna propter fidem Catholicam amissa, nisi insignem martyrem prædicant ? Sacrum ergo pignus depositum, sancte a nobis servandum accipimus : reddituri procul dubio fideliter, quando ab eis quorum interest jussi fuerimus. Deum interim Omnipotentem diu **noctuque** humillimis precibus pro animæ ejus refrigerio deprecaturi, si tamen indiguerit. De cætero, gratias agimus immortales tum Ludovico Magno, **tum** Serenissimæ Mariæ, Angliæ Reginæ, quod nos tantillos tanto honore affecerint. Quos Deus, optimus, maximus, necnon et serenissimum Jacobum III Angliæ Regem diu, non nobis tantum, sed et toti Ecclesiæ suæ sanctæ incolumes servet, gubernet et protegat.

On the royal coffin a brass plate contains these words:

Icy est le corps de Très-Haut & Très-Puissant et Très Excellent Prince Jacques II par la Grâce de Dieu Roy de la Grande Bretagne né le 24 Octobre 1633. Décédé en France au Château de St. Germain en Laye le 16 Sept. 1701.

Part of the flesh taken from his body when it was embalmed and of his bowels or entrails (of which the Jesuits of St. Omer's had the rest) are interred in the parish Church of St. Germain's en Lay with this Latin epitaph which I give paraphrased by Sr. Girardin.

> Regi regum
> Felicique memoriæ
> Jacobi II Majoris Britanniæ Regis
> Au Roy qui fait regner tous les Rois de la Terre
> Et pour transmettre aux siècles à venir
> Le précieux dépôt de l'heureux souvenir
> Du grand Roy Jacques d'Angleterre.
>
> Qui sua hìc viscera condi voluit
> Conditus ipse in visceribus Christi
> Ce lieu saint est l'azile ainsi qu'il l'a prescrit
> De ses entrailles vénérables
> Et lui même goûte le fruit
> De ses vertus incomparables.
> Dans l'azile éternel du sein de Jésus Christ
> Fortitudine bellicâ nulli secundus
> Fide christianâ cui non par
> Nul ne porta plus haut la Gloire
> Qui suit la parfait valeur
> Et par la pure Foy qui règna dans son cœur
> A qui ne peut on pas comparer sa mémoire.
> Per alteram quid non ausus?
> Propter alteram quid non passus?

Est il quelque chemin aux grandes actions
Où ne l'ait pas conduit l'ardeur de son courage
Est il de coup affreux de révolutions
Qui de sa piété n'ait été le partage ?

Illâ plus quam Heros
Istâ prope Martyr.
Il remplit d'un Héro les plus vastes désirs
Partout où des grands cœurs la vertu se signale ;
Et dans ce qu'il souffrit, sa Foy fut presque égale
A la Foy même des Martyrs.

Fide fortis accensus periculis
Erectus adversis
Fort de cette force sublime
Son cœur sans relâche agité
Parut dans les périls toujours plus magnanime
Et plus grand dans l'adversité.

Nemo Rex magis cui Regna quatuor
Anglia, Scotia, Hibernia ; ubi quartum ?
Ipse sibi
Vraiment grand Roi ! dont le pouvoir suprême
Eut quatre Empires sous ses Loix ;
L'Angleterre et l'Ecosse et l'Irlande à la fois
Et quel étoit le quatrième ?
Celui qui le rendit sage entre les grands Rois
L'Empire qu'il eut sur soy même.

Tria eripi potuêre, Quartum intactum mansit ;
Priorum defensio Exercitus, qui defecerunt ;
Postremi tutela virtutes, nunquam transfugæ.

Des trois premiers sans peine on a pu le priver
Lorsqu'on vit ses Troupes Rebelles,
Loin de périr pour le sauver,
Pousser leurs attentats jusqu'à se soulever ;
Mais du dernier les Gardes immortelles
Ses vertus, dans la Paix scurent le conserver
Et lui furent toujours fidelles.

> Quin nec illa tria erepta omnino.
> Instar Regnorum est Ludovicus hospes
> Sarcit amicitia talis tantæ sacrilegia perfidiæ;
> Imperat adhuc qui sic exulat.
>
> Encore ceux là quoique envahis
> Ne lui furent pas même entièrement ravis;
> Et dans son cœur malgré le sacrilège audace
> De tant de crimes inouïs
> L'hospitalité de Louis
> Remplit abondamment la place
> Des droits sacrez du Trône indignement trahis.
> Les augustes liens d'une amitié si forte
> Dans la Grandeur Royale ont soutenu ses jours
> Etre exilé de la sorte
> N'est-ce-pas régner toujours?
>
> Moritur ut vixit, Fide plenus,
> Eoque advolat quo Fides ducit,
> Ubi nihil perfidia potest.
> Enfin sa vive Foy sanctifia sa vie,
> Consomma par sa mort sa tendre Piété,
> Et l'enleva dans la félicité
> De nôtre Céleste Patrie,
> Inaccessible aux traits de l'Infidélité.
> Non fletibus hic; canticis locus est,
> Aut si flendum, flenda Anglia.
>
> Que de cantiques saints ce Tombeau retentisse,
> Et que toujours on en bannisse
> Et les larmes et les douleurs.
> Ou s'il y faut pleurer, s'il faut qu'on y gémisse,
> Pour l'Angleterre seule il faut verser des pleurs."

What follows is at the Scotch College at Paris, where his brains are in a fine Mausoleum.

D. O. M.

Memoriæ
Augustissimi Principis
Jocobi II. Magnæ Britan : &c, Regis

Ille partis terra ac mari triumphis clarus, sed constanti in Deum fide clarior; huic Regna, opes et omnia vitæ florentis commoda postposuit. Per summum scelus a sua sede pulsus, Absolomis Impietatem, Architophelis perfidiam, et acerba Semei convitia, invictâ lenitate et patientiâ, ipsis etiam inimicis amicus, superavit; Rebus humanis major, adversis superior et cœlestis gloriæ studio inflammatus, quod Regno caruerit sibi visus beatior, miseram hanc vitam felici, Regnum terrestre cœlesti commutavit.

Hæc domus quam pius Princeps labantem sustinuit, et patrie fovit, cui etiam ingenii sui monumenta, omnia scilicet MSS sua costodienda commisit, eam corporis partem quâ maximè animus viget religiose servandam suscepit.

Vixit annis LXVIII, Regnavit XVI
Obiit XVI Kal. Oct. An. Sal. Hum.
M. D. CCI.

Jacobus Dux de Perth Præfectus Institutioni Jacobi III Magnæ Britanniæ &c Regis, Hujus domus Benefactor mœrens posuit.

What epitaph the Jesuits have framed at St. Omer's, or the nuns of the Visitation at Challiot by Paris, where his royal heart reposes by that of his mother Henrietta of France, I have neither seen nor heard, but the English Austin Nuns having obtained part of the flesh of his right arm entombed in the wall of their choir with this epitaph:

Parva moles, ingens virtus,
Particula fortissimi brachii
Potentissimi Principis Jacobi II
Magnæ Britanniæ Regis,
Quem perduelles subditi immani scelere
In exilium pepulerunt.
Verum non nisi post quam Ipsum se captivum fecerat
In obsequium Fidei,

> Victima Religionis, Norma Pietatis, Gloria Catholicorum,
> Miraculum Regum.
> Lector, bene precare, piis ac Regiis manibus
> Et venerare Has, tantum non sacras, Reliquias
> Pretiosissimi Dono datas, ac huic allatas a Castro S. Germ.
> in Layo, 1701

To these I may well add the verses of Brother Wilfrid Reeves on Louis the Great and James the Just.

L. J.

> Quam bene junxerunt Dii te, Ludovice, Jacobo
> Dum tu defendis, sustinet ille, Crucem
> Impare sorte, pares meritis, fortesque, piique,
> Illum Palma manet; Laurea tota tua est.

Leave demanded and joyfully granted, the Reverend Dominicans of the great Convent in St. James' Street, on the 19th. of October came in solemn procession to St. Edmund's, and sung in musick a Requiem for the King.

On the fortieth (day) his Service was kept very solemn, the Church hung in black from top to bottom &c. Dom Arnoult, Lord Prior of the great royal Abbey of St. Denis, invited by the Fathers of St. Edmund's, officiated in great state with his Religious at the rate of their Abbey where all the Kings of France are interred.

CHAPTER THE SIXTY-NINTH.

EXTRAORDINARY EFFECTS BY THE INVOCATION OF KING JAMES II OF HOLY MEMORY.

ANNO 1702, the world taking alarm at miracles said to be wrought at King James' tomb, on the 18th of February the Princess of Condé came; on the 6th of April Madame Maintenon; on the 17th of April the Duchess of Burgundy made her Jubilee Stations at the Church, and was some time in prayer in the Chapel where the royal corpse reposes in state. A month after, to wit on the 17th of May, the Archbishop of Paris, Cardinal Noailles, did the same thing with the Canons of his most illustrious Cathedral in procession. And on the 15th of June following, His Eminence issued out a commission to Joachim de la Chetardie (a person of great account, Priest, Bachelor of Sorbonne and Curate of the great parish of St. Sulpice in the Suburbs of St. German at Paris, a man of eminent learning and piety who had refused a bishopric) to examine the King's miracles, which he did with great exactness and all the rigour used on such accounts, and has verified at least twenty. The great St. Charles Borromeus, Cardinal and Archbishop of Milan, was canonized upon the proof of twenty miracles. Many other great persons publicly and privately have and do visit the royal tomb. Bishops say Mass there and have Masses said for them. Particularly the late famous Bishop of Meaux, M. Bossuet, before his death had neuvaines celebrated for him; so likewise Cardinal Coïlen, Bishop of Orleans.

On the 14th of December, Doctor Moor, (Irish by nation) being chosen Rector of the University of Paris, brought the whole University of Paris in procession &c, to St. Edmund's to do the King honour. And indeed a noble ceremony it was. This was the same year the King died.

The anniversary day was kept more solemn yet than the 40th ; for the Bishop of Autun officiated.

Anno 1703, September 15th, the Queen, (her two years of mourning being out, very privately and in incognito as her Majesty does still betwixt whiles,) visited her royal Consort's tomb.

The same year on the feast of St. James the Apostle, in July, at St. Edmund's, in the chamber where his Majesty used to lie when he honoured the house with his pious retreats, died his Chaplain R. F. Joseph Aprice after a long sickness, aged about fifty three (July 25th, 1703.) He was professed of Dieulwart and so acceptable to the King, that his Majesty would have him in his service wheresoever he went. He lies with Mr. Penrodock his dear friend.

Anno 1704 on the 12th of April æt. 78, died the illustrious Bishop of Meaux, M. Bossuet. Some of his controversy books were Englished by Father Johnston.

September 30th, the Royal Princess of England visited her royal father's tomb.

CHAPTER THE SEVENTIETH.

THE 24TH GENERAL CHAPTER. DEATH OF FATHER DUNSTAN LAKE AT LA TRAPPE.

ANNO 1705, the 24th General Chapter was held at London where R. F. Bernard Gregson was the second time chosen President.

Second elect President and Provincial of Canterbury Rev. Fr. Austin Howard.

The Provincial of York, R. F. Philip Metham.

The Prior of Douay, R. F. William Philips; who refusing, R. F. Cuthbert Tatham became Prior.

The Prior of Dieulwart, by a special privilege was Rev. Fr. Francis Watmough, for he became Prior of that place in the foregoing Quadriennium upon R. F. Mather's refusing the charge.

The Prior of Paris R. F. Joseph Johnston, R. F. William Philipson refusing the office.

The Abbess of Cambray, Dame Cecilia Hussey.

Their Vicar, R. F. Placid Acton, to whom succeeded R. F. John Stourton; upon which his Secretaryship was cast upon R. F. Robert, otherwise John Hardcastle.

At Lisbon (December 31st) died Catherine of Portugal, Queen Dowager of England, a Princess of great piety and example.

Anno 1706 (September 17th, Friday) King James III communicated at his royal father's tomb; he had been there before and could not forbear his tears; but now he had outreached the ears prescribed for his being of age, which were eighteen.

CHAPTER THE SEVENTIETH.

Anno 1707, Louis the Great commanded that the English Benedictines who had any benefices in his dominions should only possess them for the public and common good of the house of their profession: so that they have only the name of them, and what the last General Chapter allows out of their benefices when they need assistance in England.

Anno 1768, his said Majesty most graciously confirmed to them what they had at La Celle which he annexes by his royal charter to the house at Paris.

Last year (Anno 1707) I had the honour of a letter from the most Reverend Abbot of La Trappe, Dom Jacques de la Cour, wherein his Reverence assured me that R. F. Dunstan, otherwise Farington Lake, who with leave of his Superiors in the beginning of October, 1697, was withdrawn thither, had exchanged this life for a better on the 30th of March, which is the solemnity of St. John Climachus, a particular patron of La Trappe, in the year 1704. They called him there Dom Bede, and in that fervourous community he appeared a Saint, and his last end answered his life. Paris house is much indebted to him for he was a fortune to it and a blessing, sparing no pains to serve his house; but dreading the functions of the Apostolical mission, he thought his salvation would be most secure in a retired life.

An. 1709, on the 15th of May, the house of St. Edmund at Paris was a second time upon public Town-duty going in Procession to the Cathedral and from thence to S. Genovefa's. The next day was the General Procession of Paris.

And this year the General Chapter was deferred for a year by reason an excessive cold and frost beginning at the Epiphany and holding about 2 weeks and taking up again betwixt whiles, had caused such hurt to the fruits of the earth that voyaging or travelling could not prove but most excessive costly and troublesome.

Anno 1710 towards the middle of February Father John Dakins was taken with something of an apoplexy at La Celle at Matins in the Choir and thought to have weathered it out, but on the 25th (Feria iij) about half an hour after his Mass he was again seized therewith so violently that he lost the use of his speech and became altogether helpless, the palsy taking away the use of his right side ; and thus notwithstanding all that art could devise he continued to a quarter before 7 o'clock in the evening of the 28th of the said Febr: (Fer. vj) and then expired, æt. 42, Relig. 22.

On the Tuesday in Easter Week the enemies began to environ Douay and a dreadful siege it proved, holding to the 26th of June. Many of our houses sheltered themselves in the neighbouring monasteries; several with the Prior abided the fatigue and dread of the siege, Fr. Pullein got with the children they take care of to Cambray, in order to beseech the Duke of Marlborough to favour their House against which all the force of their batteries stood ; the Duke received him very civilly and promised he would favour them all he could ; and so it pleased the goodness of God that the house was more frighted than hurt.

CHAPTER THE SEVENTY-FIRST.

THE TWENTY-FIFTH GENERAL CHAPTER IS HELD AT DOUAY. DEATH OF FATHER BERNARD GREGSON. DIEULWART SAVED FROM DISSOLUTION.

WHEREFORE at the Nativity of our Lady (September 8th.) 1710 the 25th General Chapter began (at Douay) in which was chosen for President the V. R. F. Gregory Riddell, Doctor of Divinity in the University of Douay.

Second elect President, R. F. Michael Pullein.
The Provincial of Canterbury, R. F. Bernard Gregson.
The Provincial of York, R. F. Laurence Casse.
The Abbot of Lambspring R. F. Augustine Tempest who was chosen last July, Father Maurus Knightley being dead on the 28th of April preceding.
The Prior of St. Gregory's, R. F. Michael Pullein.
The Prior of St. Laurence's, R. F. Robert Hardcastle.
The Prior of St. Edmund's, R. F. Anthony Turberville.
The Abbess of Cambray, Dame Scholastica Houghton.
Their Vicar, R. F. John Stourton, again.
Secretary, R. F. Edward Chorley.
The Cathedral Prior of Worcester R. F. Francis Watmough.
The Cathedral Prior of Peterborough, R. F. Joseph Berriman.

Definitores Regiminis. { 1. R. F. Benedict Gibbon.
2. R. F. Joseph Johnston.
3. R. F. Edmund Taylor.

CHAPTER THE SEVENTY-FIRST.

Adsunt 14 personaliter, 7 per deputatos.

This Chapter was to have been held last year, but as we said above, the public calamities of the times hindered.

Anno 1711, January 27th, at London died the Very Rev. Father Bernard Gregson, ex-President, then Provincial of Canterbury. The fatigues of his last Presidentship, which continued five years, quite bereaved him of the little health he enjoyed in a body broken with sickness and labour; for being forced to cross the seas often, and ramble to and fro through Flanders, France, Lorraine and Germany, he could never recover the fatigue of his late voyage, which was to the Chapter. He governed *fortiter et suaviter*. A superior very humble, modest, courteous, sweet, affable, and reasonable, so as nothing could be more satisfactory in his comportment and behaviour to his subjects, while themselves adhered to reason. For when one, forgetting God and himself, thought to baffle his duty, he knew how not to let his patience and mildness be abused, but make to ply under the severity of the law all contempt of what the law in reason and justice required as duty. Wherefore imprudent rashness rued that which true piety and prudence would have avoided. Dieulwart, the house of his profession, he laboured to exalt by all lawful means possible, and for ever, of necessity, it will stand highly indebted to the worthy memory of his generous and industrious gratitude. Æternam Deus Optimus Maximus det ei requiem, et lux sanctorum illuceat animæ ejus.

July 19th. R. F. President arrived here with his Secretary to make a visit, and so on the 11th of August departed for Cambray, while on the 10th at Douay R. F. Hitchcock departed this life, æt. 94. Relig. 65.

The queen preserved our house of Dieulwart from being dissolved by the king of France, because he said it was established without his Patents, and Her Majesty now obtained that our Fathers of Douay should be paid their money out of the Townhouse, though Douay was taken.

Anno 1712, Feb. 12th, on which we served Saint Scholastica, died the Dauphiness, formerly Duchess of Burgundy, and on the 18th, (Fer. v), in the same month died her royal consort.

CHAPTER THE SEVENTY-FIRST.

Anno 1712, April 18th. died the Princess of England of the small-pox, at S. German's en Lay, and lies in deposit at Paris with her Royal Father, King James II, at St. Edmund's.

THE END.

APPENDIX.

APPENDIX.

I

A list of the Presidents General of the English Congregation of the order of St. Benedict, from the year 1619, with the date of their election.

1619. R. F. Leander of St. Martin	1701. R. F. Augustine Howard
1621. ,, ,, Rudesind Barlow	1705. ,, ,, Bernard Gregson
1629. ,, ,, Sigebert Bagshaw †	1710. ,, ,, Gregory Riddell
1633. ,, ,, Claud White or Bennet	1713. ,, ,, Francis Watmough
1633. ,, ,, Leander of St. Martin †	1717. ,, ,, Laurence Fenwick
1635. ,, ,, Clement Reyner	1721. ,, ,, Thomas Southcot
1641. ,, ,, Jocelin Elmer	1741. ,, ,, Cuthbert Farnworth
1645. ,, ,, Wilfrid Selby	1753. ,, ,, Placid Howard †
1649. ,, ,, Placid Gascoigne	1766. ,, . Placid Naylor †
1653. ,, ,, Claud White or Bennet †	1772. ,, ,, John Fisher
1655. ,, ,, Laurence Reyner	1777. ,, ,, Augustine Walker †
1657. ,, ,, Paul Robinson	1794. ,, ,, Gregory Cowley †
1659. ,, ,, Cuthbert Horsley	1799. ,, ,, Bede Brewer †
1661. ,, ,, Augustine Hungate	1822. ,, ,, Richard Marsh
1669. ,, ,, Benedict Stapylton †	1826. ,, ,, Augustine Birdsall †
1680. ,, ,, Maurus Corker	1837. ,, ,, Richard Marsh
1681. ,, ,, Joseph Sherburne †	1842. ,, ,, Bernard Barber †
1697. ,, ,, Augustine Howard	1850. ,, ,, Alban Molyneux
1697. ,, ,, Bernard Gregson	1854. ,, ,, Placid Burchall

II

A Catalogue of the Provincials.

(I) of Canterbury   and   (II) of York.

1620. R. F. Robert Sadler †	1620 R. F. Bede Helme
1621. ,, ,, Joseph Prater	1625 ,, ,, Robert Haddock
1625. ,, ,, Mark Crowther	1629 ,, ,, John Hutton
1629. ,, ,, Claud White or Bennet	1633 ,, ,, Augustine Hungate
1633. ,, ,, Robert Sherwood	1649 ,, ,, Laurence Reyner
1641. ,, ,, Paulinus Greenwood †	1653 ,, ,, Gregory Hungate †

† *Died in office.*

APPENDIX.

Provincials of Canterbury				Provincials of York			
1645.	R.	F.	Claud White or Bennet	1653-7	R.	F.	Augustine Hungate
1653.	,,	,,	Anselm Crowther †	1661.	,,	,,	Bede Taylard
1666.	,,	,,	Gregory Mallet †	1677.	,,	,,	Francis Lawson
1681.	,,	,,	Augustine Llewellin	1685.	,,	,,	Robert Killingbeck
1693.	,,	,,	Augustine Constable	1693.	,,	,,	Michael Pullein
1697.	,,	,,	Augustine Howard	1701.	,,	,,	Augustine Tempest
1701.	,,	,,	Bernard Gregson	1705.	,,	,,	Sylvester Metham
1705.	,,	,,	Augustine Howard	1710.	,,	,,	Laurence Casse
1710.	,,	,,	Bernard Gregson †	1713.	,,	,,	Bede Halsall
1711.	,,	,,	Ildephonsus Aprice †	1717.	,,	,,	Bernard Greaves †
1712.	,,	,,	Francis Rookwood	1720.	,,	,,	Anselm Carter
1717.	,,	,,	Francis Watmough	1721.	,,	,,	Gregory Skelton †
1721.	,,	,,	William Banester	1721.	,,	,,	Laurence Casse
1725.	,,	,,	Gregory Greenwood	1725.	,,	,,	Wilfrid Helme
1737.	,,	,,	Robert Hardcastle	1729.	,,	,,	Cuthbert Farnworth
1741.	,,	,,	Francis Bruning	1741.	,,	,,	Placid Naylor
1745.	,,	,,	Placid Howard	1766.	,,	,,	Benedict Steare
1753.	,,	,,	Henry Wyburne †	1777.	,,	,,	Anselm Bolas
1769.	,,	,,	Bernard Bradshaw †	1785.	,,	,,	Michael Lacon
1774.	,,	,,	Joseph Carteret	1806.	,,	,,	Richard Marsh
1777.	,,	,,	Bernard Warmoll	1822.	,,	,,	Henry Lawson
1805.	,,	,,	Dunstan Garstang	1822.	,,	,,	Gregory Robinson. †
1806.	,,	,,	Ralph Ainsworth †	1837.	,,	,,	Anselm Brewer
1814.	,,	,,	Bernard Barr	1846.	,,	,,	Alban Molyneux
1122.	,,	,,	Augustine Birdsall	1850.	,,	,,	Ignatius Greenough
1826.	,,	,,	Benedict Deday	1858.	,,	,,	Athanasius Allanson †
1834.	,,	,,	Bernard Barber	1876.	,,	,,	Cuthbert Clifton
1842.	,,	,,	Dunstan Scott	1878.	,,	,,	Augustine Bury
1846.	,,	,,	Jerome Jenkins				
1852.	,,	,,	Paulinus Heptonstall				
1866.	,,	,,	Cuthbert Smith				

III

A list of the monks professed in, or aggregated to, the English Benedictine Congregation: and first of those admitted to profession by Father Sigebert Buckley.

1607. Nov. 21st.   Dom. Vincent, Robert Sadler *alias* **Robert Walter**, of Collier's Oak Warwickshire.
,, ,, ,, ,, ,,   Edward Maihew, of Dinton, **Wiltshire**.

† *Died in office.*

APPENDIX.

R. F. Augustine Baker, of Abergavenny, Monmouthshire.
,, ,, Sigebert Bagshaw.
,, ,, Bartholomew.
,, ,, Placid.—and several others.

(2). In the Cassinese Congregation were professed (1588-1619).

R. F. Gregory, Robert Sayr, at Monte Cassino.
,, ,, Thomas Preston.   ,,   ,,
,, ,, Augustine Smith.   ,,   ,,
,, ,, Richard Huddleston,   ,,   ,,
,, ,, Bernard Preston,   ,,   ,,
,, ,, Anselm Beech, of Manchester, professed at St. Justina's at Padua.
,, ,, Maurus Taylor, professed at St George's, Venice.
,, ,, Athanasius, Anthony Martin, professed at La Cava, near Salerno.
,, ,, Raphael, professed at St. Paul without the Walls, Rome.
,, ,, Gervase Grey.
,, ,, William Palmer.
,, ,, David Codner.
,, ,, Samuel Kennet.
,, ,, Henry Styles.
,, ,, Michael Godfrey.

(3). In the Spanish Benedictine Congregation were professed, (1600-1619)

R. F. Augustine Bradshaw, alias White, of Worcester, professed at St. Martin's, Compostella.
,, ,, John Roberts, alias Mervin, of Merionethshire,   ,,   (1595).
,, ,, Leander Jones or Scudamore, of Kentchurch, Herefordshire. ,,
,, ,, Joseph Prater   ,,
,, ,, Gregory Grange,   ,,
,, ,, Robert Haddock, alias Benson.   ,,
,, ,, John Hutton,   ,,
,, ,, William Johnson, alias Chambers   ,,
,, ,, John Harper, professed at the Abbey of St. Æmilian.
,, ,, John Baines, professed at St. Benedict's Abbey, Valladolid.
,, ,, Thomas, Torquatus Latham.   ,,   ,,   ,,
,, ,, Justus Edner, alias Rigge.   ,,   ,,   ,,
,, ,, Thomas Green, alias Houghton. ,,   ,,   ,,
,, ,, Maurus Scott professed at the Abbey of St. Facundus, Sahagun.
,, ,, Augustinus   ,,   ,,   ,,
,, ,, Thomas Emerson   ,,   ,,   ,,
,, ,, Boniface Blandy.   ,,   ,,   ,,
,, ,, Benedict Jones.   ,,   ,,   ,,
,, ,, Placid Peto, alias Badd.   ,,   ,,   ,,
,, ,, Augustine Hungate.professed at Montserrat.
,, ,, Boniface Kemp, alias Kipton, ,,
,, ,, Anselm Tuberville.   ,,

F. R. Beda Helme, professed at Montserrat.
,, ,, Andrew Shirly, professed at the Abbey of Najar.
,, ,, Nicholas Becket, professed at the Abbey of Ona.
,, ,, Paulinus. ,,
,, ,, Francis Atrobas. ,,
,, ,, Bernard Berington. ,,
,, ,, Rudesind Barlow, professed at the Abbey of Cella Nova.
,, ,, George Brown, professed at the Abbey of St. Sinbert.
,, ,, George Berington, professed at the Abbey of St. Millan.

And in other Monasteries in Spain were professed:

R. F. Maurus Hanson.
,, ,, Thomas Hungate.
,, ,, Peter Wilcock.
,, ,, Lambert Clifton.
,, ,, Constantius Nathal, *alias* Matthews.
,, ,, John Owen.
,, ,, Edward Ash.

(4). The following Religious were professed on the English Mission.

R. F. George Gervase, **of Bosham, Sussex.**
,, ,, Thomas Dyer.
,, ,, Robert Edmunds.
,, ,, Francis Foster.
,, ,, Thomas Minshall.
,, ,, Peter Warnford.
,, ,, William Middleton, *alias* Hethcote.
,, ,, George Bacon.
,, ,, John Huddleston, **of Sawston, Cambridgeshire.**

(5). The following members of the Scotch Benedictine Congregation were admitted into the English Congregation.

R. F. William Gordon.
,, ,, Celestine Anderton.
,, ,, Roland Dunn.
,, ,, Alexander Brown.

(6). The following were **members of the** Congregation **of** SS. Vanne and Hydulph in Lorraine, and were admitted into the English Congregation in 1625.

R. F. Deusdedit **Jarfield.**
,, ,, Anselm Pearson.

APPENDIX. 7

IV

The Monastery of St. Gregory the Great at Douai.

List of Priors with the date of their election.

1605. R. F. Augustine Bradshaw	1693. R. F. John Phillipson
1612. ,, ,, Leander of St. Martin	1701. ,, ,, Michael Pullein
1613. ,, ,, Rudesind Barlow	1705. ,, ,, Cuthbert Tatham
1620. ,, ,, Francis Atrobus	1710. ,, ,, Michael Pullein
1621. ,, ,, Leander of St. Martin	1713. ,, ,, Sylvester Metham †
1625. ,, ,, Rudesind Barlow	1715. ,, ,, Edwardus Chorley
1629. ,, ,, Leander of St. Martin	1717. ,, ,, John Stourton
1633. ,, ,, Joseph Frere	1721. ,, ,, William Pestel, alias Phillips
1641. ,, ,, John Meutisse	
1653. ,, ,, Bernard Palmes	1723. ,, ,, Anthony Oard
1657. ,, ,, Benedict Stapylton	1725. ,, ,, Laurence York
1662. ,, ,, Joseph Frere	1729. ,, ,, Basil Warwick †
1666. ,, ,, Godric Blount †	1732. ,, ,, Thomas Nelson
1667. ,, ,, William Hitchcock	1737. ,, ,, Benedict Steare
1673. ,, ,, Alexius Caryll	1745. ,, ,, Alexius Shepherd †
1675. ,, ,, William Hitchcock	1755. ,, ,, Augustine Moore †
1677. ,, ,, Augustine Howard	1775. ,, ,, Gregory Sharrock
1681. ,, ,, Jerome Hesketh	1781. ,, ,, Jerome Sharrock †
1685. ,, ,, William Hitchcock	

A list of the Monks of St. Gregory's, Douay, with the date of their profession, extracted from the *Liber Graduum Conventus S. Gregorii Duaci, Congregationis Angliæ, ordinis monachorum nigrorum S. Patris nostri Benedicti.* *

1607. July 18th. R. F. Joseph Haworth.
1608. May 15th. R. F. Nicholas Fitzjames, of **Redlynch, Somersetshire**.
1609. September 8th. R. F. Boniface Wilford.
 ,,   ,,   13th. R. F. Columban Malone, of Lancashire.
 ,,   ,,   14th. R. F. Mark Crowder, of Shropshire.
1610. November 16th. R. F. Thomas Monington, of All hallows, Herefordshire.
 ,,   November 16th. R. F. Gregory Hungate **of the diocese of York.**
 ,,   ,,   ,,   Brother Peter Huitson, **of Ashburne, Derbyshire**, a Lay-Brother
1611. July 3rd. R. F. Anselm Crowder, of Montgomery.
1612. January 12th. R. F. Paulinus Greenwood, of Brentwood, Essex.
1613. October 18th. R. F. Robert of St. Mary, Sherwood, of Bath, Somersetshire.

† *Died in office*   * *This manuscript is preserved at* **St. Gregory's, Downside.**

APPENDIX

1613. October 8th. R. F. Thomas Hill.
1614. March 21st. R. F. Cuthbert of St. Martin, Martin Hartbourne of Shillington, Durham.
„ „ , R. F. Anthony of St. William, **William Winchcombe**, of Henwick, Berks.
„ „ , R. F. James of St. Gregory, James Shirbourne of Little Milton, Whalley, Lancaster.
„ June 15th. Br. Edmund Arrowsmith, of Lancashire, a **Lay-Brother**.
„ July 11th. R. F. Richard of St. John, Richard Hodgson of Gromon, Yorkshire
„ „ 13th. R. F. Maurus of St. John, John Curre, of Sandonfec Berkshire.
„ „ , R. F. Moundeford, of S. Martin, of Wenhamrow, Norfolk.
„ „ 22nd R. F. Maurus of St. Mary, William Atkins, of Oatwell Norfolk.
1615. February 15. R. F. Alphonsus of St. Gregory, William Hanson or Hesketh, of Barrowfield Lancashire.
„ „ , R. F. George Hathersall
1616. January 5th. R. F. Ambrose, Edward Barlow, of Manchester.
„ „ , R. F. Augustine of St. Eugenius, *alias* Owen.
1617. Sept. 29th. R. F. Joseph of St. Mary, George Latham, of Rainfaith, Lancashire.
„ „ , R. F. Placid of St. John, Hartburn, *alias* Foorde.
1618. July 31st. R. F. Augustine of St. Benedict, John Richardson, of Somersetshire.
1620. March 12th. R. F. Joseph Frere, of Essex.
„ March 21st. R. F. Wilfrid of St. Michael, Richard Reade or Selby, of Durham.
„ May 5th. R. F. Epiphanius of St. Mary, Rudadelphus Stapylton, of Carleton, Yorkshire.
„ June 18th. R. F. Francis of St. Joseph, Cape, of Chichester, Sussex.
„ June 20th. R. F. Romuald Danvers, of Suffolk.
„ August 15th. R. F. Philip Roger or Prosser, *alias* Morgan or Powel, of Tralon, Brecknockshire.
„ „ R. F. Laurence Mabbs, of Leicestershire,
„ „ R. F. Maurus of St. Nicholas, Nicholas Pritchard, of Monmouthshire.
„ October 1st R. F. William Walter Kemble, of Herefordshire.
„ „ , R. F. Placid of St. Francis, Loader *alias* Ireland, of London.
„ „ , R. F. Bede of St. Magdalen, Gaile, of York.
„ November 25th R. F. John Lone, of Kent.
„ „ R. F. Cuthbert, John Fursden, of Thorverton, Devonshire.
1621. June 29th R. F. Augustine of St. Mary, Stoker, of Mechliu.
„ „ , R. F. Francis of St. Benedict, Crathorne, of Yorkshire.
„ October 18th. R. F. Austin of St. John, Kinder, of Nottingham.

APPENDIX.

1621	December 28th	D. Gregory of the Immaculate Conception, **Haywood**, of Cockthorpe, Oxfordshire.
1622	January 15th	D. Michael of St. Mary, Gascoigne, of Barnbow, Yorkshire.
„	June 29th	D. George of St. Ildephonsus, of Sculthorpe, Norfolk.
„	July 2nd,	D. Gregory of St. Richard, Moore, of Carlisle.
„	December 8th	D. Vincent Latham, of Lancashire.
„	——	D. Jerome Porter, *alias* Nelson.
„	——	D. Thomas Woodhope, *alias* White, of Worcestershire.
1623	January 12th	D. Leander Pritchard, of Monmouthshire.
„	October 22nd	D. Francis Morgan, of Weston, Warwickshire.
„	„ „	D. James Anderton, of Lancashire.
„	November 1st	D. Francis Tresham, of Northampton.
„	„ 21st	D. Thomas Tanke, of Pembrokeshire.
1624	May 10th	D. Gregory Grainge, or Carnaby, of Yorkshire.
„	July 4th	D. Augustine of St. Benedict, Lee, *alias* Johnson, of Mortlake, Surrey.
„	August 15th	D. John Byfleet, of Devonshire.
„	„ „	D. Placid Frere, of Essex.
„	August 24th	D. Christopher Anderton, of Lancashire.
„	„ 25th	D. John Allen, of Middlesex.
„	September 29th	D. John of St. Mary, Norton, of Sussex.
„	„ „	D. Amandus Southcot, of Devonshire.
„	October 28th	D. Christian Govaerdt, of Bruges.
1625	January 20th	D. Stanislaus Tanke, of Pembrokeshire.
„	February 2nd	D. Maurus Smith, of London.
„	„ „	D. Benedict Brychan, *alias* Thomas, of Brecknockshire
„	March 30th	D. Robert Stapylton, of Carlton, **Yorkshire**.
„	April 21st	D. Amatus Legatt, of Shaftesbury, **Dorset**.
„	September 8th	D. Michael Blakestone, of Durham.
„	November 1st	D. Thomas Swinburne, of Northumberland.
1626	April 12th	D. John Meutisse, *alias* Northall, of Shropshire.
„	October 4th	D. Francis Blackestone, of Durham.
„	December 8th	D. Anselm Cassey, of Herefordshire.
1630	November 3rd	D. Robert, Theodore Barlow, **of Manchester**.
1631	March 23rd	D. Paulinus Hird, or Laton, of Battle, **Yorkshire**.
1632	January 18th	D. Peter Salvin, of Thornton, Durham.
„	July 4th	D. Edward Wolseley, of Staffordshire.
1634	March 12th	D. Gregory Scrogges, of Chichester, Sussex.
„	„ „	D. Maurus, John Scrogges, **of** Chichester, Sussex.
„	„ „	D. Placid Scrogges, **or** Windsor, of Bray, Berkshire.
1635	April 22nd	D. Laurence Appleton, of Benfleet, Essex.
„	September 8th	D. Leander Thomson, *alias* Richard Jackson, of Durham.
1636	February 2nd	D. Michael, **W** Wytham, of Clyff, Yorkshire.
1638	May 16th	D. Andrew **of** St. Benedict, **Andrew Whitfield**, of Hexham.

APPENDIX.

1638	November 13th	D. Augustine Conyers, of Yorkshire.
1639	September 8th	D. Benedict Preston, of Lancashire.
,,	September 21st	D. Jerome Hesketh, of Lancashire.
,,	October 23rd	D. Hilarion Wake, *alias* John Merriman, of Carryhouse, Durham.
1643	October 28th	D. Cuthbert, Thomas Middelton, of Stockeld, Yorkshire.
,,	,, ,,	D. Benedict, Gregory Stapleton, or Stapylton of Carlton,* Yorkshire.
,,	November 22nd	D. Robert Corham, of Antwerp.
,,	,, ,,	D. Anselm, George Touchett, of Stalbridge, Dorsetshire.
,,	December 27th	D. Bernard, George Palmes, of Naborne Castle, Yorkshire.
1644	June 11th	D. Edward Sheldon, of Weston, Warwickshire.
1645	April 2nd	D. Thomas Stourton, of Stourton, Wilts.
1649	August 22nd	D. Serenus, Hugh Cressy, of Thorpsalvin, Yorkshire.
,,	,, ,,	D. Placid, Edward Bittenson, of Essex.
,,	,, ,,	D. Augustine, Thomas Constable, of Eagle Castle, Lincolnshire.
,,	,, ,,	D. Godric of St. Martin, Richard Blount, of Fawley, Berkshire.
,,	,, ,,	D. Bede, William Witham, of Coken Castle, Durham.
1650	February 14th	D. William of St. Catherine, Walgrave, *alias* Pleayll, of Barneston, Essex.
,,	————	D. William Hitchcock, or Nedam.†
,,	————	D. Leander Normington.
,,	————	D. Francis Lawson, of Yorkshire.
,,	————	D. Maurus Poss, or Nichols.
,,	————	D. Bernard Salkeld, of Cumberland.
c 1653	————	D. Lionel Sheldon, of Weston, Warwickshire.
,,	————	Br. John Barter, a novice, died July 1st, 1653.
1654	————	D. Basil Roan.
,,	————	D. John Barter, (the Elder).
,,	————	D. Laurence Errington.
,,	————	D. Alexius Caryll, of West Grinstead, Sussex.
,,	————	D. Joseph Berriman, Somersetshire.
1657	————	D. Ambrose Bride.
,,	————	D. Bede Tatham, of Yorkshire.
,,	————	D. Bennet, George Hemsworth.
,,	————	D. Basil Skinner.
1660	————	Br. Thomas Pickering, Lay-brother.
,,	————	D. Wolstan Crosby.
,,	————	D. Philip Constable, of Yorkshire.

* "De castro quod vocatur quousque" MS.
† The precise dates of the profession of all between D. William Walgrave and D. Bruno Jennings cannot be ascertained.

APPENDIX. 11

1660	———	D. George Beare.
1661	———	D. John Martin, of Balsbury, (Baltonsborough) Somersetshire.
1662	———	D. Placid Skinner.
1662	———	D. Augustine Howard.
1667	———	D. Thomas Wilson.
1668	———	D. Ildephonsus Willobie, or Rider.
„	———	D. Jerome, Ralph Wilson.
„	July 11th,	D. Bruno, John Jennings, (Jenyns) of Middlesex.
1670	November 30th	D. Francis, Samuel Sidgewick, of Durham.
„	„ „	D. Philip Ellis, of Waddesdon, Bucks.
„	„ „	D. Anselm, George Carter, of Worcestershire.
1672	December 8th	D. Michael Pullein, of Hampswith, Yorkshire.
„	„ „	D. Charles Sumpner of Hellingly Castle, Sussex.
a 1674	„ „	Br. Peter Holmes, Lay-brother.
1676	July 11th	D. Wilfrid, Richard Reeve, of Gloucester.
„	„ „	D. Dunstan, Joseph Porter, of Cumberland.
„	„ „	D. John Philipson of Strenly, Berkshire.
„	„ „	D. Bernard, Joseph Greeves, of Northumberland.
„	November 1st	D. Richard Holme, of Lancashire.
1678	April 17th	D. Cuthbert, James Tatham, of Burton, **Yorkshire.**
„	October 16th	D. Benedict, John Wilson, of Seftley, **Durham.**
1679	March 25th	D. Serenus, Roger Rotton, of Harborne, **Staffordshire.**
1680	May 26th	D. Edmund Taylor, of London.
„	September 13th	D. Francis Rookwood, of Suffolk.
1681	September 14th	D. Gregory, John Skelton, of Cumberland.
„	„ „	D. Joseph, Roger Hesketh, of Lancashire.
„	December 21st	D. Augustine, Francis Acton, of London.
1682	October 11th	D. William Pestell *alias* Philips, of Winchester.
1683	September 30th	D. Sylvester, Philip Metham of Yorkshire.
„	November 30th	D. Maurus, Christopher Barber, of London.
1684	February	Br. Peter Money, Lay-brother.
a 1685		Br. Thomas Brabant, Lay-brother.
1685	January 12th	D. Jerome, John Willson, of Yorkshire.
„	July 29th	Br. John Green, a Lay-brother.
„	„ „	Br. Henry Lawson, a Lay-brother.
„	December 8th	D. Placid, John Acton, of London.
„	„ „	D. Laurence, Lewis Fenwick, of Northumberland.
„	„ „	D. Cuthbert, William Hutton, of Durham.
„	„ „	D. Thomas Wytham, of Yorkshire.
„	„ „	D. Anthony, Ralph **Oard**, of Stourton Grange, Northumberland.
1687	June 19th	D. Bede, Arthur Halsall, of Oringham, Northumberland.
„	„ „	D. John Baptist Savory, of Oxford.
1688	May 3rd	D. George Canning, of Foxcote, Warwickshire.
„	August 1st	D. Gregory Greenwood, of **Brize** Norton, Oxfordshire.
„	„ „	D. William **Bannoster**, of Lancashire.

APPENDIX

1688	August 1st	D. Thomas Southcott, of Surrey.
"	" "	D. Joseph, Richard Ashton, of Lancashire.
1690	September 3rd	D. William Metcalf of Yorkshire.
"	" "	D. William Sheldon.
1692	February 24th	D. Francis Rich, of Kent.
"	" "	D. Gilbert Knowles, of Hampshire.
"	May 4th	D. Bernard Richard Bartlett, of Worcestershire.
"	October 5th	D. Benedict William Winter, of Huntingdonshire.
1693	July 14th	D. John Stourton, of Stourton, Wilts.
"	September 29th	D. Augustine, William Fenwick, of Northumberland.
1695	May	Br. Andrew, William Townson, Lay-brother.
"	August 15th	D. George Fitzwilliams, of Lincolnshire.
1698	January 5th	D. Richard Lannyng of Dorsetshire.
"	October 21st	D. Edward Chorley, of Lancashire.
"	" "	D. Basil, Thomas Warwick, of Warwick Hall, Cumberland.
1699	August 15th	D. Alexius, John Jones, of Middlesex.
1700	March 4th	D. Ambrose, William Brown, of Westmoreland.
"	" "	D. Hugh Frankland, of Yorkshire.
"	March 7th	D. Anselm, John Mannock, of Suffolk.
"	May ——	Br. Anthony Dandy, a Lay-brother.
1701	December 29th	D. Placid, Francis Haggerston, of Northumberland.
"	" "	D. Maurus, Richard Harrison, of Stokesley, Yorkshire.
1703	May 22nd	D. Thomas Nelson, of Lancashire.
"	" "	D. Joseph Starkey, *alias* Haumer, of London.
1704	August ——	Br. Gabriel Bocquet a Lay-brother.
1705	December 28th	D. Paul, Richard Chandler, of Maryland, North America.
"	" "	D. Laurence, William York, of London.
"	" "	Br. John Armston, Lay-brother.
1708	May 29th	D. Ildefonsus, William Byerley, of Leicestershire.
"	" "	D. Augustine, Francis Southcott, of Essex.
"	" "	D. Bernard, John Wythie, of Cambridgeshire.
1711	August 11th	D. Gregory, Edward Pigott, of Oxfordshire.
1712	November 21st	D. Joseph, William Howard, of Corby Castle, Cumberland.
1714	July 11th	D. Bedo Knight, of Somersetshire.
"	November 18th	D. Maurus, John Buckley, of Yorkshire.
"	" "	D. Anselm, Francis Lynch, of London.
1719	May 30th	D. Placid, John Howard, of Corby Castle, Cumberland.
"	" "	D. Ambrose, Edward Eliott, of Shropshire.
1720	October 17th	D. Benedict, Robert Stear, of London.
1721	December 21st	D. Alexius, Thomas Shephard, of Warwickshire.
1723	September 21st	D. Joseph, Francis Carteret, of London.
"	" "	D. Cuthbert, Anthony Hutchinson, of Yorkshire.
1724	November 21st	D. Gregory, John Mackay, of Northumberland.
1727	April 15th	D. Dunstan, Francis Pigott, of London.

APPENDIX. 13

	1729	May 22nd	D. Bartholomew, John Havers, of Thelveton, Norfolk.
	1731	August 15th	D. Augustine, Henry Brigham of Wyton, Yorkshire.
	„	„ „	D. Placid, William De la Fontain, of Luffwick, Northamptonshire.
	„	November 8th	D. Edward Hussey, of Marnhull, Dorsetshire.
a	1733	————	Br. Peter Deval, a Lay-brother.
	1733	October 5th	D. Basil Eyston, of Brecknock.
	„	„ „	D. Leander, Anthony Raffa, of London.
	1736	May 31st	Br. Anthony Parkinson, Lay-brother.
	„	September 8th	D. John Charlton, of Northumberland.
	„	„ „	D. Peter, Richard Walmesley, *alias* Sherburne, of Lancashire.
	1737	November 13th,	D. Bernard, John Warmoll, of Norfolk.
a	1738	————	Br. Mark Le Deux, Lay-brother.
	1738	November 16th,	Br. Dunstan, Peter Osbaldeston. Lay-brother.
	„	„ „	Br. Joseph, William Sharrock, Lay-brother
	„	„ „	Br. Andrew, Nicholas Barguet, or Berget, of Fines, in Champagne, Lay-brother.
	1740	March 12th	D. Augustine, James Moore of Fawley, Berkshire.
	1741	October 15th	D. Bede, Thomas Bennet, of Somersetshire.
	„	„ „	D. Benedict, Michael Pembridge, of London.
	1745	„ „	D. Maurus, Walter Blount, of Maple Durham, Oxfordshire.
	1746	July 3rd	D. Thomas Patten, of Lancashire.
	„	„ „	D. Gregory, John Watkinson, of London.
	„	„ „	D. Charles Smith, of London.
	1751	February 14th	D. Maurus, Jordan Langdale, of Yorkshire.
	1752	December 12th	D. Michael, George Lewis, of Hereford.
	1756	August 22nd	Br. Bennet, Dominic Mompas, of Douay, Lay-brother.
	1757	March 25th	D. Augustine, William Caldwell or Walmesley, of Lancashire.
	„	„ „	D. Anselm, Ranald Macdonald of Lochabor, Scotland.
	„	„ „	D. Laurence, Joseph Hadley, of London.
	„	September 11th	D. Benedict, Archibald Macdonald, of **Knodort**, (Lochabor.)
	„	„ „	D. Ambrose, John Naylor, of Lancashire.
	„	„ „	D. Bernard, Thomas Barr, of Hampshire.
	„	„ „	D. Placid, James **Duvivier**, *alias* Waters, of London.
	„	„ „	D. Bede, Francis **Anderton**, of Euxton, Lancashire.
	1758	September 29th	D. Gregory, William Sharrock, of Lancashire.
	1761	March 15th	D. Michael, Rowland Lacon, of Lindley, Shropshire.
	„	„ „	D. Jerome, William Digby, of Middlesex.
	„	September 20th	D. Augustine, John Hawkins, of Kent.
	„	„ „	D. Edmund, John Hadley of London, Middlesex.
	1764	April 1st	D. Cuthbert, John Edward Grime, of Essex.
	1768	August 13th	D. Jerome, Charles James Sharrock, of Lancashire.
	„	„ „	D. Anselm, Michael Lorymer, of Monmouthshire.

1768	October 3rd		D. George Johnson, of Warwickshire.
,,	,,	,,	D. Laurence, John Barnes, of Dorsetshire.
1768	October 3rd		D. Ambrose, William Allam, of London.
1776	January 1st		D. Bernard, Richard Butler, of Lancashire.
1777	January 15th		Br. Francis, Holderness, of Preston, Lancashire, Lay-brother.
1778	March 19th		Br. Silvester Quince, of Kent, Lay-brother.
1779	May 24th		D. Peter, Richard Kendall, of Bath, Somersetshire.
,,	August 22nd		D. Augustine, Thomas Lawson, of Brough, Yorkshire.
1781	July 2nd		Br. Paul Wilson, Lay-brother.
1785	January 12th		D. Henry Lawson, of York.
,,	August 7th		D. James Higginson, of Wrightington, Lancashire.
1788	July 24th		D. John Culshaw, of Latham, Lancashire.
1790	October 10th		D. Thomas Barker, of Cambridge.
,,	,,	,,	D. George Turner, of Houghton, Lancashire.
1792	October 21st		D. Raymund, John Eldridge, of London.
,,	,,	,,	D. Bernard, Joseph Hawarden, of Eccleston, Lancashire.
,,	,,	,,	D. Augustine, John Harrison, of Brough, Yorkshire.
,,	,,	,,	Br. Joseph Barber, of Macclesfield, Cheshire, Lay-brother.

V

A list of the Priors and professed religious of the Monastery of St. Laurence, at Dieulouart or Dieulwart in Lorraine.

Priors with the date of their election.

1609. D. Gabriel Giffard
1610. D. Nicholas Fitzjames
1610. D. Paulinus Appleby (de Ona)
1614. D. Edward Maihew
1620. D. Jocelin Elmer !
1621. D. Columban Malone †
1623. D. Laurence Reyner
1641. D. Cuthbert Horsley
1653. D. Laurence Reyner
1657. D. Cuthbert Horsley
1659. D. Placid Adelham
1661. D. Cuthbert Horsley
1677. D. John Girlington
1681. D. Bernard Gregson
1685. D. James Mather

1687. D. Mellitus Walmesley †
1689. D. James Mather
1693. D. Laurence Champney
1701. D. Francis Watmough
1710. D. Robert Hardcastle
1713. D. Bernard Lowick
1717. D. Laurence Champney
1721. D. Francis Watmough †
1733. D. Bernard Catteral
1753. D. Ambrose Kaye
1765. D. Gregory Cowley
1773. D. Dunstan Holderness
1781. D. Jerome Marsh
1785. D. Jerome Coupe
1789. D. Richard Marsh

† Died in office.

The Professed Monks of St. Laurence's, Dieulwart. *

1609		D. Gabriel of St. Mary, William Giffard, of Hampshire.
"		D. Joseph Haworth, of Lancashire.
1609	August 1st	D. Laurence Reyner, of Yorkshire.
"	September 8th	D. Francis Walgrave.
"		D. Mellitus, Robert Bapthorpe.
1610		D. Placid Hilton, *alias* Musgrave.
"		D. Bede Merriman.
"		D. Clement Reyner, of Yorkshire.
o 1610—11		D. Claude White, *alias* Bennet.
"		D. Placid Muttleberry, or Muttlebury of Somerset.
"		D. Bernard Edmunds, of Kent.
"		D. Jocelin Elmer.
"		D. Nicholas Curre.
1611		D. George Gaire.
1612		D. Alban, Bartholomew Roe, of Suffolk.
"		D. Augustine Heath, of Winchester.
"		D. Benedict, Robert Cox.
"		D. Benedict D'Orgain, of Dieulwart.
1614		D. Amandus Verner, *alias* Fermor, of Devonshire.
"	September 14th	D. Swithbert Latham, of Lancashire.
c 1615		D. Placid Gascoigne, of Yorkshire.
"		D. Dunstan Pottinger.
"		D. Anthony Batt.
"		D. Francis Hull, of Devonshire.
"		D. Francis Constable.
"		D. Boniface Chandler.
"		D. Peter Hunt.
"		D. Ambrose, John Langton.
"		D. Alexius Bennet.
"		D. Joseph Brookes
1620		D. Thomas Fursden.
"		D. Aldhelm Philips, of Herefordshire.
"		D. Laurence Lodwick.
c 1620		Br. Anthony Lovel, Lay-brother.
"		Br. Claudius Moliner. Lay-brother.
1622		D. Bede Taylard.
"		D. Faustus, Thomas Vincent Sadler.
c 1623		D. Anselm Williams.
e 1625		D. Paul, Robert Robinson.
"		D. Boniface Martin.
1625		D. Benedict, Anthony Jerningham.
"		Br. Oliver, John Toudelle or Tordell, of Lancashire, a Lay-brother.

* Owing to the loss of the old profession-book of St. Laurence's many of the dates in the early part of this Catalogue are only conjecturally accurate.

APPENDIX.

	1626		D. Gregory Mallet, alias John Jackson.
	"		D. Maurus Roe, of Suffolk.
	"		D. Robert Ingleby.
	"		D. Elphege, William Sherwood.
	"		D. Cuthbert, Thomas Horsley.
	1628		D. Leander Neville.
	"		D. Michael Cape, of Sussex.
	"		D. Maurus Flutot, of Dieulwart.
	"		D. Laurence Neville.
	1630		D. Joseph Foster, of Yorkshire.
	"		D. Celestine de Landres, of Lorraine.
c	1631		Br. John Gratian, of Dieulwart, Lay-brother.
o	1639		Br. Paul Waty, Lay-brother.
	1640		Br. Laurence, Paul Brocast, of Dieulwart, Lay-brother.
	1651		D. Bernard, George Millington.
	1652		D. Placid Johnson.
	1653		D. Gregory, Bartholomew Hesketh, of Lancashire.
	1655		D. Dunstan Duck.
	1656		D. Matthew Cheriton, of Oxfordshire.
	"		D. John Lumley, of Yorkshire.
	1660		D. Benedict Winchcombe, of Henwick, Worcester.
	1661		Br. Robert Richardson, Lay-brother.
	1663		D. Edward Johnson.
	"		Br. John Lockers, Lay-brother.
	1664		D. Mellitus Hesketh, of Lancashire.
	"		Br. Francis West, Lay-brother.
	1666		D. Joseph Aprice, of Northamptonshire.
	"		D. Augustine Mather, of Lancashire.
	"		D. George Whall.
	1668		D. James Mather, of Lancashire.
	"		D. Nicholas Hesketh, of Lancashire.
	"		D. Ildephonsus, Thomas Aprice.
	"		D. Bernard Gregson.
	"		D. Patrick Curwen.
	"		D. Benedict Sparrey.
	1672		Br. Austin Rumley, Lay-brother.
	1673		D. Alban, Zachary Fuller, of Norfolk.
	"		D. Ambrose, Robert Booth.
	1676		D. James Ferreyra.
	"		D. Cuthbert, Edward Brent.
	1679	May 22nd	D. Mellitus Walmesley, of Lancashire.
	1684		D. Thomas Eaves.
	"		D. Francis Watmough.
	"		D. Laurence, William Champney.
	1685		D. Joseph Kennet.
	"		D. Augustine, John Hudson.
	1686		D. Vincent Craven, of Lancashire.
	"		D. Gregory Helme.
	"		D. Anselm Brown.

APPENDIX. 17

o	1688	D. Charles Barker.
	"	D. Maurus Fermor, or Farmer.
	1690	D. Robert Hardcastle.
	"	Br. Joseph Bateson, Lay-brother.
	1693	D. John, Edmund Green.
	"	D. Placid Bagnal.
		D. Bernard Quynco.
		D. Maurus, John Rigmaiden, or Smith.
	1701	D. Cuthbert, Ralph Farnworth, of Runshaw, Lancashire.
o	1701	Br. Peter Gregson. Lay-brother.
o	1707	D. Bernard Bradley.
		D. Benedict, Simeon Rigmaiden.
	1708	D. Francis Howard.
		D. Augustine Sulyard, of Haughley Hall, Norfolk.
	1710	D. Anselm, Richard Walmesley.
	1711	D. Placid, William Naylor, of Scarisbrick, Lancashire.
		D. John Rous.
	1712	D. William Champney.
	1713	D. Edward Houghton, of Parkhall, Lancashire.
		D. Laurence Kirby.
	1715	D. Ambrose Eastgate.
	1717	D. Vincent Palin.
	1724	D. Maurus, Bertram Bulmer.
	1725	D. Bernard, Edward Catteral, of Lancashire.
a	1726	B. Robert Rowston, Lay-brother.
	1726	D. John Fisher, of Lancashire.
	1727	D. Placid, John Rigby.
		D. Augustine Gregson, of Lancashire.
o	1728	Br. Bede Houghton, Lay-brother.
	1730	D. Gregory Robinson.
	1732	D. Jerome, John Berry, or Butler.
	1735	D. Ambrose, James Kaye, of Lancashire.
		D. Robert Daniel, of Whittingham, Lancashire.
	1736	D. Francis Walmesley.
		D. Benedict, John Daniel, *alias* Simpson, of Lancashire.
	1737	D. Bernard, James Price, of Standish, Lancashire.
	"	D. Peter Wilcock, of Lancashire.
	"	D. Nicholas, John Richardson, of Lancashire.
	"	D. Thomas Simpson.
a	1739	Br. James Draper, Lay-brother.
o	1740	Br. James, Robert Johnson, Lay-brother.
	1741	D. Vincent, Richard Gregson, of Lancashire.
		D. Dunstan, Peter Holderness.
	1743	D. Placid, John Naylor, of Lancashire.
	1749	D. Alexius, Edward Pope, or Fisher, of Lancashire.
		D. Gregory, William Cowley.
	1751	D. Benedict, Richard Simpson, of Preston, Lancashire.
	"	D. Anselm, John Bolton, of Brindle, Lancashire.
	"	D. Maurus, Richard Barret, of Lancashire.

APPENDIX.

	Year	Date	Name
	1755	December 28th	D. Oswald Eaves, of Lancashire.
	1758		D. Bede, John Brewer, of Lancashire.
	,,		D. Placid, John Beunet.
	,,		D. Dunstan Worswick.
c	1759		D. Thomas, John Turner, of Lancashire.
	,,		D. Jerome, Thomas Marsh, of Lancashire.
c	1760		D. Bernard, John Slater, of Lancashire.
	1761		D. Ambrose Waring, of Lancashire.
	1766	April 27th	D. Edward, Richard Fisher, of Lancashire.
	,,		D. Basil, John Brindle of Lancashire.
	,,		D. Anselm Bromley, of Liverpool.
	1775		D. Dunstan, John Sharrock, of Lancashire.
	,,		D. Jerome, Thomas Coupe, of South hill, Chorley, Lancashire.
	1776		D. Alexius, James Pope, of Lancashire.
a	1777		Br. Christopher Osbaldeston, Lay-brother.
	1777		D. Thomas Slater, of Lancashire.
	1778		D. Edmund Pennington, of Lancashire.
	1781	April 22nd	D. Richard Pope, of Lancashire.
a	1782		Br. Andrew Burn, Lay-brother.
	1783	April 22nd	D. Richard Marsh, of Hindley, Lancashire.
	1784	December 15th	D. Ralph Ainsworth, of Liverpool.
	,,	,, ,,	D. Stephen Hodgson, of Durham.
a	1786		Br. Joseph Johnson, a Lay-brother.
	1788	January 12th	D. Anselm, Thomas Appleton, of Lancashire.
	,,		D. Bernard Robinson.
	,,		D. Augustine, Samuel Mitchell.
	1789		D. Bede, James Burgess, of Lancashire.
	,,		D. Oswald, James Talbot, ,,
	1791		D. John Dawber, of Standish, ,,
	1792		D. James Calderbank, of Liverpool.
	,,		D. Francis, Lewis Cooper, of Walton, Lancashire.
	,,		D. Alexius, William Chew.
	1793		D. Benedict, Richard Marsh.

VI

The Priors and professed religions of the Monastery of St. Benedict at St. Malo, in Britany.

Priors, with the date of their election.

1611 D. Gabriel Gifford   1649 D. Jocelin Elmer †
1620 D. Paulinus Greenwood   1651 D. Bernard Ribertierre
1625 D. Jocelin Elmer   1653 D. John Mentisse
1629 D. Deodatus L'Angevin   1657 D. Gabriel Brett
1641 D. Gabriel Brett   1661 D. Thomas Anderton
1643 D. Paul Robinson   1666 D. Benedict Nelson
1645 D. Gabriel Brett

† Died in office.

APPENDIX.   19

The professed monks of St. Benedict's St. Malo.

1613	August 6th	D. Matthew Sandeford, **of Lea**, Shropshire.
1614	July 22nd	D Deodatus **of** St. Mary, Renatus L'Angevin, of St. Malo.
,,	October	D Felix of St. **Mary, Thompson or Pratt.**
,,	——	D. Celestine of St. **John, Trembie.**
1614		Br. James Le Munier, **a Breton, Lay-brother.**
1615	——	D. Benedict, Luke Cape.
,,	November 5th	**D.** Gabriel, Robert Brett, **of White Staunton, Som-**ersetshire.
,,	,, ,,	Br. Dominic Taylor, Lay-**brother.**
1616	March 24th	D. Dunstan Everard, of **Suffolk.**
1617	October 18th	D. Francis Gicou, a Breton.
,,	,, ,,	D. Rupert Guillet, a Welshman.
1620	February 10th	D. Romanus, William Grossier, of **Paris.**
,,	September 23rd	Br. Anselm Hamoy, a Lay-brother.
1621	February 14th	D. Bernard Ribertierre, of St. Malo's.
,,	?	D. Mansuetus Powel, an Irishman, professed in Spain.
1630	April 24th	D. Maurus of the Holy Cross, Hames.
1634	September 24th	D. Bede Foster, *alias* William Thornton, of **Galley**-hill, Northumberland.
1644	December 8th	Br. Anselm Prudhomme, of Burgundy, **Lay-brother.**
1657	——	D. Anselm Williams.
a 1669		**Br.** Bennet Galli, Lay-brother
,,		**Br.** John Barbierre. ,,
,,		**Br.** Francis Chamberlain. ,,

VII

The Priors and professed Religious of the Monastery of St. Edmund the King, at Paris.

Priors, with the date of their election.

1615	D. Augustine Bradshaw	1677	D. Augustine Latham †
1616	D. Bernard Berington	,,	D. Benedict Nelson
1618	D. Matthew Sandeford	1689	D. Francis Fenwick
1619	D. Bernard Berington	1685	D. James Nelson
1620	D. Thomas Monington	1693	D. Placid Nelson
1621	D. Sigebert Bagshaw	1697	D. Joseph Johnston
1629	D. Placid Gascoigne	1698	D. William Hitchcock
1633	D. Gabriel Brett	1701	D. Anthony Turberville
1640	D. Thomas Anderton	1705	D. Joseph Johnston
1641	D. Francis Cape	1710	D. Anthony Turberville
1653	D. Augustine Latham	1713	D. Placid Anderton
1654	D. Benedict Nelson	1717	D. Francis Moore
1657	D. Francis Cape	1721	D. Laurence York
1666	D. Michael Cape †	1725	D. John Stourton
1668	D. Thomas Anderton	1729	D. Wilfrid Helme
1669	D. Joseph Sherburne	1737	D. Henry Wyburne

† Died in office.

1745 D. Maurus Coupe
1749 D. Charles Walmesley
1753 D. Augustine Walker
1757 D. Bernard Price

1765 D. Thomas Welch
1773 D. Gregory Cowley
1789 D. Henry Parker †

A list of the professed monks of St. Edmund's, Paris.

1622	March 31st	D. Gabriel Latham of Lancashire.
1623	February 8th	D. Æmilian, Ferdinand Throckmorton, of Warwickshire.
1629	May 26th	D. Dunstan Gibson, of Yorkshire.
,,	October 5th	D. Francis Whitnal of Kent.
1630	December 26th	D. Thomas Anderton, of Euxton, Lancashire.
,,	,, ,,	D. Wolstan, Richard Ingham, or Walmesley.
1632	———	D. Dunstan Craffe, or Grove.
,,	June 1st	D. Columban, John Phillips, of Pembrokeshire.
1639	January 15th	D. John Garter, of Northamptonshire.
,,	,, ,,	D. Richard King, or Scott, of Bedfordshire.
,,	,, ,,	Br. Edmund Ward, of Norfolk, Lay-brother.
1640	April 10th	D. Augustine, Henry Latham, of Mosborrow, Lancashire.
,,	April 15th	D. Benedict, William Nelson, of Maudsley, Lancashire.
,,	,, ,,	D. William Sheldon, of Warwickshire.
,,	,, ,,	D. Peter Gifford, of Whiston, Staffordshire.
,,	,, ,,	D. Wolstan, Edmund Shuttleworth, or Dalton, of Bedford, Lancashire.
,,	August 5th	D. Edward Gloster, *alias* Glasscock, of Essex.
,,	November 30th	D. Cuthbert, Thomas Risden.
1641	February 17th	D. Placid, Henry Carey, (son of Viscount Falkland).
,,	December	D. Andrew Simpson.
1642	June 8th	D. Maurus Bennet, or William Davis, of Flintshire.
,,	November 15th	D. Bede, Richard Houghton, *alias* Farnaby, of Lancashire.
1648	January 1st	Br. Bennet, Randal Hankinson, a Lay-brother.
,,	July 11th	D. Bernard Warren of Cheshire.
1650	May 22nd	Br. Gregory Wilkinson, of London, a Lay-brother.
1651	June 24th	D. Basil Cheriton, of Oxfordshire.
1652	January 1st	D. Placid, John Adelham, of Wiltshire.
,,	June 24th	D. David Guilliam, of Monmouthshire.
,,	,,	D. Joseph Sherburne, of Lancashire.
1653	March 21st	D. Maurus Robinson, of Yorkshire.
,,	May 26th	D. John Girlington, of Lancashire.
1654	November 20th	D. Augustine Cornwallis, of Norwich.
1656	November 1st	D. Laurence Woolfe, of Shropshire.
1657	July 26th	Br. Francis Mosse, Lay-brother.

† Died in office.

1658	November 13th	D. Augustine, Edward Llewellin, of Yorkshire.
"	"	D. Francis Muttlebury, of Somersetshire.
1660	March 17th	D. Charles Philip, or William Pugh, of St. Asaph's, Flintshire.
"	July 25th	D. James, Ralph Nelson, of Maudsley, Lancashire.
"	September 21st	D. Bede Shirburn, of Lancashire.
1661	January 21st	D. Alban Berriman, of Somersetshire.
1663	October 9th	D. Placid, Richard Bruning, of Hambledon Park, Hants.
"	"	D. Richard Yoward, of London.
1664	March 23rd	D. Anthony Turberville, of Ewenny, Glamorganshire.
"	"	D. Andrew Rycaut, of London.
"	November 1st	D. Francis Fenwick, of London.
1673	February 10th	D. Cuthbert Parker, of Marscough, Lancashire.
"	"	D. Thomas Hesketh, of Lancashire.
"	July 2nd	D. Bernard, Henry Lowick, of Stoxley, **Yorkshire**.
1675	May 26th	D. Joseph, Henry Johnston, of Methley, **Yorkshire**.
1676	October 5th	D. Augustine Stelling, of Durham.
1677	March 21st	D. John Smith, of Wooton, Warwickshire.
"	"	D. Gregory, Henry Timperly, of Hintlesham, Suffolk.
1679	May 22nd	D. Placid, Richard Nelson, of Fairhurst, Lancashire.
1681	November 13th	D. Bede, Benjamin Moore, of London.
"	"	D. Maurus Nelson, of Fairhurst, Lancashire.
1682	September 20th	D. Felix, Richard Tasburgh, of Flixton Hall, **Suffolk**.
1683	February 4th	D. Edmund Hawet, of Ormskirk, Lancashire.
"	April 19th	D. Anselm Nelson, of Fairhurst, Lancashire.
1683	October 26th	D. Clement Paston, of Barningham, Norfolk.
1684	November 26th	D. William Philipson, of Streitly, Berkshire.
1685	November 11th	D. Martin Stone, of Euxton, Lancashire.
"	"	D. Dunstan, Farrigton Lake, of Waretree, Lancashire.
1688	May 2nd	D. Dominic, Charles Green, of Windsor, Berkshire.
"	"	D. Ambrose, Robert Davis, of London.
"	June 13th	D. Bernard, Francis Hornyold, of Worcestershire.
"	October 2nd	D. James, Francis Poyntz, of Northamptonshire.
"	October 24th	D. John Dakins, of Leicestershire.
1689	March 6th	D. Augustine, John Southcot, of Witham Place, Essex.
"	July 27th	D. Edmund Smith, of Durham.
"	September 14th	D. Jerome, Charles Bruning, of Hambledon Park, Hants.
"	October 9th	D. Laurence Casse, of Knaresboro', **Yorkshire**.
"	December 23rd	D. Thomas, William Short, of London.
1692	January 13th	D. Joseph, William Kennedy, of Ireland.
"	"	D. Benedict, Ralph Weldon, of Swanscombe, Kent.
1696	February 2nd	D. Thomas Bruning of Hambledon Park, Hants.
"	July 11th	D. Placid, William Anderton, of Euxton, Lancashire.
"	"	D. Jerome, John Farnworth, of Runshaw, Lancashire.
1698	July 3rd	D. Francis Moore, of Fawley, Berkshire.
"	December 8th	D. Edmund, David Cox, of London.
"	———	Br. Maurus, Charles Middleton, Lay-brother.

1699	July 5th	D. Alban Ashton, of Warrington, Lancashire.
,,	,, ,,	D. Augustine, Thomas Lumley, of Yorkshire.
,,	,, ,,	D. Wilfrid, Thomas Helme, of Goosnargh, Lancashire.
,,	,, ,,	Br. Laurence Delattre, Lay-brother.
,,	November 17th	Br. Alexius Higgs, of London, Lay-brother.
,,	,, 22nd	D. Edward Sherburn, of Parrington, Essex.
,,	,, ,,	D. William Hewlett, of Winchester.
1700	October 12th	D. Joseph, John D'Ognate, of Bruges.
1706	May 2nd	D. Augustine, Edward Delattre, of London.
1708	March 25th	D. Joseph Roskow, of Runshaw, Lancashire.
,,	,, ,,	D. James Buckley, of London.
1714	July 31st	D. John Aspinwall, of Yorkshire.
,,	,, ,,	D. Dunstan, Edward Rogers, of Denbigh.
1715	August 6th	D. Benedict, William Shaftoe, of Northumberland.
1723	November 21st	D. Henry Wyburne, of Kent.
1725	July 26th	D. Wilfrid, Philip Constable, of Everingham, Yorkshire.
,,	,, ,,	D. Maurus, John Dale, of Yorkshire.
,,	,, ,,	D. Placid, Richard Ashton, of Warrington, Lancashire.
1726	December 12th	D. Edmund, William Batchelor, of Yorkshire.
,,	,, ,,	D. Joseph, Roger Whittel, of London.
1729	April 19th	D. Bernard, William Nechills, of London.
1731	July 15th	D. Anselm, Evans Eastham, of Walton-le-Dale, Lancashire.
,,	,, ,,	D. Maurus, Abram Coupe, of Owlerton, Lancashire.
1739	September 29th	D. Charles Walmesley, of Westwood Hall, near Wigan.
,,	,, ,,	D. James, George Crook, of Chorley, Lancashire.
1743	May 23rd	D. Augustine, George Walker, of Hindley, Lancashire.
,,	,, ,,	D. Benedict, Alexander Catteral, of Lancashire.
1744	May 25th	D. Thomas Welch, of Lancashire.
1746	November 1st	D. Cuthbert, John Simpson, of Preston, Lancashire.
,,	December 18th	D. John, Lewis Barnes, of London.
1750	November 8th	D. Philip Jefferson, of Hexham, Northumberland.
,,	December 19th	Br. Joseph Valentine, Lay-brother, of Samesbury, Lancashire.
1751	April 18th	D. Augustine, Robert Kellet, of Plumpton, Lancashire.
,,	,, ,,	D. Gregory, William Gregson, of Samesbury, Lancashire.
1753	November 1st	D. Benedict Harsnep, of Ormskirk, Lancashire.
,,	,, ,,	D. Dunstan, William Garstang, of Brindle, Lancashire.
1755	September 29th	D. Richard Harris, of Winchester.
,,	,, ,,	D. Robert Goolde, of London.
1757	May 12th	D. Bede, Richard Barton, of Wheaton, Lancashire.
,,	,, ,,	D. Maurus, Ralph Shaw, of Rotbbury, Northumberland.
1760	December 30th	D. Edmund, George Ducket, of Lancashire.

APPENDIX. 23

1764 September 10th D. Benedict Cawser, of Ormskirk, Lancashire.
1764 December 10th D. Cuthbert, Joseph Wilks, of Coughton, Warwickshire.
1769 March 12th D. Bernard, Andrew Ryding, of Wigan, Lancashire.
1773 November 30th D. Henry Parker of Kirkham, Lancashire.
1775 October 16th D. Bernard, James Compton, of Salisbury.
1779 December 21st D. James Berry, of Wigan, Lancashire.
  ,, ——— Br. Hugh Holden, died before profession.
1781 February 12th D. John Atkinson, of Ashton, Lancashire.
1786 September 8th D. John Turner, of Woolstan, Lancashire.
 ,, October 12th D. Francis Beswick, of St. Helen's, Lancashire.
1787 January 18th D. John Crombleholme, of Lancashire.
1788 October 13th D. Peter Marsh, of Hindley, Lancashire.
 ,, ,, ,, D. Daniel Spencer, of Crosby, ,,

VIII

The Abbey of SS. Adrian and Denis at Lambspring in Germany.
List of Abbots, with date of their accession to office.

1643 D. Clement Reyner. †	1697 D. Maurus (II), Knightley †
1651 D. Placid Gascoigne †	1708 D. Augustine Tempest †
1681 D. Joseph Sherwood †	1730 D. Joseph Rokeby †
1690 D. Maurus (I) Corker	1762 D. Maurus (III) Heatley

A list of monks professed at the Abbey of Lambspring.

1645 August 27th D. Clement, Richard Meutisse, or Northall, of Shropshire.
1649 February 2nd D. Hugh, Henry Starkey, of Darley, Cheshire.
1653 June 5th D. Adrian Kirke, of Northamptonshire.
 ,, ,, ,, D. Robert Killingbecke, of Yorkshire.
 ,, ,, ,, D. Joseph Sherwood, of the diocese of Ghent.
1655 December 8th D. Bede, Bartholomew Addye, of the county of Durham.
 ,, ,, ,, D. Placid Shafto, of the County of Durham.
1656 April 23rd D. Maurus, John Corker, of Yorkshire.
 ,, July 22nd Br. John Sherwood, of Somersetshire. Lay-brother.
 ,, ,, ,, Br. Peter Street, Lay-brother.
1658 September 16th D. Francis Porter, of the county of Durham.
 ,, December 30th D. Benedict, Robert Meryng, or Meering, of Tardebig, Worcestershire.
1660 April 11th D. Leander, Francis Greene, of Monmouthshire.
1661 December 28th D. John Tempest, of Yorkshire.
1663 January 18th Br. Thomas Tucker, of Bradford, Wilts, Lay-brother.
 ,, July 25th D. Anselm, Roger Collingwood, of Northumberland.
 ,, ,, ,, D. Bernard Sanderson, of Paris.
1664 January 15th D. Denis Sanderson, of Northumberland.
 ,, ,, ,, D. Basil, John Smeaton, of Cumberland.

† Died in office.

	1664	October 9th	D. Alban, George Porter, of Cumberland
	"	" "	D. Augustine, Francis Tempest, of Yorkshire.
	1665	September 8th	Br. Bede Barnes, of Chester-le-Street, Durham, Lay-brother.
	1666	March 25th	Br. Joseph Blakey, of Newcastle-on-Tyne, a Lay-brother.
	1668	January 11th	D. Cuthbert, William Marsh, *alias* Wall, or Marshall, of Lancashire.
a	1669	" "	Br. Ralph Hodson, Lay-brother. (?)
	1669	August 7th	D. Benedict Constable, of Yorkshire.
	"	October 15th	D. Ildephonsus Ratcliffe, or Radcliffe, of Northumberland.
	1670	May 9th	D. Ambrose Lindley, of Yorkshire.
	"	" "	D. Placid, Alban Francis, of Middesex.
	"	" "	D. Maurus, John Knightley, of Warwickshire.
	"	October 9th	D. Laurence Swale, of Yorkshire.
	"	" "	D. Gregory Dalyson, of Lincolnshire.
	1672	June 3rd	D. Celestine Shafto, of the county of Durham.
	1673	March 21st	D. Nicholas Colston, of Quarry-hill, Durham.
	"	" "	D. Benedict Gibbon, of Westcliff, Kent.
	"	" "	D. Bernard Huntley, of Shadforth, Durham, a Lay-brother.
	1674	May 7th	D. John Townson, of Lancashire.
	"	September 14th	D. Francis Mildmay, of Amersden, Oxfordshire.
	1979	November 7th	D. Wilfrid, Joseph Hutchinson, of Northumberland.
	1682	November 3rd	D. Anselm, William Blakey, of Northumberland.
	"	" "	D. Denis, Bartholomew Bishop, of Oxfordshire.
	1683	February 24th	D. Alban, Obed Dawney, of Lancashire.
	1684	December 8th	D. Willibrord, William Wilson, of the Co. of Durham.
	1685	June 27th	D. Benedict, William Lawson, of Brough, Yorkshire.
	"	" "	D. Paul, Robert Gillmore, of Ramsbury, Wiltshire.
	"	" "	D. Dunstan, Matthew Hutchinson, of Northumberland.
	"	" "	D. Richard, John Isherwood, of Lancashire.
	"	" "	D. Edward, Bertram Bulmer, of Yorkshire.
	"	" "	Br. Jerome Six, of Antwerp, a Lay-brother.
	1688	March 21st	D. Gregory, George Riddell, of Northumberland.
	"	" "	D. Maurus, Ralph Wilson, of the county of Durham.
	"	August 15th	D. Augustine, Thomas Townson, of Lancashire.
	"	" "	D. Elphege, John Skelton, of Cumberland.
	1689	April 23rd	D. Leander, John Davies of Middlesex.
	"	" "	D. Odo, William Duddell, of Middlesex.
	"	October 9th	D. Benedict Sies, of Brabant.
	1690	March 21st	D. James Winton of Middlesex.
	"	" "	D. Adrian, Martin Bernard, of Lincolnshire.
	"	" "	D. Philip Blakey, of Northumberland.
	"	" "	D. Joseph Wyche, of Middlesex.
	"	" "	D. Ambrose, William Gawen, of Middlesex.

1691	May 21st	D. Bede, John Potts, of Northumberland.
1694	December 8th	D. Oswald, John Smithers, of Middlesex.
1695	March 12th	D. Placid, John Scudamore, of Middlesex.
1696	March 21st	D. George, Richard Brent, of Worcestershire.
"	" "	D. Benedict, George Mordaunt, of Middlesex.
1699	May 1st	D. Francis Bruning, of Berkshire.
1701	April 24th	D. Denis, William Huddlestone, of Sawston, Cambridgeshire.
"	" "	D. Placid, Fairfax Robinson, of Yorkshire.
1702	March 4th	D. John Osland, of Sutton, Shropshire.
1703	February 2nd	D. Frederick Howard, of Norfolk.
"	April 15th	D. Benedict, John Comberlege, of Newcastle-under-Lyne, Staffordshire.
"	" "	D. Anselm, Thomas Crathorne, of Ness, Yorkshire.
"	December 21st	D. Joseph, George Rokeby, of Middlesex.
"	" "	D. Edward Salisbury, of Devonshire.
"	" "	D. Adrian, Thomas Hardisty, of Yorkshire.
1705	January 15th	D. James Hawkins, of Gloucestershire.
1709	April 1st	D. Elphege, Robert Dobson, of Kent.
"	October 9th	D. Michael, John Anderton, of Hardhill, Lancashire.
1711	November 15th	D. Charles, Anthony Delattre, of London.
1713	December 8th	D. Bede, William Hutton, of Eldon, Durham.
"	" "	D. Paul, Matthew Allanson, of Woodal, Yorkshire.
1714	August 15th	D. Placid, Thomas Hutton, of Eldon, Durham.
1715	January 25th	D. Wilfrid, James Witham, of Cliff, Yorkshire.
"	" "	D. Thomas, Robert Riddell, of Swinburne Castle, Northumberland.
"	" "	D. Alexius, John Wall, of Ludshott, Hampshire.
"	February 14th	Br. Adrian Muller, of Lambspring, Lay-brother.
"	" "	Br. Antony Doutch, of Lambspring, a Lay-brother.
1719	January 12th	D. Joseph, Edward Riddell, of Swinburne, Northumberland.
"	" "	D. Edward, Michael Tempest, of London.
"	" "	D. Boniface, Michael Byers, of Fenham, Northumberland.
1722	March 21st	D. Robert, George Robinson, of Middlesex.
"	July 11th	D. Augustine, Simon Dunscombe, of Devonshire.
1723	March 28th	D. Bernard Bradshaw, *alias* Handford, of Preston Goballs, Shropshire.
"	July 16th	D. Benedict, Thomas Shuttleworth of Middlesex.
a 1726	———	D. Odo Smithers.
1726	April 21st	D. Maurus, Wiliam Darell, *alias* Westbrook, of Kent.
"	" "	D. Gregory, Edward Selbye, of Yardhill, Northumberland.
1732	April 15th	D. Dunstan, James Knight, of Reasby, Lincolnshire.
"	" "	D. Bede, Lancelot Newton, of Stocksfield Hall, Northumberland.
"	" "	D. **Anselm,** John Gery, of Middlesex.
"	" "	D. **Laurence,** William Hardisty, of Middlesex.

APPENDIX.

1732	June 1st	D. Joseph Peyton, of Middlesex.
1732	September 8th	D. Denis, John Bulmer, of Middlesex.
1733	May 31st	D. Benedict, Francis Knight, of Reasby, Lincolnshire.
"	"	" D. Bernard, John Davis, *alias* Kirke, of Middlesex.
"	"	" D. Robert, Pitt Copsey, of Middlesex.
1735	August 30th	Br. Bernard, Joseph Beckman, of **Lambspring**, a Lay-brother.
1737	October 28th	D. James Le Grand, of Middlesex.
1740	May 26th	D. Placid, William Metcalfe, of Lincolnshire.
"	"	" D. Augustine, Robert Turner, of Mowdsley, Lancashire.
"	"	" D. Maurus, William Heatley, of Samsbury, Lancashire.
"	"	" D. Gregory, John Metcalfe, of Lincolnshire.
1743	July 6th	D. Wilfrid, John Strutt, or Bridgman, of Middlesex.
"	October 1st	D. Alexius, Frederick Latham, of Hamburg.
1744	April 13th	Br. John Jansen, of Lambspring, Lay-brother.
"	December 21st	D. Benedict, Bernard Bolas, of Preston Goballs, Shropshire.
"	"	" D. Ambrose, Robert Boucher, of Middlesex.
"	"	" D. Denis, John Wenham, of Middlesex.
1748	November 12th	Br. Jerome, George Clarkson, of Brindle, Lancashire, a Lay-brother.
1751	January 10th	D. Anselm, Thomas Bolas, **of Preston Goballs**, Shropshire.
"	"	" D. Joseph, John Story, of Northumberland.
"	"	" D. Laurence, Augustus Turck, of Hildesheim.
1754	May 5th	D. Gregory, John Ballyman, of Devonshire.
1756	November 7th	D. Thomas, Ballyman, of Devonshire.
"	"	" D. Boniface, Roger Hall, of Lancashire.
1758	December 29th	D. Augustine, Clare Hatton, of Norfolk.
"	"	" D. Benedict, Thomas Garner, of Barton, Lancashire.
1760	August 31st	D. Anselm, Bernard Bradshaw, of Esh, Durham.
"	"	" D. Bernard, Daniel Yonge, or Young, of Ormskirk, Lancashire.
"	"	" D. Dunstan, Joseph Scott, of Beaufront, Northumberland.
1762	June 24th	D. Basil, Francis Bradshaw, of Esh, Durham.
1763	September 18th	D. Adrian, Thomas Gurnall, of London.
"	"	" D. Bede, Robert Scott, of Beaufront, Northumberland.
"	"	" D. Maurus, James Chaplin, of Norfolk.
1770	November 1st	D. Placid, Thomas Harsnep, of Ormskirk, Lancashire.
1771	August 18th	D. Joseph, George Crook, *alias* Gregson, of Chorley, Lancashire.
"	"	" D. Denis, Matthew Allerton, of Ormskirk, Lancashire.
"	"	" D. Anselm, Michael Chaplin, of Middlesex.
"	December 15th	Br. Ambrose, Francis Pape, of Lambspring, a **Lay-brother**.
1772	November 1st	D. Boniface, Charles Taylor, of Goosnargh, Lancashire.

APPENDIX. 27

1772	November 1st	D. Oswald, James Johnson, of Wrightington, Lancashire.
1774	July 22nd	D. Clement, William Grimbaldeston, of Alston, Lancashire.
1776	August 15th	D. Joachim, Goderic Swinburn, of Durham.
,,	,, ,,	D. Lewis, John Heatley, of Samsbury, Lancashire.
1777	March 30th	D. Jerome, Hugh Heatley, of Preston, Lancashire.
,,	May 18th	D. Paul, Joseph Grimbaldeston, of Alston, ,,
,,	October 19th	D. Basil, James Kennedy, of Middlesex.
1779	March 1st	Br. Francis Tegetmeyr, a Lay-brother.
1783	May 29th	D. Joseph, William Collins, of London.
,,	,, ,,	D. Cyprian, John Barnewall, of London.
1784	November 1st	D. Dunstan, William Wobb, of Birmingham, Warwickshire.
1786	August 1st	Br. John, Francis Knacksterdt, a Lay-brother.
1787	November 11th	D. Anselm, Thomas Kenyon, of Warrington, Lancashire.
,,	,, ,,	D. Alban, Edward Clarkson, of Goosnargh, Lancashire.
,,	,, ,,	D. Vincent, John Weardon, of Walton, Lancashire.
,,	,, ,,	D. Adrian, James Horsman, of Knaresboro', Yorkshire.
,,	,, ,,	D. Wilfrid, Thomas Fisher, of Cheadle, Staffordshire.
1788	September 7th	D. Laurence, John Forshaw, of Ormskirk, Lancashire.
1790	September 12th	D. Cyril, James Mather, of Goosnargh, Lancashire.
1792	September 16th	D. Jerome, William Alcock, of Warrington, ,,
,,	,, ,,	D. Boniface, John Taylor, of Altcar, Lancashire.
1796	November 6th	D. Cyprian, George Kearton, of Ormskirk, Lancashire.
,,	,, ,,	D. Augustine, John Birdsall, of Liverpool.
1798	May 17th	D. Benedict Lacabanne, of Preston, Lancashire.
,,	,, ,,	D. Maurus, William Robinson, of Burstwick, Yorkshire.
,,	November 18th	D. Bede, John Rigby, of Warrington, Lancashire.
1802	January 1st	D. Adrian, Richard Towers, of Preston, Lancashire.

The place of profession of the following religious is uncertain.

D. Anselm Wafte, died March 20th, 1652.
Br. Anthony Tenant, Lay-brother.
Br. William Tahon, Lay-brother.
Br. John Bradstock.

IX

The Abbey of Nuns of our Blessed Lady of Comfort at Cambray.

The history of the foundation of this Abbey has been given in the *Chronological Notes.* We here subjoin a list of the Abbesses and religious of the community in the order of their decease; the loss of the Profession book and other records preventing us from furnishing a more complete list.

Abbesses with the date of their election.

1625	Dame Frances Gawen, **professed** at Brussels.	
1629	Dame Catharine Gascoigne	
1641	Dame Mary Christina Brent	
1645	Dame Catharine Gascoigne	
1673	Dame Catharine Maura Hall.	
1677	Dame Mary Christina Brent	
1681	Dame Marina Appleton †	
1694	Dame Cecilia Hussey	
1697	Dame Scholastica Houghton	
1701	Dame Margaret Swinburne	
1705	Dame Cecilia Hussey	
1710	Dame Scholastica Houghton	
1713	Dame Margaret Swinburn †	
1741	Dame Helen (Josepha) Gascoigne	
1773	Dame Agnes Ingleby †	
1789	Dame Mary Christina **Hook** †	
1792	Dame Clare **Knight** †	
1792	Dame Lucy **Blyde**	

The professed religious of Cambray.

1625	January 1st	Dame Gertrude, Helen More.
,,	,, ,,	D. Lucy, Margaret Vavasour, of Hazelwood, Yorkshire.
,,	,, ,,	D. Benedicta, Anne Morgan, of Weston, Warwickshire.
,,	,, ,,	D. Catharine Gascoigne, of Barnlow, Yorkshire.
,,	,, ,,	D. Agnes, Grace More.
,,	,, ,,	D. Anne More
,,	,, ,,	D. Mary, Frances Watson, of Parke, Bedfordshire.
,,	,, ,,	Sister Mary Hoskins, a Lay-Sister.
,,	,, ,,	Sister Martha, Jane Martin, a Lay-sister.

Owing to the loss of the Records of this Abbey we are only able to give the year of the death of its professed members.

Dame Ebba Brown		died in 1631	Dame Benedicta Boult		died in 1659
D.	Barbara Smith	,,	1635	D.	Elizabeth Brent	,, 1660
D.	Margaret Gascoigne	,,	1637	D.	Gertrude Swinburne	,, ,,
D.	Margaret Swinburne	,,	1640	D.	Anne Tavern	,, 1661
D.	Mary Frances Gawen *	,,	,,	D.	Agnes Errington	,, 1662
D.	Scholastica Timperly	,,	,,	D.	Winefride Cotton	,, ,,
D.	Mary Lucy Cape	,,	,,	D.	Mary Magdalen Ever	,, ,,
D.	Angela Mullins	,,	1641	D.	Mildred Latchmore	,, 1663
D.	Mary Frances Lucig	,,	,,	D.	Flavia Brown	,, 1665
D.	Margaret Kenyou	,,	,,	D.	Etheldreda Stapleton	,, 1668
D.	Magdalen Cary	,,	1645	D.	Mary Bridget ———	,, 1669
D.	Benedicta Roper	,,	1646	Sr.	Hilda Percy, a Lay-sister	1670
D.	Pudentiana Deacons *	,,	1648	D.	Theresa Timperley	,, 1671
D.	Cecilia Hall	,,	1650	D.	Clementina Cary	,, ,,
D.	Catharine Sheldon	,,	1651	D.	Gertrude Wrisdon	,, 1675
D.	Gertrude Hodson	,,	1652	D.	Mechtilde Frere	,, 1676
D.	Viviana Yaxley *	,,	1656	D.	Catharine Vavasour	,, ,,
D.	Helena Kenyon	,,	1657	D.	Catharine Gascoigne	,, ,,

† Died in office. * Professed at Brussels.

Dame	Lucy Vavasour	died in	1679	Dame	Joseph Dwerihouse	died in	1726
D.	Margaret Smith	,,	1680	D.	Scholastica Houghton	,,	,,
D.	Winifred Constable	,,	,,	D.	Dorothea More	,,	,,
D.	Clare Radcliffe	,,	1681	D.	Agatha Fazakerly	,,	,,
D.	Austin Cary	,,	1682	D.	Mary Gaudelier	,,	1727
D.	Catharine Trevilian	,,	,,	D.	Mary Eves	,,	1732
D.	Jane Cellar	,,	1683	D.	Agnes Widdrington	,,	1733
D.	Barbara Constable	,,	1684	D.	Isabella Kennet	,,	,,
D.	Elizabeth Lusher	,,	,,	D.	Gertrude Chilton	,,	,,
D.	Clare Crook	,,	1685	D.	Mary Astin	,,	1734
D.	Benedicta Conquest	,,	1686	D.	Martha Smith	,,	1737
D.	Frances Lusher	,,	1687	D.	Theresa Chilton	,,	1739
D.	Helen Brent	,,	1688	D.	Benedicta Fairclough	,,	1741
D.	Benedicta Middleton	,,	,,	D.	Elizabeth Fairclough	,,	1744
D.	Euphrasia Tempest	,,	1689	D.	Scholastica Addison	,,	,,
D.	Alexia Fenwick	,,	,,	D.	Paula Gascoigne	,,	1746
D.	Barbara Breton	,,	,,	D.	Monica Augustina Jenison		1747
D.	Ursula Radcliffe	,,	,,	D.	Mary Magdalen Toldorly		1749
D.	Catharine Maura Hall	,,	1690	D.	Amanda Barrister	,,	,,
D.	Scholastica Hodson	,,	,,	D.	Gertrude Belerby	,,	1750
D.	Justina Gascoigne	,,	,,	D.	Alathea Clifton	,,	1753
D.	Mary Legge	,,	1691	D.	Winifred Howet	,,	1754
D.	Anne Gill	,,	1692	D.	Anne Benedicta Warwick	,,	,,
D.	Bridget More	,,	,,	Sr.	M. Anne Moody, Lay-Sr.		1755
D.	Mary Cary	,,	1693	D.	Anne Josepha Bate	,,	1758
D.	Marina Appleton	,,	1694	D.	Bridget Coffin	,,	,,
D.	Theresa Gurney	,,	1696	D.	Anne Theresa Young	,,	,,
D.	Theresa Meynell	,,	1697	Sr.	Olivia Darell, a novice	,,	1760
D.	Placida Sheldon	,,	1700	D.	Constantia Langdale	,,	,,
D.	Catharine Kennett	,,	,,	D.	Theresa Swinburne	,,	1762
D.	Christina Brent, Abbess		,,	D.	Anne Benedicta Reeves		1763
D.	Scholastica Burgess	,,	,,	Sr.	Agnes Batchell, Lay-Sr.		
D.	Anne Batemanson	,,	1701	D.	Benedicta Maynell	,,	1764
D.	Eugenia Houghton	,,	,,	D.	Bernarda Plompton	,,	1768
D.	Susanna Phillips	,,	1705	D.	Catharine Palliser	,,	1770
D.	Mary Compline	,,	,,	D.	Mary Coffin	,,	,,
D.	Benedicta Taylor	,,	1707	Sr.	Josepha Tookey, Lay-Sr.		1772
D.	Anne Agry	,,	1713	D.	Bathildis Du Pery	,,	1773
D.	Josepha Dodd	,,	1715	Sr.	Alexia Elerby, Lay-sister		1774
D.	Mary Magdalen More	,,	1719	D.	Josepha Gascoigne, Abbess		,,
D.	Josepha O'More	,,	1720	D.	Winifred Ball	,,	,,
D.	Placida Pulleyne	,,	,,	D.	Theresa Wilks	,,	1775
D.	Maura Harrington	,,	,,	D.	Austin Widdrington	,,	,,
D.	Cecilia Hussey	,,	1721	D.	Placida Wilson	,,	1776
D.	Scholastica Reeder	,,	1722	D.	Anne Rigby	,,	,,
D.	Agnes Kennet	,,	1723	D.	Mary Mooney	,,	1778
D.	Benedicta Englefield	,,	1725	D.	Angela Plompton	,,	1779

Dame	Benedicta Walker	died in	1783	Sr.	M. Anne Le Fèvre, L.-Sr.		1802
D.	Placida Pullen	„	1786	D.	Frances Sheldon	„	1808
D.	Frances Gascoigne	„	1788	D.	Theresa Shepherd	„	1809
D.	Josepha Carrington	„	„	D.	Louisa Hagan	„	1811
D.	Agnes Ingleby, Abbess		1789	Sr.	Anne Frances Helm	„	
D.	Clare Knight, Abbess	„	1792		Lay-sister.		1812
D.	Christina Hooke, Abbess		1792	D.	Anne Joseph Knight	„	1815
D.	Margaret Burgess †	„	1794	D.	Lucy Blyde	„	1816
Sr.	Anne Pennington, Lay-Sr.†			D.	Augustina Shepherd, Abb.		1818
D.	Anselma Ann †	„	„	D.	Anne Theresa Partington		1820
D.	Theresa Walmesley †	„	„	Sr.	Martha Fryar, Lay-sister		1825
Sr.	Joseph Miller, Lay-Sr.		*1796	D.	Benedicta Partington		1826
D.	Jane Alexander	„	1799	D.	Agnes Robinson, Abbess		1830
D.	Magdalen Kimberly	„	1802	Sr.	Scholastica Caton, Lay-Sr.		1830

X

Of the other monasteries of English Benedictine Nuns.

The Abbey of the Glorious Assumption of our Lady founded at Brussels in 1598.

The Benedictine Monastery for Nuns founded at Brussels in 1598 under the title of the Glorious Assumption of the Blessed Virgin Mary was the first Monastery erected for English subjects since the destruction of religious houses by Henry VIII. Its establishment was due to the desire of many English ladies to embrace a religious life which the persecution of those days rendered impossible at home. The foundresses of this Abbey were Lady Mary Percy, daughter of that Earl of Northumberland who was put to death in the reign of Queen Elizabeth (August 1572), and Mistress Dorothy Arundell and her sister Gertrude of Lanherne in Cornwall. Lady Mary Percy after the death of her mother in 1596 had resided in Brussels where she lived a life of great piety. So great was her fervour that she used to go barefooted to visit the Blessed Sacrament of Miracles at St. Gudule's and other Sanctuaries. Her directer, Father Holt, of the Society of Jesus, finding her bent on entering religion advised and encouraged her to found a house for English subjects. About this time Mistress Dorothy Arundel was passing through Brussels on her way to Lisbon in order to enter the Bridgettine Convent there in accordance with a promise she had made under her saintly director, F. John Cornelius S. J. who was martyred at Dorchester in 1594. Whilst praying in the Church of St. Gudule she received a supernatural intimation from Almighty God that she was to join Lady Mary Percy in the foundation of a Benedictine Monastery. Her sister, Gertrude Arundel remained to share in the good work.

These Ladies, with the assistance of Father Holt and Father Parsons, of the Society of Jesus, obtained a Brief from Pope Clement VIII to erect the monastery which was to be under the government of perpetual Abbesses and subject to the

---

† Died in prison at Compiegne during the French Revolution.
* The following religious, who died subsequent to the settlement of the community in England, made their Profession at Cambray

jurisdiction of the Ordinary. The Archduke and Duchess, Governors of the Low Countries, granted their permission together with all the privileges usually conceded to convents: the offer of the Archduchess Isabella to endow the new Monastery was respectfully declined by Lady Percy as she feared that court patronage might interfere with the freedom of election which she was anxious to secure for the future Community.

The first Abbess was procured, at the request of Lady Mary Percy and the Archbishop of Mechlin, from the Royal Abbey of St. Peter at Rheims. This was Dame Joanna Berkeley, daughter of Sir John Berkeley of Beverston, Gloucestershire, a lady who had been a professed Nun in that Monastery for seventeen years. The preacher who delivered the sermon at her profession ceremony had predicted to her that she would be called to assist in the foundation of a Benedictine Community which would be the first to return to England. On November 14th, 1599, Dame Joanna Berkeley was solemnly blessed and installed as Abbess at Brussels by the Archbishop of Mechlin in presence of the Papal Nuncio; after which, on the same day, Lady Mary Percy, Dorothy and Gertrude Arundell and five other English ladies were solemnly invested with the habit of St. Benedict, together with four others who entered as Lay-Sisters, making thus twelve in all; the Archduke and Duchess and the whole court attending the ceremony. A letter* written by an eye witness, in describing the event says: "It was one of the most solemnest things that was seen this hundred years; many ladies and others could not forbear weeping."

The following year, 1600, all these novices made their profession, and several new members were admitted to the noviciate. So eager were English subjects to avail themselves of this opportunity of embracing the monastic life, that ladies crossed the sea at the peril of their lives, several in fact being apprehended in the act and imprisoned for a time to check their dangerous "popish" proclivities. The rigours of the persecution in England being extended to the property of Catholics, many were much impoverished and consequently the convent suffered often from want of means; and on this account several ladies of good family entered the community as Lay-Sisters.

In 1616 Lady Abbess Berkeley died, after having had the consolation of seeing all firmly established, the Statutes approved, the monastic buildings increased, and the Church in progress;—the way in which this was built being perhaps one of the last instances of the kind on record, of the devotion of the English people manifested so commonly during the ages of Faith,—the soldiers of Sir William Stanley's regiment, then quartered in Brussels, giving their labour to it gratis.

An other event in connection with the Church is remarkable as such occurrences had become out of date: A lady of rank a niece of Cardinal Mazarin's, who had fallen into great trouble, took sanctuary in it, and the Abbess then governing protected her for some time.

During the time of Lady Abbess Berkeley there existed a vestige of another ancient custom dating from the days when Abbesses exercised Jurisdiction beyond the precincts of their monastery. When the Archbishop of Mechlin held his Provincial Synod, he gave notice to the Abbess to send her proxy, and she

---

* Now in the Public Record Office.

thereupon delegated the Rev. Doctor **Chambers**, the Chaplain of her community to assist at the Council in her behalf.

In 1616, Lady Mary Percy succeeded D. Joanna Berkeley as second Abbess.

In 1623, the English Monks asked for some Nuns from Brussels to assist some English Ladies in the foundation of a Convent at Cambray to be under the jurisdiction of the Order. Three religious were sent, one of them, Dame Frances Gawen, becoming first Abbess there. The Community of the Abbey of our Lady of Comfort at Stanbrook near Worcester are the descendants of the Cambray nuns.

In 1624, four nuns, one novice and a Lay-Sister, went from Brussels to found a house at Ghent under the same statutes. The community after the troubles of the French Revolution finally settled at Oulton near Stone in Staffordshire.

The Ghent nuns sent a Colony, in January, 1652, to establish a monastery at Pontoise; and in the same year a filiation of the Cambray community was established at Paris. From Ghent again, in 1662, a new foundation was made at Dunkirk; this and the Pontoise community as now represented by the Abbey of St. Scholastica at Teignmouth, Devonshire. The last continental convent established by the English Benedictine nuns was that of Ypres, which still exists.

After the Brussels monastery had existed for two hundred years, the French Revolution forced the nuns to leave in 1794, and though other communities set out before them, they were the first to reach England, thus verifying the prediction made so many years previously at the profession of Dame Joanna Berkeley. The Brussels Convent, all the furniture and many valuable papers and records, were confiscated by the French. Dr. Douglas, Vicar apostolic of the London District provided the community with a house at Winchester, where they were received and assisted in their great need by Dr Milner, at that time priest of the mission in that town. Dr. Milner made every exertion to procure them the necessary furniture, giving them even his own bed, and interesting his protestant as well as his catholic friends in their behalf. After his consecration as Bishop and removal to Wolverhampton, Dr. Milner ever continued a true and valued friend to the community.*

The Nuns of this house removed from Winchester to East Bergholt, near Colchester, in 1857.

List of the Abbesses of the Monastery of the Glorious Assumption of Our Lady at Brussels with the date of their election.

1598 Dame Joanna Berkeley †	1719 Dame Mary Crispe †
1616 Dame Mary Percy †	1757 Dame Maura Whitenhall or Whitenhal †
1642 Dame Agnes Leuthall †	
1651 Dame Alexia Blanchard †	1762 Dame Etheldreda Mannock †
1651 Dame Mary Vavasour †	1773 Dame Mary Ursula Pigott
1676 Dame Anne Forester or Forster	1796 Dame Austin Tancred †
1682 Dame Dorothy Blundel †	1797 Dame Philippa Eccles
1713 Dame Theodosia Waldegrave †	

* It is worthy of note that at Winchester the first Church and Bishop were publicly consecrated and the first Abbess (Dame Austin Tancred, 1796) blessed, since the change of religion in England.   † Died in office.

APPENDIX.

A list of the Religious professed at this Abbey.

1599		Dame Mary Percy	1612	D.	Mary Cecilia Atslow
„	D.	Dorothy Arundel, of Lanherne, Cornwall	„	D.	Anne Ingilby
			„	D.	Benedicta Hawkins
„	D.	Gertrude Arundel, of Lanherne, Cornwall	„	D.	Alexia, Dorothy Blanchard
„	D.	Anne, Elizabeth Cansfield	„	D.	Margaret, Anne Curson
„	D.	Elizabeth Southcoat	„	Sr.	Magdalen Thomasina Thornburgh, a Lay-sister
„	D.	Frances Gawen or Gawine			
1600	D.	Winifred, Margaret Thomson	„	Sr.	Petronilla, Jane Williamson, a Lay-sister
„	D.	Renata, Margaret Smith	1613	D.	Catharine Paston
1601	Sr.	Scholastica, Elizabeth Tichbourne,* a Lay-sister	1614	Sr.	Jane Moro a Lay-sister
			„	Sr.	Anne Healy a Lay-sister
„	Sr.	Martha, Margaret Whitaker, a Lay-sister.	1615	D.	Elizabeth Rookwood
			„	D.	Winifred Lucy Tresham
„	Sr.	Benedicta, Sybil Banks	„	D.	Mary Renata Smith
„	Sr.	Catharine, Elizabeth Clayton, a Lay-sister	1616	D.	Mary Vavasour
			„	D.	Christina, Frances Lovel
1603	D.	Mary Watson	„	D.	Mary Philips
„	D.	Ursula Hewicke	„	D.	Columba, Elizabeth Gago
„	D.	Agnes, Anne Lenthall	1617	D.	Aurea, Anne James
„	D.	Agatha, Winifred Wiseman	„	D.	Theresa, Barbara Gage
			1618	Sr.	Barbara Ducket, Lay-Sr.
1604	Sr.	Cecily, Jane Price, a Lay-sister	1619 April 14th	D.	Etheldreda, Margaret Smith
1605	D.	Eugenia, Jane Pulton †	„	D.	Dorothy, Elizabeth Mannock
„	D.	Clare, Elizabeth Curson			
„	D.	Barbara, Jane Leake	„	D.	Mary Kempe
1608	D.	Anastasia, Sylvestra Morgan	„	D.	Placida, Alice Brooke
			„	D.	Catharine Bond
„	D.	Helen, Elizabeth Dolman	„	D.	Mary Roper †
„	D.	Mary Gage	„	Sr.	Mary Fletcher, a Lay-Sr.
„	D.	Mary Persons	1620	D.	Mary Winter
„	D.	Pudentiana, Elizabeth Deacon or Deacons ‡	„	D.	Flavia, Judoca Langdale
			„	Sr.	Agnes Bolton, a Lay-Sr
1609	Sr.	Frances Appleby, Lay-Sr.	1621	D.	Viviana, Margaret Yaxley‡
„	Sr.	Mary Margaret Strachy, a Lay-sister	„	Sr.	Alexia, Alice Shepherd, a Lay-Sister
1610	D.	Scholastica, Ursula Smith	„	Sr.	Frances, Catharine Fletcher, a Lay-Sister
1611	D.	Magdalen Elizabeth Digby †			
			1622	D.	Bridget Draycott
„	D.	Lucy, Elizabeth Knatchbull †	1623	Sr.	Mary, Mabel Corbinton or Corby, a Lay-Sister. §
„	D.	Martha Colford	„	Sr.	Dorothy Redman „

* Daughter of the Martyr, Mr. Nicholas Tichbourne.   † One of the Colony sent to Ghent.
‡ One of the Colony sent to Cambray.   § Sister to the Martyr F. Ralph Corby S. J.

1624	D.	Mechtilde, Vere Trentham.	1670	Sr.	Frances, Catharine Gargill
„	D.	Christina, Anne Paris	1672	D.	Mary Scroup
„	D.	Mary, Margaret Eure	1678	D.	Mary Errington
„	D.	Frances, Margaret Paston	1683	D.	Benedicta, Mary Collins
„	D.	Apollonia, Barbara Waldegrave	1687	D.	Mary Crispe
			1691	D.	Elizabeth Chilton
1625	D.	Constantia Joanna Penruddocke	1692	D.	Theresa, Mary Vraux
			1693	D.	Austin, Rachel Ireland
„	Sr.	Lucy, Jane Bullock, L-Sr.	1694	D.	Gertrude, Henrietta Chilton
1627	D.	Lucy, Philippa Pershall			
„	D.	Marina, Elizabeth Draycott	1695	D.	Delphina, Lucy Ireland
„	Sr.	Eugenia Corbinton or Corby, * Lay-sister.	1697	D.	Beatrix, Rebecca Deeble
			„	D.	Xaveria, Elizabeth Darrell
1634	Sr.	Elizabeth Sunley	„	D.	Anastasia, Ursula Mannock
1638	Sr.	Anne, Grace Baker			
1643	D.	Melchiora, Barbara Campbell	1701	D.	Isabella Beligny
			„	D.	Mary Magdalen Matham
1652	D.	Gertrude, Catharine Blount	1706	D.	Catharine Matham
1653	Sr.	Helen Burch, Lay-sister	1711	D.	Scholastica, Elizabeth Errington
„	Sr.	Mary Hills, „			
„	Sr.	Agatha Green, „	„	D.	Mary Joseph, Margaret Darrell
1655	D.	Anne Forester or Forster			
„	D.	Placida, Etheldreda Forester or Forster	„	D.	Ursula, Faith Mannock
			„	D.	Winifred, Margaret Berkley
„	D.	Dorothy Blundel			
„	D.	Maura, Margaret Blundel	1712	D.	Aloysia, Catharine Compton.
1656	D.	Mary Guyllim			
„	Sr.	Anne Sherburne, Lay-Sr.	1715	D.	Agnes, Anne Carew
1657	D.	Hilda, Margaret Russel	„	D.	Anne ———
„	D.	Mildred, Helena Russel	„	D.	Mary Anne Bell
1658	D.	Josepha, Bridget Dallison	1716	D.	Maura, Catharine Whitenhall
„	D.	Martha Dallison			
„	D.	Theresa, Anne Hide	1717	D.	Placida, Elizabeth Waldegrave
1659	D.	Frances Goodair			
„	D.	Philippa Garnous †	„	D.	Barbara Jackson
„	Sr.	Mary Gravenore a Lay-Sr.	1718	Sr.	M Joseph Bird, Lay-Sr.
1661	D.	Mary Bedingfield	1720	D.	Mary Ignatia, Elizabeth Collins
„	Sr.	Margaret Urmston, L-Sr.			
1662	Sr.	Mary Urmston Lay-Sr.	1723	D.	Stanislaus, Philippa Poole
1664	D.	Elizabeth Neals	1725	Sr.	Anne Brindley, Lay-Sr.
1666	D.	Marina Havelock	„	Sr.	Elizabeth Newton, „
„	D.	Henrietta, Mary Spear	1727	D.	Angela, M Anne Petre
„	D.	Theodosia, Joanna Waldegrave	1731	D.	Etheldreda Mannock
			1732	D.	Benedicta, Mary Anne Plowden
„	D.	Magdalen Street			
1669	D.	Scholastica, Dorothea Byron	„	D.	Mary, Frances Bodenham
			1733	D.	Marina, Elizabeth Byerley

* Sister to the Martyr, F. Ralph Corby S. J.   † Professed on her death bed.

1733	Dame	Austin, Anne Byerley	1755	Sr.	Frances, Catharine Damiens, a Lay-sister
„	D.	Clementina, Penelope Simpson	1756	Sr.	Mary Benedict Rulands, a Lay-sister
„	D.	Agnes, Mary Mannock			
1737	D.	Henrietta, Frances Blount	1768	D.	Scholastica, Elizabeth Roger
„	D.	Christina, Mary Stapelton			
1738	D.	Cecilia, Anne Mannock.	1770	Sr.	Winifred, Catharine Galver, a Lay-sister
1742	D.	M Theresa, Anne Collins			
„	Sr.	Barbara Wilson, Lay-Sr.	1774	D.	Mary Anne Rayment
1745	D.	M Ursula, Rebecca Pigott	„	D.	Aloysia, Dorothea Witham
„	D.	Xaveria, Catharine Pigott	1780	D.	Ignatia, Catharine Collins
1746	Sr.	Theresa, Margaret Ascough a Lay-sister	1781	D.	Joseph, Catharine Collius
			„	Sr.	Scholastica, Elizabeth Midi, a Lay-Sister
„	Sr.	Mary, Elizabeth Potts, a Lay-sister	1783	D.	Ursula, Elizabeth Scoles
1748	Sr.	Margaret Littlewood, L-Sr.	„	Sr.	Sophia, Anne Leblon
1750	Sr.	Benedicta, Anne Ascough „	1784	Sr.	Martha, Elizabeth Thielmans a Lay-Sister
1753	D.	Philippa, Anne Eccles			
1754	D.	Mechtilde, Elizabeth Debord	1785	Sr.	Magdalen, Dorothy King „
			1793	D.	Maura, Hannah Harper
„	D.	Romana, Bridget Foxe	„	D.	Josepha, Anne Elizabeth Collingridge
„	D.	M. Benedicta, Eleanor Reddy	1796	D.	Mary Benedict, Elizabeth McDouald
„	D.	M. Austin, Margaret Tancred	1798	D.	Edburga, Mary Anselma Collins
„	D.	M. Bernard, Frances Tancred			

XI

The Abbey of the Immaculate Conception of the Blessed Virgin Mary, founded at Ghent in 1624.

The community of the English Benedictine Dames at Brussels having grown very numerous, the Lady Mary Percy, 2nd Abbess of that monastery sent a colony of religious to Ghent in 1624, under the guidance of Dame Lucy Knatchbull, daughter of Reginald Knatchbull, Esq, of the county of Kent. Her companions were Dame Eugenia Poulton, or Pulton, daughter of Ferdinand Pulton, Esq, of Desborough, Northamptonshire, Dame Magdalen Digby, and Dame Mary Roper, daughter of Lord Teynham, of Linstead Lodge, Kent. The ecclesiastical authorities of Ghent having given their sanction to the undertaking, the little band of Religious set out, and were welcomed to Ghent by the magistrates and people of the town who met them in public procession and accompanied them to their new abode with every mark of kindly feeling and hospitality.

Under the government of the first Abbess, Dame Lucy Knatchbull, and her successors, the number of the nuns was much increased, so that new communities were established at Pontoise, Dunkirk and Ypres to ease the mother house at Ghent. The French Revolution forced the community to leave their Convent, and the nuns proceeded to England, where, after a long stay at Caverswall Castle in ffordshire, they finally settled down at Oulton, near Stone, in the same county.

APPENDIX.

The Abbesses of the Monastery of the Immaculate Conception of our Blessed Lady, established at Ghent, with the date of their election.

1624	Dame Lucy Knatchbull †	1711	Dame Mary Knatchbull (II) †
1628	Dame Eugenia Poulton or Pulton	1727	Dame Cecilia Tyldesley †
1645	Dame Mary Roper †	1736	Dame Magdalen Lucy (II) †
1650	Dame Mary Knatchbull (I) †	1761	Dame Baptista Philipps †
1695	Dame Justina Petre †	1781	Dame Magdalen Arden †
1698	Dame Magdalen Lucy (I) †	1797	Dame Frances Hesketh †
1703	Dame Scholastica Gerard †		

The professed Religious of this Abbey with the date of their profession.

The loss of almost all the archives of the Ghent Monastery at the French Revolution renders it impossible to provide a complete catalogue of the professed religious of that house. The following are the only names that have been preserved of a very numerous and flourishing community.

1624	August 28th	Sister	Theresa Matlock, a Lay-sister
1626	July 2nd	Dame	Catharine Wigmore
,,	,, ,,	D.	Mary Knatchbull
,,	August 12th	D.	Mary Pease
1627	June 14th	D.	Catharine Thorold
,,	November 8th	D.	Margaret Knatchbull
,,	December 8th	D.	Jeromima Waldegrave
,,	,, ,,	D.	Mary Southcote
1628	September 14th	D.	Scholastica Roper
1630	n. d.	D.	Thecla Bedingfield
,,	June 11th	D.	Mary Mounson
,,	October 6th	Sr.	Dorothy Barefoot, a Lay-sister
,,	,, 20th	D.	Mary Trevillion
1631	n. d.	D.	Aloysia Beaumont
,,	,, ,,	D.	Lucy Perkins
,,	June 24th	D.	Alexia Gray
1633	April 30th	Sr.	Benedicta Corby, a Lay-sister
,,	June 26th	D.	Eugenia Bedingfield
1634	July 2nd	D.	Anne, Mary Neville
1635	September 11th	D.	Cornelia Corham
,,	,, ,,	D.	Justina Corham
1637	August 5th	D.	Mary Digby
1638	September 14th	D.	Dorothy Cary
,,	n. d.	D.	Constantia, Catherine **Savage**
1639	September 11th	D.	Ignatia Coningsby
,,	,, ,,	D.	Margaret Markham
,,	December 27th	D.	Eugenia Thorold
1640	February 14th	D.	Bridget Guildridge
1641	January 13th	D.	Christina, Anne Forster

† Died in office.

1642	February 20th	Sister Thecla Bedingfield, a novice professed on her death bed.
,,	May 7th	Dame Theresa Gardiner
,,	May 24th	Sr. Dorothy Skrimsher, a Lay-sister
,,	July 12th	Mistress Elizabeth Wakeman, a child in the convent school, professed on her death bed
1644	n. d.	D. Scholastica Heneage
1645	July 6th	Sr. Martina de Decken, a Lay-sister
1647	n. d.	D. Agatha Webb
1648	January 28th	D. Alexia Maurice
,,	n. d.	D. Helen Wayte, or Wait
1650	n. d.	D. Mary Caryll
1652	August	Lady Honoria Burke, "a little titled lady in the school, daughter to the Marquis Clanricarde, was professed on her death bed, at her own earnest request, and died a few days after, Aug. 7th, 1652."
1655	n. d.	Dame Christina Monson
1659	n. d.	D. Anastasia Maurice
1661	n. d.	D. Xaveria Pordage
a 1665		D. Mary Beaumont
,, ,,		D. Flavia Cary
,, ,,		D. Vincentia Aire (or Viviana Eyre)
,, 1683		D. Ursula Butler
,, 1695		D. Justina Petre, daughter of Sir Francis Petre.
,, 1698		D. Magdalen Lucy
,, 1703		D. Scholastica Gerard
,, 1711		D. Mary Knatchbull
,, 1727		D. Cecilia Tyldesley
,, 1730		D. Clare Throckmorton
1736		D. Magdalen Lucy
1756		D. Magdalen Arden
a 1760		D. Baptista Philipps
1760		D. Xaveria Boone
1776		D. Anselma Tempest
1780		D. Mary Baptista Ferrars
a 1790		D. Frances Hesketh

Of the following, only the names have been preserved.

Dame Elizabeth Bradberry
D. Aloysia Langdale
D. Magdalen Mainwaring
D. Catharine Sheldon
D. Aloysia Hesketh

Dame Catharine Howard
D. Agnes Gillibrand
D. Benedicta Bedingfield, died in 1811
D. Aloysia Jefferson, died in 1818

XII

The Abbey of Pontoise, near Paris, commenced at Boulogne in 1652, and settled at Pontoise in 1658.

In January, 1652, a few of the religious of the Monastery of the Immaculate Conception of our Lady at Ghent, were sent by the Lady Abbess, Dame Mary Knatchbull, to establish a new community at Boulogne. The nuns selected for the new foundation were the following: Dame Catharine Wigmore, daughter of William Wigmore, Esq, of Lutton, Herefordshire; Dame Lucy Perkins; Dame Anne Neville, daughter of Lord Abergavenny. First Baron of England; Dame Margaret Markham; Dame Eugenia Thorold, daughter of Edmund Thorold, Esq, of Hough, near Grantham, and Dame Christina Forster, daughter of Sir Richard Forster Secretary and Treasurer to the Queen of England. When in 1658, Dunkirk fell into the power of Cromwell, the nuns of the new monastery at Boulogne were strongly advised to quit a seaport town liable to a similar fate, and to withdraw further into the country; and accordingly they removed to Pontoise near Paris. Lady Abbess Knatchbull tells us in her writings, that she was "greatly assisted in this undertaking by Monsieur Vincent" whose power and credit were exerted in her behalf, and whose name is now known throughout the Church as the great Saint Vincent de Paul. The Pontoise community flourished for many years, but meeting subsequently with heavy pecuniary losses, occasioned partly by the non-payment of large sums promised by Queen Mary Beatrice in expectation of her return to the throne, and partly by the failure of a bank in which nearly all their funds were deposited, there remained for them no alternative but the sorrowful necessity of separation. The community, at the period of its dissolution in 1786, consisted of **ten** **choir** religious and four Lay-Sisters. The Abbess, Dame Anne Clavering **and four of** her Choir nuns, Dame Mary Theresa Armstrong, Dame Placida Messenger, Dame Mary Winifred Clarke and Dame Mary Frances Markham, together with **two** Lay-Sisters, Agnes Morgan and Anne Lincoln, were received into the community of Dunkirk, the remainder **of the** community finding an asylum in other convents of the Order. The sale of the house and grounds at Pontoise enabled the nuns to discharge **their liabilities to** the tradespeople of the town who had long and faithfully served them, and who deeply regretted their **departure.**

The Abbesses of this Community.

1. Dame Catharine Wigmore, blessed Abbess at Boulogne, October 18th, 1653. Died October 28th, 1656.
2. Dame Christina Forster, blessed Abbess, May 16th, 1657. The community removed to Pontoise in 1658, where this Abbess died December 16th, 1661.
3. Dame Eugenia Thorold, blessed Abbess of Pontoise, March 7th, 1662; died December 21st, 1667.
4. Dame Anne Neville, blessed Abbess in February, 1668; died December 15th, 1689.
5. Dame Elizabeth Dabridgecourt, elected Abbess in December, 1689; resigned in 1710.
6. Dame Xaveria Gifford; elected Abbess on March 7th, 1710; died February 11th, 1711.

APPENDIX.   39

7. Dame Elizabeth Joseph Widdrington, elected Abbess on March 18th, 1711; died November 9th, 1730.
8. Dame Marina Hunloke, elected Abbess on December 6th, 1730; died March 3rd, 1753.
9. Dame Anne Catharine Haggerston, elected March 31st, 1753; died October 8th, 1765.
10. Dame Mary Anne Clavering, elected Abbess on October 24th, 1765. At the dissolution of her Abbey, June 12th, 1786, she with several of her nuns joined the Dunkirk Community, and at the Revolution settled with them at Hammersmith, where she died on November the 8th, 1795.

The Religious of Pontoise, with the date of their Profession.

1657	Dame	Christina Thorold	1672	Dame	Eugenia, Frances Greene
„	D.	Clare Vaughan	1673	D.	Mary Christina Whyte
„	D.	Gertrude, Grace Turner	„	D.	Anastasia, Persiana Bard
„	D.	Mary Joseph Butler	„	D.	Anne Nevill or Neville
„	D.	Frances, Mary Elliot	„	D.	Alexia, Cecily Weston
1658	D.	Helen, Frances Hamerton	1675	D.	Mary Bernard, Catharine Brooke
„	D.	Mary Bruning			
1659	D.	Mary Roper	1676	D.	Anne Xaveria, Anne Gifford, daughter of Sir Henry Gifford, of Burstall Leicestershire.
1660	D.	Justina, Margaret Timperly			
„	D.	Aloysia, Anne Elliot			
„	D.	Benedicta, Barbara Hamerton			
			„	D.	Maura, Elizabeth Gifford
„	D.	Anne Mary, Anne Talbot	1677	D.	M Laurentia, Mary Lawson
1661	D.	Elizabeth Dabridgecourt, daughter of Sir Thomas Dabridgecourt, Bart.	„	D.	Mary Stanislaus, Mary Culcheth
			„	D.	Francisca, Frances Culcheth
1662	D.	Placid, Elizabeth Roper			
„	D.	Angela, Margaret Riddell	1678	D.	Mary Catharine Tichborne
„	D.	Anne, Catharine Bruning	„	D.	Mary Carola, Charlotte Selby
„	D.	Mary Theresa, Mary Swift			
„	D.	Barbara Philpott	„	D.	Mary Anne, Mary Tichborne
1663	D.	Mechtilde Smythe			
„	D.	Dorothy Calvert	1679	D.	Augustina, Elizabeth Bruning
1665	D.	Xaveria, Anne Collins			
„	D.	Alexia Smythe	1680	D.	Elizabeth Joseph, Elizabeth Widdrington
1666	D.	Scholastica, Anne Bruning			
1669	D.	Catharine Roper	1681	D.	Apollonia, Anne Bellasyse
„	D.	Gertrude, Susanna Cone	„	D.	Ursula, Frances Hamerton
„	D.	Ignatia, Mary Champion	1684	D.	Constantia, Penelope Heneage
1671	D.	Anne Catharine, Catharine Thorold			
			„	D.	Mary Petre
„	D.	Mary Magdalen, Catharine Warren	1688	D.	Justina, Dorothy Green
			1689	D.	Anne Bodenham
„	D.	Victoria, Penelope Longueville	1690	D.	Henrietta, Elizabeth Pound
„	D.	Winifred, Mary Philpott	„	D.	Ignatia, Arabella Fitzjames

APPENDIX.

1691	Dame	Benedicta, **Barbara** Fitzroy			from poverty, died at Pontoise in this year.
1694	D.	Cecilia, Diana Stanihurst			
1700	D.	Agnes, Margaret Arthur	1747	Dame	Mary Bernard, Elizabeth Haggerston
„	D.	Anna Mary, **Anne** Constable	„	D.	Mary Magdalen, **Barbara** Belasyse
1711	D.	MaryCatharine, Elizabeth Maurin	1751	D.	Anne Clavering
1715	D.	M Joseph, Mary Clavering	1755	D.	Mary Theresa Armstrong
1717	D.	Anne Catharine, Jane Haggerston	„	D.	M Joseph, Susanna Fothringham
1717	D.	Mary Austin, Margaret Oxburgh	1758	D.	M Xaveria, Rachel Semmes
1718	D.	M Placida, Mary Whetanhall	1759	D.	M Henrietta Jerningham
			17 4	D.	Mary Scholastica, Bridget Preston
1721	D.	Marina Hunloke	„	Sr.	Maura, Elizabeth Preston, a choir novice.
1723	D.	M Scholastica, Mary Haggerston	1770	D.	Anne Mary, Elizabeth Thickness
?	D.	Maura, Elizabeth Tyrrell			
1727	D.	M Elizabeth Preston	1772	D.	Placida, Mary Messenger
1728	D.	Anne Preston	„	D.	Mary Winifred, Eleanor Clarke
1744	D.	M. Agatha, Anne Hunloke			
1745	D.	M Benedict, Anne Belasyse	1776	D.	Mary Frances, Catharine Harkham
„	D.	M. Pelagia Browne, a nun professed in 1724 in a French Benedictine monastery which broke up	1777	D.	Mary Scholastica, Barbara Belasyse
			1779	D.	Anne Austin, Mary Innes

The Lay-sisters of the Abbey of Pontoise with the year of their deaths.*

Sister	Agnes Pickering	died in	1666	Sister Theresa Walton	died in	1713
Sr.	Mary Hardwick	„	1668	Sr. Elizabeth Euro	„	1718
Sr.	Mechtild Pashley	„	1680	Sr. Winifred Whitfield	„	1719
Sr.	Winifred Hill	„	1688	Sr. Mary Benedict Swift	„	„
Sr.	Anne Berington	„	1690	Sr. Scholastica Higginson	„	1730
Sr.	M. Joseph Bolney	„	1691	Sr. Magdalen Huggonson	„	1739
Sr.	Magdalen Swift	„	1694	Sr. Margaret Chaddock	„	1745
Sr.	Margaret Rishton	„	„	Sr. Barbara Lockard	„	1752
Sr.	Susan Bolney	„	„	Sr. Mary Joseph Price	„	1759
Sr.	Francis Rishton	„	1700	Sr. Bernarda Pilkington	„	„
Sr.	Martha Hardwick	„	1703	Sr. Catharine Turner	„	1765
Sr.	Anne Soloman	„	1708	Sr. Placida Houghton	„	1777
Sr.	Joanna Widowfield	„	1709	Sr. M. Benedicta Valentino	„	„
Sr.	Lucy Downes	„	1711	Sr Anne Byard Ross	„	
Sr.	Dorothy Walton	„	„	Sr. Mary Chalk	„	1787
Sr.	Agnes Woolgar	„	1712	Sr. Agnes Morgan	„	1793
Sr.	Mary Peter Rashley	„	„	Sr. Mary Anne Lincoln	„	1794

* Four of five of these were probably professed at Ghent.

XIII

The Priory of our Blessed Lady of Good Hope, commenced at Paris in 1652.

In the *Chronological Notes* (page 199) a brief account has been given of the establishment of this Monastery by the Nuns of the Abbey of our Lady of Comfort at Cambray, in the Spring of 1652. The Religious of the Paris filiation, however, were not finally settled in their abode in the Champs d'Alouette until the year 1664, when M. de Touche provided them with a suitable residence. There the Community remained till the outbreak of the French Revolution when the nuns were imprisoned in the Tower of Vincennes and only reached England after great trials and losses. They settled first at Marnhull, in Dorsetshire, and after a few years moved to Cannington Court in Somersetshire, where they took up their abode in what had originally formed part of a Benedictine Convent. There, in 1829, the perpetual Adoration of the Blessed Sacrament was introduced by the community, which devotion they have since perpetuated in their Monastery at Colwich in Staffordshire, whither they moved in 1835.

The Priory of St. Scholastica at Atherstone in Warwickshire, erected in 1858, is an offshoot of this Monastery.

Prioresses with the date of their election.

1652	Mother Bridget More	1738	Mother Mary Anne Woodman
1665	Mother Justina Gascoigne †	1766	Mother Mary MagdalenJohnson †
1690	Mother Agnes Temple	1784	Mother Mary Clare Bond †
1710	Mother Agatha Gillibrord	1789	Mother Theresa Joseph Johnson, who brought the Community to England in 1785, and who died in office in 1807.
1714	Mother Agnes Temple		
1722	Mother Mary Buckingham		
1726	Mother Christina Witham		
1734	Mother Mary Benedict Dally		

The names of the Religious of this Monastery with the date of their profession.

1629	August 5th		Mother Elizabeth Brent, de Sancta Maria, professed at Cambray, died at Paris, April 1st, 1660.
1630	September 24th	,,	Bridget More, of SS. Peter and Paul, professed at Cambray; died at Paris, October 12th, 1692.
1640	——	,,	Clementina Cary, who received the habit at Cambray, April 3rd, 1639, died at Paris, April 26th, 1671.
,,	April 15th	,,	Justina Gascoigne, de S. Maria, professed at Cambray, died at Paris, May 17th, 1690.
1642	February 24th	Sister	Scholastica Hodson, de Jesu Maria, Lay-Sr. professed at Cambray, died at Paris May 31st, 1690.
1650	March 1st	,,	Gertrude Hodson, of St. Lawrence, Lay-Sister professed at Cambray, died at Paris, Oct. 7th, 1652
1654	——	,,	Margaret Green, Lay-Sister.
1660	October 9th	,,	Rachel Launing.
,,	——		Mother Etheldreda Smith, professed at Brussels in 1629, joined the Paris Community in this year.

† Died in office.

APPENDIX.

1662	July 2nd	Sister	Anne Longworth, of our Blessed Lady
"	"	"	Mary Tempest, of St. John the Evangelist.
1665	August 15th	Mother	Clare Newport, of our Lady and St. John Ev.
"	"	"	Catharine Conyers.
"	September 18th	Sister	Bridget Swales, a novice who received the habit on her death bed.
1666	November 21st	Mother	Mary Appleby, of the most Blessed Sacrament.
1667	November 24th	"	Ursula Trevillian, of the most Blessed Trinity.
1670	January 3rd	Sister	Benedicta Pease, Lay-Sister.
1677	November 21st	Mother	Gertrude Hanne.
1683	October 14th	Sister	Placid Coesneau, of all Saints.
1684	December 26th	"	Mary Hawes, of Jesus.

Nearly all the Records and Archives of this house having been seized at the French Revolution and all traces of them, having been lost, we can only give the date of the death of the following religious of this community.

Mother Maura Witham, of St. Mary Magdalen,	died Sept. 11th, 1700
Sister Dorothy Muttlebury, of St. John Baptist, Lay-Sr,	" Octob. 2nd, 1704
Mother Winifred Curtis, of the Passion	" April 17th, 1710
" Constantia Godfrey, of St. Laurence	" Aug. 12th, "
" Lucy Conyers, of Jesus Maria	" Octob. 7th, 1714
Sister Frances Longworth, of our Lady and St. John the Evangelist	" Sept. 5th, 1715
" Magdalen Nepthou, of St. Maurus	" Octob. 26th, 1719
Mother Bibiana Stones, of our Lady of Good Hope	" Dec. 6th, "
" Etheldreda Risdon "	" " "
Sister Frances Lawes, Lay-sister	" Aug. 25th, 1721
" Mechtilde Tempest, of the Holy Ghost	" Dec. 2nd, 1722
" Clementina Husbands, of St. John the Evangelist	" March 2nd, 1723
" Elizabeth Hilton, a Lay-Sister	" Jan. 26th, 1726
Mother Agatha Gillibord, of the Assumption	" Feb. 10th. "
" Martina Tempest, of the Holy Ghost	" May 17th, "
" Agnes Temple, of the Infant Jesus	" July 3rd, "
" Theresa Cook " "	" Aug. 14th, "
" Elizabeth Cook, of our Blessed Lady.	" Nov. 2nd, 1728
Sister Helen Taylor, of the Holy Cross, Lay-Sister	died Jan. 15th, 1732
" Amanda Butcher, of St. Austin, "	" March 4th, "
Mother Mary Buckingham, of the Incarnation	" March 14th, "
" Scholastica Tempest, "	" March 24th, 1735
" Christina Milfort, of St. Scholastica,	" April 24th, "
" Benedicta De la Rue, of the Blessed Sacrament.	" Dec. 5th, 1737
" Christina Witham, of the Assumption.	" Sept. 3rd, 1740
" Catharine Trumble, of the Holy Ghost.	" Aug. 14th, 1744
Sister M. Gertrude Belarby, of the Nativity, Lay-Sister.	" Aug 4th, 1750
" Margaret Lee, of the Passion, "	" Jan. 4th, 1753
Mother Alathea Clifton, of the Presentation,	" Nov. 23rd, "
Sister Anne Rawcliffe, of the Visitation, Lay-Sister,	" Oct. 16th, 1755
Mother Anne Theresa Couch, of Jesus,	" May 28th, 1757

APPENDIX.

Mother Anne Austin Wilkley, of the Presentation,	died	June 23rd,	1759
,, Maura Wills, of the Holy Ghost,	,,	Aug. 11th,	,,
,, Theresa Brennand, of the Blessed **Trinity**	,,	April 14th,	1760
,, Winifred Pattinson, of the Nativity	,,	July 13th	,,
,, Mary Dalley, of our Lady of Mercy	,,	April 16th,	1761
Sister Frances Rawcliffe, of our Lady of Mercy, Lay-Sr.	,,	May 17th,	,,
Mother Scholastica Lawrenson, of the Assumption	,,	Jan. 4th,	1767
,, Mary Joseph Constable, of the Holy Ghost	,,	April 25th,	,,
,, Philippa Ryant, of the Seven Dolours	,,	Sept. 9th,	,,
Sister Margaret Tootal, **a Postulant**	,,	Aug. 9th,	1772
Mother Gertrude Wilkinson, **of the Sacred Hearts of Jesus** and Mary,	,,	May 8th,	1774
,, Sophia Barnes, of **the Blessed Sacrament**	,,	May 28th	,,
Sister Mary Austin Wilks,	,,	Octob. 19th,	1775
Mother Maria Mooney, of the Holy Ghost,	,,	Aug. 20th,	1778
,, Magdalen Simmes, **of the** Blessed Sacrament	,,	Jan. 14th,	1780
,, Anne Woodman	,,	March 23rd,	,,
,, Mary Scholastica Berry, of the Sacred Hearts	,,	March 19th,	1781
Sister Anne Dewhurst, of the Visitation, Lay-Sister	,,	June 8th,	1784
other Mary Magdalen **Johnson,** of the Holy Cross,	,,	June 13th,	,,
,, Xaveria Simmes,	,,	Jan. 17th,	1789
,, Mary Clare Bond, **of** Jesus	,,	Nov. 22nd	,,
Sister Anne Benedict Jones, of our Lady of **Mercy,**	,,	March 30th,	1792
,, Mary Elizabeth Kirby, of the Nativity,	,,	Sept. 30th,	,,
,, Agnes Norris, of our Lady of Mercy.	,,	Jan. 7th,	1793
,, Martina Bibby, of the Blessed Sacrament, Lay-Sr.	,,	April 1st,	,,
,, Mary Lucy Parkinson, died whilst the religious were imprisoned in the Tower of Vincennes,	,,	Oct. 13th,	1794
,, Mary Knight, of the Sacred Hearts of Jesus and Mary, a Lay-Sister	,,	Oct. 10th,	1795
,, Mary Gertrude Parkinson, **of the Holy Ghost,**	,,	March 24th,	1799
Mother Theresa Joseph Johnson, of **the Holy Ghost**		died in	1807
,, Mary Placida Brindle,	,,	,,	
Sister M Scholastica Greenway,	,,	,,	1809
,, Amanda Cooper, Lay-sister	,,	,,	,,
,, M Magdalen Glynn, a Postulant **who accompanied the** community to prison, and **was professed in England** in 1798	,,	,,	1811
Sister **Anna Maria Thickness,**	,,	,,	1812
Mother **Theresa Hagan**	,,	,,	1816
,, Anne Joseph Gee	,,	,,	,,
Sister Anne Theresa Bagnal, **Lay-Sister,**	,,	,,	1820
,, Mary Joseph Worsley	,,	,,	1821
,, Mary Benedict Hardwidge	,,	,,	1823
Mother Mary Frances Simmes	,,	,,	1824
Sister Theresa Catharine Mc **Donald**	,,	,,	1831

XIV
The Abbey of Dunkirk.

In the year 1662, this Monastery was founded at Dunkirk by the Lady Abbess of the English Benedictine Dames at Ghent, Dame Mary Knatchbull. As Dunkirk then belonged to England, the consent of the King, Charles II, was asked for and obtained before the new foundation was commenced. Twelve religious, seven choir nuns and five Lay-sisters, were sent from Ghent, Dame Mary Caryll, a member of the ancient Sussex family of that name, being appointed Superior. Her companions in the work were Dame Ignatia Fortescue, D. Anne Nevil, D. Flavia Cary, D. Constantia Savage, D. Scholastica Heneage, D. Agatha Webb, D. Valeria Stanley, D. Christina Munson, D. Anastasia Maurice, D. Xaveria Pordage, and D. Viviana Eyre, all ladies of birth and singular virtue. Five of these religious afterwards returned to Ghent when the community of Dunkirk had become sufficiently numerous. The new community was established in May, 1662; the Reverend Mr. Gerard accompanying the nuns as Chaplain. Dame Mary Caryll, who though young, had won the confidence of all by her great piety and the sweetness of her disposition, was chosen the Abbess, and solemnly blessed on the 24th of June, 1664; and so rapidly did her community increase under her guidance, that before her death in 1712, she had received to profession ninety-five religious.

The donations bestowed on her by her Father, John Caryll, Esq. of Harting and West Grinstead, her uncle Lord Petre, and other benefactors, enabled her to erect a Church and other monastic buildings. In this work she received valuable assistance from her brother, Dom Alexius Caryll, a Benedictine Monk of St. Gregory's monastery at Douay, who was well skilled in architecture.

The troubles of the French Revolution which fell so heavily on all religious houses, did not spare the English Abbey at Dunkirk. On October 13th, 1793, the inclosure was invaded, all records and documents seized, and the expelled religious imprisoned, together with two other communities, at Gravelines, where they remained for eighteen months. So great were the hardships of this imprisonment that eleven of the nuns died, and several others were seriously ill when permission was at length obtained for their removal to England. The Benedictine Dames, now reduced to the number of twenty five reached London in May, 1795, and took up their abode in the old Convent at Hammersmith which was soon made over entirely to their use. There they remained till, in 1863, they removed to their present Monastery of St. Scholastica, at Teignmouth in Devonshire.

The Abbesses of Dunkirk.

1. Dame Mary Caryll, professed at Ghent, February 6th, 1650; sent to Dunkirk in 1662, blessed Abbess on June 24th, 1664, died in office, Aug. 21st, 1712.

2. Dame Benedicta Fleetwood, professed in 1686; blessed Abbess on Oct. 2nd, 1712; died October 10th, 1748.

3. Dame Mary Frances Fermor, professed on the 23rd of April, 1713; blessed Abbess on October 20th, 1748; died December 10th, 1764.

4. Dame Mary Winifred Englefield; professed in 1736; became Abbess in 1765; died February 12th, 1777.

APPENDIX. 45

5. Dame Mary Magdalen Prujean, professed June 14th, 1750; blessed Abbess May 20th, 1777. Under her guidance the community settled at Hammersmith near London in 1795. Her successor was

6. Dame Mary Placida Messenger, professed at Pontoise, August 10th, 1772; blessed Abbess at Hammersmith November 3rd, 1812; died August 30th, 1828.

The professed religious of the Abbey of Dunkirk.

a 1665	Dame	Josepha O'Bryan	a 1695	Dame	Winifred Petre
1666	D.	Alexia Mary Legge	,,	D.	Ruperta Coleman
1670	D.	M. Joseph, Mary Ryan	,,	D.	Scholastica Culcheth
,,	D.	Catharine, C. Nichols	1695	D.	Susanna Lavery
,,	D.	Mary Skinner	1696	D.	Etheldreda Middleton
,,	D.	Mary Anne Skinner*	,,	D.	M. Bede, Anne Culcheth
1671	D.	M. Benedict Culcheth	1697	D.	Paula Stafford
,,	D.	Constantia Culcheth	,,	D.	Agatha Spooner
,,	D.	Placida, Anne Morley	,,	D.	Mary, Winifred Yate
,,	D.	M. Martha, Mary Salkeld	,,	D.	Catharine Sheldon
,,	D.	Frances Pordage	,,	D.	Anastasia Vincent
1679	D.	Mary Copley	,,	D.	Placid Fermor
,,	D.	Agnes, Catharine Warner	1699	D.	M Bernard Englefield
a 1685	D.	Eugenia Caryll	a 1706	D.	M Augustine Harvey
,,	D.	Theresa Caryll	,,	D.	Agnes Anderton
,,	D.	Mary Alexia Copley	,,	D.	M. Catharine Strickland
,,	D.	Mechtilde, Frances Pulton		D.	M Magdalen Caryll
,,	D.	Justina Caryll		D.	M Baptist Anderton
,,	D.	Helena Smith		D.	HenriettaMaria,H.Pigott
,,	D.	Cecilia, C. Conyers		D.	Maura Fleming
,,	D.	Ildefonsa Guildford		Sr.	Mary Gertrude Darell, a novice
,,	D.	Gertrude, Anne Pulton			
,,	D.	Mary Beatrix Roger	1706	D.	Mechtilde, Frances Pulton †
,,	D.	Dorothy Gage			
,,	D.	Mary Benedict Clifton	1708	D.	M Romana, Mary Caryll
,,	D.	Margaret Hungate	,,	D.	M Benedict Caryll
,,	D.	Bridget Southcote	a 1713	D.	M Monica Bond
,,	D.	Elizabeth Pulton	,,	D.	M Ignatia Berkeley
,,	D.	Barbara Fleetwood	,,	D.	M Anselm Salkeld
1685	D.	Angela Gerard	,,	D.	Mary Fortescue
1686	D.	Ignatia, Susan Warner	,,	D.	Mary Anne Acton
,,	D.	Mary Baptist Thornton	1713	D.	M Frances Fermor
,,	D.	Benedicta, Ann Fleetwood	1714	D.	Benedicta,ArabellaCaryll
1688	D.	Winifred,TrothThornton	a 1720	D.	Cecilia Fitzroy
1690	D.	M Michael Fleetwood	,,	D.	M Anne, Frances Scroope
a 1695	D.	Lucy, Catharine Ireland	,,	D.	M Baptist Aylward
,,	D.	Josepha Price	,,	D.	Angela Brown

* The Baptismal name of the following four religious is wanting, one was Jane Culcheth and another was Mary Skinner, sister to Dom Placid Skinner, Professor of Theology at St. Gregory's at Douay in 1672. † The second of the name.

APPENDIX.

1720	Dame	M Bernard, Mary Preston	1745	Dame	Barbara Sheldon
a 1725	D.	M Dunstan Abercromby	1746	D.	Gertrude, Elizabeth Wells
a 1725	D.	M Xaveria Pearse	a 1750	D.	M Theresa Haliwell
1725	D.	M Agnes Pulton	,,	D.	M Augustine Belasyse
1727	D.	M Joseph, Mary Sheldon	1750	D.	Mary Magdalen, Anne Prujean
a 1736	D.	M Margaret, Margaret Meynell	1751	D.	Henrietta Strickland
	D.	Anne Augustine, Anne Meynell	1752	D.	Anne Joseph Wells
			1753	D.	M Michael Prescott
	D.	M Bernard Englefield	1755	D.	M Aloysia Tuite
	Sr.	M Michael Willis, died during her noviceship	1758	D.	M Placida Macclesfield
			,,	D.	M Barbara Acton
1736	D.	M Winifred Englefield	1762	D.	Benedicta, Margaret Willoughby
,,	D.	M Ignatia Dyve			
1740	D.	Scholastica, Cecilia Jones	1774	D.	Mary Joseph, Charlotte Mostyn
,,	D.	M Benedict, Anne Sheldon			
1742	D.	M Lucy, Anne Berkeley	1775	D.	Josepha Theresa, Florence Kane
1743	D.	M Monica White			

[In 1786 the following five professed Choir nuns of Pontoise were admitted and associated to the Dunkirk Community.

1751	Dame	Anne Clavering, Abbess of Pontoise	1776	D.	Mary Frances, Catharine Markham]
1747	D.	M Theresa Armstrong	1787	D.	M Agnes Parkes
1772	D.	Placida, Mary Messenger	1796	D.	M Victoria Whitehall
,,	D.	Mary Winifred, Eleanor Clarke	1798	D.	M Maura, Elizabeth Carrington

The Lay-Sisters of the Dunkirk Monastery*

Sister	Mary Magdalen Howard	Sr.	Benedicta Spencer	
Sr.	Elizabeth Boult	Sr.	Mechtilde Barrows	
Sr.	Dorothy Sovette	Sr.	Placida Ludkin	
Sr.	Margaret	Sr.	Bernarda Gregson	
Sr.	Xaveria	Sr.	Etheldreda Roberts	
Sr.	Scholastica	Sr.	Agnes Dallison	
Sr.	Maura	Sr.	Mary Dunstan Smith	
Sr.	Margaret	Sr.	Paula Slaughter	
Sr.	Mary Joseph	Sr.	M Winifred Farrar	
Sr.	Winifred	Sr.	Scholastica	
Sr.	Magdalen	Sr.	Theresa Connick	
Sr.	Mary Xaveria	Sr.	M Benedict Gregston	
Sr.	Anne Joseph	Sr.	M James Plumpton	
Sr.	Scholastica	Sr.	M Magdalen Harvey	
Sr.	Frances	Sr.	M Scholastica Catharel	
Sr.	Mary Magdalen	Sr.	Catharine Mills,	died in 1720
Sr.	Anne	Sr.	Elizabeth Judd,	,, 1737
Sr.	Cecilia Gerrard	Sr.	Martha Waters,	,, 1740
Sr.	Eugenia Hyde	Sr.	Frances Middleton,	,, 1755

* The years of the profession and death of many of these Sisters have not been recorded.

Sister M Joseph Dytch	died in 1755	Sr.	M Magdalen Formby	,,	1784
Sr. Ignatia Leight	,, 1760	Sr.	M Anne Johnson	,,	1787
Sr. Martha Rigby	,, 1764	Sr.	M Agnes Morgan *	,,	1793
Sr. Lucy Smith	,, 1768	Sr.	M Anne Lincoln *	,,	1794
Sr. Anne Winifred Thomby	1773	Sr.	Martha Gornal	,,	,,
Sr. Josepha Harrison	,, 1778	Sr.	M Félicité Salcement	,,	1795
Sr. M Barbara Pyser	,, 1781	Sr.	M Margaret Evans	,,	1798

Sister Elizabeth Charnley,	professed in 1758		died in 1807
Sr. Scholastica Phesackelloy	,,	1775	,,	1823
Sr. Anne Benedict Godwin	,,	1768	,,	1828
Sr. Mary Magdalen Berry	,,	1791	,,	1829
Sr. Mary Agnes Bond	,,	1778	,,	1832
Sr. Mary Winifred Tobin	,,	1781	,,	1846

XV

The Abbey of our Lady of Grace at Ypres. †

The Lady Mary Percy, daughter to Thomas, Earl of Northumberland, was the first who projected the erection of a religious house in Flanders for English subjects. She left her native country and obtained leave from the Archduke Albert, Governor of the Low Countries, to found a monastery at Brussels, and by his favourable assistance it was likewise arranged that some English nuns of the Abbey of St. Peter at Rheims might be removed to Brussels in company with Madame Noelle, the Prioress of St. Peter's, and three other French Religious, in 1598. Nothing now remained for the complete establishment of the new Abbey but the sanction of the Holy See, which his Holiness Pope Clement VIII readily granted by a Bull which reached Brussels in 1599.

[The history of the foundation of the Abbeys of Cambray and Ghent has already been related.]

In the year 1665, M. Martin de Praets, Canon of Ghent, was elected Bishop of Ypres, and made his solemn entrance into his Diocese on the 7th of March in the same year. On the 18th of May following he solicited the permission of the Magistrates of his Cathedral city for the erection of an Abbey of English Benedictine Dames, and on their consent all necessary grants and orders were issued by Philip IV, king of Spain, and registered in the great Council of the Commune of Ypres.

After these formalities his Lordship requested the Lady Abbess and Community of Ghent to send Dame Mary Beaumont to Ypres to found a monastery of her Order and nation. Thereupon the Lady Abbess and community elected the said D. Mary Beaumont, to be Abbess of the new convent, and sent with her Dame Flavia Cary, D. Helen Wait, (Wayte, or White), and D. Vincentia Aire, ‡ all professed nuns of Ghent. They arrived at Ypres about the 22nd of May, 1665, and entered the house that the Bishop had provided for them. Four years later, his Lordship solemnly blessed in his Cathedral Church Dame Mary Beaumont as first Abbess of this Monastery. On the 3rd of May, in the

---

* Professed at Pontoise.
† Abridged from an account kindly communicated by the Lady Abbess of that Monastery.
‡ Dodd (Church History, III, 485) gives her name as Viviana Eyre.

same year, Dame Josepha Carew, the first nun of this community, made her solemn profession. A Lay-sister, Sister Frances Wright, was admitted about the same time. But the Abbess, seeing that very little success attended her efforts, began to make arrangements for handing over the Abbey to the English Benedictine Nuns of Paris, but on the suggestion of Dame Mary Knatchbull, Abbess of Ghent, the project was set aside and it was determined to make the house of Ypres an Abbey for the Irish nation. At the request of the Abbess of Ghent, Dame Mary Caryll, Abbess of Dunkirk proceeded to Ypres with four of her religious, two of whom were of Irish birth, when death had removed Lady Abbess Beaumont.* The four Dunkirk religious were invited to join the Ypres community; and on their consenting, a new Abbess was to be chosen, in quality of first Abbess of an Irish Community, though the second of the establishment. On November 19th, 1682, Dame Flavia Cary was elected to the office and the choice of the community was confirmed by the Letters Patent of the Vicars General of Ypres.

Thereupon Lady Abbess Knatchbull desired the other Monasteries of the Congregation to send some of their professed Irish members in order to increase the Ypres community. From Ghent was sent the Reverend Dame Ursula Butler; the Abbess of Dunkirk sent Dame Josepha O'Bryan (or O'Byrnn); from Pontoise, Lady Abbess Neville sent Dame Mary Joseph Butler daughter of Toby Butler Esq, of Callin, and some others, upon which a legal concession and donation of the house at Ypres was made in favour of the Irish nation, and Dame Flavia Cary entered on her office as abbess of the Irish monastery, dedicated to the Immaculate Conception of our Lady under the title of "The grace of God."

After many pains and labours for propagating this establishment, it pleased God to call to Himself the Reverend Lady Abbess, D. Flavia Cary, on the 20th of February, 1686. She was succeeded in her office by Dame Mary Joseph Butler, who received the Abbatial benediction at Commines, from the Rt. Rev. Lord de Choiseul de Plessis Prastin, Bishop of Tournay, the See of Ypres being then vacant.

In 1687 King James II being desirous of establishing a convent of religious women in Ireland, ordered the Earl of Tyrconnell, his Lord Lieutenant in the said kingdom, to write to the Lady Abbess of the Irish Dames of Ypres to desire her to repair to Dublin, and to transfer her community to that city. The difficulties and obstacles which had to be overcome before the King's wish could be put into execution, were innumerable; but this valiant woman surmounted them all with heroic patience and magnanimity. When preparing to start on her journey, a portion of an old wall fell upon her, under which she was so buried that it seemed a miracle that she was not killed; a picture of the crucifixion fell on her head and kept off the bricks, yet drove a nail very deep into her forehead. This happened at a time when none of the religious were within hearing, but God, who destined his servant for further labours in his service, caused a voice to be heard by a Lay-sister who was working in the garden, saying thrice: "Go help my Lady."—Thus the Abbess was discovered, all bleeding from her wound and almost suffocated under the ruins of the wall. After her recovery fresh difficul-

* She died on August 22nd, 1682, in the 66th year of her age, and the 47th of her religious profession, and 17th of Abbatial dignity.

ties arose; but at last the Earl of Tyrconnell wrote to the Court of France to obtain the removal of all the obstacles that impeded Lady Butler's journey to Ireland, and in the meantime the Archbishop of Dublin wrote to the Grand Vicars of Ypres, informing them of the King's wish, and stating that His Majesty would protect no other establishment but that of Lady Butler, and that moreover it was the opinion of the better part of the kingdom that the new Monastery should be commenced with all possible speed, in order that it might the longer enjoy the advantages of Lady Butler's direction. It was arranged at the same time, that the Monastery at Ypres should be reserved as a refuge in case of trouble in those unsettled times.

The Lord Lieutenant had, by the king's orders, taken a house for Lady Butler and her community towards the upper end of Big Sleep Street in Dublin, and His Majesty went in person to see that it was properly fitted up for the reception of the nuns. In 1688, the Abbess departed from Ypres with some of her choir nuns, **Dame** Mary Markham, a nun of Pontoise being of the number, and a lay novice, **Sister** Placida Holmes. On arriving in London, the Abbess, wearing the choir **dress** of the Order, waited on the Queen at Whitehall, and was graciously **received, and** on the 8th of October set out with her nuns for Dublin, where they **arrived on the** Eve of All Saints.

On their arrival they were presented to the King by **the Earl** and Countess of Tyrconnell. His Majesty received them most kindly **and** promised them his royal protection; and gave orders for Letters Patent to **be** expedited granting most ample privileges in favour of the Abbess and the Community, under the honourable title of His Majesty's own First, Chief and Royal Abbey of the three kingdoms, with free permission to settle in **any** part of the Kingdom **of** Ireland: the royal patent was dated June 5th, 1689.

As soon as the religious entered their inclosure in **Big Sleep Street, the Divine Office,** Holy Mass and all regular observances **were commenced to the comfort** and edification of the Irish nobility and gentry who **hastened to place their** children for education under so venerable **an** Abbess **who excelled** in piety, virtue and every branch of true learning. Among thirty young ladies **who** were intrusted to her, eighteen had petitioned for the habit of the Order, but **the** prudent **Abbess** thought it expedient to **defer their admission till more peaceable** times, **as the** civil war had already **commenced in Ireland.** On the entry of King William's victorious army into Dublin after the battle of the **Boyne**, the monastery was sacked by the troops, but not before the Abbess had sent **back** the children of the school to their respective parents; **the nuns themselves took** refuge in a neighbouring **house,** and managed to **save some of their church plate** though all besides was lost.

After this disaster, the Abbess **resolved to return to** Ypres, notwithstanding **the many assurances given her by** the Duke of Ormond, a near relation, who **promised her a strong protection from** King **William** for herself and nuns if she **would** remain; but **the journey back** to Ypres, though facilitated by an ample passport from the new **King, was** not accomplished without great difficulty. Soon after this the Pontoise religious were recalled to their own convent, so that the Lady Mary Butler led for some time a life of great solitude; for five years she had no other companions than four Lay-sisters. Their poverty was so great that their only drink was a decoction of bran. Destitute of all human comfort, but ever united to God in prayer, never wearied of suffering, and yielding not, she awaited with an humble resignation our Lord's good pleasure, resisting the solicitations of her family to return to them, and refusing the Bishop's request that she should sell the Monastery, and live where she pleased at her ease. But her heroic soul confiding on Divine Providence would not abandon the work of God nor fly from His Cross ; and in her, the Almighty verified His word, that none put their trust in him in vain. In 1700 she had the comfort of receiving several good subjects, so that the regular observances of the Choir and other community exercises were resumed ; the worthy Abbess herself being to every one an example of fervour, regularity, union with God, and unbounded charity. Thus governing her flock in the spirit of Jesus Christ, she was called to her eternal repose on the 22nd of December, 1723, in the 82nd year of her age, the 66th of her religious profession, and the 38th of her abbatial dignity.

The community, deeply afflicted at the loss of this saintly superior, had the consolation of seeing her spirit perpetuated in their new Abbess, Dame Xaveria Arthur. This Religious was one of the first whom her predecessor had received into her community after her return from Dublin. She had passed her noviciate among the English Benedictines at Ghent, but on her return to Ypres for profession, the Bishop refused his consent. All means were tried to induce him to withdraw his opposition, Sister Xaveria herself assuring him that the Irish nuns would never be a burden to his Diocese, (which was what he apprehended), and that she would be contented to live on bread and water if only he would consent to her profession. For four years he persisted in his refusal, and only agreed when the Queen of England had joined her prayers to those of the fervent novice. When the desired permission was granted, Sister Xaveria commenced to prepare the unfinished Church of the Monastery for the profession ceremony, and with her usual energy began to dig the earth and carry it in baskets into the street, in order that the pavement might be the sooner laid. After her profession she was a model of the most exact regularity, so that she was continued in the office of Prioress from 1705 to 1724, in which year she was chosen Abbess. She endeared herself to all by her great kindness and virtue ; her conduct during the great distress caused by the severe frost of 1740 made her excellent qualities most apparent to every one.* Her devotion to the sacred wounds of our Lord, prompted her to obtain for her community the privilege of keeping the Feast instituted in their honour, and, as it seemed, in reward for her zeal she was called out of life on the very feast of the five Sacred Wounds, March 5th, 1743.

On the 3rd of April following the Reverend Dame Mary Magdalen Mandeville was elected Abbess, and on the 29th of January 1744, was blessed by Bishop Delvaulx in his own palace. The early religious life of this worthy Superior is not without interest. She had completed nine months of her Noviciate, under her great-aunt, Lady Abbess Butler, when, in the interests of the community, she obtained permission to set out for Ireland to sue for her fortune, of which her brother would deprive her. After two years labour and trouble she succeeded in her endeavours, and was fortunate enough to recover the Church

* At this trying time the provisions of the nuns were of so wretched a quality that the good Abbess took upon herself the office of baker, to try whether by mixing eggs and milk with their poor bread, it might be rendered more eatable.

plate and ornaments which had been saved from the plunder of the Dublin monastery. On her return, the vessel in which she was crossing to Flanders was wrecked off the Isle of Wight on the 9th October, 1725; from mid-night till about two o'clock in the morning she clung to the main mast, but at last the violence of the waves swept her from her position of comparative safety, and it was only with extreme difficulty, and by the mercy of God, that she was enabled to save herself from drowning by means of some floating pieces of timber on which she contrived to hold till eight o'clock, when her dangerous position was discovered and some fishermen came to her rescue. By the 17th of November she reached Ypres, and having recommenced her Noviciate on the 8th of December, was admitted to profession on the 15th day of the same month in the following year.

The siege of the town, and the many crosses and anxieties which the troubled times occasioned her, added to her own great bodily sufferings, shortened her life. She died on the 27th of November, 1760, after holding her office for seventeen years.

Her successor, Dame Mary Bernard Dalton, was not unworthy of the Abbesses who had preceded her. Her superior talents and great piety were much spoken of, while within her convent, her fervent zeal for silence, prayer and holy union with God, made her a model to her subjects. Inflamed with a great devotion towards the Sacred Heart of Jesus, and seconded by the Director of the Convent, Fr. Dalas, S. J., she obtained from Pope Pius VI a grant and Briefs for erecting in the Abbey Church a confraternity of the Sacred Heart; and on the 2nd of June, 1780, (the Feast of the Sacred Heart,) the Bishop of Ypres solemnly consecrated the Abbey and its members to the service of that Adorable Object of Catholic piety, and to the particular reparation of the injuries to which It is exposed in the Most Blessed Sacrament of the Altar.* Still further to promote the piety of the faithful, His Holiness, besides other favours, granted a plenary Indulgence to be gained daily, by all who after confession and Communion should pray before the picture of the Sacred Heart placed on the Altar in the church of the Irish Benedictines.

After receiving to profession several worthy religious, Dame Mary Bernard Dalton died on the 6th of October, 1783.

By the unanimous consent of the nuns, Dame Mary Scholastica Lynch was chosen in her place, and blessed as Abbess by Bishop Wavrans on the 30th of November following. Her excellent judgment, gravity and great piety supplied what was wanting in years, and her noble bearing during the French invasion justified the choice that had been made. On the 13th of January, 1792, she had the grief of witnessing an attack on her monastery by a band of forty or fifty armed soldiers who loudly and insolently insisted on being admitted into the inclosure. The Abbess refused to allow them to enter till proper authorisation had been obtained, whereupon they threatened to point their cannon against the house, and immediately began to batter down the gates and doors with the utmost violence, and by this means forced an entrance into the inclosure where sentinels were placed at every door, and seals set on church, sacristy, and

---

* The Acts of Consecration to the Sacred Heart, and the Act of Reparation, now so commonly in use, were drawn up by Fr. Dalas for the members of this Confraternity.

other apartments where they hoped to find anything of value. All remonstrances proved useless and the nuns with difficulty persuaded their troublesome guests (who had drunk heavily at their expense), to pass the night in the out-parlours and allow the Divine Sacrifice to be celebrated next morning in the choir.

Having heard that the officer in command of the French forces at Tournai was an Irishman, the Abbess appealed to him for help in behalf of his distressed countrywomen, with the happy result of receiving a visit from the temporary governor of Ypres, who came to make excuses and pay for the damages caused by his unruly soldiers, withdraw them from the monastery and remove the seals. In taking his leave, however, this worthy exhorted the nuns to avail themselves of the liberty which the French nation had proclaimed, to return to the world again; advice which was received with the disdain which it deserved.

The following year again saw the French endeavouring to secure their possession of Flanders, and in July 1794, they surrounded the town of Ypres with a formidable army. The Irish convent was particularly exposed to danger during the last days of the siege when the enemy's artillery was directed towards that part of the ramparts near which it lay.

The merciful providence of God preserved the entire Community from any hurt during those dreadful days, though all around the fire of the enemy took deadly effect.

On one occasion all the nuns and the children of their school had retired to the work-room to take a little repose after so many restless nights, when a bomb shell fell on the garret roof over their heads; had it fallen perpendicularly, every one had been crushed to death, but it took an oblique direction and fell into an adjoining garden. Though many of their neighbours were killed by these missiles of death, and several houses in their vicinity were in flames, the Irish monastery escaped comparatively unharmed. The courage of their venerable Abbess, and the fervent exhortations of the saintly Father Dalas who daily administered the Holy Communion to the Religious, supported the nuns in this fiery trial.

Every measure that prudence could suggest had been taken by the Abbess in readiness for any emergency; and though they had determined upon quitting Ypres in case the French obtained possession, the neglect of the Austrian Commander to warn the Abbess, (as he had promised to do), of a safe opportunity for departing, obliged the religious to stay in their monastery and abide the trials which they saw in store for them.

No exception was made in their favour when the conquerors decreed the suppression of all religious houses, though, as foreigners, more time was allowed them to prepare for departure than was vouchsafed to the other communities in the town. Nevertheless the arbitrary conduct of the new authorities, their domiciliary visits at all hours of the day and night, and on the most ridiculous pretexts, the constant presence of a rude military guard, and daily menaces and theatenings of speedy expulsion, made their position anything but an enviable one.

The grief and pain which these acts of oppression caused the holy Abbess, and her deep grief at the spread of infidelity and irreligion throughout Europe shortened her life, and on the 22nd of June, 1799, Dame Mary Scholastica Lynch, passed to her reward. Her death plunged the community into still deeper grief as they found themselves deprived of their mother and guide at a most trying time.

However in Dame Mary Bernard Lynch, Sister of the deceased, **they found a worthy** successor, and the newly elected Abbess entered on her **office in time to receive** the final sentence of the suppression **of** her monastery.

The nuns were indebted to a neighbour of theirs, a Frenchman, **for this last** annoyance; the zealous Jacobin could not endure the thought **of even one single** house of religious women, and these too, of foreign birth, being allowed to **exist.** So the Abbey was sold over the heads of its owners, the Irish Benedictine Dames, who received positive and final orders to quit their abode within ten days, leave being graciously given for each religious to take with her **the** furniture of her cell. The nuns, however, found means to secure their church plate and altar furniture before the time fixed for their departure arrived.

The 13th of November, (the solemn feast of All Saints of the **Benedictine** Order), the **day** appointed for their bidding an eternal **farewell to their sacred** inclosure, came at last, but the heavy rain which fell **that day prevented the** religious from leaving the house. The next **morning news arrived of an entire** change in the government, so **that the** decree **of expulsion was not carried into** effect; **and** though **the** Abbess **was obliged to buy back the convent from its pretended** proprietor at **a** higher price **than he had paid for it, and though for a long time** the nuns **were in** extreme **want, as no supplies could reach them from England, they cheerfully persevered through all their hardships. For many years following the only community in the Low Countries was that of the Irish Benedictines of Ypres, and their successors have perpetuated to the present day the holy traditions of their monastery.**

Abbesses of the Irish Benedictine Dames of the Monastery of Our Lady of Grace at Ypres.

Dame Mary Marina Beaumont professed at **Ghent, elected Abbess in 1665**; died August 27th, 1682.

Dame Flavia Cary **professed at Ghent, elected November** 19th, 1682; died February 20th, 1686.

Dame Mary Joseph Butler, professed at Pontoise, November 4th, **1657**; elected Abbess, August 20th, 1686; died December 22nd, 1723.

Dame Mary Xaveria Arthur, chosen Abbess in 1723; blessed on **March** 19th, 1724; died March 5th, 1743.

Dame Mary Magdalen Mandeville, elected **April 3rd, 1743; died November 27th, 1760.**

Dame Mary **Bernard Dalton, elected December 22nd, 1760; died October 6th,** 1783.

Dame Mary Scholastica **Lynch, elected October 17th, 1783; died June 22nd,** 1799.

Dame Mary Bernard Lynch, **elected June 29th, 1799; died August 21st,** 1830.

Dame Mary Benedict Byrne, elected in 1830; died January 12th, 1840.

Dame Elizabeth Jarrett, elected May 1st, 1840.

APPENDIX

The professed Religious of this Abbey.

Dame Mary Marina Beaumont, professed at Ghent, in 1636.
Dame Flavia Cary
Dame Helen Wait or Wayte
Dame Viviana Eyre or Aire, all professed at Ghent.

1657	Nov. 4th		Dame Mary Joseph Butler, professed at Pontoise.
1669	May 3rd	D.	Josepha, Susanna Carew, professed at Ypres.
a 1673	——	Sr.	Frances Wright, Lay-Sr, died Nov. 10, 1673.
1673	——	D.	Christina Whyte or White, professed at Pontoise.
,,	——	D.	Mary Anne Nevil or Nevill, ,, ,,
a 1685	——	D.	Ursula Butler, died April 10th, 1685.
1685	May 19th	Sr.	Mary Benedict Blisset, an Extern-sister.
a 1689	——	D.	Mary Susanna Fletcher, died May 18th, 1689.
1690	March 10th	Sr.	Placida Holmes, Lay-sister.
a 1697	——	Sr.	M. Helen Marlow, Lay-sister, died May 12th, 1697.
1700	Dec. 9th,	D.	Xaveria, Margaret Arthur.
,,	,, 29th,	D.	Josepha O'Conner.
1702	Sept. 18th.	D.	Mary Benedict O'Neile.
,,	,, ,,	D.	Mary Theresa Wyld or Wyre.
1703	Jan 25th,	Sr.	Mary Joseph Le Ducq, a Lay-sister.
,,	April 24th,	D.	Mary Xaveria Goulde.
,,	,, ,,	D.	Mary Ignatia Goulde.
a 1704	——	Sr.	M. Anne Jennison, Lay-sister, died Nov. 6th, 1704.
1706	June 8th,	Sr.	Mary Joseph Adkinson, Lay-sister.
,,	Oct. 10th,	D.	Gertrude Chamberlaine.
1710	July 7th,	D.	Mary Louise Macleane.
,,	,, ,,	D.	Mary Bridget Creagh.
,,	Sept. 30th,	D.	Mary Catharine Aylmer.
1711	Nov. 15th,	Sr.	Petronilla Van Mechels, a Lay-sister.
1712	April 2nd,	D.	Mary Scholastica Goulde.
1718	June 7th,	D.	Mary Theresa Butler.
1725	March 19th	D.	Anne Butler.
1726	Dec. 15th,	D.	Mary Magdalen Mandeville.
,,	Dec. 29th,	Sr.	Mary Margaret Brown, Lay-sister.
,,	——	Sr.	Anna Le Ducq, Lay-sister.
1728	May 26th,	Sr.	Praxedis, Natalie Sandermont, Lay-sister. ?
1730	April 30th,	D.	Mary Josepha Malone.
1731	Nov. 6th,	D.	Mary Maura Archbald.
1732	Oct. 7th,	Sr.	Mary Benedict Morrissy, Lay-sister.
1733	May 7th,	D.	Mary Xaveria Browne.
1734	Feb. 16th,	D.	Mary Austin Browne.
		D.	Mary Baptist O'Moore.
1736	July 11th	D.	Josepha, Helen Hamborough.
,,	,, ,,	D.	Mary Winifred Goodge.
1737	Jan. 10th,	D.	Mary Bernard Dalton.
1738	Aug. 26th	D.	Mary Mechtilde Nagle.
,,	,,	D.	Mary Anthony Nagle.
1740	May 1st	Sr.	Scholastica Stafford, Lay-Sister.

APPENDIX. 55

1747	May 23rd,	Dame	Benedicta Ley.
1753	Jan. 23rd,	D.	Mary Ignatia Sarsfield.
1771	June 16th.	Sr.	Mary Patrick Segeart, Lay-Sister.
1772	March 21st	D.	Mary Patrick Reily.
"	"	D.	Mary Scholastica, Clementina Lynch.
1775	Dec. 8th,	D.	Mary B, Esmenia Fleming.
1780	Feb. 2nd,	D.	Mary Gertrude Fleming.
1781	Jan. 16th,	Sr.	Anne Theresa Fouquet, Lay-Sister.
"	Nov. 4th,	D.	Mary Benedict, Bridget Fleming.
1782	June 1st.	D.	Mary Bernard, Bridget Lynch.
1785	Jan. 25th,	D.	Mary Placida Byrne.
1786	April 16th,	D.	Mary Mechtilde Longe.
1789	Feb. 2nd	Sr.	Mary Benedict Le Maire, Lay-sister.
1791	April 24th,	D.	Mary Scholastica Cadet.
1795	Feb. 2nd,	D.	Mary Joseph Fleming.
"	Feb. 25th,	D.	Mary Benedict Byrne.
a 1810	———	D.	Mary Scholastica O'Curren, died May 24th, 1810.
1815	Oct. 29th,	D.	Mary Aloysia Du Toit.
1816	Jan 15th,	Sr.	Mary Joseph Denis, Lay-sister.
1817	June 5th,	D.	Mary Scholastica Morris.
1819	Jan. 21st	D.	Mary Xaveria Mason
"	Oct. 29th	D.	Mary Bernard Jarrett
"	" "	Sr.	Mary Austin Tailler, Lay-sister.
1820	Feb. 7th	D.	Mary Theresa Coppe (Coppé)
"	June 21st	D.	Elizabeth Jarrett
a 1822	———	D.	Mary Bridget Fleming, died July 24th, 1822. *
"	———	D.	Mary Maura Reily, died August 19th, 1822.
1823	June 29th,	D.	Mary Baptist Morris.
"	" "	D.	Mary Sales Morris.
1825	Nov. 19th,	Sr.	Mary Magdalen Gunn, Lay-sister.
1826	July 22nd,	D.	Mary Gertrude Stockman.

* Not the same as D. Mary Fleming, professed in 1781, whose death occurred on March 27th, 1786.

INDEX.

A

Abbot, Titular of London and **Canterbury**, 77, 82, 83
Abbotsbury Abbey, 53
Abingdon Abbey, 53
Acton, D, Placid, 251
Adelham, D. Placid, 224
Aggregation by Fr. Buckley, 60, 61
Albert, Archduke of Austria, 67, 74, 86, 122
Alcester Abbey, **51**, 53
Alcuin, 12
Aldeby Priory, **55**
Aldermanshave, **59**
Alexander VII, 190, **204**
    ,,   VIII, 231
Alexandria, Church of, **19**
Allen, Cardinal, 33, 35, 103, **104**
    ,,   Letter to D. Athanasius **Martin**, 40
Anchin College, Douay, 62
Anderton family converted, **191**
Anderton, D. Christopher 185, **189**
    ,,   D. James 185
    ,,   D. **Robert**, 185
    ,,   D. **Thomas**, 185, 196, **207, 208**
    ,,   Sir Francis, 216
Andrewes, Bishop of Winchester, 83
Anne of Austria, 202
Anselm, D. of Manchester, *see* Beech
Apostolatus Benedictinorum in **Anglia**, 140
Appleton, D. Lawrence, 196
    ,,   Dame Marina, **225, 227, 232, 234**, 235
Aprice, D. Joseph, 250
Archpriests in England, **37, 129, 130**
Armagh, Archbishop of, *see* **Plunket**
Arnoult, Prior of St. Denis, 248
Arras, Abbey of St. Vedest or Vaast, 63 (*see* **Cavarel**)
    ,,   Jesuit College, 63
Arviragus, king of Britain, **11**
Athelney Abbey, 53
Atrobus, D Francis, **112, 155**
Avecot Priory, 56

B

Babthorpe or Bapthorpe, D. **Mellitus**, 80
Bacon, D George, 200
Bagshaw, D. Sigebert, 96, 99, 108, 112, 113, 115, 126, 137, 146, **166, 169, 178**
Baker, D. Augustine, 47, 49, 96, 139, 145, 178, 183, 186, 212
  „   Sir Richard, *quoted*, 36, 79, 83
Barbo, Abbot of St. Justina's at Padua, 7
Balthassar, 30.
Bardney Abbey, 51
Barking Abbey, 56
Barkworth, V Mark, or Lambert, Martyr, 43
Barlow, V Ambrose, Martyr, 183
  „   D Rudesind, 89, 105, 126, 136, 139, 143, 145, 146, 148, 183
Barnes, D. John, 78, 81, 83, 97, 131, 135, 137, 138, 170
Barnstaple Priory, 59
Baronius refuted, 13 ; elogium of St. Bennet Biscop, 22, 23
Barter, Br. John, 189
  „   D. John, (the elder), 189, 196, 205
Basil, Monks of St., 22
Bassec, Austin Friars at, 174
Bassclech Priory, 52
Batt, D. Anthony, 188
Battle Abbey, 51
Beaulieu Priory, 50
Bec Abbey, Normandy, 24
Beech, D. Anselm, of Manchester, 40, 46, 60, 76, 95, 96, 98
Bell at Lambspring Abbey, 185
Bellarmine S.J, Cardinal, 98, 103, 106, 126
Bellasis, Lord, 231
Bellieur, M. de, 120, 121
Belvere or Belvoir Priory, 50
Benedict of St. Facundo, *see* Jones
Benson, *see* Dom Robert Haddock, 187
Bentivoglio, Cardinal, 72, 86, 95, 106, 183
Berington, D. Bernard, 126, 136, 137, 146, 166, 169, 180, 200
  „   D. George, 200
Bermondsey Abbey, 56, 58
Bernard, D. Prior of Cluny College, Paris, 90
Berriman, D. Joseph, 240, 254
Bettenson, D. Placid, 207
Bingham Priory, 51
Birkenhead Priory, 55
Birkhead, Rev. G. Archpriest, 130
Bishop, Dr. Bishop of Chalcedon, 129, 130, **193**
Blackestone, D. Francis, 188
  „   D. Michael, 168, 188
Blacklo, Blacklow or White, 197, **228**
Blackwell, Rev George, Archpriest, 46, 129

Blandy, D. Boniface, 172
Blount, D. Goderic, 205
Bondage of our Lady, 156
Boniface of St. Facundo, *see* Blandy
Booth, Sir George, 205
Borromeo, Cardinal Frederick, 45
    "   St. Charles, 104
Bossuet, 219, 249, 250
Boudot, Paul, 156
Bouillon, Cardinal de, 237, 238
Bradshaw or White, D. Augustine of St. John, 45, 46, 62, 64, 65, 66, 69, 72, 73, 78, 79, 90, 94, 120, 121, 128
Bradwell Priory, 55
Brecon Priory, 51
Brent, Dame Christina, 182, 215
Brett, D. Gabriel, 182, 185, 194, 202, **236**
Bristol Priory, 52; St. James's (Cell of Tewkesbury Abbey), 54
Bristow, Dr. President of Douay College, 34
Bromholme Priory, 59
Broomfield Priory, 52
Brown, D. George 158,
Bruning, D. Placid, 225
Brussels, **72, 73**
    "   English Benedictine Abbey, 144, 185
    "   English Soldiers, at 107
Bucelinus, O. S. B, quoted, 77
Buckley, D. Sigebert, 46, 47, 49, 60, 62, 76
Burgundy, Duchess of, 249, 255
Bursfield, Congregation, O. S. B, 8, 102, 157, 167 (*see* Lambspring)
Burstall, Leicestershire, 201
Burton on Trent Abbey, 53

C

Cajetan, Abbot Constantine, 13, 128, 178, 184, 194
Caldwell or Candwell Priory, 56
Calvin, 161
Calvino-Turcismus, **163**
Cambden or Camden, the Antiquary, 14, 141
Cambray, English Benedictine Abbey at, 108, **142, 146,** 166, 169, 181, 182, 185, 187, 189, **190,** 194, 196, 199, 202, **204, 205, 207,** 209, 210, 212, 214, 215, 225, **227, 232,** 234, 235, 238, **240,** 251, 255
Cambridge, monks at, 51
    "   St. Peter's, 56
Campion V, Fr. S. J. Martyr, **36**
Canons of English Secular Chapter, **193**
Canons Regular of St. Austin, 15
Canterbury, Abbey of St. Augustine, **51**
    "   Cathedral, 11, 154, 158
    "   Archbishop of, 24

Capo, D. Francois, 182, 185, 187, 194, 205
Capo, D. Michael, 204, 205
Cardiff Priory, 54
Cardigan, Lord, 203, 241
Cardigan Priory, 53
Carmes, Discalced, 21
Carswell, Dorsetshire, 59
Carter, D. Anselm, 225
Cary, Dame Clementina, 199, 208
„ D. Placid, 187
Caryll, D. Aloxius, 207
Casse, D. Laurence, 254
Cassinese Monks on English Mission, 172
Cassy, D. Anselm, 208
Castleacre Priory, 58
Castro, D Antonio de, 114.
Catharine of Portugal, Queen Dowager, 230, 251
Cathedral Churches served by monks, 14, 19
Cauke, Staffordshire, 122
Cavarel, Abbot of St. Vedast's, 63, 67, 72, 73, 74, 88, 115, 130, 131, 148, 174
Cecil of Salisbury, 122
Cerne Abbey, Dorsetshire, 53
Chalcedon Bishop of, 193, see Bishop Smith &c.
Challiot, Visitation nuns, 247
Chambers D. William, or Johnson, 200
Champney, Dr. Anthony, 130
„ D. Laurence, 234, 238
Chapter, English Secular, 193
Chapter General of English Benedictines, 124, 125
Charles I, 102
Charles II, 188, 191, 196, 218, 223, 225, 232, 236
Charles of Lorraine, Cardinal, 65
Chelles, Abbey near Paris, 90, 105, 116, 135, 136, 158, 170
Cheriton, D. Basil, 198
Chertsey Abbey, 53
Chester Abbey (now the Cathedral), 54
Chetardie, Abbé de la, 294
Choiseul, Bishop of Tournay, 156
Choisy, Benefice of, 237
Chorley, D. Edward, 254
Church lands alienated, 29, 30, 229
Cismar Abbey, 102, 157, 178, 219
Cisneros, Garcias, O S B, 8
Cisson, Norfolk, 46
Cistercian Congregation, 15, 20
Clement VIII, 45, 46, 93, 104
„ IX, 204, 208
„ X, 208, 210

INDEX.

Clerkenwell Priory, 56
    ,,   Monastery in James II's reign, 236
Clermont, near St. Malo's, 69, 236, (*see* St. Malo)
Cliffe, D. Ildephonse, 189
Clifford Priory, Herefordshire, 59
Clink Prison, London, 187
Cluny, Congregation of, 16, 20, 58, 59, 81, 136, 139, 170
Cockersand Priory, 59
Coilen, Cardinal, 249
Colchester Abbey, 51
Coldingham Priory, 54
Colne Priory, 51
Cologne, Elector of, 233
Compostella, St Martin's Abbey, 77, 101, 186
Condé, Princess of, 249
Congregation, English Benedictine, 17, 18, 25, 110
Coniers or Conyers, D. Augustine, 185, 187, 204, 209
Constable, D. Augustine, 190, 194, 225, 234, 240
    ,,   D. Benedict, 225
Constitutions of the English Benedictines, 112
Coppens, Adrian, 216
Corby or Corvy Abbey, 180
Cork Priory, 55
Corker, D. Maurus 219, 223, 227, 232, **234, 235**
Cotton, Sir Robert, 139, 141
Cour, D. Didacus de la, 129
Cour, D. Jacques de la, 252
Coventry, Cathedral Monastery, 54
Cowick Priory, 53
Cox, D. Benedict, 187
Cranburn Priory, 54
Cranmer, Archbishop of Canterbury, 31
Crathorne, D. Francis, 205
Cressy, D. Serenus, 141, 209
Croft, Sir Herbert, 164
Crosby, D. Wolstan, 232
Crowder or Crowther, D. Anselm, 71, 89, 156, 189, **194**, 196, 202,
    ,,   ,,   D. Mark, 71
Crowland or Croyland Abbey, 51
Cumberford, Three Sisters, 205
Curr, D John, 172
Curre, D. Nicholas, 91

D

Dada, **Papal Nuncio at St. James'**, 230
Dakins, D. John, 252
Damascus, Archbishop of, **67**
Danes in England, 23, 24

Danvers, D. Romuald, 172
Darel, D. John, General of the Maurists, 190
Daventry, Priory, 59
Deacons, Dame Potentiana, 145
De la Cour, D. Didacus, 129
De la Cour, D. Jacques, Abbot of La Trappe, 252
Deping Priory, 53
Derby Priory, 58
Derehurst Priory, 54
Dieulwart, Monastery of St Laurence, 65, 69, 79, 90, 101, 104, 112, 116, 126, 136, 158, 166, 168, 169, 171, 172, 182, 185, 187, 188, 189, 190, 194, 196, 204, 205, 206, 207, 209, 210, 214, 216, 221, 225, 227, 232, 234, 238, 240, 251, 254, 255
Dobran Abbey, 178
Dorington, Sir Francis, 200
Dorset, Lord, 200
Douay, Anchin College, 62
" English College, 34
" English Franciscans, 174, 177, 203
" Monastery of St. Gregory the Great, 62, 67, 72, 78, 82, 85, 89, 101, 108, 112, 116, 118, 122, 124, 126, 130, 131, 140, 146, 148, 149, 164, 166, 168, 169, 172, 174, 177, 178, 179, 182, 183, 184, 185, 187, 189, 193, 194, 196, 201, 203, 204, 205, 207, 209, 214, 217, 218, 221, 225, 227, 231, 232, 234, 238, 240, 251, 253, 254, 255
" Marchin or Marchienne College, 67, 89, 116, 122, 146, 150
" Plague at, 189, 204
" Siege of, by the Duke of Marlborough, 253
" Trinitarians, 63
" College of St. Vaast, 150, 222
Dover Priory, 54
Down family, 191
Drury Lane, London, 190
Dudley Priory, Staffordshire, 58
Dunn, D. Roland, 210
Dunster Priory, Somerset, 55
Durham Cathedral Priory, 54
Du Sourdis, Cardinal, 129
Duval, M. 137

E

Eadmer, 14
Edgarus, King, 23
Edner, D. Justus, alias Rigg, 146, 172
Edward VI, 28
Edwardeston Priory, 51
Eleutherius, Pope St., 11
Elizabeth, Queen, 35
Ellenstowe Nunnery, 56
Ellis, D. Philip, (afterwards Bishop), 139, 229, 231, 238

Elmer, D. Jocelin, 112, 146, 166, 169, 173, 182, 187, 188
Ely Cathedral Monastery, 55
Emmerson, D. Thomas, 167
Erric of Lorraine, Bishop of Verdun, 65
d'Escars, Annas, Cardinal O. S. B. 73
Esquerchin, near Douay, 155
Eu, Seminary at, 36
Everard, D Dunstan, 188, 196
Evesham Abbey, 51
Ewenny Priory, 52
Ewyas Harold Priory, 52
Exeter Priory, 51
  ,, Cluniac Priory of St. James, 58
Eynsham Abbey, 53

F

Falkland, Lady, &c, 178, 188, 199
Faremoutier Abbey, 170
Farley Priory, Wilts, 58
Farington Hall, Lancashire, 190
Farmer or Venner, D. Amandus, 158
Feckenham, Abbot of Westminster, 31, 113
Felixstowe Priory, 55
Femy Abbey, 143
Fenwick, D. Francis, 209, 232, 235
  ,, D. Laurence, 238
Ferdinand II, Emperor, 178
Feversham Abbey, 53
Finchal Priory, 54
Fitzherbert, Mr. 42
Fitzjames, D. Nicholas, 69, 105
Fleury-sur-Loire, Abbey, 23
Flixton, Suffolk, 202
Flutot, D. Maur, 207
Fontevrault Abbey, 104
Foster, D. Bede, 245
  ,, D. Francis, 167
Foucquoi, Jean de, Abbot of Marchienne, 87
Frere, D. Joseph, 155, 169, 234
  ,, D. Placid, 168
Freston Priory, 51
Fromegham (Framlingham?), 46
Frost in 1709, 252
Fursden, D. Cuthbert, 178, 210
  ,, D. Thomas, 216

G

Gaire, D. George, 171

Galloni, 13,
Gant, *see* Ghent
Gascoigne, Dame Catharine, 142, 169, 185, 187, 189, 194, 212
  „   Dame Justina, 232
  „   D. Michael, 194
  „   D. Placid, 92, 166, 184, 187, 189, 233
  „   Sir Thomas, 228, 232
Gatehouse Prison, London, 60, 185
Gavel, Fr. Edmund, O. S. F., 46
Gawen, Dame Frances, 144, 146, 181
Gervaise, V George or Jervase, Martyr, 74
Ghent, St. Peter's Abbey, 23, 91, 128, 179
Gibbon, D. Benedict, 254
Gicou, D. Francis, 186
Gifford or Giffard, D. Gabriel, (Archbishop of Rheims), 69, 79, 81, 94, 95, 102, 112, 116, 126, 127, 128, 132, 135, 159, 202
Gifford, Sir Henry, 201
Girlington, D. John, 215
Gesenius, Dr., 91
Glastonbury Abbey, 52, 193
Gloucester Abbey, 52
Godstow Nunnery, 56
Goldcliff Priory, 54
Gordon or Gourdan, D. William, 178
Gothland Priory, 54
Govaerdt, D. Christian, 169
Grange, D. Gregory, 112, 122
Gratz in Styria, 200
Green, D. Thomas, 80
Greenwood, D. Paulin, 113, 118, 126, 152, 182, 185
Gregory XIII, 77
Gregory XV, 128
Gregson, D. Bernard, 1, 3, 225, 227, 238, 240, 251, 254, 255
Grineus, Fr. Paul, 97
Guildford, Surrey, 205
Guillet, D. Rupert, 165
Guise, Duke of, 36, 103,
  „   Louis de, Archbishop of Rheims, 103

H

Hackness Priory, 54
Haddock or Benson, D. Robert, 105, 126
Hagham Priory, 59
Hall, Dame Maura, 209
  „   Mrs. of High Meadow, 210
Hardcastle, D. Robert, 251, 254
Harding Castle, Flintshire, 120, 185
Harlay, Achilles de, Bishop of St. Malo, 186

Harper, D. John, 146, 180
Harrison, Rev. W. Archpriest, 130
Hartburne, or Foorde, D. Placid, 183
Hatfield Brodoke Priory, 55
Hatfield Peverel Priory, 50
Haworth, D. Joseph, 69
Haywood, Fr. S. J, 37
Helme, D. Bede, 122
Henrietta, Queen, 102, 199, 208
Henry VIII, 23
Hereford Priory, 52
    ,,   Mission, 200
Hertford Priory, 50
Hesketh, D. Gregory, 209
    ,,   D. Ildefonsus, 80
    ,,   D. Jerome, 225
    ,,   D. Mellitus, 209
    ,,   D. Thomas, 235
Hildesheim, 91, 232
Hill, D. Thomas, 183
Hills, Henry, King's Printer, 229
Hilton or Musgrave, D. Placid, 79, 81
Hitchcock, D. William, 204, 207, 209, 227, 232, 234, 238, 255
Hodgson, D. Richard, 186
Holiwell Priory, 56
Holland Priory, 51
Holt, Fr. S. J., 37
Horskley Priory, 59
Horton Priory, 54, 59
Horsley, D. Cuthbert, 182, 185, 187, 190, 194, 204, 207, 216
Hoskins, Sister Mary, 143
Hospitals held by Cluny, 59
Houghton, Dame Scholastica, 238, 254
Howard, D. Augustine, 215, 234, 237, 238, 240, 251
Howland Priory, 55
Hoxne Priory, 55
Huddleston, D. John, 188, 190, 198, 225, 238
    ,,   D. Richard, 190
Huitson, Br. Peter, 63, 71, 201
Hull, D. Francis, 166, 182, 186
Hulme Abbey (St. Bennet's), 52
Humbersteyn Abbey, 54
Hungate, D. Austin, 146, 169, 194, 196, 204, 208, 239
    ,,   D. Gregory, 71, 189, 194
    ,,   Sir Francis, 208
Hunsdon House, accident at, 79
Hurley Priory, 53
Hussey, Dame Cecilia, 251
Hutton, D. John, 166

Hutton, D. Nicholas, Martyr, 78
Hyde Abbey, Winchester, 52

I

Ingleby family, 191
Ingleby, Dr. 241
Innocent III, 7
Innocent X, 183, 190
Innocent XI, 203, 231
Ireland family, 191
Irish Benedictines, 210
Ishel, John, Priest, 63

J

James II, 226, 228, 235, 236, 241, 249
James III, 251 (see Prince of Wales)
Jarrow Priory, 55
Jerusalem, Church of, 19
Jersey, 188
Jervase (*see* Gervaise)
Jesuit Mission to England, 35, 37, 75
Jesuitesses suppressed, 167
Johnson or Lee, D. Austin, 180
  ,,   D. Placid, 206
  ,,   D. William, or Chambers, 200
Johnston, D. Joseph, 238, 250, 251, 254
Jones, D. Bennet, or Price, (Benedict of St. Facundus) 107, 148, 166
  ,, D. Leander (*see* Leander of St. Martin)
Julius III, 30

K

Kemp, D. Boniface, or Kipton, Martyr, 80
Kiddington, Oxfordshire, 202
Kidwilly Priory, 54
Kilenmin Priory, 52
Killingbeck, D. Robert, 226
Kilpeck Priory, 52
Kinder, D. Austin, 182, 210
Knightley, D. Maurus, 235, 254

L

La Celle, Priory of, 170, 171, 188, 205, 218, 234, 252
Lake, D. Dunstan, 252
Lambspring Abbey, 71, 91, 92, 158, 178, 184, 185, 189, 194, 204, 219, 223, 225, 228, 234, 235
Lammana Priory, 52
Lancashire families converted, 191
Landres, D. Celestine de, 168
Lanfranc, Archbishop of Canterbury, 24
L'Angevin, D. Deodatus, 166, 169

Langius, Paul, 12
Lateran Council (1215) Decrees for Benedictine Order, 7
Latham, D. Austin, 189, 209, 215
  ,,   D. Gabriel, 171
  ,,   D. Joseph, 181
  ,,   D. Swithbert, 181
  ,,   D. Thomas Torquatus, 89, 108, 181
La Trappe, Abbey of, 252
Laud, Archbishop of Canterbury, 102
Lauderdale, Lord, 235
Lawson, D. Francis, 215, 225
Leander of St. Martin, 66, 70, 73, 88, 89, 94, 95, 97, 98, 100, 105, 112, 116, 117, 126, 135, 140, 148, 149, 166, 169, 179, 183
Ledcombe Priory, 59
Lee, D. Austin, or Johnson, 180
Legan Priory, 55
Le Gouverneur, Bishop of St. Malo, 167
Leighland, Somersetshire, 200, 204
Le Mercier, M, 150, 151
Lenton Priory, 58
Leominster Priory, 52
Lewes Priory, 58
Lewis, D. Owen, Bishop of Cassano, 35, 43
Leyburn, Dr. V. A. 139, 193
Lincoln Priory, 51
Lindisfarne Priory, 55
Lisbon Seminary, 36
Lisle, Deanery of, 104
Little Milton, Lancashire, 192
Little Stoke, Oxfordshire, 200
Llewellin, D. Austin, 227
Lodwick, D, Laurence, 169
London, 43, 45, 46, 49, 60, 65, 79, 89, 90, 139, 145, 156, 186, 181, 183, 185, 186, 187, 190, 193, 194, 195, 196, 200, 203, 204, 205, 207, 208, 219, 223, 225, 226, 227, 230, 231, 233, 236, 238, 251,
  ,,   Clink Prison, 187
  ,,   Newgate, 70, 181
Longueville Priory, Normandy, 93, 120, 128
Longwood, Hampshire, 190, 205
Louis XIII, 104, 183, 197
Louis XIV, 213, 252
Louvain University, 103
Louvoy, M, 163
Lucius, king of Britain, 11
Luffield Priory, 55
Lynch Priory, 55
Lynn Priory, 55

M

Mabbs, D. Laurence, 181

Mabillon, D. 14, 164
Madrid, 173
Maihew, D. Edward, 60, 107, 112, 146, 163
Maintenon, Madame de, 249
Mallaneus, John, Bishop of Tulle, 65
Mallet, D. Gregory, 185, 187, 207, 215, 225
Malmesbury Abbey, 52
Malon, D. Columban, 70, 80, 113, 126
Malpas Priory, 59
Malvern, Great, Priory, 56
Malvern, Little, Priory, 56
Marchantius, Provincial, O. S. F., 203
Marchin or Marchienne Abbey, 87, 89
  ,,   College, Douay, 67, 89
Marlborough, Duke of, 253
Marsh Priory, 51
Martin, D. Athanasius, 40
  ,,   Sir Henry, 83
  ,,   D. John, 208
  ,,   Sister Martha, 143
Martyrs, English, 26, 43, 45, 46, 60, 74, 77, 78, 80, 82, 92, 172, 181, 183, 186, 187, 219, 223, 224
Mary, Queen of England, 29
Mary Beatrice of Modena, Queen of England, 230
Mary Louise, Princess, 213
Mather, D. Austin, 225, 251
  ,,   D. James, 225, 232, 240
Matthews or Nathal, D. Constantius, 195
Maupas, M de, Abbot of St. Denis' of Rheims, 163
Maurist Congregation, O. S. B., 8, (*see* La Celle)
May Priory, Scotland, 52
Mayne or Maine, V. Cuthbert, Martyr, 36
Meering, D. Benedict, 204
Mendham Priory, 59
Mercier or Le Mercier, M. 150, 151
Merkgate Nunnery, 51
Mervin or Roberts, John, Martyr, 45, 46
Messingham Priory, 58
Metham D. Philip, 251
Meutisse, D. John, 169, 182, 185, **187**, 189, 203
Middlesborough Priory, Yorkshire, 54
Middleton Abbey, 55
Middleton family converted, 191
Mildmay, Sir Walter, 60
Millington, D. Bernard, 194, 204
Minshall, D. Thomas, 120
Miracles at tomb of James II, 249
Missioners in England, Benedictine, 33
  ,, ,, ,,   Jesuit, 35, 37, 75

Modbury Priory, 53
Modney Priory, 52
Molesme Abbey, 20
Monaco, Prince of, 238
Monk Bretton Priory, 55
Monkton or Pembroke Priory, 51
Monnington, D Thomas, 71, 113
Montacute (Montague) Priory, 58
Montacute, Viscount, 173
Montalt, Cardinal, 67
Monte Cassino, 39, 45, 191
Montmorency, Anthony de, Abbot, 143
Moor, Dr. Rector of Sorbonne, 250
Moor or More, D. Bede, 232, 234
More, Sir Thomas, 142
  ,,   Dame Agnes, 142
  ,,   Dame Anne, 142
  ,,   Dame Bridget, 189
  ,,   Dame Gertrude, 142, 212
Morfield Priory, 52
Morgan, Dame Benedicta, 142
  ,,   Philip Powel or, Martyr, 186
Moseley, **192**
Moundeford, D. John, 186
Mount St. Michael Priory, Devon, 52
Mountaigue, L'Abbé, 213
Muchelney Abbey, 53
Munster, Bishop of, 233
Musgrave or Hilton, D. Placid, **79**
Muttlebury, D. Francis, 227
  ,,   D. Placid, 168

N

Nancy Cathedral, 65
Nathal, D. Constantius, **195**
Neddrum Priory, 51
Nelson, D. Bennet, 189, **204, 207, 225, 238**
  ,,   D. James, 227
  ,,   D. Maurus, 232
  ,,   D. Placid, 234
Neuberg, Prince of, 233
Nevill, Br. Leander, 172
Newgate Prison, London, 70, 181
Newport, Rev. Mr. Martyr, 83
Newton Longville Priory, 59
Nizar or Nizart, Dom, Prior **of St. Vaast's,** 149, 151
Noailles, Archbishop of Paris, **213, 249**
Norfolk, 195
Normansbery **Priory,** 59

Normington or Normiuton, D. Leander, 139, 194, 196, 202
Northampton Abbey, 56, 58,
    ,,   Nunnery, 58
North Elham Priory, 55
Norwich Cathedral, 55
    ,,   St. Leonard's Priory, 55
Nuce, Angelus de, Abbot of M. Cassino, 180

O

Oath of allegiance, 80, 109
Oath of Seminarists, 147
Oates' Plot, 218, 228
Ocymild Priory, 52
Offord Priory, 59
Old Bailey, London, 204
Onia Abbey, 122, 155
Orangian Revolution, 23
Ordericus Vitalis, 14
d'Orgain, D. Benedict, 80
Owen, D. John, 190
Oxford, Canterbury College, 54
    ,,   Durham College, 54
    ,,   Gloucester (St. Benedict's) College, 56
    ,,   St. Frideswide's, 51
    ,,   St. John's, 101
    ,,   Mission, 186

P

Palmer, D. William, 190
Palmes, D. Bernard, 189, 190, 194, 200
Paris, 104, 108, 113, 116, 126
    ,,   Augustinian Nuns (English,) 247
    ,,   Benedictines (English), St. Edmund's, 90, 113, 136, 163, 166, 169, 170, 171, 178, 180, 182, 185, 186, 187, 189, 190, 193, 194, 198, 200, 201, 202, 204, 205, 207, 208, 213, 215, 216, 220, 224, 225, 227, 232, 235, 236, 238, 240, 241, 249, 250, 251, 256
    ,,   Benedictine Nuns (English), 189, 190, 197, 208, 231, 232
    ,,   Carmelite Nuns, 199, 239
    ,,   Cluny College, 90
    ,,   Dominicans, 248
    ,,   Marmoutier College, 170
    ,,   St. Germain's Abbey, 190, 241
    ,,   Scotch College, 246
Parker, D. Cuthbert, 225, 227
Parsons, Fr. S. J., 36, 93
Paul V, 60, 61, 75, 93, 109, 122, 129, 147
Paul, Abbot of St. Alban's, 24
Pembroke Priory, 51
Penrodock, Mr. Charles, 220, 250

Penwortham Priory, 51
Perez, General of Spanish Benedictines, 67
Peronne in France, 130
Pershore Abbey, 53
Peterborough Abbey, 52
Petey, D. Charles, 241
Pettinger, D. Dunstan, 92, 190, 202
Philip II, of Spain, 33
Philip III, of Spain, 122
Philip, Duke of Orleans, 239
Philipson, D. William, 251
Phillipson, D. John, 234, 238
Pickering, Br. Thomas, Martyr, 219
Pilton Priory, 52
Pitts *de Scriptoribus*, quoted, 59, 163
Pitts, Dr. Arthur, 65, 66
Plague at Douay, 189, 204
"*Plantata in Agro Dominico*," 180, 184, 227
Plunket, Archbishop of Armagh, Martyr, 223
Pole or Pool, Cardinal Legate to England, 29, 113
Pont-à-Mousson University, 103
Pontefract Priory, 58
Pontoise, near Paris, 137
Port Royal, nuns of, 199
Porter, D. Jerome, 168
Possevinus, S. J., quoted, 59
Powel, D. Philip, (Prosser or Morgan), Martyr, 186
Prater, D. Joseph, 126, 167
Preston family, converted, 191
Preston D. Thomas ,40, 43, 46, 76, 94, 95, 180
Price, William, *see* D. Bennet Jones, 107
Princess of England, 256
Pritchard, D. Leander, 196
    ,,   D. Maurus, 193
Pritwell Priory, 59
Providence of God to Benedictine Order, 9
Pullein, D. Michael, 234, 238, 240, 253, 254
Pyll Priory, 56

R

Raleigh, Sir Walter, 204
Ramsey Abbey, 52
Raphael, Don, 40
Reading Abbey 52, 60
Recollects, 21
Redburn Priory, 51
Reeves, Br. Wilfred, 218, 219
Reginald or Reinald, William, 163
Remiremont Abbey, 65

Renunciation of Abbey lands, 229
Reyner, D. Clement, 89, 90 126, 128, 140, 146, 169, 178, **179**, 184, 185
    „   D. Laurence, 126, 146, 187, 189, 190, 200
    „   Dr. William, 130
Rheims, English College, 34, **103**
    „   Abbey of St. Denis (Augustinian), 159, 163
    „   „   , St. Peter (Benedictine nuns), 162
    „   „   , St. Remi, (Benedictine), 70, 101, 105, 160, 191
    „   University, 104
Ribertiero, D. Bernard, 182
Richardot, Bishop of Arras, 85
Richardson, D. John, **147**
Richelieu, Cardinal, 170
Richmond Priory, Yorkshire, **52**
Riddell, D. Gregory, 254
Rigg or Edner, D. Justus, **172**
Rindelgros Priory, 52
Rintelin Abbey, 91, 167, **168, 169**
Risbury Priory, 54
Roberts, V John or Mervin, Martyr, 45, 76
Robinson, D. Paul, 184, 185, 194, 195, 196, 205
Rochefoucault, Cardinal, 128
Rochester Cathedral Priory, 55
Rock, Our Lady of the, Wilts, **59**
Roe, V Alban, Martyr, 92
    „   D. Maurus, 194
Romburgh Priory, 51
Rome, 182, 184, 185, 190, 191, 194, 196, 209, 227, 235, 238,
    „   College of St. Gregory, 128, 178, 194, (see Cajetan)
Rookwood, D. Francis, 240
Rosary Sodality in London, 193, 203
Rouen, 193
Rumsey Abbey, 56

S

Sadler, D. Nicholas, Martyr, 78
    „   D. Thomas Vincent, 122, 156, 193
    „   D. Vincent, 60, 102. 112, 122
St. Alban's Abbey, 40, 50, 158
St. Andrew, 113
St. Andrew's Abbey, near Cambray, 143
St. Anselm, 14, 24
St. Augustine of England, 11, 12, 19, 113, **121**
St. Augustine of Hippo, 22, 191
St. Basil, 22
St. Bede the Venerable, 22
St. Bees' Priory, 51
St. Benedict, 2, &c.
St. Benedict Biscop, 22, 23
St. Benno, 20

St. Bernard, 20
St. Blandin's Hermitage, 205
St. Charles Borromeo, 70, 104
St. Dunstan, 23, 24, 113
St. Edmundsbury Abbey, 52
St. Eleutherius, Pope, 11
St. Francis de Sales, 163
St. Germain-en-Laye, 241, 244, 256
St. Gislen's Abbey, 181
St. Gregory the Great, 12
St. Helen's, Isle of Wight, 59
St. Ive's Priory, 52
St. Jacut's Abbey, Brittany, 198
St. James', London, 207, 226, 227, 230
St. Joseph of Arimathea, 11
St. Lucar, English Seminary at, 36
St. Malo, Monastery of St. Benedict, 69, 79, 104, 113, 116, 126, 127, 146, 163, 165, 166, 167, 169, 171, 172, 182, 183, 185, 186, 187, 188, 194, 196, 197, 204, 207, 208, 235, 236, 239
St. Maur, Congregation of, 208, &c.
St. Mayolus, 21, 81
St. Odo, 20
St. Omer, Seminary at, 36, 244
St. Robert, 20
St. Vanne in Lorraine, Congregation of, 8
St. Vedast, or Vaast, *see* Arras, 63
St. Wilfrid, 22, 23
Salvin, D. Peter. 210
Sandeford, D. Matthew, 135
Sandtoft and Haines Priory, 51
Sandwell Priory, 56
Sayr, or Sayer, D. Gregory, 39, 45, 180, 192
Scharnabeck Abbey, 178
Scot, V Maurus, Martyr, 82
Scotch Benedictines, 210
Scott, D. Richard, or King, 200
Scroggs, D. Gregory, 172, 208
    „   D. Maurus, 172
    „   D, Placid, 172
Segran, Père, 160
Selby Abbey, 52
Selby or Reade, D. Wilfrid, 169, **182**, **184**
Selden, the Antiquary, 14, 139
Seville, Seminary at, 36
Shaftesbury, Abbey of Nuns, 56
Shafto, D. Placid, 209, 215
Sheldon, Mr. 190
    „   D. Lionel, **217, 218, 223**
Sheppey Nunnery, 56

Sherborne Abbey, 53
Sherbourn family, 191
Sherley, D. Andrew, 75
Shirburn, Shirburne or Sherburne, D. James, 192
    „   „   D. Joseph, 207, 225, 226, 234, 237
Sherwood, D. Joseph, 92, 223, 225
    „   D. Robert, 126, 169, 202
Shrewsbury Abbey, 52
Smith, Dr., Bishop, 106, 130, 193
    „   D. Austin, 40
    „   D. Benedict, 173
Snaith Priory, 52
Snapes Priory, 51
Sneshal Priory, 56
Sopewell Priory, 61
Spalding Priory, 56
Spanish dependency abrogated, 197
Spondanus, 13
Stafford Castle, 167
Stafford, Mr. Francis, 239
Stamford Priory, 55
Stangate Priory, 58
Stanley St. Leonard's, 52
Stapylton, D. Benedict, 144, 194, 207, 215, 221
Stapylton, Br. Epiphanius, 130
Starkey, D. Hugh, 231
Stechman, Dr. a Lutheran, 91
Stiles, D. Henry, 181
Stocker or Stoker, D. Austin, 205
Stoke, Gloucestershire, 169
Stoterlingburg Abbey, 167
Stourton, Wilts, 70
Stourton, D. John, 251, 254
Strafford family, 191
Sudbury Priory, 53
Supremacy, Oath of, 33
Swinburn, Dame Margaret, 240
    „   D. Thomas, 205

T

Tatham, D. Cuthbert, 238, 251
    „   D. Bede, 215
Tavistock Abbey, 53
Taylard, D. Bede, 196, 209
Taylor, D. Edmund, 254
Tekeford Priory, 59
Tempest, D. Augustine, 240, 254
Tewkesbury Abbey, 54
Thetford Nunnery, 52

Thetford Priory, 58
Thimbleby family converted, 191
Thomas, Archbishop Elect of Cashel, 46
    " D. Eleyson, 210
Thompson, D. Felix, 171
Thorn, Relic of the Holy, 193
Thorney Abbey, 53
Thornton, D. Bede, or Foster, 235
Tivardreath Priory, 53
Touche, M de, 200
Townson, D. John, 91
Toutall or Toudelle, Br. John, 158
Towtin, M. of St. Malo, 81
Trappes family converted, 191
Tremby, D. Celestine, 165
Trescaw Priory, 53
Tresham, D. Francis, 203
Troy, Bishop of, 167
Tulle, Bishop of, 65, 66
Turberville, D. Anthony, 240, 254
Tynemouth Priory, 51

U

Ubaldin, Cardinal, 100, 106
Union of English Benedictines of various Congregations, 94, &c.
Urban VIII, 46, 129, 143, 147, 151, 183

V

Val de Grace, Abbey of Benedictine nuns in Paris, 202
Valladolid, Abbey of St. Benedict, 135
    " Benedictine Congregation of, 39, 197
    " English Seminary at, 36, 101
Vanderburgh, Archbishop of Cambray, 142, 146, 154
Vasoniensis, Bishop of, 46
Vavasour, Dame Lucy, 142
Vendivilius, Bishop of Tournay, 33, 34
Venice, Abbey of St. George, 39
Veuner or Fermor, D. Amandus, 158
Verdun, Bishop of, 65
Visitors to tomb of James II at St. Edmund's, Paris, 249

W

Wake, D. Hilarion, 187, 190
Walden Abbey, 54
Wales, Prince of, 231, 239
Walgrave, D. Francis, 90, 96, 121, 131, 135, 136, 138, 168, 170, 171, 180
    " D. William, 189, 202
Wallingford Priory, 51
Walsingham, Secretary of State, 141
Wangford Priory, 59

Warkworth Cell, 55
Warmington Priory, 51
Warnford, D. Peter, 193
Waterford Priory, 55
Waterton family converted, 191
Watmough, D. Francis, 240, 251, 254
Watson, Dame Mary, 143
Wearmouth Priory, 55
Weine Abbey, 178
Wells, Somerset, 208
Wendlam, Norfolk, 46
Wenlock Priory, 58
Westacre Priory, 58
Westminster Abbey, 31, 49, 53
Westmoreland's rebellion, Earl of, 141
Weston, Warwickshire, 91, 190
Wetheral Priory, 51
Whipheling, 12
Whitby Abbey, 54
White, or Blackow, (see Blacklow), 197, &c.
White, D. Austin Bradshaw or, (see Bradshaw), 45, &c.
   ,,   D. Claud, 166, 187, 189, 190, 196
White Stanton, Somerset, 202
Whitfield, D. Andrew, 182
Whitgrave family, 192
Wickham Skeyth Priory, 51
Wiclef, 14
Widdrington, 180, (see Preston)
Wilford, D. Boniface, 70
William of Malmesbury, 14
Williams, D. Anselm, 172
Wilson, Rev. W, Martyr, 77
Winchcombe Abbey, 53
Winchester Cathedral Priory, 55
   ,,   (see also Hyde Abbey)
Windsor, Lord, 180, 190
Worcester, 186
   ,,   Battle of, 188, 192, 225
   ,,   Cathedral Priory, 55
Wisbeach Castle, 31, 32
Wood, Anthony, quoted, 165
Woodhouse, Mr. Francis, 46
Worsley, D. John, 169
Wymundham Abbey, 54

Y

Yarmouth, Norfolk, 46
   ,,   Priory, 55
Yaxley, Dame Viviana, 145

Yepez, Abbot, 13, 77
York, Duchess of 217
 „ Duke of, 218, (*see* James II)
 „ Abbey of St. Mary, 51
 „ Priory of All Saints, 54
Yorkshire families converted, 191
Youghal Priory, 51

Z

Zieppe, Abbot, 13

INDEX

OF NAMES CONTAINED IN THE APPENDIX.

A

Abercromby, Mary Dunstan, 46
Acton, Augustine, 11
 „ Barbara, 46
 „ Mary Anne, 45
 „ Placid, 11
Addison, Scholastica, 29
Addy, or Addye, Bede, 23
Adelham, Placid, 14, 20
Adkinson, Mary, 54
Agry, Anne, 29
Ainsworth, Ralph, 4, 18
Aire, or Eyre, Viviana, 37
Alcock, Jerome, 27
Alexander, Jane, 30
Allam, Ambrose, 14
Allanson, Athanasius, 4
 „ Paul, 25
Allen, John, 9
Allerton, Denis, 26
Anderton, Agnes, 45
 „ Bede, 13
 „ Celestine, 6
 „ Christopher, 9
 „ James, 9

Anderton Mary Baptist, 45
 „ Michael, 25
 „ Placid,, 19, 21
 „ or Ashton Robert*
 „ Thomas, 18, 19, 20
Ann, Anselma, 34
Anne, Dame, 34
Anne, Sister, 46
Anselm, *see* Beech
Appleby, Frances, 33
 „ Mary, 42
 „ Paulinus, de Ona, 6, 14
Appleton, Anselm, 18
 „ Laurence, 9
 „ Marina, 28, 29
Aprice, Ildefonsus, 4, 16
 „ Joseph, 16
Archbald, Maura, 54
Arden, Magdalen, 36, 37
Armstrong, Theresa, 40, 46
Arthur, Agnes, 40
 „ Mary Xaveria, 53, 54
Arundel, Dorothy, 33
 „ Gertrude, 33
Armston, John, 12

---

* His name was accidentally omitted in the list of monks of St. Edmund's Paris. D. Robert Anderton or Ashton was professed in 1635.

Arrowsmith, Edmund, 8
Ascough, Benedicta, 35
    „   Theresa, 35
Ash, Edward, 6
Ashton, Alban, 22,
    „   Joseph, 12
    „   Placid, 22
Aspinwall, John, 22
Astin, Mary, 29
Athanasius, *see* Martin, Athanasius, 5
Atkins, Maurus, 8
Atkinson, John, 23
Atrobos, Francis, 6, 7
Atslow, Cecilia, 33
Augustine de S Facundo, 5
Aylmer, Catharine, 54
Aylward, Mary Baptist, 45

B

Bacon, George, 6
Bagnal, Placid, 17
    „   Anne Theresa, 43
Bagshaw, Sigebert, 3, 5, 19
Baker Anne, 34
    „   Augustine, 5
Ball, Winifred, 29
Ballyman, Gregory, 26
    „   Thomas, 26
Banks, Benedicta, 33
Banester or Gaile, Bede, 8
    „   or Bannester, William, 4, 11
Bapthorpe or Babthorpe, Mellitus, 15
Barber, Bernard, 3, 4
    „   Joseph, 14
    „   Maurus, 11
Barbierre, John, 19
Bard, Anastasia, 39
Barefoot, Dorothy, 36
Barguet, Andrew, 13
Barker, Charles, 17
    „   Thomas, 14
Barlow, Ambrose, 8
    „   Rudesind, 3, 6, 7
    „   Robert, 9
Barnes, Bede, 24
    „   John, (Spanish Cong), 5
    „   John, 22
    „   Laurence, 14
    „   Sophia, 43

Barnewall, Cyprian, 27
Barr, Bernard, 4, 13
Barret, Maurus, 17
Barrister, Amanda, 29
Barrows, Mechtilde, 46
Barter, Br. John, 10
    „   D. John, 10
Bartlett, Bernard, 12
Bartholomew, Don, 5
Barton, Bede, 22
Batchell, Agnes, 29
Batchelor, Edmund, 22
Bate, Anne, 29
Batemanson, Anne, 29
Bateson, Joseph, 17
Batt, Anthony, 15
Beare, George, 11
Beaumont, Aloysia, 36
    „   Mary Marina, 37, 53, 54
Becket, Nicholas, 6
Beckman, Bernard, 26
Bedingfield, Benedicta, 37
    „   Eugenia, 36
    „   Mary, 34
    „   Thecla, 36
    „   (another), 37
Beech, Anselm, 5
Belasyse, Benedicta, 40
    „   M Augustine, 46
    „   M Magdalen, 40
    „   M Scholastica, 40
Belerby, Gertrude, 29, 42
Beligny, Isabella, 34
Bell, Mary Anne, 34
Bellasyse, Apollonia, 39
Bennett, Alexius, 15
    „   Bede, 13
    „   or Davis, Maurus, 20
    „   or White, Claud, 3, 4, 15
    „   Placid, 18
Benson, Robert, *see* Haddock
Berington, Anne, 40
    „   Bernard, 6, 19
    „   George, 6
Berkeley, Ignatia, 45
    „   Joanna, 32
    „   Lucy, 46
Berkeley, Winifred, 34
Bernard, Adrian, 24

INDEX.

Berriman, Alban, 21
" Joseph, 10
Berry, James, 23
" or Butler, Jerome, 17
" Magdalen, 47
" Scholastica, 43
Beswick, Francis, 23
Bibby, Martina, 43
Bird, Mary Joseph, 34
Birdsall, Augustine, 3, 4, 27
Bishop, Denis, 24
Bittenson or Betenson, Placid, 10
Blackstone, or Blakestone, Francis, 9
" " " Michael, 9
Blakey, Anselm, 24
" Joseph, 24
" Philip, 24
Blanchard, Alexia, 32, 33
Blandy, Boniface, 5
Blisset, Benedicta, 54
Blount, Gertrude, 34
" Godric, 7, 10
" Henrietta, 35
" Maurus, 13
Blundel, Dorothy, 32, 34
" Maura, 34
Blyde, Lucy, 28, 30
Bocquet, Gabriel, 12
Bodenham, Anne, 39
" Mary Francis, 34
Bolas, Anselm, 4, 26
" Benedict, 26
Boluey, M. Josepha, 40
" Susan, 40
Bolton, Agnes, 33
" Anselm, 17
Bond, Agnes, 47
" Catharine, 33
" M Clare, 41, 43
" Monica, 45
Boone, Xaveria, 37
Booth, Ambrose, 16
Boucher, Ambrose, 26
Boult, Benedicta, 28
" Elizabeth, 46
Brabrant, Thomas, 11
Bradberry, Elizabeth, 37
Bradley, Bernard, 17
Bradshaw, Anselm, 26
" or White, Augustine, 5, 7, 19

Bradshaw, Basil, 26
" or Handford, Bernard, 4, 25
Bradstock, John, 27
Brennand, Theresa, 43
Brent, Christina, 28, 29
" Cuthbert, 16
" Elizabeth, 28, 41
" George, 25
" Helen, 29
Breton, Barbara, 29
Brett, Gabriel 18, 19
Brewer, Anselm, 4
" Bede 3, 18
Bride, Ambrose, 10
Bridget, Mary, 28
Brigham, Augustine, 13
Bridgeman, Wilfrid, see Strutt
Brindle, Basil, 18
" Placida, 43
Brindley, Anne, 34
Brocast, Laurence, 16
Bromley, Anselm, 18
Brooke, Mary Bernard, 39
" Placida, 33
Brookes, Joseph, 15
Broughton, Anselm, see Crowther
" Mark, see Crowther,
Brown, Alexander 6
" Ambrose, 12
" Angela, 45
" Anselm, 16
" Ebba, 28
" Flavia, 28
" George, 6
" Margaret, 54
Browne, Mary Austin, 54
" Pelagia, 40
" Xaveria, 54
Bruning, Anne, 39
" Augustina, 39
" Francis, 4, 25
" Jerome, 21
" Mary, 39
" Placid, 21
" Scholastica, 39
" Thomas, 21
Brychan, or Thomas, Bennet, 9
Buckingham, Mary, 41, 42
Buckley, James, 22
" Maurus, 12

Buckley Sigebert, 4
Budd, Placid, *see* Peto
Bullock, Lucy, 34
Bulmer, Denis, 26
 " Edward, 24
 " Maurus, 17
Burch, Helen, 34
Burchall, Placid, 3
Burgess, Bede, 18
Burgess, Scholastica, 29
 " Margaret, 30
Burke, Honoria, 37
Burn, Andrew, 18
Bury, Augustine, 4
Butcher, Amanda, 42
Butler, Anne, 54
 " Bernard, 14
 " Mary Joseph, 39, 53, 54
 " Theresa, 54
 " Ursula, 37, 54
Byerley, Anne Augustine, 35
 " Ildephonsus, 12
 " Marina, 34
Byers, Boniface, 25
Byflect or Worsley, John, 9
Byrne, Mary Benedict, 53, 55
 " Mary Placida, 55
Byron, Scholastica, 34

C

Cadet, Scholastica, 55
Calderbank, James, 18
Caldwell, Augustine, *see* Walmesley, 13
Calvert, Dorothy, 39
Campbell, Melchiora, 34
Canning, George, 11
Cansfield, Anne, 33
Cape, Benedict, 19
 " Francis, 8, 19
 " M Lucy, 28
 " Michael, 16, 19
Carew, Agnes, 34
 " Josepha, 54
Carnaby, Gregory *see* Grange, 9
Carrington, Josepha, 30
 " Maura, 46
Carter, Anselm, 4, 11
Carteret, Joseph, 4, 12
Cary, Clementina, 28, 41

Cary, Dorothy, 36
 " Flavia, 37, 53, 54
 " Magdalen, 28
 " Mary, 29
 " M. Austin, 29
 " Placid, 20
Caryll, Alexius, 7, 10
 " Benedicta, 34
 " Eugenia, 45
 " Justina, 45
 " Mary, 37, 44
 " Mary Benedict, 45
 " Mary Magdalen, 45
 " Romana, 45
 " Theresa, 45
Casse, Laurence, 4, 21
Cassey, Anselm, 9
Catharel, Scholastica, 46
Caton, Scholastica, 30
Catteral, Benedict, 22
 " Bernard 14, 17
Cawser, Benedict, 23
Cellar, Jane 29
Chaddock, Margaret, 40
Chalk, Mary, 40
Chamberlain, Francis, 19
Chamberlaine, Gertrude, 54
Chambers, William, *see* Johnson
Champion, Ignatia, 39
Champney, Laurence, 14, 16
 " William, 17
Chandler, Boniface, 15
 " Paul, 12
Chaplin, Anselm, 26
 " Maurus, 26
Charlton, John, 13
Charnley, Elizabeth, 47
Cheriton, Basil, 20
 " Matthew, 16
Chew, Alexius, 18
Chilton, Elizabeth, 34
 " Gertrude, 29, 34
 " Theresa, 29
Chorley, Edward, 7, 12
Clarke, Winifred, 40, 46
Clarkson, Alban, 27
 " Jerome, 26
Clavering, M Anne, 39, 40, 46
 " M Joseph, 40

INDEX.

Clayton, Catharine, 33
Cliff or Cowper, Ildephonsus.
Clifton, Alathea, 29, 42
  ,, Cuthbert, 4
  ,, Lambert, 6
  ,, M. Benedicta, 45
Codner, David, 5
Coesneau, Placida, 42
Coffin, Bridget, 29
  ,, Mary, 29
Coleman, Ruperta, 45
Colford, Martha, 33
Collingridge, Josepha, 35
Collingwood, Anselm, 23
Collins, Benedicta, 34
  ,, Edburga, 35
  ,, Ignatia, 35
  ,, Joseph, 27
  ,, Mary Ignatia, 34
  ,, Mary Joseph, 35
  ,, Theresa, 35
  ,, Xaveria, 39
Colston, Nicholas, 24
Comberlege, Benedict, 25
Commings, Placid *see* Hartburn
Compline, Mary, 29
Compton, Aloysia, 34
  ,, Bernard, 23
Cone, Gertrude, 39
Coningsby, Ignatia, 36
Connick, Theresa, 46
Conquest, Benedicta, 29
Constable, Ann Mary, 40
  ,, Augustine, 4, 10
  ,, Barbara, 29
  ,, Benedict, 24
  ,, Francis, 15
  ,, Mary Joseph, 43
  ,, Philip, 10
  ,, Wilfrid, 22
  ,, Winifred, 29
Conyers, Augustine, 10
  ,, Catharine, 42
  ,, Cecilia, 45
  ,, Lucy, 42
Cook, Elizabeth, 42
  ,, Theresa, 42
Cooper, Amanda, 43
  ,, Francis, 18

Copley, Mary, 45
  ,, Mary Alexia, 45
Coppé, Theresa, 55
Copsey, Robert, 26
Corbinton or Corby, Eugenia, 34
  ,, ,, ,, Mary, 33
Corby, Benedicta, 36
Corham, Cornelia, 36
  ,, Justina, 36
  ,, Robert, 10
Corker, Maurus, 3, 23
Cornwallis, Augustine, 20
Cotton, Winifred, 28
Couch, Anne Theresa, 42
Coupe, Jerome, 14, 18
  ,, Maurus, 20, 22
Cowley, Gregory, 3, 14, 17, 20
Cox, Benedict, 15
  ,, Edmund, 21
Craffe or Grove, Dunstan, 20
Crathorne, Anselm, 25
  ,, Francis, 8
Craven, Vincent, 16
Creagh, Bridget, 54
Cressy, Serenus, 10
Crispe, Mary, 32, 34
Crombleholme, John, 23,
Crook, Clare, 29
  ,, James, 22
  ,, or Gregson, D. Joseph, 26
Crosby, Wolstan, 10
Crowther or Crowder, Anselm, 4, 7
  ,, Mark, 3, 7
Culcheth, Constantia, 45
  ,, Frances, 39
  ,, Mary Bede, 45
  ,, Mary Benedict, 45,
  ,, Mary Stanislaus, 39
  ,, Scholastica, 45
Culshaw, John, 14
Curre, Maurus, 8
  ,, Nicholas, 15
Curson, Clare, 33
  ,, Margaret, 33
Curtis, Winifred, 42
Curwen, Patrick, 16

D

Dabridgecourt, Elizabeth, 83, 39

Dakins, John, 21
Dale, Maurus, 22
Dalley or Dally, Mary Benedict, 41, 43
Dallison, Agnes, 46
  ,, Josepha, 34
  ,, Martha, 34
Dalton, Mary Bernard, 53, 54
  ,, or Shuttleworth, Wolstan, 20
Dalyson, Gregory, 24
Damiens, Frances, 35
Dandy, Anthony, 12
Daniel or Simpson, Benedict, 17
  ,, Robert, 17
Danvers, Romuald, 8
Darell, Mary Gertrude, 45
  ,, or Westbrook, Maurus, 25
  ,, Olivia, 29
Darrell, Mary Joseph, 34
  ,, Xaveria, 34
Davies, Leander, 24
Davis Ambrose, 21
  ,, or Kirke, Bernard, 26
  ,, or Bennett, Maurus, 20
Dawber, John, 18
Dawney, Alban, 24
Deacon or Deacons, Pudentiana, 28, 33
Debord, Mechtilde, 35
De Decken, Martina, 37
Deday, Benedict, 4
Deeble, Beatrix, 43
De la Fontain, Placid, 13
De Landres, Celestine, 16
De la Rue, Benedicta, 42
Delattre, Augustine, 22
  ,, Charles, 25
  ,, Laurence, 22,
Denis, Mary, 55
Deval, Peter, 13
Dewhurst, Anne, 43
Digby, Jerome, 13
  ,, Magdalen, 33
  ,, Mary, 36
Dobson, Elphege, 25
Dodd, Josepha, 29
D'Ognate, Joseph, 22
Dolman, Helen, 33
D'Orgain, Benedict, 15
Doutch, Anthony, 25

Downes, Lucy, 40
Draper, James, 17
Draycott, Bridget, 33
  ,, Marina, 64
Duck, Dunstan, 16
Ducket, Barbara, 33
  ,, Edmund, 22
Duddell, Odo, 24
Dunn, Roland, 6
Dunscombe, Augustine, 25
Du Pery, Bathildis, 29
Du Toit, Aloysia, 55
Duvivier, Placid, see Waters, 13
Dworihouse, Josepha, 29
Dyer, Thomas, 6
Dytch, M. Josepha, 47
Dyve, Ignatia, 46

E

Eastgate, Ambrose, 17
Eastham, Anselm, 22
Eaves, Oswald, 18
  ,, Thomas, 16
Eccles, Philippa, 32, 35
Edmunds, Bernard, 15
  ,, Robert, 6
Edner or Rigge, Justus, 5
Eldridge, Raymund, 14
Elerby, Alexia, 29
Eliott, Ambrose, 12
Elliot, Aloysia, 39
  ,, Frances, 39
Ellis, Philip, 11
Elmer, Jocelin, 3, 14, 15, 18
Emerson, Thomas, 5
Englefield, Benedicta, 29
  ,, M. Winifred, 44, 46
  ,, M. Bernard, 45
  ,, (another,) 46
Errington, Agnes, 28
  ,, Laurence, 10
  ,, Mary, 34
  ,, Scholastica, 34
Eure, Elizabeth, 40
  ,, Mary, 34
Evans, Margaret, 47
Ever, Magdalen, 28
Eves, Mary, 29

Everard, Dunstan, 19
Eyston, Basil, 13

F

Fairclough, Benedicta, 29
" Elizabeth, 29
Fairfax, Placid, see Robinson
Farnworth, Cuthbert, 3, 4, 17
" Jerome, 21
Farrar, Winifred, 46
Fazakerly, Agatha, 29
Fenwick, Alexia, 29
" Augustine, 12
" Francis, 19, 21
" Laurence, 3, 11
Fermor or Venner, Amandus, 15
" or Farmer, Maurus, 17
" Mary Frances, 44, 45
" Placida, 45
Ferrars, Mary Baptista, 37
Ferreyra, James, 16
Le Fèvre, Anne, 30
Fisher, Edward, 18
" John, 3, 17
" Wilfrid, 27
Fitzjames, Ignatia, 39
" Nicholas, 7, 14
Fitzroy, Benedicta, 40
" Cecilia, 45
Fitzwilliams, George, 12
Fleetwood, Barbara, 45
" Benedicta, 44, 45
" Mary Michael, 45
Fleming, Bridget, 55
" Esmenia, 55
" Gertrude, 55
" M Benedicta, 55
" M Joseph, 55
" Maura, 45
Fletcher, Frances, 33
" Mary, 33
" Susanna, 54
Flutot, Maurus, 16
Fontaine, de la, Placid, 13
Foorde or Hartburn, Placid, 8
Forester or Forster, Anne, 32, 34,
" " Placida, 34
Formby, Magdalen, 47
Forshaw, Laurence, 27
Forster, Christina, 36, 38

Fortescue, Mary, 45
Foster, or Thornton, Bede, 19
" Francis, 6
" Joseph, 16
Fothringham, M. Joseph, 40
Foxe, Romana, 35
Fouquet, Anne Theresa, 55
Frances, Sister, 46
Francis, Placid, 24
Frankland, Hugh, 12
Frere, Joseph, 7, 8
" Placid, 9
" Mechtilde, 28
Fryar, Martha, 30
Fuller, Alban, 16
Fursden, Cuthbert, 8
" Thomas, 15

G

Gage, Columba, 33
" Dorothy, 45
" Mary, 33
" Theresa, 33
Gaile, Bede, or Banester, 8
Gaire, George, 15
Galli, Bennet, 19
Galver, Winifred, 35
Gardiner, Theresa, 37
Gargill, Frances, 34
Garner, Benedict, 26
Garnous, Philippa, 34
Garstang, Dunstan, 4, 22
Garter, John, 20
Gascoigne, Catharine, 28
" Frances, 30
" Helen Josepha, 28, 29
" Justina, 29, 41
" Margaret, 28
" Michael, 9
" Paula, 29
" Placid, 3, 15, 19, 23
Gaudelier, Mary, 29
Gawon, Ambrose, 24
" or Gawine, Frances, 28, 33
Gee, Anne, 43
George, of St. Ildephonsus, 9
Gerard, Angela, 45
" Scholastica, 36, 37
Gerrard, Cecilia, 46

Gervase or Jervase, George, 6
Gery, Anselm, 25
Gibbon, Benedict, 24
Gibson, Dunstan, 20
Gicou, Francis, 19
Gifford or Giffard, Gabriel, 14, 15, 16
   „ „ „ Maura, 39
   „ „ „ Peter, 20
   „ „ „ Xaveria, 38, 39
Gill, Anne, 29
Gillibrand, Agnes, 37
Gillibrord, Agatha, 41, 42
Gillmore, Paul, 24
Girlington, John, 14, 20
Gloster or Glasscock, Edward, 20
Glynn, Magdalen, 43
Godfrey, Constantia, 42
  „ Michael, 5
Godwin, Anne, 47
Goodair, Frances, 34
Goodge, Winifred, 54
Goolde, Robert, 22
Gordon, William, 6
Gornal, Martha, 47
Goulde, Ignatia, 54
  „ Scholastica, 54
  „ Xaveria, 54
Govaerdt, Christian, 9
Graincourt, Maurus,
Grainge or Carnaby, Gregory, 9
Grange, Gregory, 5
Gratian, John, 15
Gravenore, Mary, 34
Gray, Alexia, 36
Greaves or Greeves, Bernard, 4, 11
Green, Agatha, 34
  „ Dominic, 21
  „ John, 17
  „ Br. John, 11
  „ Justina, 39
  „ Leander, 23
  „ Margaret, 41
  „ Thomas, or Houghton, 5
Greene, Eugenia, 39
Greenough, Ignatius, 4
Greenway, Scholastica, 43
Greenwood, Gregory, 4, 11
  „ Paulinus, 3, 7, 18
Gregson, Augustine, 17

Gregson, Bernard, 3, 4, 14, 15
  „ Bernarda, 46
  „ Gregory, 22
  „ Peter, 17
  „ Vincent, 17
Gregston, Benedicta, 46
Grey, Gervase, 5
Grimbaldeston, Clement, 27
  „ Paul, 27
Grime, Cuthbert, 13
Grossier, Romanus, 19
Grove or Craffe, Dunstan, 20
Guildford, Ildefonsa, 45
Guildridge, Bridget, 36
Guillet, Rupert, 19
Guilliam, David, 20
Gunn, Magdalen, 55
Gurnell, Adrian, 26
Gurney, Theresa, 29
Guyllim, Mary, 34

H

Haddock or Benson, Robert, 3, 5,
Hadley, Edmund, 13
  „ Laurence, 13
Hagan, Louisa, 30
  „ Theresa, 43
Haggerston, Anne Catharine, 39, 40
  „ Mary Bernard, 40
  „ Placid, 12
  „ Scholastica, 40
Haliwell, Theresa, 46
Hall, Boniface, 26
  „ Catharine Maura, 28, 29
  „ Cecilia, 28
Halsall, Bede, 4, 11
Hamborough, Josepha, 54
Hamerton, Benedicta, 39
  „ Helen, 39
  „ Ursula, 39
Hames, Maurus, 19
Hamoy, Anselm, 19
Hankinson, Bennet, 20
Hanmer, Joseph, *see* Starkey, 12
Hanne, Gertrude, 42
Hanson, Maurus, 6
  „ *see* Hesketh, Alphonsus, 8
Hardcastle, Robert, 4, 14, 17
Hardisty, Adrian, 25

Hardisty, Laurence, 25
Hardwick, Martha, 40
  „   Mary, 40
Hardwidge, M Benedicta, 43
Harkham, M. Frances, 40
Harper, John, 5
  „   Maura, 35
Harrington, Maura, 29
Harris, Richard, 22
Harrison, Augustine, 14
  „   Josepha, 47
  „   Maurus, 12
Harsnep, Benedict, 22
  „   Placid, 26
Hartbourne, Cuthbert, 8
Hartburn or Foorde, Placid, 8
Harvey, M. Augustina, 45
  „   Mary Magdalen, 46
Hathersall, George, 8
Hatton, Augustine, 26
Havelock, Marina, 34
Havers, Bartholomew, 13
Hawarden, Bernard, 14
Hawes, Mary, 42
Hawet, Edmund, 21
Hawkins, Augustine, 13
  „   Benedicta, 33
  „   James, 25
Haworth, Joseph, 7, 15
Haywood, Gregory, 9
Healy, Anne, 33
Heath, Augustine, 15
Heatley, Jerome, 27
  „   Lewis, 27
  „   Maurus, 26
Helm, Anne, 30
Helme, Bede, 3, 6
  „   Gregory, 16
  „   Wilfrid, 19, 22
Hemsworth, Bennet, 10
Heneage, Constantia, 39
  „   Scholastica, 37
Heptonstall, Paulinus, 4
Heskett, Aloysia, 37
  „   or Hanson, Alphonsus, 8
  „   Frances, 37
  „   Gregory, 16
  „   Jerome, 10
  „   Joseph, 11

Heskett, Mellitus, 16
Hesketh, Nicholas, 16
  „   Thomas, 21
Hethcote, William, see Middleton, 6
Hewicke, Ursula, 33
Hewlett, William, 22
Hide, Theresa, 34
Higginson, James, 14
  „   Scholastica, 40
Higgs, Alexius, 22
Hill, Thomas, 8
  „   Winifred, 40
Hills, Mary, 34
Hilton, Elizabeth, 42
  „   or Musgrave, Placid, 15
Hird or Laton, Paulinus, 9
Hitchcock or Nedam, William, 10
Hodgson, Richard, 8
  „   Stephen, 18
Hodson, Gertrude, 28, 40
  „   Ralph, 24
  „   Scholastica, 29, 41
Holden, Hugh, 22
Holderness, Frances, 14
  „   Dunstan, 14, 17
Holme, Richard, 11
Holmes, Peter, 11
  „   Placida, 54
Hook or Hooke, Christina, 28, 30
Hornyold, Bernard, 21
Horsley, Cuthbert, 3, 14, 16
Horsman, Adrian, 27
Hoskius, Mary, 28
Houghton or Farnaby, Bede, 30
  „   Bede, 17
  „   Edward, 17
  „   Eugenia, 29
  „   Placida, 40
  „   Scholastica, 28, 29
  „   Thomas, see Green, 5
Howard, Augustine, 3, 4, 11
  „   Catharine, 37
  „   Frances, 17
  „   Frederick, 25
  „   Joseph, 12
  „   Magdalen, 46
  „   Placid, 3, 4, 12
Howet, Winifred, 29
Huddleston, Denis, 25

INDEX.

Huddleston, John, 6
" Richard, 5
Hudson, Augustine, 16
Huggonson, Magdalen, 40
Huitson, Peter, 7
Hull, Francis, 15
Huugate, Augustine, 3, 4, 5
" Gregory, 3, 7
" Margaret, 45
" Thomas, 6
Hunloke, Agatha, 40
" Marina, 39, 40
Hunt, Peter, 15
Huntley, Bernard, 24
Husbands, Clementina, 42
Hussey, Cecilia, 28, 29
" Edward, 13
Hutchinson, Cuthbert, 12
" Dunstan, 24
" Wilfrid, 24
Hutton, Bede, 25
" or Salvin, Cuthbert, 11
" John, 3, 5
" Placid, 25
Hyde, Eugenia, 46

I

Ingham or Walmesley, Wolstan, 20
Ingilby, Ann, 33
Ingleby, Agnes, 28, 30
" Robert, 16
Innes, Anne, 40
Ireland, Augustina, 34
" Delphina, 34
" Lucy, 45
" see Loader, Placid, 9
Isherwood, Richard, 24

J

Jackson, Barbara, 34
" Gregory, see Mallet
Jackson, Leander, see Thompson, 9
James, Aurea, 33
Jansen, John, 26
Jarfield, Dousdedit, 6
Jarrett, Elizabeth, 53, 55
" Mary Bernard, 55
Jefferson, Aloysia, 37
" Philip, 22

Jenison, Monica, 29
Jenkins, Jerome, 4
Jennings or Jenyns, Bruno, 11
Jennison, Mary Anne, 54
Jerningham, Benedict, 15
" Henrietta, 40
Johnson, Anne, 47
" Augustine, see Lee, 9
" Edward, 16
" George, 14
" James, 17
" Joseph, 18
" Mary Magdalene, 41, 43
" Oswald, 27
" Placid, 16
" Theresa, 41
" Theresa Joseph, 43
" or Chambers, William, 5
Johnston, Joseph, 19, 21
Jones, Alexius, 12
" Anne Benedict, 43
" or Price, Benedict, 5
" or Scudamore, see Leander of St.
Martin, 3, 5, 7
" Scholastica, 46
Judd, Elizabeth, 46

K

Kane, Josepha, 46
Kaye, Ambrose, 14, 17
Kearton, Cyprian, 27
Kellet, Augustine, 22
Kemble, William, 8
Kemp or Kipton, Boniface, 5
Kemp, Mary, 33
Kendall, Peter, 14
Kennedy, Basil, 27
" Joseph, 21
Kennet, Agnes, 29
" Isabella, 29
" Joseph, 16
" Samuel, 5
Kennett, Catharine, 29
Kenyon, Anselm, 27
" Helena, 28
" Margaret, 28
Killingbecke, Robert, 4, 23
Kimberly, Magdalen, 30
Kinder, Augustine, 8

INDEX.

King, Magdalen, 25
  ,, or Scott, Richard, 23
Kirby, Elizabeth, 43
Kirke, Laurence, 17
  ,, Adrian, 23
  ,, or Davis, Bernard, 25
Knacksterdt, John, 27
Knatchbull, Lucy, 33, 36
  ,, (another), 36
  ,, Margaret, 36
  ,, Mary, 36
  ,, (another), 36, 37
Knight, Anne Joseph, 30
  ,, Bede, 12
  ,, Benedict, 26
  ,, Clare, 28, 30
  ,, Dunstan, 25
  ,, Mary, 43
Knightly, Maurus, 23, 24
Knowles, Gilbert, 12

L.

Lacabanne, Ambrose, 15
Lacon, Michael, 4, 13
Lake, Dunstan, 21
de Landres, Celestine, 16
Langdale, Aloysia, 37
  ,, Constantia, 29
  ,, Flavia, 33
  ,, Maurus, 13
L'Angevin, Deodatus, 18, 19
Langton, Ambrose, 15,
  ,, John,
Lanning, Rachel, 41
  ,, Richard, 12
Latham, Alexius, 26
  ,, Augustine, 19, 20
  ,, Gabriel, 20
  ,, Joseph, 8
  ,, Swithbert, 15
  ,, Torquatus, 5
  ,, Vincent, 9
Latchmore, Mildred, 28
Laton, Paulinus, see Hird, 9
Lavery, Susanna, 45
Lawes, Frances, 42
Lawrenson, Scholastica, 43
Lawson, Augustine, 14
  ,, Benedict, 24

Lawson, Francis, 4, 10
  ,, Henry, 4, 14
  ,, Br, Henry, 11
  ,, Laurentia, 39
Leake, Barbara, 33
Leander, of St. Martin, 3, 5, 7
Leblon, Sophia, 35
Le Ducq, Anne, 54
  ,, Mary Joseph, 54
Lee or Johnson, Augustine, 9
  ,, Margaret, 42
Legatt, Amatus, 9
Legge, Alexia, 45
  ,, Mary, 29
Le Deux, Mark, 13
Le Fèvre, Anne, 30
Le Grand, James, 26
Light, Ignatia, 47
Le Maire, Mary Benedict,
Le Munier, James, 19
Lenthall, Agnes, 32, 33
Lewis, Michael, 13
Ley, Benedicta, 55
Lincoln, Mary Anne, 40, 47
Lindley, Ambrose, 24
Littlewood, Margaret, 35
Llewellin, Augustine, 4, 21
Loader or Ireland, Placid, 8
Lockard, Barbara, 40
Lockers, John, 16
Lodwick, Laurence, 15
Lone, John, 8
Longe, Mechtilde, 55
Longueville, Victoria, 39
Longworth, Anne, 42
  ,, Frances 42
Lorymer, Anselm, 13
Love, Christopher
Lovel, Anthony, 15
  ,, Christina, 33
Lowick, Bernard, 14 21
Lucig, Mary Frances, 28
Lucy, Magdalen, 36, 37
  ,, (another), 26, 27
Ludkin, Placida, 46
Lumley, Augustine, 22
  ,, John, 16
Lusher, Elizabeth, 29
  ,, Frances, 29

Lynch, Anselm, 12
" Mary Bernard, 53, 55
" Scholastica, 53, 55

M

Mabbs, Laurence, 8
Macclesfield, Placida, 64
Macdonald, Anselm, 13
" Benedict, 13
Mackay, Gergory, 21
Macleane, Mary Louise, 54
Magdalen, (2), 46
Mathew, Edward, 4, 14
Le Maire, Mary Benedict, 55
Mainwaring, Magdalen, 37
Mallet or Jackson, Gregory, 4, 16
Malone, Columban, 7
" Mary Josepha, 54
Mandeville, Magdalen, 53, 54
" Agnes, 35
" Anastasia, 34
Maunock, Anselm, 12
" Cecilia, 35
" Dorothy, 33
" Etheldreda, 32, 34
" Ursula, 34
Markham, Mary Frances, 40, 46
" Margaret, 36
" Margaret, (2), 36
Marlow, Mary Helen, 54
Marsh, Benedict, 18
Marsh or Marshal, Cuthbert see Wall, 24
" Jerome, 14, 18
" Peter, 23
" Richard, 3, 4, 14, 18
Martin, Athanasius, 5
" Boniface, 15
" Joseph,*
" Martha, 28
Mason, M. Xaveria, 55
Matham, Catherine, 34
" Magdalen, 34
Mather, Augustine, 16

Mather, Cyril, 27
" James, 14, 16
Matlock, Theresa, 36
Matthews, Constance, see Nathal, 6
" Maura, 46
Maurice, Alexia, 37
" Anastasia, 37
Maurin, Catherine, 40
Maynell, Benedicta, 29
Mc Donald, M. Benedicta, 35
" Theresa, 3
Mechels, Petronilla van, 5
Meering or Meryng, Benedict, 23
Merriman, Bede, 15
" Hilarion. see Wake, 10
Mervin, John. see Roberts, 5
Messenger, Placida, 40, 45, 46
Metcalf, Gregory, 26
" Placid, 26
" William, 12
Metham, Sylvester, 4, 7, 11
Meutisse or Northall, Clement, 23
" " " John, 7, 9, 18
Meynell, Anne Augustine, 46
" Margaret, 46
" Theresa, 29
Middleton or Middelton, Benedicta, 29
" " " Cuthbert, 10
" " " Etheldreda, 45
" " " Frances, 46
" " " Maurus, 21
" " " Michael,†
" or Hethcot, William, 6
Midi, Scholastica, 35
Mildmay, Francis, 24
Milfort, Christina, 42
Miller, Josepha, 30
Millington, Bernard, 16
Mills, Catharine, 46
Minns, James, ‡
Minshall, Thomas, 6
Mitchell, Augustine, 18
Moliner, Claudius, 15

---

* His name occurs in the Necrology of the Congregation on April 8th, 1663, but nothing more is known about him.

† He was a Conventual at St. Gregory's, Douay, in 1646, but his name is not in the Profession book nor does it occur elsewhere.

‡ Br. James Minns, whose name was accidentally omitted from the Catalogue of St. Edmund's, Paris, was a Lay-Brother professed there on June 16th, 1772.

Moliner, or Le Munier, James, 19
Molyneux, Alban, 3, 4
Mompas, Bennet, 13
Money, Peter, 11
Monington, Thomas, 7, 19
Monson, Christina, 37
Moody, Anne, 29
Mooney, Mary, 29, 43
Moore, Augustine, 7, 13
  ,, Bede, 21
  ,, Francis, 19, 21
  ,, George, 9
Mordaunt, Benedict, 25
More, Agnes, 28
  ,, Anne, 28
  ,, Bridget, 29, 41
  ,, Dorothy, 29
  ,, Gertrude, 28
  ,, Jane, 33
  ,, M. Magdalen, 29
Morgan, Agnes, 40, 47
  ,, Anastasia, 33
  ,, Benedicta, 28
  ,, Francis, 9
  ,, or Powel, Philip, 8
Morley, Placida, 45
Morris, M. Baptist 55
  ,, M. Sales, 55
  ,, Scholastica, 55
Morrissy, M. Benedicta, 54
Mosse, Francis, 20
Mostyn, Mary Joseph, 45
Moundeford or Munford, John, 8
Mounson, Mary, 36
Muller, Adrian, 25
Mullins, Angela, 28
Musgrave, Placid, see Hilton, 15
Muttlebury, Dorothy, 42
  ,, Francis, 21
  ,, or Muttleberry, Placid, 15

N

Nagle, Mary Anthony, 54
  ,, Mechtilde, 54
Nathal or Matthews, Constantius, 6
Naylor, Ambrose, 13
  ,, Placid, 4, 17
  ,, another, 17
Neals, Elizabeth, 34

Nechills, Bernard, 22
Nedam, William, see Hitchcock,
Nelson, Anselm, 21
  ,, Benedict, 18, 19, 20
  ,, James, 19, 21
  ,, Jerome, see Porter, 9
  ,, Maurus, 21
  ,, Placid, 19, 21
  ,, Thomas, 7, 12
Nepthou, Magdalen, 42
Neville or Nevill, Anne, 36, 38
  ,, ,, Anne, (another) 39
  ,, ,, Laurence, 16
  ,, ,, Leander, 16
  ,, ,, Mary Anne, 54
Newport, Clare, 42
Newton, Bede, 25
  ,, Elizabeth, 34
Nicholls, Maurus, see Poss, 10
Nichols, Catharine, 45
Normington or Norminton, Leander, 10
Norris, Agnes, 43
Northall, Clement, see Meutisse, 23
  ,, John, ,, 9
Norton, John, 9

O

Oard, Anthony, 7, 11
O'Bryan, Josepha, 45
O'Connor, Josepha, 54
O'Curren, Scholastica, 55
D'Oguate, Joseph, 22
O'Moore, Mary Baptist, 54
O'More, Josepha, 29
O'Neile, Benedicta, 54
D'Orgain, Benedicta, 15
Osbaldeston, Christopher, 18
  ,, Dunstan, 13
Osland, John, 25
Owen, Augustine, 8
  ,, John, 6
Oxburgh, Mary Austin, 40

P

Palin, Vincent, 17
Palliser, Catharine, 29
Palmer, William, 5
Palmes, Bernard, 7, 10
Pape, Ambrose, 26
Paris, Christina, 34

Parker, Cuthbert, 21
,, Henry, 20, 23
Parkes, Agnes, 46
Parkinson, Anthony, 13
,, Gertrude, 43
,, Mary Lucy, 43
Partington, Anne, 30
,, Benedict, 30
Pashley, Mechtilde, 40
Paston, Catharine, 33
,, Clement, 21
,, Frances, 34
Patten, Thomas, 13
Pattinson, Winifred, 43
Paulinus de Onia, 6
Pearse, Xaveria, 46
Pearson, Anselm, 6
Pease, Benedict, 42
,, Mary, 36
Pembridge, Benedict, 13
Pennington, Anne, 30
,, Edmund, 18
Penruddocke, Constantia, 34
Percy, Hilda, 28
,, Mary, 32, 36
Perkins, Lucy, 36
Du Pery, Bathildis, 29
Pershall, Lucy, 34
Persons, Mary, 33
Pestell, Pestel or Phillips, William, 7, 11
Peto or Budd, Placid, 5
Petre, Angela, 34
,, Justina, 36, 37
,, Mary, 39
,, Winifred, 45
Pettinger, Dunstan, 15
Peyton, Joseph, 56
Phesackelly, Scholastica, 47
Philip or Pugh, Charles, 21
Philipps, Baptist, 36, 37
Philips, Aldhelm, 15
,, Mary, 33
Philipson or Phillipson, John, 21
,, William, 7, 11
Philips, Columban, 20
,, Susanna, 29
Philpott, Barbara, 32
,, Winifred, 39
Pickering, Agnes, 40

Pickering, Thomas, 10
Pigott, Dunstan, 12
,, Gregory, 12
,, Henrietta, 45
,, Ursula, 32, 35
,, Xaveria, 35
Pilkington, Bernarda, 40
Placid, Dom, 5
Pleyal, *see* Walgrave, William
Plompton, Angela, 29
,, Bernarda, 29
Plowden, Benedicta, 34
Plumpton, Mary James, 46
Poole, Mary Stanislaus, 35
Pope or Fisher, Alexius, 17
,, ,, Alexius, (another), 18
,, ,, Richard, 18
Pordage, Frances, 45
,, Xaveria, 37
Porter, Alban, 24
,, Dunstan, 11
,, Francis, 23
,, or Nelson, Jerome, 9
Poss or Nichols, Maurus, 10
Potts, Bede, 25
,, Mary, 35
Pound, Henrietta, 39
Powel, Mansuetus, 19
,, Prosser, or Morgan, Philip, 8
Poyntz, James, 21
Prater, Joseph, 3, 5
Pratt, Felix, *see* Thompson, 19
Prescott, Mary, Michael, 46
Preston, Anne, 40
,, Benedict, 10
,, Bernard, 5
,, Elizabeth, 40
,, Mary Bernard, 46
,, Maura, 40
,, Scholastica, 40
,, Thomas, 5
Price, Benedict, *see* Jones.
,, Bernard, 17, 20
,, Cecily, 33
,, Josepha, 45
,, Mary Joseph, 40
Pritchard, Leander, 9
,, Maurus, 8
Prosser, or Powel, &c. Philip, 8

Prudhomme, Anselm, 19
Prujean, Magdalen, 45, 46
Pugh or Philip, Charles, 21
Pullen, Placida, 30
Pulleyne, Placida, 20
Pullein, Michael, 4, 7, 11
Pulton, Agnes, 46
  ,, Elizabeth, 42
  ,, or Poulton, Eugenia, 33, 36
  ,, Gertrude, 45
  ,, Mechtilde, 45
  ,, (another), 45
Pyser, Barbara, 47

Q

Quince, Sylvester, 14
Quynes, Bernard, 17

R

Radcliffe, Clare, 29
  ,, Ursula, 29
Raffa, Leander, 13
Raphael, Don, 5
Rashley, Mary, 40
Ratcliffe, Ildephonsus, 24
Raweliffe, Anne, 42
  ,, Frances, 43
Rayment, Mary Anne, 35
Reddy, Benedicta, 35
Redman, Dorothy, 33
Reede or Selby, Wilfrid, 8
Reeder, Scholastica, 29
Reeve, Wilfrid, 11
Reeves, Anne, 29
Reily, Mary Patrick, 55
  ,, Maura, 55
Reyner, Clement, 3, 15, 23
  ,, Laurence, 3, 14, 15
Ribertierre, Bernard, 18, 19
Rich, Francis, 12
Richardson, Augustine, 8
  ,, Nicholas, 17
  ,, Robert, 16
Riddell, Angela, 39
  ,, Gregory, 1, 24
  ,, Joseph, 25
  ,, Thomas, 25
Rider or Willoughby or Willobie, Ildephonsus, 11

Rigby, Anne, 29
  ,, Bede, 27
  ,, Martha, 47
  ,, Placid, 17
Rigge or Edner, Justus, 5
Rigmaiden, Benedict, 17
  ,, or Smith, Maurus, 17
Risden, Cuthbert, 20
Risdon, Etheldreda, 42
Rishton, Frances, 40
  ,, Margaret, 40
Roan, Basil, 10
Roberts, Etheldreda, 46
  ,, or Mervin, John, 5
Robinson, Agnes, 30
  ,, Bernard, 18
  ,, Gregory, 4, 17
  ,, Maurus, 20
  ,, (another), 27
  ,, Paul, 3, 15, 18
  ,, or Fairfax, Placid, 25
  ,, Robert, 25
Roe, Alban, 15
  ,, Maurus, 16
Roger, Beatrix, 45
  ,, Scholastica, 35
Rogers, Dunstan, 22
Rokeby, Joseph, 23, 25
Rookwood, Elizabeth, 33
  ,, Francis, 4, 11
  ,, Ignatius, (date uncertain).
Roper, Benedicta, 28
  ,, Catharine, 39
  ,, Mary, 33, 35
  ,, (another), 39
  ,, Placida, 39
  ,, Scholastica, 36
Roskow, Joseph, 22
Ross, Anne, 40
Rotton, Serenus, 11
Rous, John, 17
Rowston, Robert, 17
De la Rue, Benedicta, 42
Rulands, Mary, 35
Rumley, Augustine, 16
Russel, Hilda, 34
  ,, Mildred, 34
Ryan, Philippa, 43
Rycaut, Andrew, 21

Ryding, Bernard, 23

S

Sadler, Faustus, 15
", or Walter, Vincent, 3, 4
Salcemont, Felicitas, 47
Salisbury, Edward, 25
Salkeld, Bernard, 10
", Martha, 45
", Mary Anselm, 45
Salvin, Peter, 9
Sandeford, Matthew, 19
Sandermont, Praxedis, 54
Sanderson, Bernard, 23
", Denis, 23
Sarsfield, Ignatia, 55
Savage, Constantia, 36
Savory, John Baptist, 11
Sayr, Gregory, 5
Scholastica. Three Lay-sisters so named, 46
Scoles, Ursula, 35
Scott, Bede, 26
", Dunstan, 4
", (another), 26
Scott, Maurus, 5
", or King, Richard, 20
Scrogges, Cuthbert,
", Gregory, 9 *
", Maurus, 9
", or Windsor, Placid, 9
Scroope, Anne, 45
Scroup, Mary, 34
Scudamore, Placid, 25
Segeart, Mary Patrick, 55
Selby or Selbye, Gregory, 25
", ", ", Mary Carola, 39
", or Reade, Wilfrid, 3
Semmes, Xaveria, 40
Shafto or Shaftoe, Benedict, 22
", Celestine, 24
", Placid, 23
Sharrock, Dunstan, 18
", Gregory, 7, 13
", Jerome, 7, 13

Sharrock, Joseph, 13
", William, †
Shaw, Maurus, 22
Sheldon, Barbara, 46
", Catharine, 28
", ", (another), 37
", ", ", 45
", Edward, 10
", Frances, 30
", Mary Benedict, 46
", Mary Joseph, 46
", M Placida, 29
", William, 12
", ", (another), 20
Shepherd or Shephard, Alexia, 33
", Alexius, 7, 12
", Augustina, 30
", Theresa, 30
Sherburn, Edward, 21
Sherburne, Anne, 34
", or Shirburne, Joseph, 3, 19,
", or Isherwood, Richard, 24
", or Walmesley, Peter, 13
Sherley or Shirley, Andrew, 6
Sherwood, Elphege, 16
", John, 23
", Joseph, 23
", Robert, 3, 7
Shirbourne, James, 8
Shirburn, Bede, 21
Short, Thomas, 21
Shuttleworth, Benedict, 25
", or Dalton, Wolstan, 20
Sidgewicke, Francis, 11
Sies, Benedict, 24
Simmes, Magdalen, 43
", Mary Frances, 43
", Xaveria, 43
Simpson, Andrew, 20
", or Daniel, Benedict, 17
", Clementina, 25
", Cuthbert, 22
", Thomas, 17
Six, Jerome, 24
Skelton, Elphege, 24

---

* Though his name does not occur in the Profession books, it is entered in the Necrology of the Congregation (November 10th, 1663).

† A Lay-Brother professed at St. Laurence's some time before 1780.

Skinner, Basil, 10
" Mary, 45
" Mary Anne, 45
" Placid, 11
Skrimsher, Dorothy, 37
Slater, Bernard, 18
" Thomas, 18
Slaughter, Paula, 46
Smeaton, Basil, 23
Smith, Augustine, 5
" Barbara, 28
" Benedict, *
" Charles, 13
" Cuthbert, 4
" Edmund, 21
" Etheldreda, 33, 41
" Helen. 45
" John, 21
" Lucy, 47
" Margaret, 29
" Martha, 29
" Mary Dunstan, 46
" Mary Renata, 43
" Maurus, 9
" or Rigmaiden, Maurus, 17
" Renata, 33
" Scholastica, 33
Smithers, Odo, 25
" Oswald, 25
Smythe, Alexia, 39
" Mechtilde, 39
Soloman, Anne, 40
Southcoat, Elizabeth, 33
Southcot or Southcott, Amandus, 9
" Augustine, 12
" " (another), 21
" or Southcote, Bridget, 45
" " Mary, 36
" Thomas, 3, 12,
Sovette, Dorothy, 46
Sparrey, Benedict, 16
Spear, Henrietta, 34
Spencer, Benedicta, 46
" Daniel, 23

Spooner, Agatha, 45
Stafford, Scholastica, 54
" Paula, 45
Stanihurst, Cecilia, 40
Stapelton, Christina, 35
Stapleton, Etheldreda, 28
Stapylton, Benedict, 3, 7, 10
" Epiphanius, 8
" Robert, 9
Starkey, Hugh, 23
" or Hanmer, Joseph, 12
Stear or Steare, Benedict, 4, 7, 12
Stelling, Augustine, 21
Stocker or Stoker, Augustine, 8
Stockman, Gertrude, 55
Stone, Martin, 21
Stones, Bibiana, 42
Story, Joseph, 26
Stourton, John, 7, 12, 19
" Thomas, 10
Strachy, Mary Margaret, 33
Street, Magdalen, 34
" Peter, 23
Strickland, Henrietta, 46
" Mary Catharine, 45
Strutt or Bridgman, Wilfrid, 26
Styles, Henry, 5
Sulyard, Augustine, 17
Sumpner, Charles, 11
Sunley, Elizabeth, 34
Swale, Laurence, 24
Swales, Bridget, 42
Swift, Magdalen, 40
" Mary Benedict, 40
" Theresa, 39
Swinburn or Swinburne, Gertrude, 28
" " " Joachim, 27
" " " Margaret, 28
" " " Theresa, 29
" " " Thomas, 9

T

Tahon, William, 27
Tailler, Mary Austin, 55

---

* D. Benedict, of the most Holy Trinity, (Edward Smith) was professed at Chelles by Fr. Walgrave in 1617.

Talbot, Anne Mary, 39
Talbot, Oswald, 18
Tancred, Mary Austin, 32, 35
   ,, Mary Bernard, 35
Tanke, Stanislaus, 2
   ,, Thomas, 9
Tasburgh, Felix, 21
Tatham, Bede, 10
   ,, Cuthbert, 7, 11
Tavern, Anne, 28
Taylard, Bede, 4, 15
Taylor, Anthony, *
   ,, Benedicta, 29
   ,, Boniface, 26
   ,, ,, (another), 27
   ,, Dominick, 19
   ,, Edmund, 11
   ,, Helen, 42
   ,, Maurus, 5
Tegetmeyr, Francis, 27
Tempest, Anselma, 37
   ,, Augustine, 4, 23, 24
   ,, Edward, 25
   ,, Euphrasia, 29
   ,, John, 23
   ,, Martina, 42
   ,, Mary, 42
   ,, Mechtilde, 42
   ,, Scholastica, 42
Temple, Agnes, 41, 42
Tenant, Anthony, 27
Thickness, Anne, Mary, 40
   ,, Anna Maria, 43
Thielmans, Martha, 35
Thomas or Brychan, Benedict, 9
Thomby, Anne Winifred, 47
Thomson or Jackson, Leander, 9
   ,, Winifred, 33
Thompson or Pratt, Felix, 19
Thornburgh, Magdalen, 33
Thorton or Foster, Bede, 19
   ,, Mary Baptist, 45
   ,, Winifred, 45
Thorold, Anne Catharine, 39
   ,, Catharine, 36

Thorold, Christina, 39
   ,, Eugenia, 36, 38
Throckmorton, Æmilian, 20
   ,, Clare, 37
Tichborne, Mary Anne, 37
   ,, Mary Catharine, 39
Tichbourne, Scholastica, 33
Timperly, Gregory, 21,
   ,, Justina, 39
   ,, Scholastica, 28
   ,, Theresa, 28
Tobin, Mary Winifred, 47
Tolderly, Mary Magdalen, 29
Tookey, Josepha, 29
Tootal, Margaret, 43
Touchett, Anselm, 10
Toudelle or Tordell, John, 15
Towers, Adrian, 27
Townson, Andrew, 12
   ,, Augustine, 24
   ,, John, 24
Trembie, Celestine, 19
Trentham, Mechtilde, 34
Tresham, Francis, 9
   ,, Winifred, 33
Trevilian, Catharine, 29
Trevillian, Ursula, 42
Trevillion, Mary, 36
Trumble, Catharine, 42
Tucker, Thomas, 23
Tuite, Aloysia, 46
Turberville or Tuberville, Anselm, 5
   ,, Anthony, 19, 21
Turck, Laurence, 26
Turner, Augustine, 26
   ,, Catharine, 40
   ,, George, 14
   ,, Gertrude, 39
   ,, John, 23
   ,, Thomas, 18
Tyldesley, Cecilia, 36, 37
Tyrrell, Maura, 40

U

Urmston, Margaret, 34

---

* Br. Anthony Taylor, whose name was accidently omitted in the Catalogue, died a Choir novice ot St. Laurence's, September 24th, 1762.

Urmston, Mary, 34

V

Valentine, Joseph, 22
" Mary Benedicta, 40
Van Mechels, Petronilla, 54
Vaughan, Clare, 39
Vavasour, Catharine, 28
" Lucy, 28
" Mary, 32, 33
Venner or Fermor, Amandus, 15
Vincent, Anastasia, 45
Vraux, Theresa, 34

W

Wafte, Anselm, 27
Wait or Wayte, Helen, 37, 54
Wake or Merriman, Hilarion, 10
Wakeman, Elizabeth, 37
Waldegrave, Apollonia, 34
" Jeronima, 36
" Placida, 34
" Theodosia, 32, 34
Walgrave, Francis, 15
" or Pleayll, William, 10
Walker, Augustine, 3, 20, 22
" Benedicta, 30
Wall, Alexius, 25
" or Marsh or Marshall, Cuthbert, 24
Walmesley, Anselm, 17
" or Caldwell, Augustine, 13
" Charles, 20, 22
" Francis, 17
" Mellitus, 14, 16
" or Sherburne, Peter, 13
" Theresa, 30
" or Ingham, Wolstan, 20
Walton, Dorothy, 40
" Theresa, 40
Ward, Edmund, 20
Wareham, Denis, *see* Wenham
Waring, Ambrose, 18
Warmoll, Bernard, 4, 13
Warner, Agnes, 45
" Ignatia, 45
Warnford or West, Peter, 6
Warren, Bernard, 20
" Mary Magdalen, 39
Warwick, Basil, 7, 12

Warwick, Benedicta, 29
Waters, Martha, 46
" or Duvivier, Placid, 13
Watkinson, Gregory, 13
Watmough, Francis, 3, 4, 14, 16
Watson, Frances, 28
" Mary, 33
Waty, Paul, 16
Wearden, Vincent, 27
Webb, Dunstan, 27
" Agatha, 37
Welch, Thomas, 20, 22
Weldon, Benedict, 21
Wells, Anne Joseph, 46
" Gertrude, 46
Wenham or Wareham, Denis, 26
West, Francis, 16
Westbrook or Darrell, Maurus, 25
Weston, Alexia, 39
Whall, George, 16
Whetenhall, Mary Placida, 40
Whitaker, Martha, 33
White or Bradshaw, Augustine, 5, 7, 19
" or Bennett, Claud, 3, 4, 15
" Monica, 46
" or Woodhope, Thomas, 9
Whitehall, Victoria, 46
Whitenhal or Whitnal, Frances, 20
" or Whitenhall, Maura, 32, 34
Whitfield, Andrew, 9
" Winifred, 40
Whittel, Joseph, 22
Whyte or White, Christina, 39, 54
Widdrington, Agnes, 29
" Elizabeth Joseph, 39
" Mary Austin, 29
Widowfield, Joanna, 40
Wigmore, Catharine, 39, **38**
Wilcock, Peter, 6
" (another), 17
Wilford, Boniface, 7
Wilkinson, Gertrude, 43
" Gregory, 20
Wilks, Cuthbert, 23
" Mary Austin, 43
" Theresa, 27
Williams, Anselm, **15**
" (another), 19
Williamson, Petronilla, 33

Willis, Mary Michael, 46
Willoughby, Willobie or Rider, Ildephonsus, 11
      ,,   Benedicta, 46
Wills, Maura, 43
Willson, Jerome, 11
Wilson, Barbara, 35
  ,,   Benedict, 11
  ,,   Jerome, 11
  ,,   Maurus, 24
  ,,   Paul, 14
  ,,   Placida, 29
  ,,   Thomas, 11
  ,,   Willibrord, 24
Winchcombe, Anthony, 8
      ,,   Benedict, 16
Winkley, Anne Austin, 43
Windsor or Scrogges, Placid, 9
Winifred, Sister, 46
Winter, Benedict, 12
   ,,   Mary, 33
Winton, James, 24
Wiseman, Agatha, 33
Witham, Aloysia, 35
  ,,   Bede, 10
  ,,   Christina, 41, 42
  ,,   Maura, 42
  ,,   or Wytham, Michael, 9

Witham, Thomas, 11
   ,,   Wilfrid, 25
Wolsley, Edward, 9
Woodhope or White, Thomas, 9
Woodman, Mary Anne, 41, 43
Woolfe, Laurence, 20
Woolgar, Agnes, 40
Worsley or Byfleet, John, 9
    ,,   Mary Joseph, 43
Worswick, Dunstan, 18
Wright, Frances, 54
Wrisdon, Gertrude, 28
Wyburn, Henry, 4, 19, 22
Wyche, Joseph, 24
Wyld or Wyre, Mary Theresa, 55
Wythie, Bernard, 12

X

Xaveria, Sister, 46

Y

Yate, Mary, 45
Yaxley, Viviana, 28, 33
York, Laurence, 7, 12, 19
Young or Yonge, Bernard, 26
    ,,   Anne Theresa, 29
Yoward, Richard, 21

THE END.

𝔍𝔫 omnibus glorificetur 𝔇eus.

www.ingramcontent.com/pod-product-compliance
Lightning Source LLC
Chambersburg PA
CBHW030344230426
43664CB00007BB/523